J. Ranade Workstation Series

CPI-C Programming in C

An Application Developer's Guide to APPC

John Q. Walker II

Peter J. Schwaller

McGraw-Hill, Inc.

New York   San Francisco   Washington, D.C.   Auckland   Bogotá
Caracas   Lisbon   London   Madrid   Mexico City   Milan
Montreal   New Delhi   San Juan   Singapore
Sydney   Tokyo   Toronto

Library of Congress Cataloging-in-Publication Data

Walker, John Q.
    CPI-C programming in C : an application developer's guide to APPC
/ John Q. Walker II, Peter J. Schwaller.
        p.   cm. — (J. Ranade workstation series)
    Includes index.
    ISBN 0-07-911733-3
    1. C (Computer program language) 2. Application software.
I. Schwaller, Peter J.   II. Title.   III. Series.
QA76.73.C15W3546   1995
005.7′12—dc20   94-20879
                                                                      CIP

    2 3 4 5 6 7 8 9 0   DOC/DOC   9 0 9 8 7 6

P/N 0-07-067848-0
PART OF
ISBN 0-07-911733-3

The sponsoring editor for this book was Jerry Papke and the production
supervisor was Donald F. Schmidt. This book was set in Century Schoolbook
by North Market Street Graphics.

Printed and bound by R. R. Donnelley & Sons Company.

To our parents for their loving support, and their tolerance of our adventures in book writing

Contents

Foreword   xv
Acknowledgments   xvii

Chapter 1. Welcome to CPI-C Programming 1

    What Is CPI-C? 2
    How Is This Book Organized? 4
    What Do I Need to Use the Coding Examples? 5
    What's on the Accompanying Diskette? 7
    We'd Like to Hear from You! 8

Chapter 2. An Introduction to CPI-C and APPC 9

    APPC and CPI-C: A Technical Overview 9
        Understanding APPC Concepts 10
        What's the Difference Between APPC and APPN? 10
        APPC and Client/Server Computing 11
    The Evolution of APPC 12
    CPI-C: The Best Way to Use APPC 13
    Communicating in an Open, Multivendor World 13
        Improving Productivity 14
        Improving Performance 15
    Selecting a Communications API 15
        Message Queuing 16
        Remote Procedure Calls (RPCs) 16
        Conversational Interfaces 16
    The Evolution of CPI-C 17

Part 1   Getting Started

Chapter 3. Sending "Hello, World" (Where Else to Start?) 23

    Setting Up a Conversation 25
    Ending a Conversation 25
    Creating Our First Application 27
    Synchronizing a Pair of Programs 32

Chapter 4. CPI-C Coding in C   37

Issuing CPI-C Calls   37
   Passing Integer Parameters   38
   Passing Strings and Lengths   39
   Using Your Native Character Set for Names   41
   Handling Conversation IDs   42
   Understanding Function Call Names   42
Building Your CPI-C Programs   43
   Compiling Your Programs   44
   Linking Your Programs   46
   Looking at our Makefiles   46
   Migration to Other Environments   49
Pulling It All Together   49
   Understanding the CPI-C Include File   50
   Finding the CPI-C Libraries   53
Understanding Our Coding Style in This Book   54

Chapter 5. Setting Up Your Computers to Run CPI-C Programs   55

Using Symbolic Destination Names and Side Information   56
Understanding Links, Sessions, and Conversations   58
Learning About the Three CPI-C Configuration Parameters   61
   Partner LU Name   61
   TP Name   63
   Mode Name   64
Setting Up Your Computers   65
   On Each Computer: LUs, Modes, and Links   66
   On the Client Computer: A CPI-C Side Information Entry   67
   On the Server Computer: A TP Definition   67

Chapter 6. Replying to "Hello, World"   69

Knowing Who Has the Permission-to-Send   75
Viewing the Current Conversation State   76

Chapter 7. Creating One Server for All Three Clients   79

Updating TP Definitions on the Server Side   83
Simple Error-Handling Procedures   84
Viewing the Return Code Name   87
Viewing the Status_Received Name   89

Chapter 8. Multiple Sends and Receives   91

Logical Records   91
An Example of Using Data_Received   92
Data_Received Values   96
Viewing the Data_Received Name   97

Chapter 9. Data Buffering: A Paradigm Shift   101

Rules for Sending a Network Packet   102
Network Flow Control   103

Data Buffering Examples   103
CPI-C Buffers Attaches   106
Illustrating Data Buffering   107

Part 2   CPI-C Application Design

Chapter 10. Building Blocks   117

An Umbrella File of CPI-C Procedures   118
Using These Building Blocks as a Reference   118

Chapter 11. Getting Connected: The Client Side   121

Getting a Conversation ID and Naming the Partner   122
  Initialize_Conversation (CMINIT)   122
  Using an All-Blank Symbolic Destination Name   125
Getting a Session   127
  Allocate (CMALLC)   128
Setting Conversation Characteristics   130
  Set_Conversation_Type (CMSCT)   132
  Set_Return_Control (CMSRC)   133
  Set_Sync_Level (CMSSL)   134
Overriding Side Information Table Fields   136
  Set_Partner_LU_Name (CMSPLN)   137
  Set_Mode_Name (CMSMN)   139
  Set_TP_Name (CMSTPN)   141

Chapter 12. Getting Connected: The Server Side   143

Starting the Server Program   144
Waiting for an Incoming Attach   145
  Accept_Conversation (CMACCP)   145
Inheriting and Extracting Conversation Characteristics   147
  Extract_Conversation_Context (CMECTX)   148
  Extract_Conversation_State (CMECS)   148
  Extract_Conversation_Type (CMECT)   149
  Extract_Maximum_Buffer_Size (CMEMBS)   150
  Extract_Mode_Name (CMEMN)   150
  Extract_Partner_LU_Name (CMEPLN)   151
  Extract_Security_User_ID (CMESUI)   152
  Extract_Sync_Level (CMESL)   152
  Extract_TP_Name (CMETPN)   153

Chapter 13. Sending Data   155

Getting Ready to Send Data   155
  Send_Data (CMSEND)   156
Flush (CMFLUS)   158
  Set_Send_Type (CMSST)   159
Getting Ready to Receive, After Sending   160
  Prepare_to_Receive (CMPTR)   161
  Set_Prepare_to_Receive_Type (CMSPTR)   162

Chapter 14. Receiving   **165**

   Receiving Whatever Arrives   166
      Receive (CMRCV)   166
   Receive-Immediate   169
      Set_Receive_Type (CMSRT)   169
   A General-Purpose Receive() Routine   170
   Reusable Receive Wrappers   177
      Procedure Do_Receive_Pipe()   178
      Procedure Do_Receive_Credit()   180
      Procedure Do_Receive_Inquiry()   182

Chapter 15. Exchanging Synchronization and Error Reports
with Your Partner   **185**

   Synchronizing Programs   186
      Confirm (CMCFM)   186
      What Your Partner Sees When You Issue Confirm()   187
      Confirmed (CMCFMD)   187
   Reporting Errors   188
      Send_Error (CMSERR)   188
      What Your Partner Sees When You Issue Send_Error()   190
      Set_Error_Direction (CMSED)   190
   Using Send_Error() versus Send_Data()   191

Chapter 16. Ending Conversations and Programs   **193**

   Using the Deallocate() Call   194
      Deallocate (CMDEAL)   194
      Set_Deallocate_Type (CMSDT)   194
      What Your Partner Sees When You Issue Deallocate()   197
   Cleaning Up a Conversation   198

Chapter 17. Rarely Used Techniques   **201**

   Begging and Signaling   201
      Begging, with the Request-to-Send Signal   202
      Request_to_Send (CMRTS)   204
      Test_Request_to_Send_Received (CMTRTS)   204
   Basic Conversations   205
      Building an LL Field   205
      Set_Fill (CMSF)   207
      Set_Log_Data (CMSLD)   208

Part 3   Building Robust Applications

Chapter 18. Five Classic Transactions   **211**

   The Pipeline Transaction (Datagram)   212
   The Credit Check Transaction (Confirmed Delivery)   218
   The Inquiry Transaction (Request and Reply)   226
   The File Transfer (Batch Send)   232
   The Database Update Transaction (Conversational Reply)   243

Chapter 19. Improving Performance   255

General Guidelines   255
CPI-C Coding Tips and Techniques   256
Improving Processing Overlap   257
  Use Flush() to Allow Timely Processing of Data   257
  Use Prepare_to_Receive()   259
Using Your Conversation as an Optimized Pipeline   260
  Use the Confirm() Call Appropriately   260
  Use Implicit Confirmation Instead of Confirm()   261
Reducing Data Flows   261
  Use Flush() Judiciously   261
  Minimize Use of Send_Error()   262
  Avoid Using Deallocate-Abend   262
Reducing the Number of Send_Data() and Receive() Calls   262
Using Shared Data Buffers on OS/2 Communications Manager   262
  Send as Much Data as Possible on Each Send_Data()   265
  Receive as Much Data as Possible with Each Receive() Call   265
Reducing Call Overhead   266
  Combine Functions on Send_Data()   266
  Minimize the Number of Required Set Calls   267
  Remember the Information Obtained from Extract Calls   268
Making the Most of Underlying APPC Sessions   268
  Have Multiple Conversations Serially Reuse a Session   268
  Keep Conversations Active When Using APPC Frequently   269
Understanding the Speed of Individual Calls   269

Chapter 20. Handling Errors   271

Expecting the Unexpected   271
Learning of Failures   272
Dealing with CPI-C Return Codes   273
  Categories of Return Codes   274
  Additional Diagnostic Information   277
Handling Other Unexpected Returned Values   278
  Data_Received   278
  Status_Received   279
Choosing the Right Mechanism for Handling Errors   279
Retrying Conversations   280
  Handling Other Retry Return Codes   281
  Deciding How Often to Retry   282
  Lowering the Impact of Retrying a Conversation   282
Testing Your CPI-C Programs   283

Chapter 21. Reporting (and Avoiding) Failures   289

Capturing Network and Application Information   290
Reporting Failures: Locally   291
  Error Message Text   292
  Separate Error Text from Code   292
Reporting Failures: Remotely   292
Reducing the Opportunity for Failure   293
  Avoiding User Interaction During Installation   293
  Preparing for the Worst   294

Checking for a Good Connection   295
Anticipating Requirements and Tracing   296

Part 4   Configuration

Chapter 22. Client Side: Building a Robust, Reusable
Setup Routine   305

Getting a Valid Conversation ID   306
   Hardcoding the Symbolic Destination Name   306
   Obtaining a Symbolic Destination Name   307
   Using the All-Blank Symbolic Destination Name   308
Implementing the Setup Conversation Technique   309
   Defining the Input Variables   310
   Getting a Conversation ID   311
   Setting Conversation Characteristics   315
Using Set_Up_conversation()   320

Chapter 23. Server Side: Taking Advantage of an Attach Manager   323

Setting Up the TP Name   323
   Client Specifies the TP Name   324
   Server Configures a List of TP Names   324
Understanding TP Definition versus TP Name versus TP Filespec   325
Checking Conversation Attributes First   326
   Sync Level   326
   Conversation Type   327
   Conversation Security   327
Matching Attaches with Programs   328
   When the Attach Manager Starts a New Program   328
   When Connecting an Attach to an Existing Application 329
Estimating Conversation Start-Up Overhead   329
Debugging Attach-Manager-Started Programs   331
   Determining Why the Server Program Wasn't Started 331
   Loading Your Server Program Under a Source Debugger 332

Part 5   Advanced Topics

Chapter 24. Converting Data Between Different Computers   337

Using Existing Data Conversion Tools   338
Converting Characters   339
   Handling C's Special Characters   339
   Converting from ASCII-EBCDIC Using CPI-C 1.2 Functions 340
   Convert_Outgoing (CMCNVO)   341
   Convert_Incoming (CMCNVI)   341
   Converting from ASCII-EBCDIC Using Tables   342
   Handling National Language Code Pages   346
   Handling Double-Byte Character Sets   346
Converting Other Data Types   347
   Converting Integers   347
   Converting Floating-Point Numbers   353

Converting Records with Multiple Data Types   354
  Handling C Data Structures   355
  Encoding Data   356

Chapter 25. Interacting with Security   357

Introducing APPC Security   357
  APPC Route Security   358
  APPC Session Security   359
  APPC Conversation Security   360
Additional Security Measures   363
Configuring Your Server Transaction Program   363
  Disabling Security: Public Transaction Programs   364
  Handling Security Program   364
  Allowing Persistent Verification   364
  Tightening Security: Enabling Already Verified   365
  Avoiding User Mistakes   365
Coding Your Client Program   365
  Set_Conversation_Security_Type (CMSCST)   366
  Set_Conversation_Security_User_ID (CMSCSU)   366
  Set_Conversation_Security_Password (CMSCSP)   367
  Setting a Conversation Security Type   367
  Avoiding User Interaction Until Last Possible Option   370
  Letting Users Tell You What to Use   374
  Prompting Your Users for What They Want to Use   375

Chapter 26. Nonblocking Operation   377

Nonblocking Calls   378
  Set_Processing_Mode (CMSPM)   379
  Cancel_Conversation (CMCANC)   380
  Wait_for_Conversation (CMWAIT)   380
  Initialize_for_Incoming (CMINIC)   381
  Accept_Incoming (CMACCI)   381
Windows CPI-C Extensions for Nonblocking   382
  WinCPICStartup()   383
  WinCPICCleanup()   384
  WinCPICSetBlockingHook()   384
  WinCPICUnhookBlockingHook()   386
  WinCPICIsBlocking()   386
  Specify_Windows_Handle (XCHWND)   386

Chapter 27. Designing Servers with CPI-C   389

Using Short Conversations   390
  Advantages for Server Processing   390
  Breaking Up Long Conversations   391
  Correlating Short Conversations   393
  Dealing with Conversation Start-Up Overhead   393
Servers Before CPI-C 1.2   394
Using Accept Multiple Without CPI-C 1.2   394
Using Accept Multiple in CPI-C 1.2   395
  Specify_Local_TP_Name (CMSLTP)   398
  Release_Local_TP_Name (CMRLTP)   399

Using Accept Multiple with Multiple Threads   399
Using CPI-C 1.2 Nonblocking and Accept Multiple   402

Part 6   Appendixes

Appendix A. CPI-C Return Codes, A Practical Guide   **405**

Appendix B. Definitions for Five Predefined Modes   **441**

Appendix C. CPI-C Header File <cpic.h>   **443**

Appendix D. A Guide to Helpful Information   **467**

Index   475
CPI-C Calls and Conversion Characteristics   485

Foreword

The need to access and exchange information readily across diverse platforms has given rise to the phenomenal growth of client/server networks.

Most large enterprises have understood the value of networked computers for years, and are continually evolving their systems. But networks are no longer the province of business alone; they are being implemented everywhere from health care to transportation to entertainment.

We expect this trend to accelerate throughout the decade, as new communications technology and applications emerge. A major advance was the development of Asynchronous Transfer Mode (ATM), which can integrate data, voice, text, image, and video, and deliver it over a single network at speeds a thousand times faster than before.

Consider the potential applications: multimedia lessons delivered to students' desks at school and home; scientists exchanging huge files of satellite pictures and seismic data around the world, enabling more precise assessments of earthquake and volcano dangers; movies and television programs distributed to homes on demand, creating new options for people to customize their environment.

The 21st-century global information superhighway is now under construction. Its infrastructure requires powerful client/server networks which, in turn, require applications to make it all work.

By opening this book, you've expressed interest in client/server. That's very good news for our customers and our industry. In fact, the full promise of client/server networks depends on software innovation. Once people are linked to the global network, they need applications that put the information in their hands and help them make good use of it. Therefore, a ground swell of programming activity is urgently needed.

As you can imagine, development in this environment offers exciting rewards to those who enjoy a complex challenge. I personally hope many of you accept the challenge.

When writing programs for stand-alone computers, developers have control over the entire environment. Not so in the communicating environment. Consideration must extend to the client, the server, and the whole network in between. In the client/server environment, portability is a top priority for developers. Application must run on diverse platforms to meet open systems requirements and protect customers' investments in multivendor hardware and software.

Developers who accept these challenges deserve excellent tools. One is APPC, a very popular distributed protocol, used worldwide on both IBM and non-IBM machines. With this network software, programs can communicate across platforms.

For APPC, the preferred programming interface is CPI-C, the Common Programming Interface for Communications. It lets your applications cross different kinds of computers and networks. CPI-C has become an international standard for conversational network programming, adopted by the X/Open Consortium.

Knowing how valuable CPI-C programming can be to developers, I am very glad to see a book completely devoted to the topic. The authors, Peter Schwaller and John Q. Walker, have extensive experience with APPC and CPI-C. They are distinguished programmers who have taught CPI-C and used it extensively to write client/server applications. I can't imagine experts more suited to produce a practical, how-to guide to this important interface.

I hope you're planning to contribute your talents to client/server network applications. If so, I know this volume will become one of the most useful tools in your development kit.

Ellen M. Hancock
IBM Senior Vice President and Group Executive

Acknowledgments

Suzanne Schwaller, Peter's wife, cheerfully tolerated many evenings and weekends of us hackers, writing and rewriting until our ideas achieved readable English. She read the manuscript several times, with a strong eye toward making things understandable. Her patience is ever appreciated.

Tim Huntley read and marked up every page of two drafts, and offered many helpful comments. Look for his upcoming book on APPN.

Lance Bader was a fount of ideas. He designed most of the "Five Classic Transactions" chapter, the retry guidelines, the discussion of request-to-send, and offered lots of other ideas.

Matt Briggs, an impressive programming talent who is now a sophomore at Virginia Tech, gave us an early review of the first seven chapters.

We had a set of experienced C gurus and CPI-C programmers review the manuscript during the final month. They found innumerable bugs and inconsistencies, and offered many suggestions for improvements. We are grateful for their volunteer help; we hope we've given them the book they wished to see. These friends and reviewers were, alphabetically, Richard Brooks, Bob Gibson, Richard Gray, Dave Kaminsky, Alan Oursland, Dave Sanders, and Bruce Walker.

Brad Mehlenbacher did the mercenary work of page-by-page editing the manuscript (as it was changing underneath him).

IBM gave us the time and resources we needed to complete this book. We especially thank our managers, Rick McGee, Steve Joyce, and Kim Murray.

Alex Berson, a long-time APPC advocate, got us in touch with Jay Ranade and reviewed a late draft of the manuscript.

Jay Ranade and Jerry Papke at McGraw-Hill have been great to work with. May every author be so fortunate.

John Q. Walker II
Peter J. Schwaller

CPI-C Programming in C

Welcome to CPI-C Programming

If you are a C or C++ programmer wishing to create high-speed programs for communicating between computers, this book is for you. In it, we describe a library of C functions used to communicate among programs. This library of calls has the long name *Common Programming Interface for Communications,* or *CPI-C* for short (pronounced "sip'-ick").

If you're an experienced C programmer, you'll be able to skip quickly through some of the earlier sections of this book. If you're new to C, don't worry. The CPI-C calls are as easy to use as the standard calls in C, such as strcpy() or printf(). Finally, if you prefer a programming language other than C, read on. You'll find that CPI-C was designed for remarkable portability across programming languages. You can easily apply what you learn in this book to other programming languages. Join us for the adventure, and we think you'll learn a fair amount about C along the way.

Programmers praise the C language because it lets them build programs that are fast, robust, and portable. Part of standard C is a rich library of robust functions that are portable across platforms, that allow construction of high-performance programs, and that provide easy-to-use building blocks common to many programs.

When you look at the library section of a C compiler manual, you see many sets of run-time routines, grouped by category. For example, there are file I/O routines like fopen() and fwrite(), and string manipulation routines like strlen() and strcpy(). Each set of routines is accompanied by a C header file, which is a file of definitions and declarations that accompany the routines. You include this header file in the top of your source files to let you use any of the routines in the library. For example, to use fopen() or fwrite(), you include the header file named `stdio.h`. CPI-C is simply another set of C run-time routines, with an accompanying C header file. To give you a hint as to CPI-C's size, there are roughly the same number of CPI-C routines as there are file I/O routines in the standard C library.

Like the standard C run-time routines, CPI-C calls are *platform-independent;* that is, they work the same on all operating systems and computers on which they are available. Even better, not only do the CPI-C routines work the same across platforms, but they also allow you to use the same calls and parameters among all programming languages. For example, when porting a C program to FORTRAN, wouldn't it be great to have the printf() function? In CPI-C, every call, parameter, constant, and structure has the same name across all programming languages, as well as the same structure size and constant values. In addition, while CPI-C has traditionally been associated with one type of underlying network software, namely *APPC,* you'll find that programs that make CPI-C calls can run on a variety of underlying communication protocols.

When you write a successful program, you almost always want to port it! CPI-C was designed to let you write portable, yet powerful, communicating programs.

WHAT IS CPI-C?

If you are familiar with data communications, you may wonder why yet another communications programming interface exists. To answer this question, we need to provide a little historical context. We begin by introducing *Advanced Program-to-Program Communication* (APPC).* APPC is a protocol stack, which is network software designed to let programs talk to one another between computers. APPC was a pioneering effort in creating communications software that allows programs to work the same, regardless of the type of computers or the type of networks being used.

The original APPC specification was a general, open architecture, without details for particular computer platforms. It described the format and sequencing of the network messages that flowed between the computers. When APPC was designed in the early 1980s, program portability was less important than it is today. APPC architecture did not define a common programming interface between an application program and the underlying implementation of the communication function.

As APPC was implemented on many different computers, the programmers on each system made the syntax of their native APPC programming interface look like that of their operating system interfaces. Many different computer vendors implemented the APPC architecture; each invented a native APPC programming interface that resembled its operating system. Most of these APPC interfaces are designed around control blocks and interrupts.

---

* You may also hear APPC referred to as *LU 6.2.*

There's a similar situation in C programming that you may have already encountered. Think about how you do file I/O in your programs. You have two choices: you can use the portable C run-time routines, such as fopen() and fwrite(), or you can choose to use the native operating system functions. The native operating system functions vary from computer to computer. For example, in DOS, your program can issue "interrupt 21" after placing parameter values in registers; in OS/2, you can call DosOpen() with its parameters; in MVS, you can make supervisor calls with the correct parameters in a control block. The native APPC verbs similarly vary from computer to computer. So, while the high-level concept of program-to-program communication is straightforward, porting applications that used APPC to different platforms is not a trivial task.

Writing and testing file I/O routines for all the platforms on which you intend to run your application would be arduous. Likewise, creating platform-specific APPC communication calls would be equally time-consuming. CPI-C resulted from the realization that it is preferable to standardize communications calls across platforms. This allows programmers to spend the bulk of their time where it counts: designing the application logic, not fiddling with platform nuances.

We discussed in the opening that CPI-C was designed to work the same with any computer language. This attribute is commonly known as *language independence*. The CPI-C programming interface is identical across every programming language; the names of all the calls, constants, and parameters are identical in C, COBOL, Pascal, REXX, or whatever programming language you choose.

There are several different styles for creating communicating programs. The three most popular styles are probably the conversational style, remote procedure calls, and message queuing. CPI-C is for programmers who choose the conversational style. One's choice of programming style is motivated by many factors, which we'll discuss in the next chapter. If you are familiar with other styles, such as remote procedure calls or message queuing, you'll be learning two things as you read this book: how the conversational style works, and how to use CPI-C's programming interface.

In programming organizations that develop communicating applications, you frequently find a mix of several groups with different skills: mainframe programmers, midrange programmers, UNIX™ programmers, and PC programmers. In practice, these groups use different programming languages and tools, and rarely talk to one another (and sometimes barely like each other!). Yet, we ask them to develop complex, cooperative programs that exchange data with one other. Together, this diverse set of programmers must design, code, test, debug, and maintain these programs. With CPI-C, your programmers can work together as a team: cooperating on their design, sitting in code reviews with one another, and even maintaining each others' code.

Although you develop a program for your favorite operating system, say OS/2 or UNIX, you may find that someone needs to run the program on MVS. If you use CPI-C, you can count on the communications code porting cleanly, even though you don't know much about programming on MVS. Using CPI-C as the starting point, along with a little help with the compiler and environment, you can port your own code without having to become a guru on the new platform.

HOW IS THIS BOOK ORGANIZED?

This book is organized in five parts, each part containing several related chapters. We've approached our discussion in a breadth-first manner, as opposed to the depth-first approach you'll find in the CPI-C references. This results in a book with a lot of forward pointers, that is, references to the places later in the book where a given topic is presented in more depth.

Before we actually get started with the first part, we give you an introduction to CPI-C and APPC, to help you understand a little of their history and future. The first part of the book describes a small application which sends the phrase "Hello, world" from one program to another. The program helps us introduce the major techniques necessary to program successfully with CPI-C. Avid C programmers want to know right away how CPI-C syntax works, how it differs from what they're used to, and how to write their makefiles. This information comprises the next chapter in Part 1. The following chapter continues with an overview of the steps necessary to get this program running.

When running communicating programs, it is essential that the programs, operating system, hardware, and the intervening network be set up in a coordinated way. These additional complexities make writing communicating programs much more challenging than programs that stand alone in one computer. Because of this, we'll spend a lot of time in this book discussing techniques for making your programs robust and for reporting on unrecoverable problems. The first part of the book concludes with some examples that expand the "Hello, world" program's capabilities: how to reply to it from a partner program, how to create a partner program that is more general in handling what it receives, and how to group multiple sends and receives in the two programs.

The second part of the book is an extended discussion of the building blocks of CPI-C programs. It expands on the first part of the book by organizing its techniques into a set of useful templates and reusable code snippets. After you've written a few CPI-C programs, you'll see that there are lots of techniques that occur frequently, and you'll want to apply them in all your programs. In addition, we discuss the fundamental CPI-C calls and parameters and how to use them. C programmers familiar with the whole set of C runtime routines find there are some that they rarely use (how frequently, for example, do you use atof() or some of the string functions?). CPI-C also has some functions that we think you'll rarely use; we'll give you our opinion in the last chapter of this part.

The third part of the book focuses on combining and expanding on the building blocks. It introduces five classic transactions from which most communicating programs are constructed, techniques to improve transaction performance, and other tips and hints. It also covers techniques for error handling and reporting.

The fourth part is an extensive discussion of the issues outside of your program logic: how to assure a successful configuration and setup. The CPI-C calls that modify their environment are discussed, along with reasons why you would want to use them—and where to use them in your programs.

Finally, the fifth part rewards the patient reader with some interesting advanced topics. How should your application programs convert data when transferring it between computers that use different character sets? What are good design principles to use when building high-capacity server programs? How do you add security measures to your programs to authenticate user IDs and allow their users correct authorization to resources they want to use?

The appendixes contain a practical guide to CPI-C return codes, based on our years of CPI-C programming. It also lists the CPI-C platforms we know of today, and a full listing of the CPI-C header file, `<cpic.h>`.

We intend this book to be a companion to C programmers who are working to master CPI-C. There should be enough information and examples here so that this is the only book you'll need. However, this book is not a reference manual; it doesn't discuss every possible parameter and hexadecimal value, nor does it cover other programming languages. In addition to this book, you may want to have one of the following four reference books handy:

- *IBM SAA CPI Communications Reference,* IBM document number SC26-4399-06, March 1993. This is the reference for **CPI-C version 1.1,** which is what you'll find today on most platforms.

- *Common Programming Interface Communications Specification,* IBM document number SC31-6180-00, March 1993. This is the reference for **CPI-C version 1.2,** which contains the newest calls.

- *Microsoft Windows CPI-C version 1.0 Specification,* 1993. This spec adds Windows-specific calls to CPI-C version 1.2.

- *X/Open CAE Specification, CPI-C,* document number C210, ISBN 1-872630-35-9, February 1992. The 1992 X/Open CPI-C spec has largely been superseded by CPI-C version 1.2.

"CPI-C specifications" on p. 467 explains how to get copies of these specs. Special mention goes to an inexpensive CD-ROM from IBM, *The Best of APPC, APPN, and CPI-C.* It contains softcopies of the CPI-C specs, along with lots of related papers, source code, and programs. Get it!

WHAT DO I NEED TO USE THE CODING EXAMPLES?

First of all, you'll need to have CPI-C itself for the operating system you plan to use. CPI-C is available for a broad range of environments; we've listed the CPI-C platforms we know of on our diskette, since we expect to continue updating it. CPI-C is a software package that is either purchased separately or is shipped as part of the operating system. For example, CPI-C is shipped along with the operating systems on the IBM AS/400. For other operating systems, such as Microsoft Windows, there are CPI-C platform products available from several different vendors.

In addition to a C compiler, the two things you'll need for CPI-C programming are a CPI-C header file and a library of CPI-C calls to link to. Some of the CPI-C vendors ship their libraries and header files as part of their platform, while others have them in a separately priced toolkit. Be sure you have a copy of the libraries, header files, and other development tools you need for your platform.

The standard C header file: ‹cpic.h›

Today, each of the platforms offering CPI-C differs slightly in the content and name of the C header file it ships. To make it easier for you to get started, we've put the standard header file, `cpic.h`, on the diskette, and listed it in the back of the book.

Although we haven't compiled and tested our samples on every platform, we *have* worked with many of the compilers and platforms. Our focus is on the powerful, low-cost compilers for DOS, Windows, OS/2, and UNIX. These operating systems have the latest, state-of-the-art compiler features, are frequently enhanced with new versions, and have attained a cost and quality that allow most programmers to use one of them at home. Thus, we have assured error-free compilation and execution of the sample programs with the following compilers:

- Borland C++ version 3.1, and C++ for OS/2
- IBM C Set/2 and C Set++
- Microsoft C, versions 6.00A, 7.0, and Visual C++

Our assumption is that you will use an ANSI-compatible C compiler on the platforms for which you are developing.

We illustrate our points throughout the book with small, useful procedures and programs—much in the flavor of Kernighan and Ritchie in their landmark C programming book. The samples are designed to be portable among platforms, taking advantage of one of CPI-C's strengths. We've also avoided depending on any C header files specific to target operating systems. For example, when compiling for the OS/2 Communications Manager, you do not need to include the ‹os2.h› header file in order to use these sample programs.

On most platforms,* you can talk between the two sides of an application all on one computer. In one process or window, you can start the client program and have it talk to its partner in another process or window. This makes it exceptionally easy to develop, test, and debug CPI-C applications without disturbing anyone else. It eliminates complexities caused by network setup problems, and you'll get excellent performance. We recommend you try out all the samples in this book on a single computer as you're learning how everything works together.

---

* Except single-tasking DOS and, surprisingly, mainframe CICS.

Although ANSI C compilers and CPI-C allow portable programs to be compiled and run across different types of computers, most platforms differ in their assumptions about character sets and country codes. Your program cannot simply send data from an ASCII-based computer, such as a personal computer running DOS, to an EBCDIC-based computer, such as an IBM AS/400, and expect the target computer to understand the data. Coding techniques for data conversion are covered in Chap. 24.

Finally, while CPI-C programming syntax may be portable across platforms, the names of the terms needed to install and set up your programs are somewhat inconsistent. Some translation of terms may be necessary to set up CPI-C programs on your computer. IBM has created an excellent, free guide for matching the setup terminology among computers. Look for the *Multi-Platform Configuration Guide* (MPCONFIG) on CompuServe and as part of recent product platforms.

WHAT'S ON THE ACCOMPANYING DISKETTE?

There's a diskette accompanying this book with all the source code we show, as well as lots of other goodies. Here's a quick summary of its contents; for more details, see the README.TXT file on the diskette.

- README.TXT
- The sample code in the book
- CPIC.H, the standard header file
- WINCPIC.H and WINCPIC.DEF, for programming with WinCPIC
- APING and APINGD: all their source code and makefiles
- Working .NDF files for the OS/2 Communications Manager
- Working .NSD files for Networking Services/DOS
- Makefiles for
  Borland C++ for OS/2 (OS/2, 32-bit)
  IBM C Set/2 (OS/2, 32-bit)
  IBM C Set++ (OS/2, 32-bit)
  Microsoft C 6.00A and 7.0 (DOS, Windows, or OS/2, 16-bit)
- Makefiles that show how to build family-API programs between Networking Services/DOS and the OS/2 Communications Manager
- CPI-C return codes in .INF format, for the OS/2 VIEW command
- APPC/APPN sense data in .INF format, for the OS/2 VIEW command
- A table of all the CPI-C product platforms, with the version of CPI-C they support in each of their releases
- A table of the CPI-C product platforms and kind of conversation security they support

- An order form to get *The Best of APPC, APPN, and CPI-C* CD-ROM from IBM, as well as a listing of its contents
- An order form to get additional copies of this book

The very latest version of the diskette is available for download on the APPC Forum on CompuServe. Once you log on to CompuServe, type GO APPC to reach the APPC Forum.* Go to the Sample Programs [5] library, and download the `CPICC1.ZIP` file. If you find any bugs or have code suggestions, check first to make sure you have the latest version of the diskette. If that version still doesn't solve your problem, please contact us. We enjoy solving problems, and we're happy to update the diskette.

WE'D LIKE TO HEAR FROM YOU!

Seen on the menu of a favorite restaurant[†]:

> *Your compliments keep us going.*
> *Your criticism helps us improve.*
> *Please keep us informed.*

Modern programming is all about iterative refinement. We've given you the highest quality book and diskette we could today. Happily, we know that you'll find things we missed or think of better ways to illustrate some of these concepts. We also know you'll think of code improvements, and—believe it or not—you may even find bugs. Finally, CPI-C itself is continuing to evolve, and we plan future editions of this book. So, . . .

We want to hear from you. Much of this book is the result of our ongoing collaboration with programmers around the world. We'd like to collaborate with you on future refinements. Therefore, here are two ways to reach us via electronic mail:

	John Q.	Peter
CompuServe:	72440,1544	73602,3201
Internet:	72440.1544@compuserve.com	73602.3201@compuserve.com

If you can't reach us via e-mail, you'll always be able to reach us by traditional mail, via our publisher:

CPI-C Programming in C
McGraw-Hill Books
Jay Ranade Series
P.O. Box 338
Grand Central Station, New York 10163-0338
U.S.A.

---

* Directions for getting access to CompuServe are described in "The APPC Forum on CompuServe" on p. 471.

† The Old West Steakhouse, Steamboat Springs, Colorado.

## Chapter 2

An Introduction to CPI-C and APPC

Millions of computers worldwide are running APPC. If you're surprised, you're not alone. Many people believe that APPC is available only on IBM mainframes. The truth is that most major vendors support APPC on a wide range of systems, from portables and workstations to midrange and mainframe computers. APPC is rapidly becoming the protocol of choice for developing mission-critical, client/server applications.

This chapter introduces you to APPC: what it is, how it works, and how it evolved. The chapter also examines issues to consider if you plan to design or implement client/server applications that use APPC and CPI-C. (If you're already experienced with APPC, you might want to jump ahead to the next chapter and dive right into the coding issues.)

APPC AND CPI-C: A TECHNICAL OVERVIEW

APPC is software that enables high-speed communication between programs on different computers. APPC software is available for many different computer operating systems, either as part of the operating system or as a separate software package.

APPC serves as an interface between application programs and a data communications network. When a program on your computer passes information to the APPC software, APPC takes the information and sends it on to a network interface, such as an asynchronous modem or a token-ring adapter card. The information travels across the network to another computer, where the APPC software receives the information from its network interface. Finally,

APPC puts the information back into its original format and passes it to the corresponding communications program.

Understanding APPC concepts

When people talk with each other, we say that they are having a conversation. Likewise, when two programs communicate with one another using APPC, we say they are having a conversation.

A conversation between two programs is similar to a conversation between two people. When you have a conversation with another person, you follow unwritten rules—that is, protocols that govern how you begin and end the conversation, how you take turns speaking, and how you exchange information. Similarly, APPC is called a protocol because it provides the rules that govern how conversations between programs start and stop, which program "speaks" first, and how data is exchanged. APPC consists of a set of well-defined and thorough rules to cover all possible communications situations.

Every program needs a partner to communicate with. Thus, APPC programs are developed in pairs. A program that's using APPC may have several conversations active at one time, with the same partner program or with different partners. Like some people you may know, a cleverly designed APPC program can even talk to itself.

People use nouns, verbs, objects, modifiers, and so on to communicate with each other. APPC programs are more limited in their communications; they use only verbs (function calls) to communicate with each other. These verbs, however, can be very useful and effective in that they allow your programs to start, stop, and control conversations. APPC programs use verbs such as:

ALLOCATE	Starts a conversation with a partner program
SEND_DATA	Sends data to a partner program
RECEIVE	Receives information from a partner program
DEALLOCATE	Ends a conversation with a partner program

What's the difference between APPC and APPN?

You may have seen the terms APPC and APPN, and wondered what they mean. APPC, Advanced Program-to-Program Communication, deals with *programs,* while APPN, Advanced Peer-to-Peer Networking, deals with *networks.* APPC enforces the rules by which programs exchange information. These rules do not deal with the details of network setup and routing. It is APPN that defines how APPC traffic gets from one point in a network to another. A reasonable comparison between APPC and APPN is the difference between a person using the telephone and the services offered by the telephone company.

APPC   If you want to call a friend, you look up the person's telephone number and dial the telephone. Both people identify themselves and the exchange of information begins. When the conversation is over, both of you say "Good-bye" and hang up. This protocol, although informal, is generally accepted and makes your communication efficient. APPC provides the same functions and rules for communication between application programs instead of people. An application program tells APPC that it needs a conversation with another application program. APPC starts a conversation between the programs so they can exchange data. When all the data has been exchanged, APPC provides a way for the programs to end the conversation.

APPN   APPN provides networking functions similar to those provided by the telephone companies. After you dial a telephone number, the telephone network routes the call through trunks, switches, branches, and so on. To make the connection, the network uses what it knows about available routes and current problems. This happens without you understanding the details of the network. You can talk on the telephone to another person no matter where the person is or no matter how the call is routed. APPN provides these functions for APPC applications and their data. It computes routes through the network, dynamically calculating which route is best. Like the telephone company, APPN's routing is done transparently. APPC applications cannot tell whether their partner in the APPN network is located in the same computer, in the next office, or in another country. Similarly, if someone moves within the same city and retains the same phone number, the telephone network handles the change with no other user impact.

If you connect to an APPN network, you simplify the setup needed for your computer and make it easier for other computers in the network to find you. APPN includes many functions that help reduce the amount of information that you need to set up and maintain a network. These APPN features automate many tasks that were time-consuming, complicated, and error-prone with the first wave of APPC software. For example, if you're installing a new workstation that uses APPN, you don't have to set up configuration information for every workstation you want to communicate with. You simply provide the name of the computer itself and the address of the intermediate node that handles your traffic. APPN takes care of the rest of the information needed to route APPC traffic to and from your workstation. To learn more about APPC and APPN, see the books listed in "APPC and APPN Books" in App. D.

APPC and client/server computing

Client/server computing is popular in our industry today. In fact, a recent article in *Network Computing* proclaimed that client/server is the "next generation computing architecture" and the "open computing platform for the 1990s."* Although everyone seems to have a different definition for the term, many companies follow the same set of steps to implement client/server applications.

Client/server computing requires sophisticated communications technology which is designed to perform well on many different machines, in both local

---

* David Litwack, "Client/Server Technology: The Open Computer Platform for the 1990s," *Network Computing,* November 1, 1992, pp. 13–14.

area networks and wide area networks. That's why APPC plays such an important role in client/server computing. APPC was designed specifically for communicating between computers that are treated as peers of one another, no matter the hardware or software used by those computers. APPC was also designed so that programs can run unchanged over any communications link, from token-ring and Ethernet LANs to asynchronous connections with Hayes-compatible modems. Alex Berson, author of *Client/Server Architecture,* affirms that APPC provides the most complete architecture and set of services for client/server communications. So, it's no surprise that, among companies surveyed by BRG, APPC is the most widely used protocol for implementing client/server applications.

THE EVOLUTION OF APPC

APPC is part of a family of communications protocols known as Systems Network Architecture, which is abbreviated SNA (and pronounced where we work as "snah"). The early members of this family provided communications between mainframe computers and specialized devices, like displays and printers. There was a hierarchical relationship in the network between the larger computers and the smaller, "dumber" devices. Different types of devices used different ways to communicate. The members of the SNA family are known as *LU types,* where LU stands for logical unit, which is simply the software that handles data communications.

The first protocols developed within the SNA framework supported communications between host programs and dumb terminals. Each time a new type of device was included in the network, a new communications protocol was developed for that particular device. As a result, different LU types were developed to accommodate these devices. For instance, LU 2 supports communications between host programs and 3270 terminals, and LU 3 supports communications between host programs and 3270 printers.

To support the distributed processing required by client/server applications, new LU types were developed. It became apparent, however, that the communications protocol for distributed processing should not be tied to a particular type of hardware or operating system; there would simply be too many different protocols. For this reason, LU 6.2 was designed in 1985 as a generic protocol to support distributed, peer-to-peer processing between different types of computers. The name LU 6.2 captures its evolutionary history; there have been LU types 0, 1, 2, ..., and 6.1 preceding it. Because the name LU 6.2 is not very meaningful, the term APPC is now used synonymously. APPC, the last LU type to be developed, is flexible enough to support all communications between any set of programs that understand APPC.

APPC was originally designed to optimize the use of expensive, low-speed data links. Today we see LANs everywhere and high-speed WAN networks just around the corner. APPC's initial investment in reducing overhead and optimizing link utilization has made it the fastest protocol on the LAN for bulk data transfer. And, APPC will perform equally well on tomorrow's frame relay and asynchronous transfer mode (ATM) networks, as well as on the gigabit APPN networks of the future. The best news of all: today's APPC applications will run unchanged over tomorrow's gigabit networks.

CPI-C: THE BEST WAY TO USE APPC

APPC provides a consistent set of functions for program-to-program communication across different platforms. But, APPC's original design did not specify a common application programming interface (API) for implementing these functions. As a result, each operating system that supports APPC developed its own native API, a set of verbs that closely resemble the operating system itself. These differences do not pose a problem if you are writing programs for two computers that use the same operating system. However, to take advantage of the strengths of each computer, most client/server applications run on different types of computers.

The Common Programming Interface for Communications (CPI-C) was designed to address the problem of different syntax on different computers. CPI-C provides a standard set of verbs, known as CPI-C calls, for all systems that support CPI-C. When CPI-C was first developed, it included the base set of functions required to write robust client/server applications. Recent versions of CPI-C have added functions, such as nonblocking calls and calls to accept multiple conversations, that simplify the design and coding for the server side of client/server applications. As CPI-C continues to evolve, all applications written to any particular version of CPI-C will work with future versions of this interface. You choose when or if you want to update your applications to take advantage of these new functions.

Future versions of CPI-C will ensure portability, not only across platforms and languages, but also across transport protocols. This means that you will be able to run your CPI-C programs over TCP/IP and OSI without having to make any changes to the programs. In the near future, we expect to see CPI-C conversations being used for all types of data networks.

COMMUNICATING IN AN OPEN, MULTIVENDOR WORLD

Why is APPC the protocol of choice for many communicating applications? Many users cite its openness, its advanced features, its common programming interface, and its exceptional performance. IBM and other vendors are constantly improving both the architecture and the products to ensure greater usability and performance in your network.

According to an article in *Beyond Computing,** a system must meet several criteria to be considered truly open. An open system must be based on widely accepted standards, run on a wide variety of platforms, enable programs to be moved from platforms as technology grows and changes, and allow true interoperation between hardware and software modules.

---

* Larry Marion, "Targeting Open Systems," *Beyond Computing,* December 1992, pp. 21–26.

This definition of an open system sounds very much like a description of APPC. Standards for the APPC architecture have been available to vendors since 1985; CPI-C standards have been available since 1990. More than 50 vendors support APPC or APPN in their platforms, routers, and gateways, including major vendors such as Apple, Data General, DEC, DCA, Eicon, Hewlett-Packard, Microsoft, NetSoft, Novell, Sun, Unisys, and Wall Data. APPC implementations run on everything from the latest pen-based and portable computers to minicomputers and mainframes, and even in cash registers! APPC protocols ensure that you can connect any two APPC products.

Improving productivity

The advanced features of APPC help speed the development of robust client/server applications and keep development costs down.

Client/server applications often prove to be especially challenging to the programmer. It's not enough to understand the details about the computer and operating system that your application uses. If you're designing client/server applications, you have to deal with the computers used by both sides of the application as well as the intervening network. For instance, implementing effective security measures is more important and more complicated since you must ensure security throughout the network. In addition, synchronization and error reporting are often problematic in a distributed environment because both sides of the application must coordinate their work.

One reason APPC has become so widely used in client/server applications is that it furnishes a complete set of useful functions like security, synchronization, and error reporting. If you use other protocols, you must build these functions into every application you write. For example, if you program to the NetBIOS programming interface, you must design and implement a strategy for security for each application. Not only does this approach require additional work, but it may also result in a number of incompatible security systems in your network. By contrast, APPC includes a common set of security services that are consistent across all APPC platforms.

Similarly, most protocols do not include synchronization functions. Synchronization is required by any program that cannot continue processing data until the data sent to the partner program has been received and processed. Rather than writing your own synchronization routine, APPC provides a Confirm() call that you can use to handle synchronization between two programs.

Some applications, such as transaction-processing programs in banking, require more sophisticated synchronization facilities. If you are using an automated teller machine to withdraw money from one account and deposit it in another account, the applications must agree that the transaction has taken place. Imagine what would happen if a large withdrawal was processed, and then a construction crew dug up the phone link before the deposit was completed. APPC's advanced synchronization services, sync point (also known as *CPI-Resource Recovery* and abbreviated *CPI-RR*), ensure that the two databases are reconciled when these sorts of accidents occur. In such cases, the sync point services automatically reconnect to the partner platform and compare transactions to determine whether to commit the previous transaction. Sync point saves you an enormous amount of work; implementing all of the functions provided by sync point would require at least 20,000 lines of code.

APPC also offers error reporting features that enable a program to notify its partner that an error was discovered in the data by the program itself. The APPC Send_Error() call transmits a special record to the partner program, indicating the error condition. The applications can then exchange error information and determine how to recover from the error.

We discussed in the first chapter why CPI-C is the preferred programming interface for APPC. Incidentally, a CPI-C program can have conversations just fine with programs that use the native APPC verbs. If you have a mainframe program that's already written to use APPC, you don't need to touch it. You should write all your *new* clients, however, using CPI-C.

Improving performance

Client/server computing is growing as the demand for quick access to vital information increases. For example, *Computerworld* reports that "the need for speed" is responsible for moving financial departments in many companies to client/server applications.* Thus, communication protocols that support client/server computing must demonstrate exceptional levels of performance.

The performance of APPC rivals and often exceeds that of other communications protocols. InterLAB, an independent network testing and consulting organization, used APPC in recent tests of token-ring adapters because of its high performance in a real-world application environment. According to Kevin Tolly, president of InterLAB, "we were looking for top performance and found it in APPC. Using OS/2 version 2.0 and OS/2 Extended Services version 1.0, we were able to move over 12 million bits per second across a 16-Mbps token-ring, end-to-end throughput." Similarly, recent independent tests indicate that, for both small and large data transfers on a LAN, APPC is much faster than TCP/IP. So, APPC gives you the performance you need to support new client/server applications.

SELECTING A COMMUNICATIONS API

If you develop client/server applications, you have several important design decisions to make. One decision involves selecting a protocol to provide communications support; examples of communications protocols include APPC, TCP/IP, NetBIOS, and IPX. A separate, but related, decision is determining which application programming interface (API) to use. When you use APPC, you can choose among three popular API styles: message queuing, remote procedure calls

---

* Kim S. Nash, "Financial Departments Move to Client/Server," *Computerworld,* December 28, 1992, p. 34.

(RPCs), and conversational. All of these interfaces run easily atop APPC; CPI-C is the preferred API when you choose conversational programming.

Message queuing

With message queues, a program sends messages to a queue serviced by a partner program and receives messages sent to its own queue by other programs. Message queuing is an asynchronous API; the program does not wait for its partner to return a response to its message. As a result, message queuing makes efficient use of network and system resources.

Message queuing makes programming easier, since the verbs are simple and most programmers understand how queues work. Nevertheless, additional programming is required to correlate requests and responses. Plus, you have to use timeouts to start error-recovery processing.

Examples of applications that typically use message queuing include electronic mail, reservation systems, and other high-volume transaction processing applications. Message queuing is probably not the best choice for applications like telnet that require many small blocks of data which are all dependent upon one another.

Remote Procedure Calls (RPCs)

Remote Procedure Calls (RPCs) enable a program to start a subroutine in the same or a different computer. When the program issues a call, the RPC code takes the parameters passed with the call and sends them to a remote subroutine. Any information returned by the remote subroutine goes back to the program that made the call.

RPCs simplify programming for distributed applications, since no communication verbs are required in the partner programs. In fact, the calls look like standard subroutine calls running on one system. Unlike message queuing, the RPC code automatically correlates the requests and responses. In addition, most RPC implementations provide automatic data conversion functions.

Although the calls are simple, RPCs require a significant amount of setup and configuration. Also, RPCs are synchronous; that is, the program waits during the call until the partner responds. So, RPCs are usually not intended for programs that support a high transaction volume. In addition, because the program can't detect network failures, error handling and recovery can be complicated.

RPCs are a good choice if you are designing request/response programs like database queries or programs that distribute work to other, faster computers. With these types of applications, it's faster to "farm out" the work than to handle it locally, as long as you don't mind waiting for the response.

Conversational interfaces

Conversational APIs enable two programs to establish a dialog or "conversation" to exchange data and status information. Examples of conversational

APIs include the Common Programming Interface for Communications (CPI-C), NetBEUI (for NetBIOS), and Sockets (for TCP/IP). These interfaces often provide more flexibility than other APIs. In fact, RPC and message queuing are often built on top of conversational APIs.

Conversational APIs give you more control as a programmer. These APIs let you control the amount of data you want to send or receive; they handle both large and small blocks of data efficiently. Because conversational APIs make detailed error information available, you also have more control over how the application recovers from errors and how much error information is available to users. In addition, the conversations serve as correlators to handle synchronization between programs.

Because conversational APIs provide you with many calls, a good understanding of communications is essential. Conversational APIs, therefore, often require more programming. A simple transaction requires several communication calls, and the program must handle all errors and data exchanges. Also, if the application requires data conversion, you have to build it into the application. That's why most programmers who use conversations create libraries and reuse their code.

Conversational APIs are ideal for applications that handle large blocks of data, like file transfers, as well as those that handle small blocks of data, including terminal emulators like telnet. These APIs are also a good choice for applications, such as distributed databases, that require synchronization across multiple partners. You should also use conversational APIs if you need to provide detailed error-handling information to your application's users.

THE EVOLUTION OF CPI-C

The development of a standard programming interface for the conversational style, CPI-C, has been an evolutionary process that has progressed dramatically over the past five years. The definition of CPI-C has principally involved the work of IBM, with additional work in the X/Open and OSI standard organizations. In recent years, CPI-C has been developed in an open forum, called the *CPI-C Implementers Workshop*. These groups have gone through several iterative steps, which are described here.

Appendix D provides the information you need to get printed books and on-line versions of the following CPI-C specifications. The following section gives you an overview of the different CPI-C versions available in the marketplace. If you're interested in getting on with the programming, skip over this section, and come back someday while you're waiting for a big program to Make.

CPI-C 1.0.   IBM's initial specification of CPI-C provided a standard base for conversational communications. It included the following support:

- Starting and ending conversations
- Sending and receiving data
- Synchronizing programs through confirmation flows

- Reporting on errors
- Optimizing conversation flows (using Flush and Prepare_To_Receive calls)

CPI-C 1.1. As more IBM computers supported CPI-C, additional functions were added in 1990 to widen CPI-C's usefulness:

- Additional parameter and return code support for sync point (CPI-RR)
- Automatic parameter conversion
- Support for communication with programs that use the native APPC API
- Local/remote transparency, allowing programs to communicate with one another within a single computer

Note that CPI-RR is a separate API. Support for CPI-RR is not required to claim full support for any CPI-C version.

X/Open CPI-C. X/Open adopted CPI-C at the 1.1 level (with the exception of sync point support for CPI-RR) to allow X/Open-compliant systems to communicate with systems implementing APPC. The X/Open developers' specification published in 1990 included several new functions not found in IBM's CPI-C 1.1:

- Support for nonblocking calls
- Ability to accept multiple conversations
- Support for conversion of data between ASCII and EBCDIC
- Support for security parameters

CPI-C 1.2. CPI-C 1.0 was designed to provide a consistent programming interface for communications programming. Its derivatives, CPI-C 1.1 and X/Open CPI-C, diverged in the function they provided. CPI-C 1.2 offers a single spec that incorporates everything added to CPI-C 1.1 and X/Open CPI-C.

- Nonblocking calls—same as the X/Open calls
- Conversation security parameters—similar to the X/Open calls, but the user ID and password parameters have been expanded to 10 bytes
- Multiple conversations—multiple calls to accommodate both the X/Open and CPI-C 1.1 approaches

WinCPIC 1.0. In 1993, a group of PC software vendors, including Microsoft and IBM, defined a CPI-C specification to be used when programming CPI-C applications for Windows environments. The Windows CPI-C specification (WinCPIC) was designed within the framework of WOSA (Windows Open Services Architecture). The committee that developed the WinCPIC spec started with CPI-C 1.2 as it was nearing completion, but varied from it a little in these areas:

- It adds five calls to do nonblocking operations in a way that is consistent with other WOSA APIs, to accommodate Windows' process and threading structure.
- It adds a CPI-C extension call, Specify_Windows_Handle(), as an alternate way to service nonblocking calls.

- It supports only the old-style (8-byte) calls for setting and extracting user IDs and passwords.
- It adds three CPI-C extension calls to Set, Extract, and Delete side information entries, consistent with the CPI-C extensions in the OS/2 Communications Manager.

CPI-C 2.0.   The development of the newest CPI-C version is being finalized at the time of the printing of this book. It's being created by the CPI-C Implementers Workshop, a group of vendors who meet quarterly to hammer out further improvements to CPI-C. CPI-C 2.0 will contain support for full-duplex conversations, improved support for nonblocking conversations, and improved diagnostics through secondary return codes.

This book discusses the CPI-C calls and parameters up through CPI-C 1.2 and WinCPIC 1.0. We don't focus on X/Open CPI-C, which was a stepping stone toward CPI-C 1.2. The X/Open and OSI standards bodies are working with members of the CPI-C Implementers Workshop to adopt CPI-C 2.0 as their standard for conversational programming. Many more months will elapse before you see the widespread installation of CPI-C 2.0 on all the platforms you might use.

Although CPI-C 1.2 is not widely available at the printing of this book, its support will blossom in 1994. We've carefully identified the calls in the text that are new to CPI-C 1.2, in case the platforms you're programming for don't yet support that version. However, we think your CPI-C platform should be providing full support for CPI-C 1.2 today. If it isn't, call the vendor of your CPI-C software and demand it. A common programming interface is of greatest benefit when it is truly common across all platforms.

Getting Started

Sending "Hello, world" (Where Else to Start?)

Let's begin at a place familiar to most C programmers. When we first learned C, we started with a program that displayed the phrase "Hello, world" on the screen. You'll remember this program (derived from Kernighan and Ritchie) looked like this:

```c
#include <stdio.h>

void main(void)
{
    (void)printf("Hello, world\n");
}
```

This program may differ in detail from the one you learned from, depending on how and when you learned C. We've added several `void` statements that Kernighan and Ritchie didn't have. For example, since we know we're not going to look at the value returned by the printf() function, we cast it to void. Similarly, our main() procedure takes no parameters and returns nothing, so it gets a couple of voids added to its declaration.

We intend the code examples we show to compile free of warnings when using modern ANSI C compilers. The code is strongly typed and passes the checks in the Lint programs we use. Thus, our style explicitly places voids, casts, consts, and so on where appropriate. We recommend you do the same.

We'll use the term *program* throughout this book to refer to a single executable file. If you were to compile and link the preceding "Hello, world" example for DOS, Windows, or OS/2, you'd probably create a file named `HELLOW.EXE`.

We refer to HELLOW.EXE as a program. Some programs are very simple and are built from just one source file—in this case, the source file HELLOW.C. Most commercial programs are much more complex; they're made from lots of source files, which are individually compiled and then linked together.

We'll use the term *application* to refer to all the programs and parts needed to make a single package work. If you're a spreadsheet user, for example, you know that an application such as *Lotus 1-2-3* consists of lots of separate programs and files. All its programs and files must be built to work together, which is usually done by version or release.

Every CPI-C application consists of at least two programs, one program for each computer where part of the application will be running. As the programmer, you have to design, code, and test both programs.* With our first CPI-C example, we'll send the phrase "Hello, world" from one program to another, which will display it. We'll create two programs: one to send the phrase "Hello, world," and one to receive the incoming phrase and display it. In these two programs, we'll use many of the typedefs and constants that are defined in the CPI-C header file, cpic.h. We'll discuss these typedefs, variables, constants, and function prototypes thoroughly in the next chapter. In the meantime, we thought you'd enjoy getting to see running code before we go into all the details of the syntax.

As you might guess, the key portion of the receiving program will look like this:

```
(void)printf("%s\n", buffer_ptr);
```

where buffer_ptr points to a string received from the sending program (hopefully the string will say "Hello, world").

Let's sketch out how the two programs work. The originator program (which we call the *client*) sends the string; the target program (which we call the *server*) receives and displays the string. The client program does not send a null-terminating character ('\0') to delimit the string, and it does not send a newline character ('\n'), either. We'll let the server program add these characters, since it controls the display of the output. Figure 3.1 shows the skeleton for these two programs, without the steps to set up and take down the communications connection.

In this first excerpt of the design, we've introduced the names of two important CPI-C calls:

- Send_Data(), which is used to send a memory block to the partner
- Receive(), which waits for data to be received, and places it into the buffer you point to

SETTING UP A CONVERSATION

To begin exchanging data, a pair of programs must be involved in a *conversation*. To do this, the client program must supply the name of the server program it wishes to contact before it issues its Send_Data() call.

---

* If you're familiar with programming for HLLAPI or mainframe 3270 terminal emulation, you've probably come to expect that you only have to write code for one side of your application. CPI-C offers a true peer-to-peer relationship between the programs, meaning that you have to create both programs in tandem.

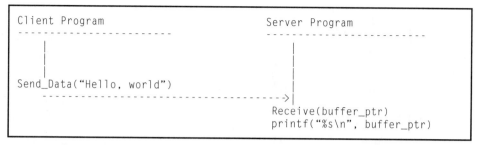

```
Client Program                                    Server Program
- - - - - - - - - - - - - - - - - - - - -         - - - - - - - - - - - - - - - - - - - - -
      |                                                 |
      |                                                 |
      |                                                 |
Send_Data("Hello, world")                               |
- - - - - - - - - - - - - - - - - - - - - - - - - - - ->|
                                                  Receive(buffer_ptr)
                                                  printf("%s\n", buffer_ptr)
```

Figure 3.1 Initial sketch for sending "Hello, world". The arrow in this sketch shows when the message flows from the client program to the server program. The Receive() call issued by the server program won't return from CPI-C until the message from the client arrives.

Setting up a CPI-C conversation is analogous to starting a telephone conversation. In a telephone conversation, you first need the telephone number of the person you're calling. Next, you dial the number and assure that someone answers the phone at the other end. At that point, you can begin talking back and forth, that is, exchanging information.

In CPI-C, your client program issues a call known as Initialize_Conversation() to supply the name and location of the server program. By analogy, Initialize_Conversation() is equivalent to having the telephone number in your hand, picking up the phone, and getting a dial tone.

The next call your CPI-C program issues is named Allocate(). Allocate() is like dialing the phone number and listening to it ring. You use the Allocate() CPI-C call to assure that you can get a good connection with that partner. At the server program, there's a CPI-C call that's equivalent to picking up the receiver of the ringing telephone; it's named Accept_Conversation(). In our first, simple program, we're going to say "Hello, world," then hang up quickly. Like many beginners, its behavior is a little antisocial; it doesn't even wait to make sure there is someone to hear what is said.

Figure 3.2 puts together the pieces we have so far.

ENDING A CONVERSATION

Among the communicating CPI-C programs you write, many of the housekeeping steps will be similar. One side issues the Initialize_Conversation() and Allocate() calls; the other side calls Accept_Conversation(). Similarly, there are some things that are always done at the end of a CPI-C program. In a telephone conversation, you may say "Good-bye," and plan to hang up—but you generally wait until the person you're talking to agrees before you actually hang up the receiver. In this example, the client side issues the CPI-C Deallocate() call to end the conversation. The Deallocate() call operates quickly; CPI-C returns to the client program without waiting for the server side to acknowledge that it's ready to end the conversation (again, antisocial behavior). In CPI-C, only one side needs to issue a Deallocate() call; one Deallocate() call ends the conversation for both sides.

Examine Fig. 3.3. Notice that the arrow showing the underlying flow of conversation data occurs after the last call on the client side, but before the first

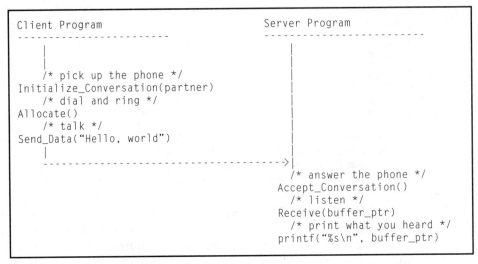

Figure 3.2 Evolving program sketches with conversation setup calls.

call on the server side. This placement isn't an accident. Data actually flows on the conversation for the first time after it has been deallocated by the client. This behavior is because of CPI-C's default buffering operation. CPI-C holds everything it's handed until it knows it has to send it. In this case, the end of a conversation tells CPI-C that it should send everything that it's holding to the partner. This results in the odd behavior we see here: one side is all done before the other side even sees anything arrive. We'll spend a whole chapter talking about how and why this occurs; its effect is excellent performance.

We've added a call to the getchar() routine on the server side. On some computers, the server program can be automatically started, pop up in a window, receive the string from the client and call printf(), then quickly close the window. By calling getchar(), the server program will at least wait for a user to press a key before it vanishes.

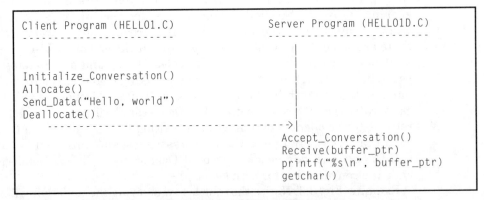

Figure 3.3 Full sketch for paired "Hello, world" programs.

It's easy to see how the two programs work together as a single application when they're sketched side by side. Sketching your applications in this way is a simple design technique we recommend you use.

CREATING OUR FIRST APPLICATION

The source code files for our first two programs are named HELLO1.C and HELLO1D.C. We're using a naming convention that's been adopted by UNIX programmers. The server side (the side sitting and waiting for something to do) is referred to as the *daemon*. Its name is constructed by adding a D to the name of its partner, the client program. Thus, the client's name is HELLO1 and server's name is HELLO1D.

We'll show the source for HELLO1.C first. You'll see that it consists of four CPI-C calls and a return statement. The four CPI-C calls are the same four we showed in the preceding sketch. When you see them in the program, they'll look a little strange, since we're using CPI-C's six-character short names for each call. We'll talk in more detail in the next chapter about why each call has a long and a short form. In the meantime, here are the CPI-C calls we use in the two programs, with their long names and their corresponding short names.

Long Name	Short Name
Initialize_Conversation()	cminit()
Allocate()	cmallc()
Send_Data()	cmsend()
Deallocate()	cmdeal()
Accept_Conversation()	cmaccp()
Receive()	cmrcv()

Each of these calls takes at least two parameters; one of these calls, the Receive() call, takes eight parameters. You'll see that every parameter on every call is a pointer. CPI-C calls only by reference, which lets it work the same across all programming languages.

The values that these parameters point to either supply input to CPI-C as part of the call, or get output information back from CPI-C. For example, the first call in HELLO1 is Initialize_Conversation(). It has three parameters: conversation_ID, symbolic_destination_name, and cpic_return_code, and looks like this:

```
cminit(                    /* Initialize_Conversation      */
    conversation_ID,       /* O: returned conversation ID  */
    SYM_DEST_NAME,         /* I: symbolic destination name */
    &cpic_return_code);    /* O: return code from this call */
```

The conversation_ID parameter is an output parameter; it points to a field into which CPI-C will return information. The symbolic_destination_name is an input parameter; it points to the name that CPI-C uses to decide who and where the partner program is. The cpic_return_code parameter is an output parameter;

it points to a field where CPI-C will write an integer that represents the return code from the call. In the early examples, we're showing the input and output parameters with an "I:" or "O:" in the comments next to the parameters.

Example client program HELLO1.C. This program contains two CPI-C calls to set up the conversation, one call to send the data, and one call to take down the conversation:

```
/*-----------------------------------------------------------------
 *  CPI-C "Hello, world" program
 *  Client side (file HELLO1.C)
 *-----------------------------------------------------------------*/
#include <cpic.h>                   /* conversation API library    */
#include <string.h>                 /* strings and memory          */
#include <stdlib.h>                 /* standard library            */

/* this hardcoded sym_dest_name is 8 chars long & blank padded     */
#define SYM_DEST_NAME   (unsigned char*)"HELLO1S "

/* this is the string we're sending to the partner                 */
#define SEND_THIS       (unsigned char*)"Hello, world"

int main(void)
{
    unsigned char   conversation_ID[CM_CID_SIZE];
    unsigned char * data_buffer = SEND_THIS;
    CM_INT32        send_length = (CM_INT32)strlen(SEND_THIS);
    CM_RETURN_CODE  cpic_return_code;

    CM_REQUEST_TO_SEND_RECEIVED rts_received;

    cminit(                     /* Initialize_Conversation          */
        conversation_ID,        /* O: returned conversation ID      */
        SYM_DEST_NAME,          /* I: symbolic destination name     */
        &cpic_return_code);     /* O: return code from this call    */

    cmallc(                     /* Allocate                         */
        conversation_ID,        /* I: conversation ID               */
        &cpic_return_code);     /* O: return code from this call    */

    cmsend(                     /* Send_Data                        */
        conversation_ID,        /* I: conversation ID               */
        data_buffer,            /* I: send this buffer              */
        &send_length,           /* I: length to send                */
        &rts_received,          /* O: was RTS received?             */
        &cpic_return_code);     /* O: return code from this call    */

    cmdeal(                     /* Deallocate                       */
        conversation_ID,        /* I: conversation ID               */
        &cpic_return_code);     /* O: return code from this call    */

    return(EXIT_SUCCESS);
}
```

The symbolic destination name is CPI-C's way of letting you say whom you want to talk to. We'll spend a lot more time with it in later chapters. We just want to mention now that it's the strangest field for C programmers. The field is eight characters long, and if your name is less than eight characters long, you need to pad it on the right with blanks.

You can see that every CPI-C call has a return code. Due to space limitations, we haven't put any error checking in this sample. One of the most important aspects of communications programming is checking all returned values, and we'll do a lot of it in the later programs we discuss.

Once you've looked through the code for the client side, HELLO1, you'll find the code for the server, HELLO1D, to be even shorter. It contains just two CPI-C calls. Accept_Conversation() gets a good conversation ID for the server side. The call to Receive() gets the arriving data, as well as the notification that the conversation has already been deallocated. There's nothing more to do at that point other than print what's arrived, wait for someone to see it and press a key, and exit.

We set aside a data_buffer to receive into. We've arbitrarily made it 101 bytes long. On the Receive(), we set the requested length to only 100 bytes. In case we receive exactly 100 bytes, we want to have room to stick a '\0' on the end, so we can use printf() to display it.

Example server program HELLO1D.C. Here we have just two CPI-C calls and a call to printf and getchar.

```
/*------------------------------------------------------------------
 *  CPI-C "Hello, world" program
 *  Server side (file HELLO1D.C)
 *------------------------------------------------------------------*/
#include <cpic.h>                /* conversation API library    */
#include <stdio.h>               /* file I/O                     */
#include <stdlib.h>              /* standard library             */

int main(void)
{
    unsigned char   conversation_ID[CM_CID_SIZE];
    unsigned char   data_buffer[100+1];
    CM_INT32        requested_length =
                        (CM_INT32)sizeof(data_buffer)-1;
    CM_INT32        received_length = 0;
    CM_RETURN_CODE  cpic_return_code;

    CM_DATA_RECEIVED_TYPE data_received;
    CM_STATUS_RECEIVED    status_received;
    CM_REQUEST_TO_SEND_RECEIVED rts_received;

    cmaccp(                      /* Accept_Conversation          */
        conversation_ID,         /*  O: returned conversation ID */
        &cpic_return_code);      /*  O: return code from this call */

    cmrcv(                       /* Receive                      */
        conversation_ID,         /*  I: conversation ID          */
        data_buffer,             /*  I: where to put received data */
        &requested_length,       /*  I: maximum length to receive */
        &data_received,          /*  O: data complete or not?    */
        &received_length,        /*  O: length of received data  */
        &status_received,        /*  O: has status changed?      */
        &rts_received,           /*  O: was RTS received?        */
        &cpic_return_code);      /*  O: return code from this call */

    data_buffer[received_length] = '\0';   /* insert the null    */
    (void)printf("%s\nPress a key to end the program...\n",
                data_buffer);

    (void)getchar();             /* pause for any keystroke      */

    return(EXIT_SUCCESS);
}
```

You can see that there are lots of programming details we need to introduce, but we won't do them all at once. We'll start with four of the most important parameters in any CPI-C application: return codes, conversation IDs, and the parameters called "data_received" and "status_received" on each Receive() call. These details are key to understanding the source code you've just seen.

Return code

For every CPI-C call that your program issues, CPI-C replies with a return code. The CPI-C return code tells you what happened on a call. Every CPI-C return code is discussed in App. A, with an explanation of what the return code means, likely reasons why it was returned, and steps you can take as a programmer to avoid the problem.

In these first few source code examples, we haven't put in any code to look at the return codes. We did this to make the program listings shorter, giving you a better chance of seeing the calls and logic. Ignoring CPI-C return codes *is a bad idea!* There are some C routines where you might dare to ignore what they return, but we've all probably been stung by ignoring the return code from a malloc() call—when we were actually out of memory. Ignoring CPI-C return codes is as problematic as ignoring what malloc() returns.

We generally expect the CPI-C return code to be zero, which is represented by the constant CM_OK. Another return code to expect is the one that tells you the conversation has been deallocated. If the return code is not zero, your programs might do something like print the return code and exit. In Chap. 20, we'll delve into more sophisticated techniques for error recovery and reporting, where programs expect and take special actions upon getting some of the nonzero return code values.

Conversation ID

Although we only have a single conversation going on in this first example, complex programs can have many conversations going on simultaneously. When your program successfully issues an Initialize_Conversation() or Accept_Conversation() call, CPI-C returns a unique 8-byte identifier for the new conversation, called a *conversation ID*. Your program then supplies a pointer to this conversation ID on all the subsequent calls as a handle for this conversation. When a conversation is deallocated, CPI-C invalidates the conversation ID.

There are five CPI-C calls that don't require a conversation ID, which means you can issue them whenever you want.* Three calls, Initialize_Conversation(), Accept_Conversation(), and Initialize_For_Incoming(), ask CPI-C for a new conversation ID; on these three calls, the conversation ID is an output

---

* For the curious, the five calls with no conversation ID are Convert_Incoming(), Convert_Outgoing(), Extract_Maximum_Buffer_Size(), Release_Local_TP_Name(), and Specify_Local_TP_Name().

parameter. On all the rest of the CPI-C calls, the conversation ID is a required input parameter.

Data received and status received

You'll notice two returned parameters on the Receive() call: *data_received* and *status_received*. A Receive() call in CPI-C lets you receive whatever there is new that your program should know about. Often the new news is that data has arrived, but sometimes the Receive() returns because the partner has changed some aspect of the conversation—for example, the partner no longer wants to be the sender. That's why CPI-C has these two parameters that get filled in on each Receive() call.

The *data_received* parameter tells your program whether or not data was actually received. If data was received, it tells your program whether it was a complete chunk of data (called a *record*) or just part of one.

The *status_received* parameter helps guide your program in what programming logic to execute next. It tells you whether the state of the conversation (that is, who is the sender and what calls are allowed) has changed since the last call.

CPI-C buries a lot of power in these two parameters; we'll devote more discussion to them in Chap. 8. For simplicity, we've written both sides of this example in such a way that we avoid looking at these parameters. This simplifying assumption of ignoring these two parameters is also a poor idea, since you can never be sure your partner program will always send you exactly what you expect long into the future of later versions of your programs.

At this point, we have covered the important parameters on the calls we've used so far. There are other parameters on these calls that we haven't used and thus haven't discussed. The table at the back of this book points you to a discussion of every call and parameter.

SYNCHRONIZING A PAIR OF PROGRAMS

Our telephone analogy gets a little stretched at this point. The example application we've just shown is like sending a message as soon as the target phone starts to ring—without making sure anyone ever picks up the phone. The message can be delivered only if someone picks up the phone. If the server program starts up fine or is already started, the previous example will accomplish what we want. But if the server program isn't set up right to answer the call, the client will never know there was a problem. That's not how we handle our phone conversations, and it's probably not how you'll design most of your CPI-C applications.

CPI-C provides an easy way for your programs to verify that what they send is successfully received and processed. The sending program asks for a confirmation (an acknowledgment), and the receiving program either confirms it or rejects the confirmation request. To use this mechanism, your programs must set the *synchronization level* (known as *sync_level*) to allow confirmation. The default sync_level for a conversation is to have no synchronization, which is represented by the constant CM_NONE. We used the default sync_level in the HELLO1 program. Relying on the default is certainly easy, but not very interesting; sync_level(CM_NONE) means that the programs will not and cannot ask each other for confirmation.

The simplest place to perform confirmation is just before the end of a conversation. You can verify that all the work done during that conversation was completed successfully and do so with only one set of synchronization calls instead of many sets.

To continue our telephone analogy, there are two ways to end a conversation:

- Politely, where we wait for an acknowledgment before hanging up
- Impolitely, where we can just hang up

To make sure that the server program is successfully started, we probably want to opt for politeness. The default in CPI-C is to be impolite,* so we need to specify that we're using the polite type. We indicate this with a CPI-C call named Set_Sync_Level(), changing the sync_level to CM_CONFIRM from its default of CM_NONE. Issuing a call to Confirm() causes the originator to wait until the partner acknowledges. The server program issues a Confirmed() call to acknowledge that everything has been received *and* processed successfully. As with many CPI-C conversation characteristics, only the client program can set the synchronization level; the server program inherits whatever value the client chose.

We'll create a new pair of programs by taking our first example and adding the CPI-C calls needed to perform confirmation. Refer to Fig. 3.4. The first addition is a call to Set_Sync_Level() on the client side. Set_Sync_Level() requires a valid conversation ID in order to work, so it's placed after the Initialize_Conversation() and before the Allocate() call.

You'll see that there is no explicit Confirm() call on the client side. The Deallocate() looks at the current sync_level, which we've set to CM_CONFIRM. The Deallocate() call doesn't complete until CPI-C sees that the partner has issued Confirmed().

What follows is the full C source code for two new programs, now with confirmation to acknowledge successful processing:

Example client program HELLO2.C.   The Deallocate() call causes CPI-C to internally make a Confirm() call. The Deallocate() call does not return from CPI-C until the partner replies with a Confirmed().

---

* Why would any communication program ever want to use this default (impolite and unsafe) technique?

- It does not consume as much network resource.
- The client doesn't have to wait for the server to become available and respond.

```
Client Program (HELLO2.C)                Server Program (HELLO2D.C)
------------------------                 --------------------------
    |                                        |
    |                                        |
Initialize_Conversation()                   |
Set_Sync_Level(CONFIRM)                      |
Allocate()                                   |
Send_Data("Hello, world")                    |
Deallocate(SYNC_LEVEL)                       |
    ------------------------------------->|
    .                                    Accept_Conversation()
    .                                    Receive(buffer_ptr)
    .                                    printf("%s\n", buffer_ptr)
    .                                    Confirmed()
    <-------------------------------------
    .                                    getchar()
```

Figure 3.4 Sketch for the "Hello, world" programs, with confirmation.

```c
/*-------------------------------------------------------------------
 * CPI-C "Hello, world" program, with confirmation.
 * Client side (file HELLO2.C)
 *-----------------------------------------------------------------*/
#include <cpic.h>              /* conversation API library     */
#include <string.h>            /* strings and memory           */
#include <stdlib.h>            /* standard library             */

/* this hardcoded sym_dest_name is 8 chars long & blank padded  */
#define SYM_DEST_NAME   (unsigned char*)"HELLO2S "

/* this is the string we're sending to the partner             */
#define SEND_THIS       (unsigned char*)"Hello, world"

int main(void)
{
    unsigned char   conversation_ID[CM_CID_SIZE];
    unsigned char * data_buffer = SEND_THIS;
    CM_INT32        send_length = (CM_INT32)strlen(SEND_THIS);
    CM_RETURN_CODE  cpic_return_code;
    CM_SYNC_LEVEL   sync_level = CM_CONFIRM;

    CM_REQUEST_TO_SEND_RECEIVED rts_received;

    cminit(                    /* Initialize_Conversation       */
        conversation_ID,       /* O: returned conversation ID   */
        SYM_DEST_NAME,         /* I: symbolic destination name  */
        &cpic_return_code);    /* O: return code from this call */

    cmssl(                     /* Set_Sync_Level                */
        conversation_ID,       /* I: conversation ID            */
        &sync_level,           /* I: set sync_level to CONFIRM  */
        &cpic_return_code);    /* O: return code from this call */
```

```
    cmallc(                        /* Allocate                     */
        conversation_ID,           /* I: conversation ID           */
        &cpic_return_code);        /* O: return code from this call */

    cmsend(                        /* Send_Data                    */
        conversation_ID,           /* I: conversation ID           */
        data_buffer,               /* I: send this buffer          */
        &send_length,              /* I: length to send            */
        &rts_received,             /* O: was RTS received?         */
        &cpic_return_code);        /* O: return code from this call */

    cmdeal(                        /* Deallocate                   */
        conversation_ID,           /* I: conversation ID           */
        &cpic_return_code);        /* O: return code from this call */

    return(EXIT_SUCCESS);
}
```

Example server program HELLO2D.C.   The Confirmed() call is issued, assuming
the client issued a corresponding Confirm().

```
/*-------------------------------------------------------------------
 *  CPI-C "Hello, world" program, with confirmation.
 *  Server side (file HELLO2D.C)
 *-----------------------------------------------------------------*/
#include <cpic.h>                 /* conversation API library     */
#include <stdio.h>                /* file I/O                     */
#include <string.h>               /* strings and memory           */
#include <stdlib.h>               /* standard library             */

int main(void)
{
    unsigned char      conversation_ID[CM_CID_SIZE];
    unsigned char      data_buffer[100+1];
    CM_INT32           requested_length =
                           (CM_INT32)sizeof(data_buffer)-1;
    CM_INT32           received_length = 0;
    CM_RETURN_CODE     cpic_return_code;

    CM_DATA_RECEIVED_TYPE data_received;
    CM_STATUS_RECEIVED    status_received;
    CM_REQUEST_TO_SEND_RECEIVED rts_received;

    cmaccp(                        /* Accept_Conversation          */
        conversation_ID,           /* O: returned conversation ID  */
        &cpic_return_code);        /* O: return code from this call */

    cmrcv(                         /* Receive                      */
        conversation_ID,           /* I: conversation ID           */
        data_buffer,               /* I: where to put received data */
        &requested_length,         /* I: maximum length to receive */
        &data_received,            /* O: data complete or not?     */
        &received_length,          /* O: length of received data   */
```

```
        &status_received,     /*  0: has status changed?         */
        &rts_received,        /*  0: was RTS received?           */
        &cpic_return_code);   /*  0: return code from this call  */
    data_buffer[received_length] = '\0'; /* a null for safety    */
    (void)printf("%s\nPress a key to end the program...\n",
             data_buffer);

    cmcfmd(                   /* Confirmed                       */
        conversation_ID,      /* I: conversation ID              */
        &cpic_return_code);   /* 0: return code from this call   */

    (void)getchar();          /* pause for any keystroke         */

    return(EXIT_SUCCESS);
}
```

HELLO2 is the version of the "Hello, world" program that you'll want to use as your first running CPI-C program. With its confirmation processing, you can make sure that the server program actually starts and runs properly. If it runs, you know you've set up everything properly between the two programs.

The next two chapters cover what you'll need to build and run CPI-C programs. We discuss the details of C coding in CPI-C first, followed by guidelines for setting up your computers to run CPI-C programs.

CPI-C Coding in C

At this point, you've seen our first two CPI-C applications. These two applications showed a lot of CPI-C's details; this chapter covers the questions you may have about the details of the C source code.

The first section discusses some of the differences between issuing CPI-C calls and issuing calls to most standard C routines. We cover details of the CPI-C header file and CPI-C library linking in the second section. The third section covers the things you'll need to know in order to *make* CPI-C programs. In the last section, we explain the rationale behind the programming style we use for these sample programs.

ISSUING CPI-C CALLS

Although this book is about writing CPI-C programs using C, the CPI-C programming interface is not actually tied to any particular programming language. CPI-C's language-independent interface has several implications for a C programmer who is accustomed to C-specific interfaces. The adjustments you have to make in your C programming style occur because:

- All parameters on CPI-C calls are passed by reference, that is, with pointers to parameters, not the parameter values themselves.

- CPI-C knows nothing about C's null-terminating character (`'\0'`), so it's not used by CPI-C to end strings.

You only have to modify your C programming style a little to accommodate these concessions to CPI-C's multiple language support. In this section, we discuss the passing of parameters like strings, integers and constants, and the CPI-C conversation ID.

Passing integer parameters

All parameters that your programs exchange with CPI-C are passed by reference, rather than by value. This means that all parameter passing, for both supplied and returned parameters, is done with *pointers to variables*—never with the actual values themselves. The requirement that all parameters be passed by reference is due to CPI-C's support of many programming languages, some of which do not allow passing parameters by value.

In C, you're probably already used to passing strings and buffers, and getting returned parameters, by reference. This leaves input constants and integers as the only kind of parameters affected by the lack of parameters passed by value.

As C programmers, we are accustomed to calling functions with constant values or even with the results from other function calls. But, we've just learned that all parameters in CPI-C are passed by reference. So, while you may want to pass a constant value on a supplied parameter, you must instead pass a pointer to a variable that contains that constant. The requirement to declare a variable in order to pass a constant can sometimes make your code a little more difficult to read.

The following code shows how to pass a constant value in a parameter. In this example, the variable named sync_level is set to the constant CM_CONFIRM. This variable has a typedef of CM_SYNC_LEVEL, which you'll find in the cpic.h file. This variable is then used in the CPI-C call named Set_Sync_Level(), which is shortened to "cmssl" when you use it in your code. The three parameters on the Set_Sync_Level() call are thus a pointer to the conversation_ID, a pointer to the sync_level variable, and a pointer to the cpic_return_code.

```
{

    {
        /* the sync_level variable is used only for this call */
        CM_SYNC_LEVEL sync_level = CM_CONFIRM;

        cmssl(                      /* Set_Sync_Level           */
            conversation_ID,        /* conversation ID          */
            &sync_level,            /* set the sync level       */
            &cpic_return_code);     /* return code from this call */
    }

}
```

All the numbers that are used as parameters on CPI-C calls are pointers to signed 32-bit integers. The CPI-C header file provides a typedef for you to use when defining these integers: CM_INT32. There are also a number of typedefs for use when passing symbolic values, like the typedef of CM_SYNC_LEVEL we used for the variable sync_level and the constant CM_CONFIRM we used in the preceding example.

Here is the list of CPI-C's integer typedefs, as you'll find in the C header file:

```
#define CM_INT32 signed long int

typedef CM_INT32 CM_CONVERSATION_SECURITY_TYPE;
typedef CM_INT32 CM_CONVERSATION_STATE;
typedef CM_INT32 CM_CONVERSATION_TYPE;
typedef CM_INT32 CM_DATA_RECEIVED_TYPE;
typedef CM_INT32 CM_DEALLOCATE_TYPE;
typedef CM_INT32 CM_ERROR_DIRECTION;
typedef CM_INT32 CM_FILL;
typedef CM_INT32 CM_PREPARE_TO_RECEIVE_TYPE;
typedef CM_INT32 CM_PROCESSING_MODE;
typedef CM_INT32 CM_RECEIVE_TYPE;
typedef CM_INT32 CM_REQUEST_TO_SEND_RECEIVED;
typedef CM_INT32 CM_RETURN_CODE;
typedef CM_INT32 CM_RETURN_CONTROL;
typedef CM_INT32 CM_SEND_TYPE;
typedef CM_INT32 CM_STATUS_RECEIVED;
typedef CM_INT32 CM_SYNC_LEVEL;
```

The `cpic.h` file has function prototypes for each of the CPI-C calls. In these function prototypes, you can see the correct typedef to use for the input parameters. For an example, the function prototype for the Set_Sync_Level() call is shown in "Set_Sync_Level (CMSSL)" on p. 134.

All integer parameters, except for lengths, have associated constant values defined. Always use these constant values in your programs, instead of a hard-coded literal number. For example, here's how the constant CM_CONFIRM is defined in `cpic.h`:

```
#define CM_CONFIRM      (CM_SYNC_LEVEL) 1
```

We're sure you've learned the lessons of strong typing in your study of programming. Using typedefs and symbolic constants protects you from portability problems and changes in the future. Thus, always use the CM_CONFIRM constant rather than the number 1.

Passing strings and lengths

All strings exchanged with CPI-C (save one) have a length parameter associated with them.* As with C's memcpy() call, CPI-C does not use C's null-

---

* The exception is the *symbolic destination name,* a parameter on the Initialize_Conversation() call, which is always 8 bytes long. If the actual name is less than 8 bytes, you pad it on the right with blanks.

terminating character, '\0', to indicate or detect the end of a string. This enhances CPI-C's portability among computer languages that use other techniques to decide how long a string is. For example, it is much easier for a C programmer to pass the length of a string than for a COBOL programmer to insert a null character into a string.

However, no C programmer wants to pass up a chance to use C's string-handling routines. This means that you'll want to use null-terminated string variables on both your CPI-C calls and on your other C library calls. You can use null-terminated strings everywhere if you'll follow these steps:

- For strings to be supplied to CPI-C, call strlen() to get the length of the supplied string.
- For strings returned from CPI-C, add a null-terminating character ('\0') at the offset in the returned length field returned by CPI-C.

The next two code examples illustrate the code for these two steps. Both of these examples involve a string called the *partner_LU_name* (which we'll cover in greater depth in Chap. 5). What you need to know here is that a partner_LU_name is a string that is up to 17 bytes long. It can be both a supplied parameter to CPI-C (you can Set the partner_LU_name) and a returned parameter from CPI-C (you can Extract the partner_LU_name). Since it's a string that's up to 17 bytes long, we'll declare partner_LU_name as an 18-byte array of characters, allowing room for the null-terminating character ('\0') at the end. In your code, use the SIZE constants defined in the cpic.h file, rather than trying to remember the maximum size of each string parameter. Here are those SIZE constants:

```
#define CM_CID_SIZE      (8)      /* conversation ID             */
#define CM_CTX_SIZE      (32)     /* context ID                  */
#define CM_LD_SIZE       (512)    /* log data                    */
#define CM_MN_SIZE       (8)      /* mode name                   */
#define CM_PLN_SIZE      (17)     /* partner LU name             */
#define CM_PW_SIZE       (10)     /* password                    */
#define CM_SDN_SIZE      (8)      /* symbolic destination name   */
#define CM_TPN_SIZE      (64)     /* TP name                     */
#define CM_UID_SIZE      (10)     /* userid ID                   */
```

The following example shows how to supply a null-terminated string as in input parameter. The CPI-C call to set the partner_LU_name is named Set_Partner_LU_Name(), which is shortened to "cmspln" in your code. In this example, we'll again assume that the variables cpic_return_code and conversation_ID were declared earlier in the program, since they are generally used on many calls. The constant named CM_PLN_SIZE defines the maximum size of a partner_LU_name.

```
{
    {
        /* this is the length of the partner_LU_name to be set    */
        CM_INT32 partner_LU_name_length;
```

```
        /* this is the 18 byte array that will hold the name      */
        unsigned char partner_LU_name[CM_PLN_SIZE+1];    /* 17+1    */

        /* copy a null-terminated string into the name field      */
        strcpy((char *)partner_LU_name, "CPICNET.JOHNQ");

        /* set the length of the name, using strlen()             */
        partner_LU_name_length =
            (CM_INT32)strlen((char *)partner_LU_name);

        cmspln(                    /* Set_Partner_LU_Name          */
            conversation_ID,       /* conversation ID             */
            partner_LU_name,       /* fully-qualified LU name      */
            &partner_LU_name_length, /* length of the LU name      */
            &cpic_return_code); /* return code from this call     */
    }

}
```

To retrieve a string, your program needs to pass a pointer to a character array long enough to hold the returned string, and a pointer to a CM_INT32 field where CPI-C will place the length of the returned string. In Fig. 4.5, we call Extract_Partner_LU_Name() to ask CPI-C to give us the current partner_LU_name. We then add a null-terminating character to the end of the array, since CPI-C never adds this character. This makes it easy to use the C string-handling functions on the returned string.

```
    {
        {
        /* this is the length of the returned partner_LU_name     */
        CM_INT32 partner_LU_name_length;

        /* this is the 18 byte array that will hold the name      */
        unsigned char partner_LU_name[CM_PLN_SIZE+1];    /* 17+1    */

        cmepln(                      /* Extract_Partner_LU_Name      */
            conversation_ID,       /* conversation ID             */
            partner_LU_name,       /* fully-qualified LU name      */
            &partner_LU_name_length, /* length of the LU name      */
            &cpic_return_code); /* return code from this call     */

        if (cpic_return_code == CM_OK) {
            /* add a null terminator, making it easier to work
               with this string in C */
            partner_LU_name[partner_LU_name_length] = '\0';
        }
        }
    }

}
```

Using your native character set for names

You may have noticed in both of these examples that we didn't do any conversion of the characters in the partner_LU_name string. If you have some previous experience with SNA programming, you may have seen that all the names you used had to be in EBCDIC. If you were to read a trace of the bytes sent and received on the communication line, you would see that the key SNA names are always in EBCDIC.

CPI-C makes things easy for you to program, by requiring that you use the native character set of your computer, not necessarily EBCDIC. If you're programming on an ASCII-based computer, like most personal computers, you use ASCII for all the SNA names. CPI-C internally converts the input parameters from ASCII to EBCDIC, and converts its output parameters from EBCDIC to ASCII. Certainly, if you're programming on an EBCDIC computer, like an AS/400 or IBM mainframe, you use their native EBCDIC strings. CPI-C always makes sure the names get out on the line in the proper format. This is another attribute of CPI-C that makes your program source code quite portable among computers.

While CPI-C lets you use your native character set for all the names it deals with, it does no conversion of your data. If one computer in a conversation uses ASCII and the other uses EBCDIC, you'll have to decide which side converts incoming and outgoing data, so both sides can interpret it correctly. This involves not only character data, but integers of different types and sizes, floating-point numbers, currency symbols, and so on. This is a complex topic, which we'll cover in more detail in Chap. 24.

Handling conversation IDs

The conversation ID is an eight-character block of binary data. CPI-C invents this ID at the beginning of a conversation, and marks it as invalid at the end of a conversation. Use the constant CM_CID_SIZE when declaring the array to hold the conversation ID.

Treat the conversation ID as an "opaque" type. Your programs never need to look at it or display it; it's not of use anywhere but in your active program, and it never gets sent to the partner. Your programs should never try to interpret or modify any of the bytes within the conversation ID.

Understanding function call names

Each function call in CPI-C has a long name and a short name. The long name is descriptive, and often consists of several words joined by underscores. For example, thus far we've discussed calls named Initialize_Conversation() and Set_Sync_Level(). CPI-C's short names are much more cryptic. They're always four to six characters long, and they start with the two letters "cm," which stands for communications.* Corresponding to the long names Initialize_Conversation() and Set_Sync_Level() are their equivalent short names: cminit() and cmssl(), respectively.

---

* Our friends who are familiar with programming on parallel systems have noted that the function calls on the Connection Machines, made by Thinking Machines, also start with the letters "cm."

Why do the names of the short calls look this way? Well, remember that CPI-C calls have the same names regardless of the computer language they're being used in (for example, C, COBOL, REXX, or Pascal). CPI-C's short names were designed to meet the requirements of a wide range of compilers and operating systems. They're only six characters long in order to satisfy the most restrictive linker on the most restrictive computer in the most restrictive language (COBOL on some host systems, we think).

Throughout this book, we'll use the long names in all our discussions. The long names are much easier to read—no one likes to read acronyms, and the names look so much alike that they're frequently a source of error. However, in all the code examples, we'll use the short names, with a comment next to them showing the long name. All the function prototypes in the C header file you'll be compiling with are expressed in short names. The C header file for CPI-C on the computer where you're compiling should contain a set of macros that map the long names to their equivalent short name. This will let you code in long names, if you choose. However, if you're working with a team that's coding CPI-C across several languages and computers, you'll probably want to stick with the short names to get the most portability.

Any platform that offers CPI-C can also offer additional calls that it deems necessary for its operating environment. These may provide additional platform-specific communications features or help the CPI-C program interact with the operating environment. To distinguish these extension calls from the standard CPI-C calls, their short names begin with the two letters "xc." For example, in the section entitled "Specify_Windows_Handle (XCHWND)" in Chap. 26, we discuss a WinCPIC call named Specify_Windows_Handle(); its short name is "xchwnd," which follows the six-character rule, and begins with "xc."

We do not explain how to use the extension calls on each platform, though we do mention a few of them. For details of which extensions are available on each platform and how to use them, consult the CPI-C programming reference for your platform. See "CPI-C Specifications" in App. D for information about how to obtain some of these references.

BUILDING YOUR CPI-C PROGRAMS

The best way to learn how to compile and link your own CPI-C programs is to build from existing samples that are known to work. To help you out, we've provided all of the sample programs and sample procedures found in this book on the accompanying diskette. Each of these can be compiled with makefiles that are also provided. The README.TXT file on the diskette contains all the information you'll need to compile and run the sample programs.

In this section, we discuss some of the general principles we use in compiling and linking our CPI-C programs. These range from simple details of compiling to techniques that help you to find more bugs and find them earlier in your development cycle.

Compiling your programs

There are many options provided by compilers to allow you control over how your programs are compiled. These options vary from compiler to compiler, and from release to release. We've tried to be comprehensive in our diskette samples; in particular, we've included about a dozen different makefiles for the APING application. This section provides some general guidelines for selecting which compiler options to use.

Using CPIC.H on your platform

The `cpic.h` file on the diskette can be used on most CPI-C platforms. Like all C header files, however, it is sensitive to the operating system and the release of the particular compiler being used. Until we see `cpic.h` shipped with the compilers, we've had to resolve many of the differences in the single header file. It's been a good study in portability.

`cpic.h` keys off a set of #define constants, indicating a particular platform. For example, these constants have names like CM_OS2, CM_DOS, and CM_AIX. When a platform's constant is defined, the definitions for that platform are used. Within the scope of these definitions, compiler-defined constants are examined; for example,_BORLANDC_and _MSC_VER.

When the `cpic.h` file is shipped with a platform, it should hardcode the platform constant so you won't have to define it in your program. Since our `cpic.h` can be used on any platform and we don't know which platform you will use, our file does not predefine any of the constants.

When you compile your programs, you should define the platform constant for the platform you use. This can usually be done on the compiler command line with the -D flag. For example, the following command line option enables the parts of `cpic.h` appropriate for the OS/2 Communications Manager:

```
-DCM_OS2
```

Here is the list of platform constants currently supported by our `cpic.h` file:

```
CM_AIX
CM_DOS
CM_MVS
CM_OS2
CM_OS400
CM_VM
```

Compiler warning levels

Always compile and link your CPI-C programs with the compiler warning level set as high as possible. You want the compiler to give you as much diagnostic information as possible. With the use of function prototypes and typedefs for all the variables exchanged with CPI-C, there should be little chance for syntactic problems.

A common programming error in C is to pass a variable to CPI-C, rather than a pointer to that variable. For example, here's an easy mistake to make: passing the sync_level itself, instead of a pointer to the sync_level value. The following code snippet is wrong. All modern C compilers should give at least a warning that the following code is syntactically incorrect.

```
CM_RETURN_CODE cpic_return_code;
CM_SYNC_LEVEL sync_level = CM_CONFIRM;

cmssl (                       /* Set_Sync_Level           */
    conversation_ID,          /* conversation ID          */
    sync_level, /* <-- bug:  should be a pointer          */
    &cpic_return_code);       /* return code from this call */
```

The following code snippet is correct; it differs from the preceding code only in the "&" symbol, indicating a pointer to the sync_level variable.

```
CM_RETURN_CODE cpic_return_code;
CM_SYNC_LEVEL sync_level = CM_CONFIRM;

cmssl (                       /* Set_Sync_Level           */
    conversation_ID,          /* conversation ID          */
    &sync_level,              /* sync_level               */
    &cpic_return_code);       /* return code from this call */
```

Debug and production versions

We strongly recommend that you build two versions of your program: a debug version and a production version. The debug version contains code and options to help detect bugs and to help locate where bugs are in your code. The debug version may have extra code to verify the correctness of your program during its execution. This extra code may slow down your program, so you'll also want to build a production version which you'll ship to your customers. The production version should be the smallest and fastest it can, while still maintaining the error handling that makes a program easy to use.

We recommend that you build your debug version with the following:

- Enable assert() calls within your code. The extra code generated by assert() occurs automatically when you include the <assert.h> header file. You need to #define the constant NDEBUG to disable this code.

- Use the compiler options that allow you to use a source level debugger.

- Enable all memory-management checking.

- Turn off all optimizations.

You should use the opposite of these for your production versions.

Using an optimizing compiler

Most C compilers have options to turn on optimization. Although optimization in compilers is mostly beyond the scope of this book, we do feel compelled to mention a few things that we've found while developing CPI-C programs.

We recommend that you turn off all optimization during the early development of your programs. This reduces your compilation times during the period when you are compiling frequently. Turning off optimization also frees you from the hassles of trying to debug an application problem that later turns out to be an optimization bug. We have yet to encounter an optimizing compiler that never produces buggy code.

After your programs are up and running and significantly tested, then add the optimization options. If your regression tests fail, you can then try to determine if an optimization bug has been encountered. You may have to disable optimization permanently on one or more of your source code modules until you get fixes for your compiler.

Linking your programs

Although there are generally fewer options when linking your programs, it is important to get the right library names and stack size.

The CPI-C library

Perhaps the most obvious part of linking your CPI-C program is also the most important: linking with the CPI-C library provided by the platform you're using. See "Finding the CPI-C libraries" later in this chapter for some information about how to find the CPI-C library for your platform.

Stack sizes

Choosing the correct stack size is always a perplexing problem. Determining the exact stack requirement of your program is often difficult or impossible. So you must try to balance giving your programs extra stack space versus reducing the memory required to run your program.

We recommend that, when starting development of your program, you use a stack size much larger than you think your program will ever need. After you have progressed in your program development and have a suite of regression tests, you can reduce the stack size to more reasonable levels. If you encounter out-of-stack-space conditions, increase the stack size by more than the minimum required to execute that particular test case; another code path probably requires yet more stack space.

Debug and production versions

As with compiling, there should be linking differences between your debug and production versions. One difference in linking between your debug and production versions will be the inclusion of source-level debug information in the debug version. Another difference is that production-level files are generally packed or compressed to reduce their size.

Looking at our makefiles

Here's one of the makefiles we have provided on the diskette. It compiles the HELLO programs you've already seen, as well as HELLO programs that you'll see in the following chapters.

```
all: hello1.exe hello1d.exe\
     hello2.exe hello2d.exe\
     hello3.exe hello3d.exe\
     hello4d.exe \
     hello5.exe hello5d.exe

#--------------------------------------------------------------------

.c.obj:
     $(CPICCC) $*.c

hello1.exe: hello1.obj
     $(CPICLINK) $**, $*.exe, , $(CPICLIB), ;

hello1d.exe: hello1d.obj
     $(CPICLINK) $**, $*.exe, , $(CPICLIB), ;

hello2.exe: hello2.obj
     $(CPICLINK) $**, $*.exe, , $(CPICLIB), ;

hello2d.exe: hello2d.obj
     $(CPICLINK) $**, $*.exe, , $(CPICLIB), ;

hello3.exe: hello3.obj
     $(CPICLINK) $**, $*.exe, , $(CPICLIB), ;

hello3d.exe: hello3d.obj
     $(CPICLINK) $**, $*.exe, , $(CPICLIB), ;

hello4d.exe: hello4d.obj docpic.obj
     $(CPICLINK) $**, $*.exe, , $(CPICLIB), ;

hello5.exe: hello5.obj docpic.obj
     $(CPICLINK) $**, $*.exe, , $(CPICLIB), ;

hello5d.exe: hello5d.obj docpic.obj
     $(CPICLINK) $**, $*.exe, , $(CPICLIB), ;
```

Using environment variables

You'll notice that the makefile doesn't actually contain the compiler and linker flags used to build the programs. It instead references the environment variables CPICCC, CPICLINK, and CPICLIB. This allows us to support a number of compilers with the same makefile. Before you use this makefile, you must externally define these environment variables.

On the diskette, we've provided .CMD and .BAT files for the compilers we support that you can use to set the environment variables. Here is the .CMD to set up the environment variables for the Microsoft C 6.0 compiler when running under OS/2:

```
@echo off
REM-------------------------------------------------------
REM  MSC6.CMD -- Set up environment for Microsoft C 6.0
REM
REM  This sets up environment variables that are used
REM  by the .MAK files. All of the compiler options
```

```
REM  and link options used in this file are explained
REM  at the bottom.
REM  ----------------------------------------------------
REM  This .CMD file is currently set up to build a DEBUG version
REM  of the programs. To build PRODUCTION versions, REM out
REM  the "@goto :debug" line below.
REM
@echo on
@goto :debug
@REM   Set up the production environment
SET CPICCC=cl -c -AS -W4 -Zelpi -DCM_OS2 -DNDEBUG -Ozax -Gs
SET CPICLINK=link /F /L /MAP /NOD /NOE /NOI /PMTYPE:VIO /PACKC /PACKD /EXEPACK
SET CPICLIB=slibce+os2+cpic
@REM   Set up the multi-threaded production environment.
SET MT_CPICCC=cl -c -AL -W4 -Ozax -Gs -Zelpi -DCM_OS2 -DNDEBUG -MT
SET MT_CPICLINK=link /F /L /MAP /NOD /NOE /NOI /PMTYPE:VIO /PACKC /PACKD /ST:4000 /EXEPACK
SET MT_CPICLIB=llibcmt+os2+cpic
@REM
@goto :end
@REM
:debug
@REM   Set up the debug environment
SET CPICCC=cl -c -AS -W4 -Zelpi -DCM_OS2 -DDEBUG -Od
SET CPICLINK=link /F /L /MAP /NOD /NOE /NOI /PMTYPE:VIO /PACKC /PACKD /CO
SET CPICLIB=slibce+os2+cpic
@REM   Set up the multi-threaded production environment.
SET MT_CPICCC=cl -c -AL -W4 -Od -Zelpi -DCM_OS2 -DDEBUG -MT
SET MT_CPICLINK=link /CO /F /L /MAP /NOD /NOE /NOI /PMTYPE:VIO /PACKC /PACKD /ST:4000
SET MT_CPICLIB=llibcmt+os2+cpic
@goto .end
REM
REM   Compiler switches:
REM   -c = compile only, no link
REM   -AS = using the small memory model.
REM   -Ox = maximum optimization
REM   -Oz = turn on maximum loop optimization
REM   -Oa = cancel alias checking
REM   -Od = disable all optimizations
REM   -Gs = remove stack probes - Use only on fully debugged
REM         program.
REM   -Zl = suppress default library selection.
REM   -Zp = pack structure members - OS/2 API calls expect packed
REM         structures.
REM   -Ze = enable special keywords.
REM   -Zi = compile for debugging
REM   -W4 = maximum warning level
REM   -DCM_OS2 = indicates to CPIC.H that we're on OS/2
REM   -DNDEBUG = turns off assert() macros
REM   -DDEBUG = turns on debug code within our source
REM
REM   Linker options:
REM   /CO = include Codeview information (source level debugging)
REM   /F = farcall translation
REM   /NOD = no default library search
REM   /NOE = no extended directory search
```

```
REM    /NOI = no ignore case
REM    /L = adds line numbers and addresses to the MAP file
REM    /MAP = causes a MAP file to be created
REM    /PMTYPE:VIO = sets the video mode of the program in OS/2
REM    /PACKC = pack code
REM    /PACKD = pack data
REM    /EXEPACK = optimize load-time relocation table
REM    /ST:4000 = sets the stack size to 0x4000 bytes
REM
:end
```

Our practice in the example .CMD and .BAT files is to have two sets of environment variable settings: one for debug and one for production. By default, each batch file sets up the debug environment. To switch to building the production version, you can comment out the "@goto :debug" line.

Implicit targets

One way that we've been able to reduce the size of our makefiles is by using implicit targets. The implicit target in the previous makefile is:

```
.c.obj:
    $(CPICCC) $*.c
```

Translating this implicit target to English, it says that .obj files are built from .c files. To build the .obj, the $(CPICCC) command should be used.

ALL: as the first target

One of the differences between MAKE and NMAKE is whether only the first target is built or whether all of the targets are built. To work around this difference, all of our makefiles specify as their first target a dummy target named ALL. This target lists as dependencies everything that we want built. Whether we use MAKE or NMAKE, the same set of programs is built.

Migration to other environments

You may want to move our samples or your programs to other CPI-C platforms. One place to look for samples of how to build programs on other platforms is the APING application, which is provided on the diskette. The APING program comes complete with source and makefiles which can be used on OS/2 CM/2, NS/DOS, AIX, MVS, VM, and AS/400.

One of the things you will need to change when moving to another platform is the link step; every operating system seems to have its own way of linking files. In fact, the file extensions for the object files you link varies. For example, on OS/2 they are .OBJ files, on AIX they are .o files, and on VM the file extension is TEXT.

PULLING IT ALL TOGETHER

To create a CPI-C program in C, you need to have the following items:

- The C header file for CPI-C, `cpic.h`
- Your C source code files (at least one of which includes `cpic.h`)
- A C compiler, and directions for the right compiler options to set
- A CPI-C library to link to, or directives for how your compiled program resolves its external CPI-C calls
- A linker (you may also hear this called a "linkage editor"), to bring together all the parts into an executable file

This section guides you through these parts, and how to combine them into makefiles to use on your platform.

Understanding the CPI-C include file

All of the typedefs and constants that you've seen used in our examples are specified in the CPI-C header files supplied with each CPI-C platform. The function prototypes and linkage conventions are also specified in this file.

As you develop programs that run on different computers, you may find differences in the file name of this header file and in its contents. On many of today's IBM platforms, the CPI-C header file for C is named CMC.H. This name was chosen for its consistency across a wide set of languages. For example, the CPI-C header file for COBOL is named CMCOBOL, the CPI-C header file for REXX is named CMREXX, and the CPI-C header file for Pascal is named CMPASCAL. On some other platforms, the header file was named to meet local operating system conventions. For example, the CPI-C header file for C on MVS/ESA is named ATBCMC. Unfortunately, the files had begun to diverge, and the difference among these files was enough that porting even a simple program requires at least minor editing.

CPI-C version 1.2 (and X/Open CPI-C) now specify a single file, named `cpic.h`, to be included when using CPI-C with C. However, our testing with the X/Open `cpic.h` file (listed as an appendix of the X/Open standard) has uncovered some bugs (sigh). To eliminate this as another hurdle for you to master, we've refined a superportable CPI-C header file, also called `cpic.h`, which is included by each of the samples in this book. This file, with this same name, will eventually be shipped with each CPI-C platform as part of the standard. Appendix C shows a listing of our `cpic.h` header file, known to work for all IBM CPI-C platforms.

`cpic.h` operates across many platforms because it depends upon a constant being defined for each platform. For example, to use it with the OS/2 Communications Manager, you need to define constant CM_OS2. In the future, we think the old header file, CMC.H, will be reduced to following:

```
#define CM_OS2
#include <cpic.h>

/* platform-specific CPI-C extensions follow... */
```

When you include the header file, use `<cpic.h>`, not `"cpic.h"`. Be sure to place the file in an appropriate place or change your setup or environment variables so that it's found by the rules used on your system for include files.

If you are programming on a platform not supported by our `<cpic.h>` file, you should look in the platform documentation for the header file shipped by that platform. If you discover that there appear to be many differences between your platform's header file and `<cpic.h>`, you may consider modifying `<cpic.h>` we've supplied to support your platform, and using it instead. This helps ensure the portability of your programs in the future.

The `cpic.h` file provides a number of types of definitions to help you program and to isolate you from platform dependencies. Many of these definitions are transparent to your programs; they are never used directly in your source code. We explain them here so that you'll know what you're looking at if you read the `cpic.h` file.

Typedefs, constant values, and function prototypes

All of the typedefs and constant values needed by CPI-C are defined in `cpic.h`. In addition, there are function prototypes for each CPI-C call and platform-specific extension. The function prototypes use the old K&R style rather than ANSI prototypes. This was done so that `cpic.h` can be used on systems that are as yet without an ANSI compiler. Although the prototypes are non-ANSI, we have provided the name of each parameter in a comment to its right.

These data types and constants protect you from differences among operating systems. You should always use them rather than their underlying C data types and constants. Since all of the data types, symbolic constants*, and function prototypes are in the `cpic.h` file, we think you can probably use it as a handy CPI-C reference when printed books aren't within reach.

Pointer differences among operating systems

CPI-C was designed to accommodate the pointer structures for a wide variety of hardware architectures. On some platforms, CPI-C requires specific pointer types peculiar to that platform. For example, you must use *far* (32-bit) pointers with DOS if you are programming in the small (16-bit) data model.

To isolate your program from these pointer differences, the CPI-C header file provides a #define for you to use in your programs, named CM_PTR. On 32-bit systems, `CM_PTR` means the exact same thing as an asterisk; its definition looks like:

```
#define CM_PTR (*)
```

In contrast, on 16-bit systems, the definition will look like:

```
#define CM_PTR (far *)
```

---

* In case you're wondering, the reason that enums are not used is that enums are always `int` in C. The integer parameters in CPI-C are defined to be 32-bit integers. On many systems, `int` is not 32-bit, thus enums wouldn't be the right size to pass to CPI-C.

CM_PTR is used in all the function prototypes for calling CPI-C. Since the function prototype is declared correctly, you will never need CM_PTR in your programs. For example, declare the pointer your programs are using to send a data buffer as:

```
unsigned char * buffer;
```

Never use:

```
unsigned char CM_PTR buffer;
```

Entry point differences among operating systems

The cpic.h file uses a #define to hide operating system linkage convention differences from your programs. The macro used for this is named CM_ENTRY. You'll see it on all the function prototypes in cpic.h.

As with CM_PTR, you should never need to use CM_ENTRY in your programs. But, for your information, here are some examples of how CM_ENTRY is defined.

On 32-bit systems, the definition in cpic.h looks like:

```
#define CM_ENTRY (extern void)
```

On 16-bit systems, the definition in cpic.h looks like:

```
#define CM_ENTRY (extern void pascal far _loadds)
```

When programming to the WinCPIC specification, CPI-C calls are native Windows calls. Here's how CM_ENTRY is defined in wincpic.h.

```
#define CM_ENTRY extern VOID WINAPI
```

On some platforms, the linkage convention must be identified in a #pragma statement. For example, on VM/ESA CMS, cpic.h defines the Initialize_Conversation() call in the following way:

```
#    pragma linkage (cminit, OS)
```

Name differences among operating systems

On some platforms, notably OS/400 and MVS/ESA, the CPI-C entry points are in uppercase. Also, the linkers on these platforms do not allow you to specify that your program's calls are case-insensitive. To avoid requiring you to change all of your CPI-C calls to uppercase, the cpic.h file does this for you. This lets you code all your calls in the lowercase, short name form, for the widest possible portability. Here's what the macro definition for the lowercase name looks like for the Initialize_Conversation() call:

```
#define cminit CMINIT
```

This should never affect your programs at all; just code your calls in lowercase and everything works fine.

Macros mapping long names to short names

At the bottom of the `cpic.h` file is a set of `#define` statements to map long names to the short entry points. For example:

```
#define Initialize_Conversation(v1,v2,v3)
               cminit(v1,v2,v3)
```

To use these long names in your programs, you must first `#define` the constant READABLE_MACROS.

Finding the CPI-C libraries

After you have compiled your programs, you need to combine them with code that resolves the external CPI-C calls. This is traditionally done by linking your object files together with the libraries they need to execute the routines you've called. Most CPI-C toolkits ship a CPI-C library for you to link to, which handles all the CPI-C calls available for the platform you're using.

The names and linking methods vary from platform to platform. Here are the libraries for some popular platforms:

AIX SNA Services/6000.   Link with `cpic.a`.

CICS/ESA.   Include the DFHCPLC stub in your CICS program.

MVS/ESA CMS.   Link with `ATBPBI`, which is in `SYS1.CSSLIB`.

Networking Services/DOS (NS/DOS).   Link with `CPICNSDR.LIB` (for DOS real mode) or `CPICNSDW.LIB` (for Windows).

OS/2 Communications Manager.   Link with `CPIC.LIB`. This library file causes `CPIC.DLL` to be loaded at run time.

VM/ESA CMS.   Link with `VMLIB TXTLIB`.

WinCPIC.   Link with `WINCPIC.DEF`.

On most (if not all) platforms, the CPI-C code itself is not actually linked in with your program; it is dynamically loaded when your program is run. This makes your executable smaller and allows the software developers for the platforms to fix defects and improve performance without requiring you to recompile your programs.

Before we leave library files, we need to mention an opportunity that results from the heritage that OS/2 shares with DOS. It is possible to create a "family-API" program, which is a single executable program that can run in either OS/2 or DOS. To create a family-API program for OS/2 Communications Manager and NS/DOS:

1. Compile your program for OS/2 with the Microsoft C 6.00A compiler.

2. Link your program with `CPIC.LIB` and the OS/2 run-time libraries.

3. BIND your program to the NS/DOS CPI-C library with the following command:

```
BIND yourprog.exe CPIC.LIB CPICNSDR.LIB
```

This requires the BIND program from the Microsoft C 6.00A compiler and the library files from both OS/2 Communications Manager and NS/DOS.

UNDERSTANDING OUR CODING STYLE IN THIS BOOK

Throughout this book, we use a consistent style for all of the source code examples. This style is a combination of different influences and requirements. Our style may not match yours, but we think you'll read along with us anyhow. For those of you who are curious or looking for new ideas, we'll provide some background on how and why we arrived at the style we've used.

One of our primary considerations was that all of the code be as free as possible of compiler warnings. You'll notice that in the makefiles, we use most (if not all) of the warning levels available in each compiler. To help us reach our goal of no compiler warnings, we have explicitly placed voids, casts, consts, and so on wherever appropriate.

Since the source code is to be read by you and others, we have placed a strong emphasis on readability. To make the code easier to understand, we have chosen long names which explain the purpose of our variables and functions. We have found that it is much easier to read code that uses a variable named `status_received` rather than `sr`.

In conflict with our goal of readability was the obvious requirement that the code had to be formatted for a book. This means that all of the code must fit into 65 columns, which means less horizontal white space. To reduce the number of pages taken up by source code, we used fewer blank lines, resulting in less vertical white space. We have had to make trade-offs between adding white space for readability and still being able to fit the source into the book.

Since our real goal is to make you a better and more productive CPI-C programmer, we have also taken steps to make our code as reusable as possible. We've used small, self-contained subroutines, and linked together the separate objects, rather than lumping everything into one big module.

We use braces liberally to allow us to define variables with limited scope. For example, many of the Set calls use variables that aren't needed except on that call. The braces let us easily limit the scope of those variables.

We use `unsigned char` instead of `signed char`. The main reason is that when supporting the character sets of other languages, especially double-byte character sets, the characters can fall in the range X'80' through X'FF'. The `signed char` propagates the sign bit, which makes character string comparisons fail (the collating sequence reverses for any character above X'7F').

Last, in some C compilers, you can change the setting so that a declaration of char implies `unsigned char`, not `signed char`. Unfortunately, this feature is not portable, so we always explicitly declare them as `unsigned char`.

Setting Up Your Computers to Run CPI-C Programs

Now that you have your first pair of CPI-C programs compiled and linked, you'll want to run them to see if they work. Do the two programs talk to each other inside one computer, or do they run over a network? What are the names of the computers that the client and server programs are on? What is the name of the executable file for the server program? What route characteristics through the network are needed from one computer to the other?

These are just some of the decisions to be made when setting up programs that communicate with one another. With CPI-C, the answers and configuration values can be stored outside of the programs, making the executable programs very portable. As you answer each of these questions, you will set up names and other values in the computers where the programs run. The term for this setup process is *configuration*; this section gets you started with the fundamentals you'll need, no matter what computers you run your programs on.

One of the challenges of communications programs is that in order to run and debug them, you need to get both computers—and the network between them—set up and activated correctly. To reduce this hurdle, we'll help you configure an application that is already debugged, named APING, and get it running first. This will assure the computers and network are set up right. After doing that, adding the simple definition needed for each additional application will be easy.

USING SYMBOLIC DESTINATION NAMES
AND SIDE INFORMATION

From the point of view of a programmer, it is easy for your program to connect to its partner program using CPI-C. All you need to do is specify one name on the client side, the *symbolic destination name*. You saw this in the previous Hello samples; for example, on the Initialize_Conversation() call, we used a symbolic destination name of HELLO2S. (Actually, we did this with a C macro definition, so it would be easy to reuse this code.)

The symbolic destination name is the only name that needs to appear in your programs' source code. In fact it is only used on the client side of an application; the server program does not have to specify any names (see Fig. 5.1). If you'll remember our telephone analogy: the caller has to know the name and phone number of the person he or she is calling, but the person answering the phone doesn't have to know who's calling—all the person does is answer the phone.

As you might guess, there is a lot going on in CPI-C to make things easy for you to write your programs. CPI-C maps the symbolic destination name it

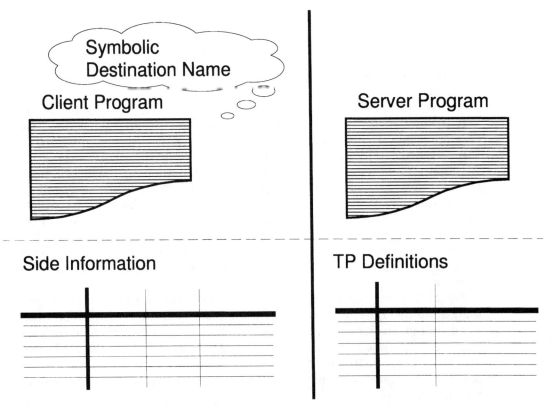

Figure 5.1 Only the client program needs a symbolic destination name.

receives on an Initialize_Conversation() call to three other fields. Although CPI-C makes coding your programs simple, it requires some setup to run the programs. This setup must be done before the program is run.

The three fields we just mentioned are analogous to the information needed to use a telephone. Think about what you need in order to have a telephone conversation:

- You need to identify the remote telephone—what is its telephone number?

- You need to identify whom you want to talk with—what is the name of the person you want to talk with? This is necessary whenever more than one person can use the same telephone.

- Sometimes, you need to identify that you want special telephone service. Is the call operator-assisted? Is it a collect call? Is this an emergency? (Generally, you just make a regular call, but sometimes you want special handling and ask for one of these services.)

The phone number, the person you want to talk to, and the type of service you want have their equivalents in CPI-C; they're called the *partner LU name,* the *TP name,* and the *mode name,* respectively. The partner LU name identifies the remote computer—much like a telephone number. The TP (transaction program) name indicates which program (of the many available programs) to connect to on the remote computer. The mode name is used to identify what kind of service you want between the pair of programs. These terms will be used a lot; plan to memorize them!

Your program, though, does not always need to specify each of these fields. When your client program issues an Initialize_Conversation() call, it supplies a symbolic destination name as a parameter. CPI-C, in turn, uses the symbolic destination name as an index into what is called *side information.* The side information maps a symbolic destination name to the three fields that are required for connecting to the target program. Configuring an entry in the side information takes place only on the client computer; it is necessary in order to run a client program. (See Fig. 5.2.)

Different computer systems have different ways to set up their side information and add entries to it. Let's look at an example of an entry in a side information table in OS/2. Figure 5.3, which shows an excerpt from an OS/2 Communications Manager configuration file, shows how we might have set up the side information table entry for our HELLO2 example.

In Fig. 5.3, we've said that the place we want to get to is CPICNET.JOHNQ and the application we want to talk to is known at the server as HELLO2D. The mode name value, #INTER, indicates the type of connection needed; in this case, we're looking for a connection for interactive traffic. For these examples, we have decided to configure a new side information table entry for each new version of the Hello program, and a new TP name for each new version.

Symbolic Destination Name	Partner LU Name	TP Name	Mode Name
HELLO1S	CPICNET.PJS	HELLO1D	#INTER
HELLO2S	CPICNET.JOHNQ	HELLO2D	#INTER
APINGS	USIBMNR.C132	APINGD	#INTER

Figure 5.2 Side information has one record for each symbolic destination name.

```
DEFINE_CPIC_SIDE_INFO
    symbolic_destination_name  ( HELLO2S        )
    fq_partner_lu_name         ( CPICNET.JOHNQ  )
    tp_name                    ( HELLO2D        )
    mode_name                  ( #INTER         );
```

Figure 5.3 Example side information table entry (needed on client side). You'll need something like this on the computer running the client program. This example shows the syntax for an entry in the side information table for the OS/2 Communications Manager.

UNDERSTANDING LINKS, SESSIONS, AND CONVERSATIONS

Communications software is structured in layers. This makes it easier for its designers to understand it, to design it, and to modify it. The CPI-C programming interface that your programs use probably sits at the top of several layers of communications software that look something like that shown in Fig. 5.4.

Your program calls CPI-C for the services it needs. CPI-C calls APPC for the services it needs to complete your calls. When the APPC layer needs help with

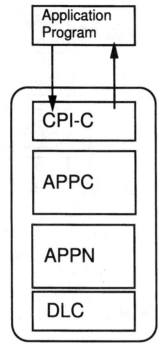

Figure 5.4 Your CPI-C program, and the software layers below it.

its function, it calls the underlying APPN software. When APPN is ready to put something on the line or receive something, it calls the data link control layer.

Your application programs generally need know nothing about what's below the CPI-C software. The client program uses a symbolic destination name to tell CPI-C about the partner, and CPI-C handles the rest. You, as the programmer, however, will probably want to know a little more about the underlying layers. You'll need to give your users some direction about setting them up correctly, and you'll want to know what's going on whenever things don't work right. You'll also find that most of the ways to improve performance come from tuning the packet sizes and buffering capabilities of the lower layers.

Designers of communications software refer to the hiding of detail about the lower layers as *abstraction*. The programs in your application think they are in a conversation with one another; one side sends, and if the other side receives, it gets what the partner sent, almost magically. The APPC and DLC layers in our picture also establish their own connections with one another. The lowest layer connection must be established before the next higher one can be successful, and on up to the top. This is important because a conversation is at the highest level of abstraction. If you can't get a conversation established, it's probably because one of the lower-layer connections couldn't be established.

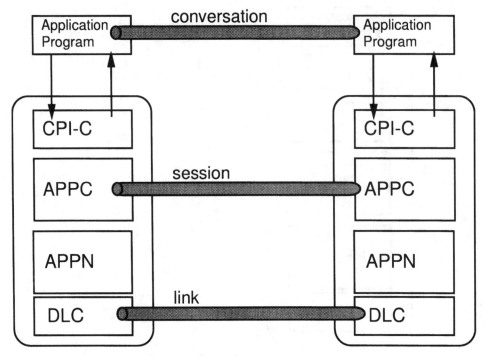

Figure 5.5 Connections between software layers.

Let's look at our picture again in Fig. 5.5, this time with the connections between the layers in two computers shown. The three connections you'll need to know about are links, sessions, and conversations.

A *link* is the connection between two communications adapters. The two adapters have to agree on the shape and speed of the bits they exchange. They have to agree on how they're going to detect if packets are in error, and how they may choose to recover. You'll need to have an active link out of your computer before you can talk to any other computer.

A *session* is the connection between the APPC software. A session needs a link underneath it to get between computers. A link can carry lots of sessions at the same time. A session, on the other hand, can only carry one conversation at a time. We'll talk a lot more about sessions, since they're the most likely culprit when you can't get a conversation.

An exchange of messages occurs between the respective layers for each of these connections. A link gets started when one DLC sends an *XID* to its partner. A session gets started when APPC sends a *Bind* to its partner. A conversation gets started when an *Attach* flows from the client computer to the server. These three messages become very important for debugging. If I can't get a link, what was in the XID? If I can't get a session, what happened to the Bind? If I can't talk to the partner in a conversation, what was the story on the Attach? Figure 5.6 shows our picture again, with the connections and the messages that start them.

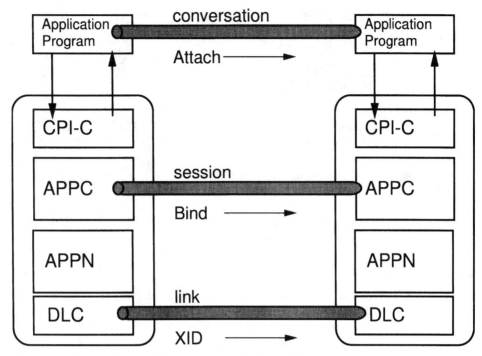

Figure 5.6 Connections and the messages that start them.

Finally, let's talk about the units of data that flow over each of these connections. Each has a name, a maximum size, and a maximum number that can be outstanding without hearing from the partner. You'll find that making the size as large as possible and maximizing the buffering gives you the best performance, but it also costs the most in memory and CPU usage.

At the DLC layer.   The packets that flow on a link are called *frames.*

At the APPC layer.   The packets that flow on a session are called *request units,* which is abbreviated *RUs.*

At the application layer.   The packets that your programs send and receive are called *records.*

LEARNING ABOUT THE THREE CPI-C CONFIGURATION PARAMETERS

We've introduced the three key CPI-C configuration parameters through an analogy to a telephone conversation. You have seen how the symbolic destination name maps to three fields that are stored in the CPI-C side information on the client side: partner LU name, TP name, and mode name. From our previous discussion, you'll see that the partner LU name and mode name are part of a Bind, which is the message that starts a session. A TP name is part of an

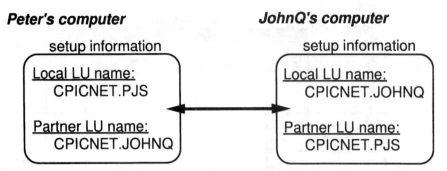

Figure 5.7 The local and partner LUs depend on your point of view.

Attach, the message which starts a conversation. Let's look again at these three parameters in more detail.

Partner LU name

A partner LU name is used to identify the computer on which the partner application will run. Each computer in the network needs an LU name. When a program on another computer wants to communicate with your local computer, it will need to know your local LU name. From the point of view of the remote computer, this is its "partner LU name." As seen in Fig. 5.7, a "fully qualified partner LU name" (or "fq_partner_LU_name") consists of two portions: a network name and an LU name, separated by a period. Each of these two portions can be up to eight characters long. The LU name of each computer must be unique within its SNA network. Thus, you cannot have two computers named JOHNQ in the CPICNET network.

How do you choose a good fully qualified LU name for your local computer? Usually, this isn't done in isolation. If your computer already has one, you're in great shape. If your computer isn't going to be connected to any others in a network (that is, you are using CPI-C to communicate among programs in the same computer), you are free to select whatever fully qualified LU name you would like.

Otherwise, your computer is probably in an SNA network with one or more other computers. Find and use the network name that is used by the other computers. If you are the one inventing a network name for the first time, assure that it is unique among all the other networks you'll ever connect to. To make this easier, there is an international registry of network names. Users of your programs should consider obtaining a block of globally unique names for their company.*

For the second portion of the name, the LU name, assure that this name is unique among all the other LU names in the same network. You don't usually

---

* See *The APPC Resource Book,* described in "APPC and APPN Books" in App. D, for more information about how to register your network name.

```
502G209A
bbbllln
|   |   |
|   |    computer number at a location (user may choose)
|   location or office number
building or site identifier
```

Figure 5.8 Example of partitioning a network's LU name space.

need more than one LU name for each computer; see if there is an administrator who is keeping track of LU names, and assigning new ones. If you are inventing the LU name scheme, try to use something practical. For example, can employee serial numbers be used as part of the LU name? How about the computer user's surname or office number? Remember, people are increasingly likely to have more than one computer in the future—they're also likely to have portable computers that they carry from place to place. Leave some space in the name to identify multiple computers per user or office. Figure 5.8 shows an example of partitioning a network's LU name space.

TP name

A TP name is simply a string that is sent by the client program to the CPI-C software on a partner computer. The partner uses it to decide which server program the client wishes to connect to. The TP name isolates your client program from file-naming differences among partner computers.

Different computers have different naming conventions for the programs they run. For example, the names can have different lengths; on DOS systems, program names look like COMMAND.COM or XCOPY.EXE; in UNIX, the three-character extensions are not necessary in program names; on a Macintosh or OS/2, the program name can be quite long: LongExampleHere. Program names can also vary in the character sets they use for names and in the characters allowable in a file name. For example, most personal computers and workstations use the ASCII character set, while most mainframe computers use EBCDIC. Character sets also vary from country to country. A TP name is the tool that allows you to write programs that talk to others on any type of computer, without knowing the naming structure for programs on *every* type of computer.

In computer science terminology, TP names give you one level of indirection. CPI-C doesn't send the executable program name of the partner program, but it sends a key, the TP name, used by the server platform to look up that actual name. On the partner computer (where the server program resides), a table of "TP definitions" must be set up. These TP definitions map incoming TP names to executable program names on that computer. TP definitions can also contain other attributes of the program, such as where to run it (for example, in a window, full-screen, or in the background), whether additional command-line parameters are to be supplied, and whether multiple copies of the server program can be running at the same time.

So, the TP name is only used as a lookup string on the computer that will be running the server program. The requirement for this string is that it be unique within that computer's table of TP definitions. Since you have up to 64 bytes to use for this string, it is helpful if the string can identify the program's name or what the program does. On some computers, if the TP name is the same as the executable program's file name, the executable name can be generated using a template, and a separate TP definition can be avoided altogether.

In most cases, the TP name you suggest when you build your application is the name your customers will configure and use. Thus it is important that you not choose a trivial name like "SERVER." In this book and in our applications, we tend to use a TP name that matches the executable name of our server program (for example, "HELLO1D"). For commercial applications which will be installed in a wide variety of networks, consider using more of the TP name space to ensure the uniqueness of your TP name. For example, consider "MoodyWare.CHEMISTRY.SOLVER" as a good name for a server marketed by the MoodyWare Company that solves chemistry puzzles.

Mode name

Many kinds of data traffic can be running on a network at the same time. For example, some programs exchange data that consists of small messages that require fast throughput. Other kinds of traffic, like network mail, don't need to arrive within a split second; they can yield to other types of traffic. Also, some traffic requires the highest data security, while other traffic is public.

When you run a program, you can choose which type of handling its data traffic will get in the network. This is done by selecting a *mode name*. A mode name maps to a set of detailed network characteristics that control flow, congestion, routing, and security in a network.

We've learned that we need a conversation between a pair of programs in order to begin exchanging information between them. Before a conversation can be started, the underlying network software on the two computers needs to be in a dialog. We call this connection between the network software a *session*. As we discussed in the last section, you need to have a session active before you can have a conversation.

We liken a session to a pipe that's carrying water. To run water from one place to another, you need to set up the pipe. As long as the pipe is set up, different people can choose to use it whenever it's free. Lots of pipes can be set up between any two locations. If a pipe gets cut, you have to replace it. In addition, water flows through the pipe in only one direction at a time.

The job of the Allocate() call you make in the client program is to get a session between the local LU and the partner LU. If it can get a free session, the Allocate() call will return with a CM_OK return code, and your program can use that session for a conversation. The mode name lets your program specify, at a very late time (that is, when the Allocate() call is issued), exactly what kind of a route it wants to the partner. Once the Allocate() call gets you a session, the session guarantees you the same kind of service through its lifetime.

The LU software at each end of the session attempts to get your program the bandwidth it needs, based on the mode name your user chose.

There are five mode definitions shipped with every computer in the network. They have the following names and characteristics:

#INTER (interactive data)	Find a session through the network that takes a fast route, suitable for interactive traffic.
#INTERSC (interactive, secure data)	Find a session through the network that takes a fast route, just like #INTER, but assure that the route is secure from the local computer to the partner.
#BATCH (batch data)	Find a session through the network for bulk data that yields to interactive traffic.
#BATCHSC (batch, secure data)	Find a session through the network for bulk data that yields to interactive traffic, just like #BATCH, but assure that the route is secure from the local computer to the partner.
all blanks	For traffic that can take the cheapest route. Find a session through the network that takes the route with the lowest cumulative cost. The cost of each hop in a route is something that's configured by network personnel; presumably low-speed, long-distance telephone links are set up as being more expensive than underutilized, high-bandwidth LANs.

One of these five mode names is probably appropriate for most applications you'll write. Because they are already predefined in each computer, these modes make life much easier for beginning users, since there will be one less field to set up in each computer. You should strongly encourage the users of your applications to use one of these modes.

SETTING UP YOUR COMPUTERS

To pull it all together, here's what you'll need to set up to run a CPI-C application between any pair of machines. We'll do this the same way we want you to train your users to set up their machines. We'll get a solid application up and running, one which gives lots of diagnostic information when it fails. This application is named APING.

APING is a "ping" program for APPC, which means it sends some data to a partner program, which simply echoes the data back. It never reads from or writes to any files on the two computers, so it's safe to distribute widely and use freely. Like many CPI-C applications, APING consists of two programs: the client side, named APING, and the server side, named APINGD. We'll get APING running first, before we try any of our HELLO applications, because they have no diagnostic information in them at all.

When a setup error occurs in a distributed application, there is usually some doubt about what caused the error: your programs, your configuration, or the network. APING helps eliminate some of the guesswork, since it is such a simple and thoroughly tested program. If your programs encounter an error, run APING. If APING also hits a setup error, the problem is probably with the configuration or the network.

You'll inevitably use CPI-C to create applications that are much more complex than APING. For example, CPI-C applications commonly access local and remote databases, and have extensive interaction with users. There will often be lots of setup steps related to these functions that will have to be correct, in addition to the communications details. Separate the complexity of getting the communications right from the other parts of your application. To do this, package APING along with your applications (if it is not already shipped with the APPC platform). Have your application installer get APING running first, which will assure that the CPI-C software on each computer—and the network in between them—are working correctly. Then add to this the two additional steps needed for your application:

On the client side: a CPI-C side information entry

On the server side: a TP definition

On each computer: LIUs, modes, and links

You'll need to define three elements on both the client and server computers. If you're adding your application to a computer that's already set up for CPI-C, these three may already be defined and you won't have to do the following three definitions. Otherwise, they have to be done before any CPI-C programs can be run.

The three definitions you'll need on each computer are a local LU name (to identify uniquely this computer in the network), a mode name (to get a session to the partner), and a link (to say what kind of communications adapter to use to get into the network).

Local logical unit (local LU) name.   Every computer running CPI-C programs will need to have a name that is unique in the network where it is running. This is called an *LU name.*

A computer can have more than one LU name, if you choose. This lets it be known by multiple names in the network. On host computers, this is often done to tie particular applications to specific LU names; no other applications run on that LU software. Most PCs and workstations should have only one local LU name, however. If you have more than one LU defined, you'll need to specify which one of them is the *default LU,* which is the one that CPI-C will use for its outgoing communications. Some platforms let you specify in the side information a local LU which is to be used.

Define a local LU as a fully qualified name, that is, a network name and an LU name, separated by a period. Computers using APPN have a special LU defined on them called the *control point.* Each computer must have at least one LU name; in most workstations, only one LU, the control point LU, will be necessary. For APING, use the default local LU, preferably the control point LU.

Mode name. If possible, your application should use one of the five predefined mode names (#INTER, #INTERSC, #BATCH, #BATCHSC, or all blanks); these mode names should already be defined on your computer. If these modes aren't available or sufficient, define a mode name that identically matches a mode name in the partner computer.* For APING, use #INTER.

Link. Define what kind of adapter card you'll be using for conversations that leave this computer. This will be something like a token-ring or Ethernet LAN card, an async modem, or a coax or twinax card.

This will be used to form a communications connection with a partner computer or with some intermediate computer in the network. You'll need to know the "address" of whatever is at the other end of the link. The format of this address is a little different for each different kind of adapter.

Unfortunately, link configuration details differ from platform to platform and from adapter type to adapter type. You should consult your platform's configuration documentation for more information about how to define and set up links.

On the client computer: a CPI-C side information entry

We'll simplify your setup assumptions by starting from the following place: the client program needs an entry in its local CPI-C side information for every partner to be contacted. Later, in Chap. 22, we'll describe some advanced procedures that you can put in your code to reduce this amount of setup.

Each entry in the side information uses a symbolic destination name as a key for that entry.

Symbolic destination name. Using a symbolic destination name, define an entry in the side information for each partner program. It maps to three fields which you'll need to coordinate with the server program:

Partner LU name. Provide the fully-qualified LU name of the computer where the server program is located.

TP name. Provide the TP name matching that in the server's TP definition.

Mode name. Provide the mode name to be used for constructing a session with the partner LU.

These steps will differ slightly among computers, operating systems, and software releases. See Chap. 22 for more details.

On the server computer: a TP definition

The server computer needs to decide what to do with each arriving TP name. This is decided based on the TP definition created for each incoming TP name.

---

* Directions for creating your own definitions for these five mode names are given in App. B.

TP name. Create a TP definition for each incoming TP name. The TP name in the TP definition on the server must match the TP name sent by the client. On the client side, the TP name is probably set up as part of the symbolic destination name definition in the side information. For APING, use APINGD.

In each TP definition on the server, you'll need to include the appropriate attributes of the program that is to be started. Here are some of the attributes to consider:

- The drive, directory, library, and file name of the executable program
- How the program is to be started
- Whether multiple copies of the program are allowed to run at the same time
- Whether security is required

You'll want to ensure that your users create good TP definitions for your applications; the TP definition has lots of implications on the performance and capacity of your server program. The ideas underlying TP definitions are new to many programmers; we've devoted a whole chapter to the topic, for you to read as your applications become a little more sophisticated. To read more, see Chap. 23.

Replying to "Hello, world"

We'll return now to our Hello example and make it a little more interesting. In the first example (HELLO1), the client program sends the phrase "Hello, world" to the server, but it isn't really sure if it arrives. In our second example (HELLO2), the client program waits to be sure the message arrives; the server explicitly issues the Confirmed() call to signal its success. In this third example (which we'll call HELLO3), the server will reply with a reversed copy of the string, which the client prints.

This will introduce an important design concept: only one side at a time can send information. It's up to the sending side to decide when it is finished sending; in the meantime, the partner continues to receive and process what it receives from the sender.

You are now familiar with the calls that are the building blocks of any conversation: Send_Data() and Receive(). The side that issues an Allocate() is the side that starts out sending; the other side, which issues Accept_Conversation() must next issue a Receive() call. So, how do things ever get turned around, as we want to do in this new example?

It's up to the current sender to change from sending to receiving. The easiest way is for the sender to call Receive(). When the current sender issues a Receive() call, it causes the partner to become the sender. The partner, who has been receiving while the other side has been sending, has been examining one of the returned parameters on each of its Receive() calls. This special parameter is named status_received, and its job is just that: to notify the receiver when a new status for the conversation has been received. In this case, your program would see the value CM_SEND_RECEIVED in the returned status_received parameter.

The values returned by the Receive() call in the status_received parameter tell your program whether there has been a change in the *conversation state*. Only one program at a time can be the sender. The program that is the current sender is referred to as being in **Send** state. Its partner is said to be in **Receive** state at the time.

CPI-C maintains a *finite state machine* for each active conversation. A finite state machine is just a simple way to describe how software, in this case CPI-C, should react when it is called. CPI-C's operation depends on calls arriving in the right sequence. CPI-C keeps track of the last call made by a program, and knows what calls are allowed next. This knowledge is the current state of the conversation.

In the back of each of the CPI-C specs,* you'll find a two-dimensional array that specifies the finite state machine for the CPI-C conversation states. Across the top of the array are the CPI-C states, and down the left side are the CPI-C calls and their parameters. The cells in this array show what the next state will be if the call shown on the left-hand side is issued. For example, if your program successfully issues a Receive() call while in **Send** state, it will make a transition to **Receive** state.

If you're not familiar with finite state machines (and even if you are), fear not! We think CPI-C's handling of conversation states is easy to understand, and we'll discuss our approach in just a few pages (see "Knowing who has the Permission-to-Send" later in this chapter). It should save you a lot of time thumbing through those state tables in the back of the CPI-C specs (which was the way we learned).

A program issuing calls to Receive() should always look at the return_code and the status_received parameters after each call. Here's a code snippet that shows how to look at the status_received parameter to see what to do next:

```
    .
    .
    .
    cmrcv (conversation_ID,     /* Receive()                   */
           data_buffer,         /* where to put received data  */
           &max_receive_length, /* maximum length to receive   */
           &data_received,      /* returned data_received      */
           &received_length,    /* length of received data     */
           &status_received,    /* returned status_received    */
           &rts_received,       /* request-to-send received?   */
           &cpic_return_code);  /* return code from this call  */

    if (cpic_return_code == CM_OK) {
        if (status_received == CM_NO_STATUS_RECEIVED) {
            /* you're still in Receive state */
        }
```

─────────────

* See "CPI-C specifications" in App. D.

```
            else if (status_received == CM_SEND_RECEIVED) {
                /* you're now in Send state */
            }
            else {
                /* check for the other values */
            }
        }
            .
            .
            .
```

If the CPI-C return code is CM_OK, check the status_received value to determine if the conversation state has changed.

Since there are many different values returned in the status_received parameter, we'll later want to make this code more general. For this example, though, here's a pseudocode sketch of these two new samples. Along the side, we've shown what conversation state each side is in before and after each CPI-C call.

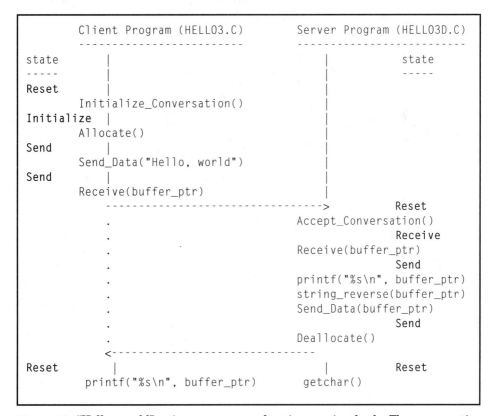

```
            Client Program (HELLO3.C)        Server Program (HELLO3D.C)
            -------------------------        --------------------------
state       |                                |                   state
-----       |                                |                   -----
Reset       |                                |
        Initialize_Conversation()            |
Initialize  |                                |
        Allocate()                           |
Send        |                                |
        Send_Data("Hello, world")            |
Send        |                                |
        Receive(buffer_ptr)                  |
            ------------------------------------->        Reset
            .                           Accept_Conversation()
            .                                            Receive
            .                           Receive(buffer_ptr)
            .                                               Send
            .                           printf("%s\n", buffer_ptr)
            .                           string_reverse(buffer_ptr)
            .                           Send_Data(buffer_ptr)
            .                                               Send
            .                           Deallocate()
            <-------------------------------
Reset       |                                |            Reset
        printf("%s\n", buffer_ptr)       getchar()
```

Figure 6.1 "Hello, world" going out, reversed string coming back. The conversation state, before and after each CPI-C call, is shown in bold.

A successful Deallocate() call, issued by either program, ends the conversation for both programs. Only one Deallocate() call needs to be made between any two programs, not one for each program. Your program finds out that the partner has deallocated the conversation via a return code, since the notification can show up on just about any call in a conversation. When your program sees one of the return codes that says the conversation is over, it knows that the conversation ID it has been using is no longer valid.

It's surprisingly easy to keep track of your conversation state—if you're sending, you are in **Send** state. You stay in **Send** state until you choose to do something else, or your return code signals that your conversation state has changed. If you're in **Receive** state, you stay there until the return_code or status_received parameter signals something different.

This example illustrates a simple "request and reply" transaction that you will use frequently in your applications. This is different from the first two examples (HELLO1 and HELLO2), which showed a single data transfer with no reply or acknowledgment, and a request with an acknowledgment, respectively.

Here's the code for HELLO3. It starts like HELLO1 did, but follows the call to Send_Data() with a call to Receive(). It's the Receive() call on the client side that both gets the returned data and discovers that the conversation has been deallocated.

```
/*----------------------------------------------------------------
 * CPI-C "Hello, world" program, waiting for a reply.
 * Client side (file HELLO3.C)
 *                                                              */
#include <cpic.h>              /* conversation API library    */
#include <stdio.h>             /* file I/O                     */
#include <string.h>            /* strings and memory           */
#include <stdlib.h>            /* standard library             */

/* this hardcoded sym_dest_name is 8 chars long & blank padded */
#define SYM_DEST_NAME (unsigned char*)"HELLO3S "

/* this is the string we're sending to the partner            */
#define SEND_THIS      (unsigned char*)"Hello, world"

int main(void)
{
    unsigned char    conversation_ID[CM_CID_SIZE];
    unsigned char    data_buffer[100+1];
    CM_INT32         send_length;
    CM_INT32         requested_length =
                         (CM_INT32)sizeof(data_buffer)-1;

    CM_INT32         received_length = 0;
    CM_RETURN_CODE   cpic_return_code;

    CM_DATA_RECEIVED_TYPE data_received;
    CM_STATUS_RECEIVED    status_received;
    CM_REQUEST_TO_SEND_RECEIVED rts_received;
```

```
cminit(                         /* Initialize_Conversation    */
    conversation_ID,            /* O: returned conversation ID  */
    SYM_DEST_NAME,              /* I: symbolic destination name */
    &cpic_return_code);         /* O: return code from this call */

cmallc(                         /* Allocate                   */
    conversation_ID,            /* I: conversation ID          */
    &cpic_return_code);         /* O: return code from this call */

(void)strcpy(data_buffer, SEND_THIS);
send_length = (CM_INT32)strlen(SEND_THIS);
cmsend(                         /* Send_Data                  */
    conversation_ID,            /* I: conversation ID          */
    data_buffer,                /* I: send this buffer         */
    &send_length,               /* I: length to send           */
    &rts_received,              /* O: was RTS received?        */
    &cpic_return_code);         /* O: return code from this call */

cmrcv(                          /* Receive                    */
    conversation_ID,            /* I: conversation ID          */
    data_buffer,                /* I: where to put received data */
    &requested_length,          /* I: maximum length to receive */
    &data_received,             /* O: data complete or not?    */
    &received_length,           /* O: length of received data  */
    &status_received,           /* O: has status changed?      */
    &rts_received,              /* O: was RTS received?        */
    &cpic_return_code);         /* O: return code from this call */

data_buffer[received_length] = '\0';    /* insert the null    */
(void)printf("%s\n", data_buffer);

return(EXIT_SUCCESS);
}
```

The source code for program HELLO3D begins with a procedure that reverses the sequence of characters in the string it is provided. This procedure is named string_reverse(). After receiving the string from the client and reversing it, HELLO3D uses Send_Data() to send the string back to the client. It then issues Deallocate() to end the conversation. The server side inherits its deallocate_type from the client, whose default is to use the current sync_level. Since the client program never explicitly set the sync_level, it remains at its default value of CM_NONE; thus the Deallocate() call issued by the server is a Deallocate-Flush. Here's the code for server program HELLO3D.C:

```
/*--------------------------------------------------------------
 *  CPI-C "Hello, world" program, with reply.
 *  Server side (file HELLO3D.C)
 *------------------------------------------------------------*/
#include <cpic.h>              /* conversation API library   */
#include <string.h>           /* strings and memory         */
#include <stdio.h>            /* file I/O header file        */
#include <stdlib.h>           /* standard library           */
```

```
void string_reverse(unsigned char * string)
{
    unsigned char temp;
    size_t count = 0;
    size_t length = strlen((char*)string);
    size_t middle = length / 2;

    if (length != 0) {
        for (length--; count < middle; count++, length--) {
            temp = string[count];
            string[count] = string[length];
            string[length] = temp;
        }
    }
}

int main(void)
{
    unsigned char    conversation_ID[CM_CID_SIZE];
    unsigned char    data_buffer[100+1];
    CM_INT32         requested_length =
                        (CM_INT32)sizeof(data_buffer)-1;
    CM_INT32         received_length = 0;
    CM_RETURN_CODE   cpic_return_code;

    CM_DATA_RECEIVED_TYPE data_received;
    CM_STATUS_RECEIVED    status_received;
    CM_REQUEST_TO_SEND_RECEIVED rts_received;

    cmaccp(                      /* Accept_Conversation             */
        conversation_ID,      /* O: returned conversation ID     */
        &cpic_return_code);   /* O: return code from this call   */

    cmrcv(                       /*Receive                         */
        conversation_ID,      /* I: conversation ID              */
        data_buffer,          /* I: where to put received data   */
        &requested_length,    /* I: maximum length to receive    */
        &data_received,       /* O: data complete or not?        */
        &received_length,     /* O: length of received data      */
        &status_received,     /* O: has status changed?          */
        &rts_received,        /* O: was RTS received?            */
        &cpic_return_code);   /* O: return code from this call   */

    data_buffer[received_length] = '\0';    /* insert the null     */
    (void)printf("%s\n", data_buffer);

    string_reverse(data_buffer);            /* reverse the string  */

    cmsend(                      /* Send_Data                      */
        conversation_ID,      /* I: conversation ID              */
        data_buffer,          /* I: send this buffer             */
        &received_length,     /* I: length to send               */
        &rts_received,        /* O: was RTS received?            */
        &cpic_return_code);   /* O: return code from this call   */
```

```
cmdeal(                        /* Deallocate                    */
    conversation_ID,           /* I: conversation ID            */
    &cpic_return_code);        /* O: return code from this call */
(void)printf("Press a key to end the program...\n");
(void)getchar();                        /* pause for any keystroke   */
return(EXIT_SUCCESS);
}
```

One ramification of conversation states is that some CPI-C calls only work in certain states. For example, if your program is in **Receive** state, a Send_Data() call won't work. If you try this, you'll see that the call to Send_Data() will return the return code CM_PROGRAM_STATE_CHECK. If your program sees this return code, it knows the conversation is still alive and its state hasn't changed. Your program simply made a call that wasn't valid for the conversation state that it was currently in.

KNOWING WHO HAS THE PERMISSION-TO-SEND

Many programmers find the idea of conversation state a little baffling until they've written several CPI-C programs and have had to debug an occasional CM_PROGRAM_STATE_CHECK return code. If you've had any experience with APPC or CPI-C programming in the past, you've probably seen the infamous *conversation state table*. This table defines the conversation states, which calls can be issued in each state, and how state changes occur. The table takes up four or more pages; we think it's unwieldy at best, and opaque at its worst.

But handling conversation states really isn't all that difficult. By examining the return codes on each call and the status_received value on the Receive() call, your programs always know what to do next.

The most important aspect of conversation states is known as the *permission-to-send,* which simply says which side is allowed to send data and is thus in control of the conversation. Only one side at a time is allowed to send data. Think of this side as owning the permission-to-send baton, similar to the baton passed from one runner to another in relay races. It is impossible for both sides to have the baton at the same time. The program holding the baton can choose at any time to pass it to its partner (normal operation); the partner can choose at any time to grab the baton from its partner (in an error condition).

Usually the sending side (that is, the side that owns the permission-to-send) chooses when to hand it off to the partner. A program can pass the baton by using the Receive or Prepare_To_Receive operations. As the receiver, the only way to find out that you have the permission-to-send baton is to issue a Receive() call and look at the status_received value.

However, the partner can grab the permission-to-send baton by using a Send_Error() call. As the sender, the only way to find out that the baton has been grabbed from you is via a return code that indicates the partner issued Send_Error().

One common question arises. What happens in that moment that the sender hands off the permission-to-send baton to its partner? The confusion arises from the apparent contradiction of both sides thinking they are in **Receive** state. The real reason behind this is that the baton takes time to reach the partner and to be received by the partner. As soon as the partner issues a Receive() call and gets that changed status_received value, it has the permission-to-send baton and can begin sending.

There are aspects of *conversation state* other than the permission-to-send. These can all be handled on the Receive() side by watching and responding to the status_received return value. For a general-purpose method of handling all the status_received return values, see "A General-Purpose Receive() Routine" in Chap. 14.

VIEWING THE CURRENT CONVERSATION STATE

Here's a useful procedure you can call from anywhere in a CPI-C program, to find out what the current conversation state is. It relies on a CPI-C call named Extract_Conversation_State(); this call (not surprisingly) takes as its input parameter the current conversation ID. The only time this call won't work is if you pass it a bad conversation ID, such as before Initialize_Conversation() or Accept_Conversation() have been issued, or after the conversation has been deallocated.

```
struct {
    CM_CONVERSATION_STATE value;
    char *                text;
} cpicerr_states_conv[] = {
    0,                                    "Null"                 ,
    1,                                    "Reset"                ,
    CM_INITIALIZE_STATE,                  "Initialize"           ,
    CM_SEND_STATE,                        "Send"                 ,
    CM_RECEIVE_STATE,                     "Receive"              ,
    CM_SEND_PENDING_STATE,                "Send-pending"         ,
    CM_CONFIRM_STATE,                     "Confirm"              ,
    CM_CONFIRM_SEND_STATE,                "Confirm-send"         ,
    CM_CONFIRM_DEALLOCATE_STATE,          "Confirm-deallocate"   ,
    CM_DEFER_RECEIVE_STATE,               "Defer-receive"        ,
    CM_DEFER_DEALLOCATE_STATE,            "Defer-deallocate"     ,
    CM_SYNC_POINT_STATE,                  "Syncpoint"            ,
    CM_SYNC_POINT_SEND_STATE,             "Syncpoint-send"       ,
    CM_SYNC_POINT_DEALLOCATE_STATE,       "Syncpoint-deallocate" ,
    INT_MAX,                              "Bad-Conversation-State"
};

void show_conversation_state(unsigned char *conversation_ID)
{
    /*------------------------------------------------------------------
     * Print the current conversation state to stdout.
     *----------------------------------------------------------------*/
```

```
CM_RETURN_CODE cpic_return_code;     /* CPI-C return code   */
CM_CONVERSATION_STATE conversation_state; /* current state */
char * state_name;                   /* state name to print    */

cmecs(                               /* Extract_Conversation_State */
    conversation_ID,                 /* conversation ID           */
    &conversation_state,             /* returned conversation state */
    &cpic_return_code);              /* return code from this call */

if (CM_OK == cpic_return_code) {
    /* Find the right message text in that array */
    unsigned int   count;
    for (count = 0;
        cpicerr_states_conv[count].value < INT_MAX;
        count++) {
        if (cpicerr_states_conv[count].value ==
            conversation_state) {
            break;
        }
    }
    state_name = cpicerr_states_conv[count].text;
}
else {  /* non-zero return code on CMECS call */
    state_name = "Reset";
}

(void)fprintf(stderr,
        "The CPI-C conversation state is %s\n",
        state_name);
}
```

Given a good conversation ID, this procedure displays the current state of that conversation. Call this from anywhere in your CPI-C programs; you may find it helpful for debugging state-check bugs. On the diskette, you can find it in file DOCPIC.C.

Creating One Server for All Three Clients

In these introductory example programs, we've meticulously crafted our clients and servers in pairs, each one created to interact with its partner and little else. With what we've learned about conversation states, however, we can start using CPI-C and its underlying transaction-oriented model to generalize the server program. For our fourth example, which we'll call HELLO4D, we'll create a single server program that will interact correctly with any of the first three clients: HELLO1, HELLO2, and HELLO3. This is also the program in which we start checking the return codes from each CPI-C call.

If you've studied even a little psychology, you may have heard of the concept of stimulus and response. A subject is said to behave normally if, for every stimulus, it returns the expected response. Transactions can be designed along a similar model. As long as the client gets the right response to every stimulus it provides, it views the server as behaving normally. What we're going to do here is learn how to make a server that generates the correct response, given the stimulus by one of these three clients. First, let's examine the behavior of each of the three client and server programs we've created.

HELLO1 sends a string and immediately deallocates the conversation. The server side recognizes the status of the conversation with its first Receive() call. It receives data and an indication that the conversation has been deallocated (the return_code says CM_DEALLOCATED_NORMAL).

HELLO2 sends a string and requests a confirmation before deallocating the conversation. On the server side, it recognizes these conditions via a Receive() call. The server receives data and an indication that a confirma-

tion is requested (the status_received parameter says CM_CONFIRM_
DEALLOC_RECEIVED).

HELLO3 sends a string, then goes into Receive state, waiting to get a
reversed copy of the string back before deallocating the conversation. On the
server side, it recognizes this condition on a Receive() call. The server
receives data and an indication that it is now to be the sender (the
status_received parameter says CM_SEND_RECEIVED).

So, let's sketch out the logic for a single server program. It issues the
Accept_Conversation() and Receive() calls, to accept the incoming Attach and
see what's arrived. Its first decision is based on the return_code from the
Receive() call. If the return_code is CM_DEALLOCATED_NORMAL, the program assumes it has been contacted by program HELLO1. If the return_code
is CM_OK, then it needs to look at the status_received parameter. When the
status_received parameter says CM_CONFIRM_DEALLOC_RECEIVED, it
knows the partner has issued a Deallocate() and is waiting for an acknowledgment of its confirmation. The server should then execute the code appropriate
for communicating with HELLO2. Otherwise, if the status_received is
CM_SEND_RECEIVED, the partner has relinquished its permission to send,
and the server is presumably communicating with HELLO3.

```
Accept_Conversation()
if (return_code != CM_OK) handle_cpic_error();
Receive()
if (return_code != CM_OK) handle_cpic_error();

if (return_code == CM_DEALLOCATED_NORMAL) {
    /* we're talking to HELLO1...
        the conversation's already gone away */
}
else if (return_code == CM_OK) {
    if (status_received == CM_CONFIRM_DEALLOC_RECEIVED){
        /* we're talking to HELLO2...
            which is asking for confirmation before going away */
    }
    else if (status_received == CM_SEND_RECEIVED) {
        /* we're talking to HELLO3...
            the partner has made us the sender */
    }
    else { /* return code wasn't CM_OK */
        handle_error();
    }
}
```

Program HELLO4D, which follows, thus incorporates some source code
from its predecessors, HELLO1D, HELLO2D, and HELLO3D. Notice the
addition of the handle_cpic_rc() and handle_error() calls. After we show you
the source for HELLO4D, we'll show you what happens in these functions.

```c
/*-------------------------------------------------------------
 *  CPI-C "Hello, world" program, general purpose server.
 *  Server side (file HELLO4D.C)
 *-------------------------------------------------------------*/
#include <cpic.h>                  /* conversation API library   */
#include <string.h>                /* strings and memory         */
#include <stdio.h>                 /* file I/O header file        */
#include <stdlib.h>                /* standard library            */

#include "docpic.h"                /* do_ and handle_ calls       */
void string_reverse(unsigned char * string)
{
    unsigned char temp;
    size_t count = 0;
    size_t length = strlen((char*)string);
    size_t middle = length / 2;

    if (length != 0) {
        for (length--; count < middle; count ++, length--) {
            temp = string[count];
            string[count] = string[length];
            string[length] = temp;
        }
    }
}

int main(void)
{
    unsigned char  conversation_ID[CM_CID_SIZE];
    unsigned char  data_buffer[100+1];
    CM_INT32       received_length;
    CM_INT32       requested_length =
                        (CM_INT32)sizeof(data_buffer)-1;

    CM_RETURN_CODE cpic_return_code;

    CM_DATA_RECEIVED_TYPE data_received;
    CM_STATUS_RECEIVED    status_received;
    CM_REQUEST_TO_SEND_RECEIVED rts_received;

    cmaccp(                        /* Accept_Conversation         */
        conversation_ID,           /* returned conversation ID    */
        &cpic_return_code);        /* return code from this call  */
    if (cpic_return_code != CM_OK) {
        handle_cpic_rc(
            conversation_ID, cpic_return_code, "CMACCP");
    }

    cmrcv(                         /* Receive                     */
        conversation_ID,           /* conversation ID             */
        data_buffer,               /* where to put received data  */
        &requested_length,         /* maximum length to receive   */
        &data_received,            /* returned data_received      */
```

```
                    &received_length,       /* length of received data    */
                    &status_received,       /* returned status_received   */
                    &rts_received,          /* ignore this parameter      */
                    &cpic_return_code);     /* return code from this call */
        if (cpic_return_code == CM_DEALLOCATED_NORMAL) {
            printf("We're talking to HELLO1\n");
            data_buffer[received_length] = '\0';     /* insert null */
            printf("%s\n", data_buffer);     /* write the string    */
        }
        else if (cpic_return_code == CM_OK) {
            if (status_received == CM_CONFIRM_DEALLOC_RECEIVED) {
                printf("We're talking to HELLO2\n");
                data_buffer[received_length] = '\0';/* insert null */
                printf("%s\n", data_buffer);    /* write the string */

                cmcfmd(                 /* Confirmed                  */
                    conversation_ID, /* conversation ID */
                    &cpic_return_code); /* return code from call    */
                if (cpic_return_code != CM_OK) {
                    handle_cpic_rc(
                        conversation_ID, cpic_return_code, "CMCFMD");
                }
            }
            else if (status_received == CM_SEND_RECEIVED) {
                printf("We're talking to HELLO3\n");
                data_buffer[received_length] = '\0';/* insert null */
                printf("%s\n", data_buffer);    /* write the string */

                string_reverse(data_buffer); /* reverse the string */

                cmsend(                 /* Send_Data                  */
                    conversation_ID,    /* conversation ID            */
                    data_buffer,        /* send this buffer           */
                    &received_length,   /* length to send             */
                    &rts_received,      /* ignore this parameter      */
                    &cpic_return_code); /* return code from call      */
                if (cpic_return_code != CM_OK) {
                    handle_cpic_rc(
                        conversation_ID, cpic_return_code, "CMSEND");
                }

                cmdeal(                 /* Deallocate                 */
                    conversation_ID,    /* conversation ID            */
                    &cpic_return_code); /* return code from call      */
                if (cpic_return_code != CM_OK) {
                    handle_cpic_rc(
                        conversation_ID, cpic_return_code, "CMDEAL");
                }
            }
            else {
```

```
                    /* an unexpected status_received value */
                    handle_error(conversation_ID,
                        "Unexpected status_received value: %ld",
                        (long)status_received);
                }
            }
            else {
                handle_cpic_rc(
                    conversation_ID, cpic_return_code, "CMRCV");
            }
            (void)getchar();    /* pause for any keystroke */

            return(EXIT_SUCCESS);
        }
```

This single server program will respond correctly to HELLO1, HELLO2, or HELLO3.

UPDATING TP DEFINITIONS ON THE SERVER SIDE

There's an additional step we need to do outside of these programs to ensure that they run correctly. Remember that our three existing client programs each have a symbolic destination name hardcoded inside them. We hardcoded those symbolic destination names in the programs using a #define in each program. Presumably you've created CPI-C side information entries on the client computer for each of these symbolic destination names. (See Table 7.1.) Notice that it's only the TP name that differs among these three entries—the TP name is the string sent to the server to find the right TP definition there. Remember that the server has a set of TP definitions, one for each incoming TP name (see Table 7.2). For example, the attach manager on the server side starts program c:\cpicpgms\hello1d.exe when it sees the arriving TP name HELLO1D.

TABLE 7.1   CPI-C Side Information for the First Three Client Programs

Symbolic destination name	Partner LU name	TP name	Mode name
HELLO1S	partner_LU_name	HELLO1D	#INTER
HELLO2S	partner_LU_name	HELLO2D	#INTER
HELLO3S	partner_LU_name	HELLO3D	#INTER

TABLE 7.2   TP Definitions for the First Three Server Programs

TP name	Executable file	Start option
HELLO1D	c:\cpicpgms\hello1d.exe	attach-manager-started
HELLO2D	c:\cpicpgms\hello2d.exe	attach-manager-started
HELLO3D	c:\cpicpgms\hello3d.exe	attach-manager-started

TABLE 7.3 Example CPI-C Side Information, Modified
These are the modified TP definitions for the first three server programs. Now all point
to the same executable program, which will internally differentiate among its clients.

TP name	Executable file	Start option
HELLO1D	c:\cpicpgms\hello4d.exe	attach-manager-started
HELLO2D	c:\cpicpgms\hello4d.exe	attach-manager-started
HELLO3D	c:\cpicpgms\hello4d.exe	attach-manager-started

The change we want to make is on the server side; we want to change its TP
definitions so that no matter which of these three TP names arrives, program
HELLO4D.EXE is executed. (See Table 7.3.)

For more details on TP definitions and how the attach manager reads the
TP definitions and acts upon their contents, see Chap. 23.

SIMPLE ERROR-HANDLING PROCEDURES

We've created a set of simple error-handling procedures that we use in the
code we show in the rest of the book. Procedure handle_error() processes a formatted input string, sends it to stderr, waits for a keystroke, and cleans up.
Procedure handle_cpic_rc() takes a CPI-C return code as an input parameter,
as well as the name of the CPI-C call that it was returned on, and calls han-
dle_error(). Procedure do_error_cleanup() cleans up the conversation and exits
the program.

We designed these procedures to illustrate the kind of procedures you might
want to have. We've made some design trade-offs that may not be the ones you
would make. For example, handle_error() calls do_error_cleanup(), which calls
exit(); in all but the simplest applications, you'll probably want to have control
return to your program. We think you'll find these three procedures to be good
jumping-off points as you make your applications robust.

Here's procedure handle_error(), for simple error reporting.

```
void
handle_error(
    unsigned char * conversation_ID,
    const char * format,
    ...)
{
    /*------------------------------------------------------------
     *  Write the passed arguments to stderr, then wait for a
     *  key to be pressed.
     *------------------------------------------------------------*/
    va_list args;
    const char text_to_display[] = {
        "\nPress a key to end the program\n" };

    assert(format != NULL);

    va_start(args, format);
    (void)vfprintf(stderr, format, args);
    va_end(args);
```

```
    (void)fprintf(stderr, "%s", text_to_display);
    (void)fflush(stderr);        /* assure the text is displayed */

    (void)getchar();                      /* wait for a keystroke */

    /*------------------------------------------------------------
     * Clean up, as appropriate for the calling program, its
     * platform, and operating system.
     *----------------------------------------------------------*/
    do_error_cleanup(conversation_ID);
}
```

Procedure handle_error() uses C's variable argument handling to accommodate anything you pass, much like printf() does. It only uses the conversation_ID pointer it gets for one thing: as an input parameter for the do_error_cleanup() procedure. We'll see that, as we elaborate on the do_error_cleanup() procedure, we'll use the conversation_ID to help end the conversation cleanly.

When we get CPI-C return codes we don't expect, we call procedure handle_cpic_rc(). Here it is:

```
void
handle_cpic_rc(
    unsigned char        * conversation_ID,
    const CM_RETURN_CODE cpic_return_code,
    const char    * call_name)
{
    /*------------------------------------------------------------
     * Construct a buffer describing the unexpected CPI-C
     * return code, calling handle_error().
     *----------------------------------------------------------*/
    const char text_to_display[] = {
        "\nPress a key to end the program\n" };

    assert(cpic_return_code >= CM_OK);
    assert(call_name != NULL);

    (void)fprintf(stderr,
        "Unexpected return code on CPI-C %s call.\n",
        call_name);
    show_cpic_return_code(cpic_return_code);

    (void)fprintf(stderr, "%s", text_to_display);
    (void)fflush(stderr);        /* assure the text is displayed */

    (void)getchar();                      /* wait for a keystroke */

    /*------------------------------------------------------------
     * Clean up, as appropriate for the calling program, its
     * platform, and operating system.
     *----------------------------------------------------------*/
    do_error_cleanup(conversation_ID);
}
```

This procedure is tailored for CPI-C return codes. It expects as input parameters the CPI-C return code (not a pointer to the return code) and a pointer to the text name of the call that failed unexpectedly. Since we're designing these procedures to work in C, we don't need to pass around a pointer to the return code any more; we can now pass it around directly. Passing around a pointer to the text name of the call isn't too sophisticated; a slightly more efficient way to do this would be to have an array with an index to all the calls and their names, and then pass around the index. We thought the approach we show here is easier to read and, besides, it's errors handling code anyway; it doesn't have to be highly efficient, just correct and complete.

There are times, when calling Receive(), that we will get a return code we expected, but won't get the expected data_received or status_received values. For these cases, we call procedure handle_receive_error(). Here it is:

```
void
handle_receive_error(
    unsigned char *        conversation_ID,
    unsigned char *        message,
    CM_RETURN_CODE         cpic_return_code,
    CM_DATA_RECEIVED_TYPE  data_received,
    CM_STATUS_RECEIVED     status_received)
{
    const char text_to_display[] = {
        "\nPress a key to end the program\n" };

    fprintf(stderr, "%c\n", message);

    show_cpic_return_code(cpic_return_code);
    if (cpic_return_code == CM_OK ||
        cpic_return_code == CM_DEALLOCATED_NORMAL) {
        show_data_received(data_received); /*if CM_OK*/
        show_status_received(status_received);
    }
    show_conversation_state(conversation_ID);

    (void)fprintf(stderr, "%s", text_to_display);
    (void)getchar(); /* wait for a keystroke */

    /*------------------------------------------------------------
     * Clean up, as appropriate for the calling program, its
     * platform, and operating system.
     *------------------------------------------------------------*/
    do_error_cleanup(conversation_ID);
}
```

The handle_receive_error() procedure is similar to the handle_cpic_rc() procedure. Instead of passing just the CPI-C return code, you also pass it the data_received and status_received values. If the return code indicates that the data_received and status_received values were set by CPI-C, the values will be shown, as well as the return code value.

The handle_cpic_rc(), handle_receive_error(), and handle_error() procedures call do_error_cleanup(), which currently doesn't return to the original
calling program. This certainly cleans up unexpected return codes, but doesn't
give a real user much diagnostic information. We'll talk about more responsible reporting of errors in Chap. 20.

Here's a first version of procedure do_error_cleanup().

```
void
do_error_cleanup(unsigned char * conversation_ID)
{
    /*-----------------------------------------------------------
     * A simple-minded procedure for cleaning up a program.
     * conversation_ID is not used in this procedure.
     *-----------------------------------------------------------*/

    exit(EXIT_FAILURE);          /* operating system cleanup     */
}
```

Calling exit() is effective, but simple-minded. The partner program doesn't get to
learn much about why the local program went away. For example, it can't distinguish whether the local program called exit() or whether its user pressed
Ctrl+Break. Although the current conversation ID is passed as an input parameter, it isn't used. We'll turn do_error_cleanup() into a much more responsible
citizen when we discuss the nuances of deallocating conversations in Chap. 16.

VIEWING THE RETURN CODE NAME

When your program encounters an unexpected CPI-C return code, it is important that it be handled properly. In the handle_ procedures shown previously,
we've given you some tools that can make this handling easier.

It is also important to make the information about an unexpected event useful and readable to the person who will look at it. The most obvious example is
the return code value; very few people have all of them memorized, but most
can recognize the constant names.

We've provided a show_cpic_return_code() procedure that simply prints
out the constant name, given a return code value. Here is the code for
show_cpic_return_code():

```
struct {
    CM_RETURN_CODE          value;
    char *                  text;
} cpicerr_cpic_return_code[] = {
    {CM_OK,                            "CM_OK"                            },
    {CM_ALLOCATE_FAILURE_NO_RETRY,    "CM_ALLOCATE_FAILURE_NO_RETRY"     },
    {CM_ALLOCATE_FAILURE_RETRY,       "CM_ALLOCATE_FAILURE_RETRY"        },
    {CM_CONVERSATION_TYPE_MISMATCH,   "CM_CONVERSATION_TYPE_MISMATCH"    },
    {CM_PIP_NOT_SPECIFIED_CORRECTLY,  "CM_PIP_NOT_SPECIFIED_CORRECTLY"   },
    {CM_SECURITY_NOT_VALID,           "CM_SECURITY_NOT_VALID"            },
```

```
                   {CM_SYNC_LVL_NOT_SUPPORTED_LU,        "CM_SYNC_LVL_NOT_SUPPORTED_LU"      },
                   {CM_SYNC_LVL_NOT_SUPPORTED_PGM,       "CM_SYNC_LVL_NOT_SUPPORTED_PGM"     },
                   {CM_TPN_NOT_RECOGNIZED,               "CM_TPN_NOT_RECOGNIZED"             },
                   {CM_TP_NOT_AVAILABLE_NO_RETRY,        "CM_TP_NOT_AVAILABLE_NO_RETRY"      },
                   {CM_TP_NOT_AVAILABLE_RETRY,           "CM_TP_NOT_AVAILABLE_RETRY"         },
                   {CM_DEALLOCATED_ABEND,                "CM_DEALLOCATED_ABEND"              },
                   {CM_DEALLOCATED_NORMAL,               "CM_DEALLOCATED_NORMAL"             },
                   {CM_PARAMETER_ERROR,                  "CM_PARAMETER_ERROR"                },
                   {CM_PRODUCT_SPECIFIC_ERROR,           "CM_PRODUCT_SPECIFIC_ERROR"         },
                   {CM_PROGRAM_ERROR_NO_TRUNC,           "CM_PROGRAM_ERROR_NO_TRUNC"         },
                   {CM_PROGRAM_ERROR_PURGING,            "CM_PROGRAM_ERROR_PURGING"          },
                   {CM_PROGRAM_ERROR_TRUNC,              "CM_PROGRAM_ERROR_TRUNC"            },
                   {CM_PROGRAM_PARAMETER_CHECK,          "CM_PROGRAM_PARAMETER_CHECK"        },
                   {CM_PROGRAM_STATE_CHECK,              "CM_PROGRAM_STATE_CHECK"            },
                   {CM_RESOURCE_FAILURE_NO_RETRY,        "CM_RESOURCE_FAILURE_NO_RETRY"      },
                   {CM_RESOURCE_FAILURE_RETRY,           "CM_RESOURCE_FAILURE_RETRY"         },
                   {CM_UNSUCCESSFUL,                     "CM_UNSUCCESSFUL"                   },
                   {CM_DEALLOCATED_ABEND_SVC,            "CM_DEALLOCATED_ABEND_SVC"          },
                   {CM_DEALLOCATED_ABEND_TIMER,          "CM_DEALLOCATED_ABEND_TIMER"        },
                   {CM_SVC_ERROR_NO_TRUNC,               "CM_SVC_ERROR_NO_TRUNC"             },
                   {CM_SVC_ERROR_PURGING,                "CM_SVC_ERROR_PURGING"              },
                   {CM_SVC_ERROR_TRUNC,                  "CM_SVC_ERROR_TRUNC"               },
                   {CM_TAKE_BACKOUT,                     "CM_TAKE_BACKOUT"                   },
                   {CM_DEALLOCATED_ABEND_BO,             "CM_DEALLOCATED_ABEND_BO"           },
                   {CM_DEALLOCATED_ABEND_SVC_BO,         "CM_DEALLOCATED_ABEND_SVC_BO"       },
                   {CM_DEALLOCATED_ABEND_TIMER_BO,       "CM_DEALLOCATED_ABEND_TIMER_BO"     },
                   {CM_RESOURCE_FAIL_NO_RETRY_BO,        "CM_RESOURCE_FAIL_NO_RETRY_BO"      }
                   {CM_RESOURCE_FAILURE_RETRY_BO,        "CM_RESOURCE_FAILURE_RETRY_BO"      },
                   {CM_DEALLOCATED_NORMAL_BO,            "CM_DEALLOCATED_NORMAL_BO"          },
                   {INT_MAX,                             "Bad cpic_return_code value"        }
               };
       void show_cpic_return_code(CM_RETURN_CODE cpic_return_code)
       {
           /*-------------------------------------------------------------
            *  Print the current cpic_return_code value to stdout.
            *-------------------------------------------------------*/
           char *rc_name;                /* cpic_return_code name        */

           /* Find the right message text in that array */
           unsigned int   count;
           for (count = 0;
                cpicerr_cpic_return_code[count].value < INT_MAX;
                count++) {
                if (cpicerr_cpic_return_code[count].value ==
                       cpic_return_code) {
                   break;
                }
           }
           rc_name = cpicerr_cpic_return_code[count].text;
```

```
            (void)fprintf(stderr,
                    "The CPI-C cpic_return_code value is %s\n",
                    rc_name);
    }
```

VIEWING THE STATUS_RECEIVED NAME

What we've seen in the server program example is the importance of the returned status_received parameter after a successful Receive() call. In the CPI-C programs you write, you will use the status_received value to guide their flow of execution. In the previous chapter, we introduced a utility procedure to display the current conversation state. Since the indication of a state change is generally found in the returned status_received parameter, you may find the following procedure helpful in your early transaction design-and-debug activities. In this procedure, we pass in the current status_received parameter rather than the conversation ID. The status_received value is valid only if the Receive() call gets a CM_OK return_code, so calling this procedure isn't too interesting unless the return_code is CM_OK.

As with conversation states, there are many status_received values that will be unfamiliar to you right now. Most of them you will never use; we'll cover the ones you'll use frequently in "A General-Purpose Receive() Routine" in Chap. 14.

```
    struct {
        CM_STATUS_RECEIVED      value;
        char *                  text;
    } cpicerr_status_received[] = {
        CM_NO_STATUS_RECEIVED,          "No Status Change",
        CM_SEND_RECEIVED,               "Send",
        CM_CONFIRM_RECEIVED,            "Confirm",
        CM_CONFIRM_SEND_RECEIVED,       "Confirm Send",
        CM_CONFIRM_DEALLOC_RECEIVED,    "Confirm Deallocate",
        CM_TAKE_COMMIT,                 "Take Commit",
        CM_TAKE_COMMIT_SEND,            "Take Commit Send",
        CM_TAKE_COMMIT_DEALLOCATE,      "Take Commit Deallocate",
        INT_MAX,                        "Bad Status_Received"
    };

    void show_status_received(CM_STATUS_RECEIVED status_received)
    {
        /*------------------------------------------------------------
         *  Print the current status_received value to stdout.
         *----------------------------------------------------------*/
        char * status_name;            /* status_received name       */

        /* Find the right message text in that array */
        unsigned int   count;
        for (count = 0;
             cpicerr_status_received[count].value < INT_MAX;
```

```
                count++) {
            if (cpicerr_status_received[count].value ==
                    status_received) {
                break;
            }
        }
        status_name = cpicerr_status_received[count].text;

        (void)fprintf(stderr,
                "The CPI-C status_received value is %s\n",
                status_name);
    }
```

Multiple Sends and Receives

Let's review the four sample programs we've created so far:

HELLO1 sent a string, but didn't wait to see if HELLO1D was started and received the string.

HELLO2 sent a string, and waited for a confirmation from HELLO2D that it arrived safely. We learned how to use Confirm() and Confirmed().

HELLO3 sent a string, then went into Receive state, waiting for HELLO3D to return it. We learned about conversation states.

HELLO4D acted as a server for any of the preceding client programs. We learned about using CPI-C return_codes and the status_received parameter to control a program's flow of execution.

HELLO5, our next example, will send extended amounts of data, and HELLO5D, its partner, will use the value of the returned data_received parameter to help control its program logic.

LOGICAL RECORDS

In CPI-C, the sender sends data in chunks called *logical records,* or just *records.* Each call to Send_Data() causes one record to be sent. On the receiving side, a successful call to Receive() retrieves one of the following indications, in the data_received parameter:

- one full record
- a portion of a record
- no data at all

The receiving program uses the value in the returned data_received parameter to distinguish among these three conditions.

As a C programmer, you are probably already familiar with the idea of records if you've used C's fread() and fwrite() library routines. It's part of your application design to decide exactly what a record is—that is, what it contains and how big it is.

Let's say we're sending our name and address to a partner. The sending program could send the entire name and address at one time. If it does that, the partner must be designed to receive and process an entire name and address. This means that the sender must assemble the record in such a way that the receiver can correctly break it back into its component parts.

A different way to build records is to make each line of the name and address a separate record. The partner must then know that each record it receives is a new line, and it needs to know how many lines there are (in case multiple names and addresses are being sent).

Still another way of building records is to break the name and address into separate fields—say one record for the first name, one for the middle name or initial, one for the surname, and so on. In order to reassemble the pieces, the partner must then be designed to know that these fields exist.

Some types of data don't invite natural or sensible record boundaries. A binary file is one common example. In such cases, you'll probably want to send it in large chunks—say 32 Kbytes—which the partner receives a record at a time and reassembles.

AN EXAMPLE OF USING DATA_RECEIVED

The client side of this example, HELLO5, sends each of its command line parameters to the partner. The number of command line arguments is available to the main() procedure in C with a variable traditionally called argc (for "argument count"). Each string on the command line is pointed to in an array of pointers traditionally called argv (for "argument variable"). To illustrate the use of records, the client will send each command line string as a single logical record. No null-terminating characters ('\0') are sent. When the client has finished sending these records, it will deallocate the conversation.

The server side of this example, HELLO5D, receives records until the conversation is over. HELLO5D receives the incoming data into small 100-byte buffers, which lets you see the techniques for handling incomplete records. HELLO5D assembles the incomplete records into complete records, which it prints, adding a newline character after each complete record. Because no null-terminating characters are sent, we'll use fwrite() and fputc() calls to print the records to stdout.

Since the logic on the server side is becoming more complicated, we'll sketch this pair of programs in two pieces, shown in Figs. 8.1 and 8.2.

The source code for the two programs, HELLO5.C and HELLO5D.C, follows.

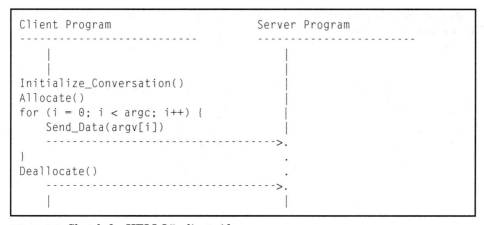

```
Client Program                          Server Program
-------------------------               -------------------------

      |                                       |
      |                                       |
Initialize_Conversation()                     |
Allocate()                                     |
for (i = 0; i < argc; i++) {                   |
    Send_Data(argv[i])                         |
    ------------------------------------->.
}                                            .
Deallocate()                                 .
    ------------------------------------->.
      |                                       |
```

Figure 8.1 Sketch for HELLO5, client side.

```
Client Program         Server Program
--------------         -----------------------

      |                     |
      |                     |
    ------------------->|
      .              Accept_Conversation()
      .              while (done == FALSE) {
      .                  Receive(100 bytes into buffer)
    ------------------->|
      .                    if (return_code == OK or DEALLOCATED_NORMAL)
      .                       if (data_received != NO_DATA_RECEIVED)
      .                          if (data_received == DATA_INCOMPLETE)
      .                             fwrite(buffer, 1, bytes, stdout)
      .                          else if (data_received == DATA_COMPLETE)
      .                             fwrite(buffer, 1, bytes, stdout)
      .                             fputc('\n', stdout)
      .                       else
      .                          handle_error()
      .                    if (return_code != OK)
      .                       done = TRUE
      .                  }
```

Figure 8.2 Sketch for HELLO5D, server side.

Example client program HELLO5.C. This program sends each of the command line parameter strings to the server:

```c
/*-------------------------------------------------------------
 *  CPI-C example program, sending command line parameters.
 *  Client side (file HELLO5.C)
 *----------------------------------------------------------*/
#include <cpic.h>               /* conversation API library    */
#include <string.h>             /* strings and memory          */
#include <stdlib.h>             /* standard library            */

#include "docpic.h"             /* do_ and handle_ calls       */

/* this hardcoded sym_dest_name is 8 chars long & blank padded */
#define SYM_DEST_NAME   (unsigned char*)"HELLO5S "

int main(int argc, char *argv[])
{
    unsigned char   conversation_ID[CM_CID_SIZE];
    CM_RETURN_CODE  cpic_return_code;

    cminit(                     /* Initialize_Conversation     */
        conversation_ID,        /* returned conversation ID    */
        SYM_DEST_NAME,          /* symbolic destination name   */
        &cpic_return_code);     /* return code from this call  */
    if (cpic_return_code != CM_OK) {
        handle_cpic_rc(
            conversation_ID, cpic_return_code, "CMINIT");
    }

    cmallc(                     /* Allocate                    */
        conversation_ID,        /* conversation ID             */
        &cpic_return_code);     /* return code from this call  */
    if (cpic_return_code != CM_OK) {
        handle_cpic_rc(
            conversation_ID, cpic_return_code, "CMALLC");
    }

    {
        /* send each command-line argument, one per send       */
        int index;
        for (index = 0; index < argc; index++) {
            CM_REQUEST_TO_SEND_RECEIVED rts_received;
            CM_INT32 send_length = (CM_INT32)strlen(argv[index]);
            cmsend(                     /* Send_Data               */
                conversation_ID,        /* conversation ID         */
                argv[index],            /* send this buffer        */
                &send_length,           /* length to send, no null */
                &rts_received,          /* ignore this parameter   */
                &cpic_return_code);     /* return code             */
            if (cpic_return_code != CM_OK) {
                handle_cpic_rc(
```

```
                              conversation_ID, cpic_return_code, "CMSEND");
                }
            }
        }

        cmdeal(                          /* Deallocate                  */
            conversation_ID,             /* conversation ID             */
            &cpic_return_code);          /* return code from this call  */
        if (cpic_return_code != CM_OK) {
            handle_cpic_rc(
                conversation_ID, cpic_return_code, "CMDEAL");
        }

        return(EXIT_SUCCESS);
}
```

Example server program HELLO5D.C. This program displays each of the records
sent by the client:

```
/*----------------------------------------------------------------
 *  CPI-C example program, displaying received records.
 *  Server side (file HELLO5D.C)
 *-----------------------------|----------------------------------*/
#include <cpic.h>                /* conversation API library    */
#include <stdio.h>               /* file I/O                     */
#include <stdlib.h>              /* standard library             */

#include "docpic.h"              /* do_ and handle_ calls        */

int main(void)
{
    unsigned int done = 0;

    unsigned char    conversation_ID[CM_CID_SIZE];
    unsigned char    data_buffer[100+1];
    CM_INT32         received_length;
    CM_INT32         requested_length =
                         (CM_INT32)sizeof(data_buffer)-1;
    CM_RETURN_CODE   cpic_return_code;

    CM_DATA_RECEIVED_TYPE data_received;
    CM_STATUS_RECEIVED     status_received;
    CM_REQUEST_TO_SEND_RECEIVED rts_received;

    setbuf(stdout, NULL);        /* assure unbuffered output    */

    cmaccp(                          /* Accept_Conversation         */
        conversation_ID,             /* returned conversation ID    */
        &cpic_return_code);          /* return code from this call  */
    if (cpic_return_code != CM_OK) {
        handle_cpic_rc(
            conversation_ID, cpic_return_code, "CMACCP");
    }
```

```
        while (done == 0) {
            cmrcv(                          /* Receive                    */
                conversation_ID,    /* conversation ID            */
                data_buffer,        /* where to put received data */
                &requested_length,  /* maximum length to receive  */
                &data_received,     /* returned data_received     */
                &received_length,   /* length of received data    */
                &status_received,   /* returned status_received   */
                &rts_received,      /* ignore this parameter      */
                &cpic_return_code); /* return code from this call */

        if ((cpic_return_code == CM_OK) ||
            (cpic_return_code == CM_DEALLOCATED_NORMAL)) {

            if (data_received != CM_NO_DATA_RECEIVED) {
                /* write the received string to stdout */
                (void)fwrite((void *)data_buffer, (size_t)1,
                            (size_t)received_length, stdout);

                if (data_received == CM_COMPLETE_DATA_RECEIVED) {
                    /* write a newline character */
                    (void)fputc((int)'\n', stdout);
                }
            }
            else {
                /* unexpected data_received */
                handle_error(conversation_ID,
                    "Unexpected data_received value; %ld",
                    (long)data_received);
            }
        }
        else {
            handle_cpic_rc(
                conversation_ID, cpic_return_code, "CMRCV ");
        }
        if (cpic_return_code != CM_OK) {
            done = 1;   /* CM_DEALLOCATED_NORMAL or unexpected */
        }
    }

    (void)printf("Press a key to end the program...\n");
    (void)getchar();                /* pause for a keystroke      */

    return(EXIT_SUCCESS);
}
```

DATA_RECEIVED VALUES

The data_received parameter is returned on the Receive() call. Its job is simple: it tells your program whether any data was returned on the call, and whether that data completes a logical record.

The Receive() call isn't just for receiving data; it returns several different pieces of information each time it is called. The return_code parameter tells whether the call worked and whether the conversation is over. The status_received parameter tells whether the conversation state changed. The data_received parameter tells whether data was actually received and whether there is more data yet to receive.

Your programs should look at the data_received parameter if the return_code on the Receive() call is CM_OK or CM_DEALLOCATED_NORMAL. If the return_code is anything else, don't bother looking—the value of the data_received parameter isn't defined except for these two return codes.

A valid data_received parameter will have one of the following four values:

CM_NO_DATA_RECEIVED. No data was received on this Receive() call. If the return_code is CM_OK, be sure to look at the returned status_received parameter because it will be a value other than CM_NO_STATUS_RECEIVED. The received_length parameter on the Receive() call is not valid for this data_received value.

CM_COMPLETE_DATA_RECEIVED. This is the value that you like to see. The Receive() call received data into the data buffer your program provided, and the data it received was either a complete logical record or the last part of one that you had previously received. Your program should next look at the received_length parameter to see how much data was received.

CM_INCOMPLETE_DATA_RECEIVED. This means your program has more work to do. The Receive() call could not fit the entire record into the buffer you provided, so it filled your buffer as much as it could. Your program should continue issuing Receive() calls until it has received the rest of this record. Your program should still look at the received_length parameter to see how much data was received. The data can either be processed now, or after the rest of the record has been received; it will depend on what you are receiving and how your program processes it.

CM_DATA_RECEIVED. A type of conversation called a *basic conversation* allows you to receive chunks of data regardless of the boundaries of the record. This value indicates that the Receive() call got a chunk of data; it is up to your program to parse the data and figure out where the record boundaries are. Your program should next look at the received_length parameter to see how much data was received.

We recommend that you not use basic conversations in your programs. For more information about how records are handled in basic conversations see "Basic Conversations" in Chap. 17.

VIEWING THE DATA_RECEIVED NAME

In HELLO5D, the value of the data_received parameter returned from the Receive() call is used to guide the logic of the program. As in the previous

example, you may find times while debugging when you want to watch the
current value for data_received.

The following procedure works like the procedure in the previous chapter
that displayed status_received. Here, the calling program passes the current
data_received parameter (which is valid only if the Receive() call got a CM_OK
or CM_DEALLOCATED_NORMAL return_code). And, while we're on the
topic, don't look at the received_length value unless data_received is a valid
value other than CM_NO_DATA_RECEIVED. Even though you might expect
it to be zero if there's no data, CPI-C doesn't make any promises about what
will be in any field if its conditions for validity aren't met.

```
struct {
    CM_DATA_RECEIVED_TYPE value;
    char *                text;
} cpicerr_data_received[] = {
    CM_NO_DATA_RECEIVED,              "No Data Received",
    CM_DATA_RECEIVED,                 "Data Received",
    CM_COMPLETE_DATA_RECEIVED,        "Complete Data Received",
    CM_INCOMPLETE_DATA_RECEIVED,      "Incomplete Data Received",
    INT_MAX,                          "Bad Data_Received"
};

void show_data_received(CM_DATA_RECEIVED_TYPE data_received)
{
    /*-------------------------------------------------------------
     * Print the current data_received value to stdout.
     *                                                          */
    char * data_name;          /* data_received name         */

    /* Find the right message text in that array */
    unsigned int   count;
    for (count = 0;
        cpicerr_data_received[count].value < INT_MAX;
        count++) {
      if (cpicerr_data_received[count].value ==
            data_received) {
          break;
      }
    }
    data_name = cpicerr_data_received[count].text;

    (void)fprintf(stderr,
            "The CPI-C data_received value is %s\n",
            data_name);
}
```

The Receive() call is powerful because it receives not only data from the
partner, but also information about the status of the conversation. It looks like
there are a lot of things to check after each Receive(), and there are! However,
you can make them manageable if you always check the returned parameters
in the following order:

1. *return_code.*   Always check this first.

2. *data_received.*   Valid if the return_code is CM_OK or CM_DEALLOCATED_NORMAL.

3. *received_length* and the *data_buffer.*   Valid if data_received is valid (see above) and isn't CM_NO_DATA_RECEIVED.

4. *status_received.*   Valid if the return_code is CM_OK. Check and process data_received and any received data before acting on the status_received value.

5. *request_to_send_received.*   Valid if the return_code is CM_OK. Request-to-send is essentially a signal that either side can send at almost any time. Handling the signal well is challenging. Use of this signal isn't recommended for most applications.*

---

* See "Begging and Signaling" in Chap. 17 for some rare circumstances in which you can use request-to-send.

Data Buffering: A Paradigm Shift

In this chapter, we discuss an idea that may be new to you:

Buffering for performance

Data doesn't necessarily leave your computer at the moment your program issues a Send_Data().

You want your distributed applications to delight their users, despite the type and speed of the networks they run on, and despite the needs of other distributed applications running at the same time. Those who manage networks want consistently high performance across all distributed applications in an error-free production environment.

Today's computer networks are self-tuning or are tuned by specialists. It's up to you, the programmer, to tune the application logic among the programs you create, regardless of the speed of the computers and networks they run on. CPI-C lets you separate your application logic from the behavior of the underlying network. We'll describe program design principles that let your applications achieve outstanding performance and high utilization of the available network resources when running in a well-tuned environment.

Packets, packets, packets! The job of the underlying network software that your applications use is handling *packets*.* Network software endeavors to

---

* Packets are the unit of delivery at the data link layer. In a LAN environment, these are also known as *frames*.

send packets that are as large as possible, since every packet to be sent adds processing overhead. Furthermore, in some types of networks, like X.25, you may be billed on a per-packet basis. Therefore, the network software works to send full packets instead of partial ones.

The size and rate of the packets sent by any network software will, of necessity, be limited. For example, each packet sent into the network is limited in size by the device drivers and communications cards used in your computer. It is the job of the network software to hide the limitations of any particular network and computers from your distributed programs so that your application has the widest possible applicability.

The network software used by CPI-C assembles packets from the logical records and status information provided by your programs. If your program sends lots of small records, for example, CPI-C accumulates them into a network buffer until it has enough bytes for a full network packet, which it then sends. If your program sends a large logical record, say the same size or larger than the size of a network packet, CPI-C sends it immediately.

Using CPI-C, your application and its network software are effectively decoupled. This means that your program never knows the size of the network packets, be they large or small. In CPI-C applications, the sending program does not know when packets are actually delivered into the network; it also doesn't know when the packets are received by the partner application. When they actually need to know that records have arrived, the applications use their conversational dialog to exchange information about what records have been received and processed. If the network can't deliver any packet, it reports to both sides that there is a network-level problem.

When CPI-C was first created, most networks consisted of slow data links and expensive wires. To achieve the most performance for the least cost (that is, to improve link utilization), it was important for CPI-C to optimize the use of network buffers and minimize network overhead. With today's high-speed data links and relatively inexpensive networks, CPI-C's investment in optimization makes it the fastest protocol with the least network and CPU overhead.

RULES FOR SENDING A NETWORK PACKET

How does CPI-C figure out when to place a packet into the network? It follows two simple rules. A packet is sent into the network when:

1. CPI-C's internal packet buffer is full
2. A program indicates that it has finished sending or that a partial packet should be sent. This can be done by:
   a. Issuing a Receive() call
   b. Requesting a confirmation (for example, issuing a Confirm() call)
   c. Reporting an application error (using the Send_Error() call)
   d. Using the Flush() call (a CPI-C call designed to cause a network packet to be sent)
   e. Deallocating the conversation

Each Send_Data() call is hence a simple hand-off of your program's data to CPI-C. The underlying CPI-C software works in parallel with your application program to construct and send network packets. Thus, Send_Data() calls usually execute quickly—there's nothing for your program to wait for. Of course, your program has no idea when its data actually leaves your computer and goes into the network. If it wants to control this, it issues the Flush() call, which causes the packets to be sent without giving up the permission to send.

The last record that your program sends almost never exactly fills a network buffer. That's why a Deallocate() call causes this last partial buffer to be sent.

NETWORK FLOW CONTROL

There is an exception to the rule that says Send_Data() calls always go fast. The laws of queuing are immutable: your programs can potentially hand records to CPI-C faster than it can get them out into the network reliably. The worst combination for this is, of course, a fast CPU and a slow network.

CPI-C sets aside a number of internal buffers to be used for each session. This number is tunable and is normally about eight. Once these internal buffers are completely filled (that is, they're not being placed into the network quickly enough) the next Send_Data() call will "block." Blocking means that the call won't return from CPI-C until CPI-C has handled it successfully.* In this case, CPI-C won't return to your program until all your data has been accepted into its internal buffers.

On most computers, you can set this "pacing window" from 1 to 63. Each session will set aside the specified number of buffers when the session is allocated. For example, if your network packets are 4 Kbytes each and you set your pacing to 63, each session will consume about 252 Kbytes. You can see that this will be a challenge if you expect to have lots of concurrent sessions on a memory-constrained operating system like DOS.

DATA BUFFERING EXAMPLES

In this section, we'll show examples of programs which send small and large records, and look at when network packets are actually sent.

In the example shown in Fig. 9.1, program SENDER1 (which is the current sender) will send three records, each 100 bytes long. We'll assume that the network packet size is 1000 bytes, a typical value. So, all three records will fit into one network packet. CPI-C puts the 300 bytes of data into the internal network buffer, along with some separators that it uses to keep track of where the records begin and end. This network packet is not delivered into the network until the sender calls Receive(), which causes CPI-C to flush its internal packet buffer.

---

* A new feature of CPI-C 1.2 is nonblocking operation. We discuss it in Chapter 26.

```
Program SENDER1                        Program RECEIVER1
---------------                        -----------------

Send_Data(rec1, 100 bytes)
  rc = OK
Send_Data(rec 2, 100 bytes)
  rc = OK
Send_Data(rec 3, 100 bytes)
  rc = OK
Receive()
                 ---rec1,rec2,rec3-->
                                       Receive(), 32 Kbytes
                                         rc = OK
                                         buffer = rec1, 100 bytes
                                       Receive(), 32 Kbytes
                                         rc = OK
                                         buffer = rec2, 100 bytes
                                       Receive(), 32 Kbytes
                                         rc = OK
                                         status = SEND
                                         buffer = rec3, 100 bytes
```

Figure 9.1 Data is buffered into a single network packet.

On the other side of the network, program RECEIVER1 (the current receiver) expects to receive the three records, one at a time. In this example, program RECEIVER1 receives each record into a 32-Kbyte buffer. It uses this one buffer to receive and process each record, before receiving the next one. Program RECEIVER1 is designed to conserve the number of times it issues the Receive() call, so it uses a large buffer, with the intention of getting a complete record with each Receive() call.

See Fig. 9.1 for the calls and line flows for this example. In this example, no data flowed through the network until program SENDER1 issued a Receive() call, telling CPI-C that it was done sending. CPI-C packed all of the buffered data into one network packet and delivered it to program RECEIVER1, which received one record each time it issued a Receive() call.

One implication of this data buffering is that if a network error occurs, your program has no way of knowing how much of the sent data was actually received and processed by the partner. You may need to go back and recover all of the data that was sent since you last synchronized with your partner program.

But this isn't the only way the data could be sent on the wire. Let's consider an example, shown in Fig. 9.2, where the data buffers being sent are larger than the network packet size. And again, let's assume that the network packet size is 1000 bytes. This time, we'll send 2400 bytes with each Send_Data() call, which is obviously larger than the packet size (although your program doesn't know this). The Receive() calls in program RECEIVER2 again use 32-Kbyte buffers, larger than the buffers used in the Send_Data() calls.

```
Program SENDER2                        Program RECEIVER2
---------------                        -----------------

Send_Data(rec1, 2400 bytes
  rc = OK
              ---part of rec1----> 1000 bytes
              ---part of rec1----> 1000 bytes

Send_Data(rec2, 2400 bytes)
  rc = OK
              ---end rec1, rec2--> 400 + 600 bytes
              ---part of rec2----> 1000 bytes
                                   Receive(), 32 Kbytes
                                     rc = OK
                                     buffer = rec1, 2400 bytes

Send_Data(rec3, 2400 bytes)
  rc = OK
              ---end rec2, rec3--> 800 + 200 bytes
              ---part of rec3----> 1000 bytes
              ---part of rec3----> 1000 bytes
                                   Receive(), 32 Kbytes
                                     rc = OK
                                     buffer = rec2, 2400 bytes
Receive()
              ---end rec3--------> 200 bytes
                                   Receive (), 32 Kbytes
                                     rc = OK
                                     buffer = rec3, 2400 bytes
                                     status = SEND
```

Figure 9.2 Data buffering, records span multiple network packets.

In the example shown in Fig. 9.2, some of the data buffer was sent as soon as network packet was filled. The last part of each data buffer was not placed on the network until the next Send_Data() call supplied more data—which filled the next network packet.

In both of these examples, the program logic and ordering of events is the same regardless of how data buffering occurs. Your programs should never be concerned with the size of the network buffers and when data actually gets sent. When a program finishes sending, CPI-C will make sure that all of its data is sent. In "Illustrating Data Buffering" later in this chapter, we will talk about telling CPI-C to send its buffered data immediately, using the Flush() call. In many cases, this can improve the performance of your application since both sides can do work simultaneously.

In the preceding two examples the program logic is exactly the same; regardless of how the network packages your data, your programs don't have to change. Your programs do not and should not exercise any control over how the CPI-C software uses network packets. Network packet sizes are a global network tuning issue and should not be dealt with in your programs.

CPI-C BUFFERS ATTACHES

Remember that the Allocate() call was named because it allocates sessions for use by a conversation. When a session is successfully allocated, no messages actually flow to its partner. The information associated with an Allocate() call is held by CPI-C in an internal network buffer, just like any other data. In particular, the data associated with an Allocate() includes the *TP_name* being sent, and optional security information, such as a user ID and password.* The information record that is sent by the client because of an Allocate() is called an *Attach*. The Attach doesn't travel to the server until the network packet containing it is sent (see the rules described in "Rules for Sending a Network Packet" earlier in this chapter).

By treating the Attach message like any other logical record, CPI-C and the network software simplify their internal code for optimizing the construction of packets. However, there are times when you may want to ensure that the server program is running before you continue with a data transfer. Further discussion of this topic and a code example are shown in "Checking for a Good Connection" in Chap. 21.

Special software handles the Attach record when it arrives at the computer where the server program is located. This software is called the *attach manager*. The attach manager understands the Attach message, TP definitions, and how to start executable programs in the target operating system. For an in-depth discussion of the attach manager, see Chap. 23.

One implication of buffering the Attach is that if the server program could not be started for any reason, your program doesn't discover it until sometime after the Allocate() call completes. In fact, if your program never issues a call requiring the server program to respond, your program might not find out that the server never started!

The Confirm and Receive operations are the only ones that force these return codes related to starting the server program. Once your program gets a CM_OK return code from one of these operations, it can never get one of these server-not-loaded return codes for that conversation. However, it is possible, but not guaranteed, that your program could get one of these server-not-loaded return codes on a Send_Data() or a Send_Error() call, issued before a Confirm() or Receive() call.

The following return codes from the server's attach manager indicate a failure before the server program issued an Accept_Conversation().

---

* Other parts of Allocate() information, such as the partner LU name and mode name, are handled during session initiation.

```
#define CM_CONVERSATION_TYPE_MISMATCH         (CM_RETURN_CODE) 3
#define CM_PIP_NOT_SPECIFIED_CORRECTLY        (CM_RETURN_CODE) 5
#define CM_SECURITY_NOT_VALID                 (CM_RETURN_CODE) 6
#define CM_SYNC_LVL_NOT_SUPPORTED_PGM         (CM_RETURN_CODE) 8
#define CM_TPN_NOT_RECOGNIZED                 (CM_RETURN_CODE) 9
#define CM_TP_NOT_AVAILABLE_NO_RETRY          (CM_RETURN_CODE) 10
#define CM_TP_NOT_AVAILABLE_RETRY             (CM_RETURN_CODE) 11
```

ILLUSTRATING DATA BUFFERING

Let's wrap up this chapter with a pair of programs that show how CPI-C buffers data. This pair is most illustrative if you can see both sides of the application while it is running. The client side issues Send_Data() calls in a loop. Before each Send_Data(), it calls getchar(), waiting for a keystroke, so you can control exactly when the Send_Data() occurs.

When the client program is started, it looks for a command-line flag which tells it whether to issue a Flush() call inside the loop. If the client side is issuing Flushes, you'll see the server program start immediately (because the Attach record is flushed after the Allocate() call). You'll also see the server's Receive() calls match up with each keystroke at the client.

If the client program doesn't issue any Flush() calls, it probably issues several Send_Data() calls before the server program even starts. The number of Send_Data() calls depends on the size of the network packets and the size of the records being sent. You'll then see the server's Receive() calls bunched up, corresponding to the arriving network packets—which contain multiple records. Remember, only one record (or less) is received on each Receive() call.

Here is the client side:

```
/*---------------------------------------------------------------
 *   Demo of the Flush call, client side.
 *   (file FLUSH.C)
 *--------------------------------------------------------------*/
#include <cpic.h>               /* conversation API library    */
#include <stdarg.h>             /* variable arguments          */
#include <stdio.h>              /* file I/O                    */
#include <stdlib.h>             /* standard library            */
#include <string.h>             /* strings and memory          */

#include "docpic.h"             /* CPI-C do_calls, BOOL        */

#define MAX_LOOP_COUNT (10)

int main(int argc, char *argv[])
{
    /*---------------------------------------------------------
     *   This side sends records in a loop. If the flag is set,
     *   issue a Flush before each Send_Data. When the loop is
     *   complete, issue Deallocate Flush.
     *--------------------------------------------------------*/
```

```
CM_RETURN_CODE   cpic_return_code;
unsigned char    conversation_ID[CM_CID_SIZE];
unsigned         count;
BOOL             flush_flag;

/*------------------------------------------------------------
 * Get the symbolic destination from the command line and
 * initialize a conversation.
 *----------------------------------------------------------*/
{
    unsigned char sym_dest_name[CM_SDN_SIZE+1];

    if (argc > 1) { /* is there at least one argument? */
        /* first, set it to 8 blanks, then copy the name */
        (void)strcpy((char*)sym_dest_name, "        ");
        (void)memcpy(sym_dest_name, argv[1],
            min(strlen(argv[1]), sizeof(sym_dest_name) - 1));
    }
    else {
        handle_error(
            conversation_ID,
            "A symbolic destination name must be provided");
    }

    cminit(                      /* Initialize_Conversation    */
        conversation_ID,         /* returned conversation ID   */
        sym_dest_name,           /* symbolic destination name  */
        &cpic_return_code        /* return code from this call */
    if (cpic_return_code != CM_OK) {
        handle_cpic_rc(
            conversation_ID, cpic_return_code, "CMINIT");
    }
}

/*------------------------------------------------------------
 *  If there's anything on the command line after the
 *  symbolic destination name, then Flush after every
 *  Send_Data() call.
 *----------------------------------------------------------*/
if (argc > 2) {          /* are there at least two arguments? */
    flush_flag = TRUE;
}
else {
    flush_flag = FALSE;
}

{
    /*------------------------------------------------------------
     * Allocate a session for this conversation.
     *----------------------------------------------------------*/
    cmallc(                  /* Allocate                   */
        conversation_ID,     /* conversation ID            */
        &cpic_return_code);  /* return code from this call */
```

```
        if (cpic_return_code != CM_OK) {
            handle_cpic_rc(
                conversation_ID, cpic_return_code, "CMALLC");
        }
    }


    /*-------------------------------------------------------------
     *  Flush the Attach header so we can see the server program
     *  started as we send the data records.
     *-----------------------------------------------------------*/
    cmflus(                         /* Flush                    */
        conversation_ID,            /* conversation ID          */
        &cpic_return_code);         /* return code              */
    if (cpic_return_code != CM_OK) {
        handle_cpic_rc(
            conversation_ID, cpic_return_code, "CMFLUS");
    }

    for (count = 1; count < MAX_LOOP_COUNT; count++) {

        unsigned char   data_buffer[80];
        CM_INT32 send_length;
        CM_REQUEST_TO_SEND_RECEIVED rts_received;   /* ignored */

        (void)sprintf((char*)data_buffer,
                "This is message %u", count);
        (void)printf("Sending \"%s\", ", data_buffer);

        /*-------------------------------------------------------
         *  Send a the next record.
         *-----------------------------------------------------*/
        send_length = (CM_INT32)strlen((char*)data_buffer);
        cmsend(                     /* Send_Data                */
            conversation_ID,        /* conversation ID          */
            data_buffer,            /* send this buffer         */
            &send_length,           /* length to send           */
            &rts_received,          /* ignore this parameter    */
            &cpic_return_code); /* return code from this call   */
        if (cpic_return_code != CM_OK) {
            handle_cpic_rc(
                conversation_ID, cpic_return_code, "CMSEND");
        }

        if (flush_flag == TRUE) {
            cmflus(             /* Flush                        */
                conversation_ID, /* conversation ID             */
                &cpic_return_code); /* return code              */
            if (cpic_return_code != CM_OK) {
                handle_cpic_rc(
                    conversation_ID, cpic_return_code, "CMFLUS");
            }
        }
```

```
            (void)printf("Press a key to continue\n");
            (void)getchar();

        }

        {

            /*-------------------------------------------------------------
             *  Deallocate this conversation. The default sync_level
             *  is CM_NONE, so do Deallocate-Flush.
             *-----------------------------------------------------------*/
            cmdeal(                     /* Deallocate                    */
                conversat               /* conversation ID               */
                &cpic_return_code); /* return code from this call    */
            if (cpic_return_code != CM_OK) {
                handle_cpic_rc(
                    conversation_ID, cpic_return_code, "CMDEAL");
            }
        }

    return EXIT_SUCCESS;          /* program was successful        */
}
```

This client program FLUSH.C illustrates the effect that Flush() has on data buffering,

On the server side, FLUSHD.C simply prints out data records as they arrive. The program logic is identical whether or not the client issues Flush() calls.

Here is the server side:

```
/*-------------------------------------------------------------
 *  Demo of the Flush call, server side.
 *  (file FLUSHD.C)
 *-----------------------------------------------------------*/
#include <cpic.h>                /* conversation API library    */
#include <stdio.h>               /* file I/O                     */
#include <stdlib.h>              /* standard library             */

#include "docpic.h"              /* CPI-C do_ calls, BOOL        */

#define RECEIVE_SIZE (1000)      /* size of each Receive()       */
#define BUFFER_SIZE (32767)      /* largest possible record      */

int main(void)
{
    /*-------------------------------------------------------------
     *  The client side should have sends multiple records,
     *  followed by a Deallocate Flush.
     *
     *  We've arbitrarily bounded the size of the incoming
     *  record to 32767 bytes.
     *-----------------------------------------------------------*/
    unsigned char   conversation_ID[CM_CID_SIZE];
    CM_RETURN_CODE  cpic_return_code;
```

```
BOOL            done;
CM_INT32        received_length;
CM_INT32        requested_length;
size_t          offset;
unsigned char * data_buffer;

CM_DATA_RECEIVED_TYPE data_received;
CM_STATUS_RECEIVED    status_received;

cmaccp(                         /* Accept_Conversation      */
    conversation_ID,            /* returned conversation ID */
    &cpic_return_code);         /* return code from this call */
if (cpic_return_code != CM_OK) {
    handle_cpic_rc(
        conversation_ID, cpic_return_code, "CMACCP");
}

/*----------------------------------------------------------
 * Allocate enough memory for whatever you expect to
 * receive from the partner...
 *--------------------------------------------------------*/
data_buffer = (unsigned char *)malloc((size_t)BUFFER_SIZE);
if (data_buffer == NULL) {
    handle_error(conversation_ID,
        "Can't allocate %u bytes for data_buffer",
        (size_t)BUFFER_SIZE);
}

/*----------------------------------------------------------
 *   Receive one complete data record.
 *   This loop continues until two conditions are met:
 *   - a complete data record is received, and
 *   - Deallocate Normal is received in the return code.
 *   It receives directly into the data buffer, with a
 *   requested length that's less than or equal to the size
 *   of the buffer. It diagnoses the following conditions:
 *   - the record sent by the partner was too large
 *   - the partner sent multiple records before deallocating
 *   - any unexpected return_code or status_received value
 *--------------------------------------------------------*/
done = FALSE;
offset = 0;
requested_length = RECEIVE_SIZE;

do {                /* continue while there's more to receive */
    CM_REQUEST_TO_SEND_RECEIVED rts_received;

    cmrcv (                     /* Receive                  */
        conversation_ID,    /* conversation ID          */
        &data_buffer[offset], /* put received data here   */
        &requested_length,  /* maximum length to receive */
        &data_received,     /* returned data_rcvd value */
        &received_length,   /* length of received data  */
```

```
                &status_received,   /* returned status_rcvd value  */
                &rts_received,      /* ignore this parameter        */
                &cpic_return_code); /* return code from this call   */
        /* check first for usable return codes */
        if ((cpic_return_code == CM_OK) ||
            (cpic_return_code == CM_DEALLOCATED_NORMAL)) {

            /*------------------------------------------------------
             *  The data_received value is very important!
             *------------------------------------------------------*/
            switch (data_received) {
                case CM_INCOMPLETE_DATA_RECEIVED:
                    if (requested_length == (CM_INT32)0) {
                        /* We're already seen DATA_COMPLETE,
                           yet there's still more. Give up! */
                        done = TRUE;
                        handle_error(conversation_ID,
                            "Multiple records sent");
                    }

                    /* update the offset, to receive more */
                    offset += (size_t)received_length;
                    if (offset == BUFFER_SIZE) {
                        /* We're at the end of the buffer, yet
                           there's still more. Give up! */
                        done = TRUE;
                        handle_error(conversation_ID,
                            "Too much data was sent");
                    }

                    /* don't ask for more than we can hold */
                    requested_length = (CM_INT32)
                        min(RECEIVE_SIZE, BUFFER_SIZE - offset);
                    break;

                case CM_COMPLETE_DATA_RECEIVED:
                    offset += (size_t)received_length;
                    if (requested_length == (CM_INT32)0) {
                        /* We've encountered multiple records,
                           since this is the flag that we've
                           been here before. */
                        done = TRUE;
                        handle_error(conversation_ID,
                            "Multiple records sent");
                    }
                    /*---------------------------------------------
                     * This is where your program processes the
                     * received data. For this example, we just
                     * display it, using fwrite().
                     *---------------------------------------------*/
```

```
                              if (offset > 0) {
                                  (void)fwrite(
                                  (void *)data_buffer, 1, offset, stdout);
                                  printf("\n");
                              }
                              else {
                                  handle_error(
                                      conversation_ID,
                                      "No data was sent");
                              }
                              offset = 0;
                              requested_length = RECEIVE_SIZE;
                              break;

                        default:
                            /* other values are ignored */
                            break;
                  } /* end of switch */

                  /*----------------------------------------------------
                   * The status_received value isn't very interesting,
                   * since the partner's presumably gone already.
                   *---------------------------------------------------*/
                  if (cpic_return_code == CM_DEALLOCATED_NORMAL) {
                      done = TRUE;        /* the conversation is over */
                  }
                  else { /* the return code is CM_OK */
                      /* we don't expect a status_received value */
                      if (status_received != CM_NO_STATUS_RECEIVED) {
                          /* partner unexpectedly changed the status */
                          done = TRUE;
                          handle_error(conversation_ID,
                              "Unexpected CPI-C status_received: %ld",
                              (long)status_received);
                      }
                  }
              }
          else {  /* this isn't a return code we expected */
              done = TRUE;
              handle_cpic_rc(
                  conversation_ID, cpic_return_code, "CMRCV");
          }
      } while (done == FALSE);

      (void)printf("\nPress a key to end the program\n");
      (void)getchar();

      return EXIT_SUCCESS;          /* program was successful */
  }
```

This server program FLUSHD.C illustrates the effect that client Flush() calls
have on data buffering.

CPI-C Application Design

## Chapter 10

Building Blocks

In this chapter and the ones that follow in this part of the book, we present a set of building blocks for creating CPI-C programs. These chapters explain all the calls you'll need to write communications programs. In each chapter, we'll discuss the calls in the order you'll likely use them, not in alphabetical order. Table 1 at the back of the book lists all the CPI-C calls, with an index to where they're discussed in the book.

The first two chapters of building blocks cover starting the client and server sides of the conversation, respectively. The next chapter discusses sending data, and the chapter that follows discusses receiving information. To round out this discussion, we describe synchronizing a pair of programs, and reporting errors to each other. CPI-C offers several ways to clean up a conversation when it's over, which we cover in Chap. 26. You might choose to skip the last chapter in this part of the book; it discusses techniques that we think you'll rarely use, but occasionally may need in special situations.

We'll give you a set of reusable procedures to accomplish each of the tasks we discuss in the chapters that follow. We've collected these together in one file, which you can include in your programs. We've also created a set of simple error-handling routines, which you already saw in "Simple Error-Handling Procedures" in Chap. 7. The error-handling procedures are modular enough that you can later modify them for use in your own programs, without needing to change your core CPI-C procedures.

AN UMBRELLA FILE OF CPI-C PROCEDURES

We've put a dozen or so of these CPI-C building-block procedures into a single file named docpic.c. If you'd like to use any or all of these procedures in your programs, you'll need to do two things. First, include its header file, docpic.h, in the top of the files that use any of these procedures. Put file docpic.h in a directory where you keep your toolkit include files; you should use it as

```
#include "docpic.h"
```

not

```
#include <docpic.h>
```

Second, you'll need to compile and link file docpic.c. This file contains the includes for the calls from the standard C run-time libraries that we make in the building-block procedures; for example, it includes <stdio.h> and <stdlib.h>.

Separating these procedures from the core of your program logic keeps them modular. You can choose to add additional logic to these procedures, say adding additional return code handling to your Receive() calls, and it will benefit all the Receive() calls you issue throughout your programs. You're probably seeing the same programming trends we're seeing: keep things modular, portable, and reusable.

We make calls to the C run-time macro assert() throughout the building-block procedures. assert() is a wonderful tool for helping you capture programming bugs. We strongly recommend you use it in your programs. A great book for C programmers that really convinced us of the efficacy of using C's assert() call is *Writing Solid Code.**

You may notice that each of the do_ procedures returns zero on success and nonzero on a failure condition, like many of the C run-time routines. Since each of the do_ routines actually calls our handle_error procedure (which then call C's exit() call), we have not worried about checking the return value on the do_ calls. If you modify the do_error_cleanup() procedure so that it doesn't call exit(), you should also add code to check the do_ call return values.

USING THESE BUILDING BLOCKS AS A REFERENCE

Starting in these building-blocks Chaps. 11 to 16, each CPI-C call is described in detail. These calls are described in the order you are likely to use them in your programs and during your development as a CPI-C programmer.

Although these call descriptions are not a replacement for the real CPI-C references, we believe you will find them useful as a reference. Therefore, when you read these sections straight through you may find that we repeat some information that is common across a number of calls. It may seem redun-

---

* This book is listed in "C Programming Books" in App. D.

dant now, but bear with us; you'll appreciate it later when you need to look up a specific call for clarification of some point.

One of the things you may notice is that our call descriptions do not list each return code possible on each call. This is partly due to our philosophy that return codes can and should be handled by a common routine. You and your programs should handle a CM_PROGRAM_PARAMETER_CHECK return code the same way regardless of which call it occurred on. Thus, we have included the complete list of CPI-C return codes in App. A, with the actions appropriate for your programs to take.

If you're interested in finding out where a particular CPI-C call is described, consult the CPI-C calls (Table 1) at the back of this book.

Getting Connected: The Client Side

This chapter describes the CPI-C calls that a client program uses to start a conversation. You'll see that the CPI-C calls themselves are easy. However, you'll probably write additional code around these calls because the network hardware, software, and all their parameters have to be set up correctly to establish the connection. Your challenge with this additional code will be to tell your program's users what went wrong and how to fix it, whenever there's a problem.

For a pair of CPI-C programs to converse, they need to establish a conversation between them. As with human conversations, one side initiates the conversation and the other side acknowledges that a conversation has indeed begun. In talking about these two roles, we've referred to the side that initiates the conversation as the *client* and the side that accepts the conversation as the *server*. In general, the client side of an application starts a conversation in order to get resources from a server program. Any kind of computer can play either role; apparent role reversals, such as a program on MVS being a client or a program on DOS being a server, are common.

As with a telephone conversation, there's a certain asymmetry here. One side has to start the conversation, and the other side has to answer. Similarly, the information required for a client to start a conversation is not the same as that required for a server to accept an incoming conversation. This is because the client must specify how to connect to the server: where it is, how to get to it, and which server program to run. The client's conversation characteristics are set when the conversation is started; the server just accepts the characteristics of the incoming conversation. The server does not need to know the identity of a client beforehand to converse with it.

Thus, the client program takes four steps to start a conversation:

1. Get a conversation ID.
2. Specify how to get to the server application.
3. (Optionally) change conversation characteristics from their default values.
4. Allocate a session for this conversation to use. This also builds an Attach— the message that contains the TP name and other characteristics needed to start the partner program.

Using CPI-C's defaults and the client side information, a program can accomplish these tasks with just two calls: Initialize_Conversation() and Allocate(). Additional calls, whose names start with the word *Set,* can override the defaults, override the local side information, or allow your program to avoid using side information entirely.

This chapter has four sections. In the first section, we discuss the Initialize_Conversation() call, which is used to identify the partner and to get a "handle" for the other calls that follow. Next, we cover the Allocate() call, which requests a connection to the partner computer (this connection is called a *session,* in APPC terminology). Allocate() is the call that is most susceptible to setup problems or any kind of failure. In the third and fourth sections, we discuss calls that you can put between the Initialize_Conversation() and Allocate() calls to change CPI-C's default values. These calls come in several categories; we'll discuss changing operational characteristics and overriding the names used to reach the partner. Security parameters are also set between the Initialize_Conversation() and Allocate() calls, but we'll save the detailed discussion of conversation security for Chap. 25.

Later on, in Chap. 22, we'll integrate these initialization building blocks into one cohesive unit that you can reuse in your client programs.

GETTING A CONVERSATION ID AND NAMING THE PARTNER

CPI-C allows any program to have many conversations active simultaneously. This number can be hundreds or thousands. We'll look at a small program later in this section that gives you an idea of this number on the computer you're using. The conversations can be with one partner program or with many partner programs. CPI-C creates a unique identifier for each conversation, so they can't get confused in your programs. This identifier, called a *conversation ID,* is returned to the client program on its first CPI-C call for each conversation, which is Initialize_Conversation().

Initialize_Conversation() is also the CPI-C call you use to point to the network configuration fields needed to reach the partner. If these local fields have been set up already, the Initialize_Conversation() call will be successful and return a good conversation ID to your program.

Initialize_Conversation (CMINIT)

Usually, the first CPI-C call issued by the client program is Initialize_Conversation(). If this call is successful, CPI-C returns a conversation ID, which your program uses as a handle for all the other CPI-C calls in this same conversation. The conversation ID is valid until the conversation is deallocated.

Initialize_Conversation() is also used to tell CPI-C who the partner will be. You can get to your partner with just one name: the *symbolic destination name.*

Here's the function prototype for the Initialize_Conversation() call.

```
CM_ENTRY                            /* Initialize_Conversation    */
cminit(unsigned char CM_PTR,        /* O: conversation_ID         */
       unsigned char CM_PTR,        /* I: sym_dest_name           */
       CM_RETURN_CODE CM_PTR);      /* O: return_code             */
```

Every CPI-C program must declare or malloc() an 8-byte array for the conversation ID, and point to it when calling CPI-C. CPI-C fills the array you've pointed to with a valid value, if the Initialize_Conversation() call is successful.

Your program will probably never need to look at or display a conversation ID; it's a hexadecimal array that never leaves your computer. In addition, the partner program has no idea what it is (and doesn't care).

Each conversation ID is unique among all the other valid conversation IDs being used in the same computer (remember, many CPI-C programs can be running at the same time in one computer). Once a conversation has been deallocated, its associated conversation ID is invalid and can't be used successfully on another CPI-C call.

Your program must also supply a pointer to a symbolic destination name as input to the Initialize_Conversation() call. As you may remember from "Using Symbolic Destination Names and Side Information" in Chap. 5, the symbolic destination name serves as an index into a local table of information about how to connect to the server program. The symbolic destination name is always an eight-byte string. Unlike all other strings used by CPI-C, no length field is associated with it. This is the one string that you'll have to handle a little differently from other strings.

If your symbolic destination name is less than eight bytes long, your program must pad it on the right (that is, out to the eighth byte) with blanks. Never put a null-terminating byte ('\0') before the ninth byte. In our C programs, we declare the symbolic destination name as nine bytes (CM_SDN_SIZE + 1), and always put a '\0' in the ninth byte. This makes it easy to use with other C run-time routines, such as printf().

The following example using Initialize_Conversation() also shows how to ensure that your symbolic destination name is specified correctly.

```
int
do_initialize_conversation(unsigned char * conversation_ID,
                           unsigned char * input_string)
{
  /*-----------------------------------------------------------
   * Get the symbolic destination from the caller, and
   * initialize a conversation, returning the new
   * conversation ID into the pointed-to input parameter.
   *-----------------------------------------------------------*/
```

```
unsigned char   sym_dest_name[CM_SDN_SIZE+1];
CM_RETURN_CODE cpic_return_code;
int             ret_val;

assert(conversation_ID != NULL);

/*-----------------------------------------------------------
 * Initialize the symbolic destination name to all-blanks
 * to assure it's padded on the right. Add a '\0', in case
 * you want to use printf() to show it.
 *---------------------------------------------------------*/
(void)memset((char *)sym_dest_name, ' ',
             sizeof(sym_dest_name) - 1);
sym_dest_name[sizeof(sym_dest_name) - 1] = '\0';

if (input_string != NULL) {
    /*-------------------------------------------------------
     * Copy the name from the input string. This will
     * truncate the name, if it's too long.
     *-----------------------------------------------------*/
    (void)memcpy(sym_dest_name,
                 input_string,
                 min(strlen(input_string),
                     (sizeof(sym_dest_name) - 1)));
}
else {
    /* Leave the symbolic destination name all blanks. */
}

/*-----------------------------------------------------------
 * Ensure the symbolic destination name is in uppercase.
 *---------------------------------------------------------*/
{
    size_t i;
    for (i=0; i < CM_SDN_SIZE ; i++) {
        sym_dest_name[i] =
            (unsigned char)toupper(sym_dest_name[i]);
    }
}

cminit(                         /* Initialize_Conversation   */
    conversation_ID,            /* returned conversation ID  */
    sym_dest_name,              /* symbolic destination name */
    &cpic_return_code);         /* return code from this call */
if (cpic_return_code == CM_OK) {
    /*-------------------------------------------------------
     * The symbolic destination name was either all blanks,
     * or was configured in the local CPI-C side
     * information. The new conversation ID is returned in
     * the string pointed-to by the input parameter.
     *-----------------------------------------------------*/
    ret_val = 0;
```

```
        }
    else {
        /*-----------------------------------------------------
         *  Either the symbolic destination name was spelled
         *  wrong or has not been configured in the local CPI-C
         *  side information, CPI-C is all out of internal
         *  control blocks, or something else.
         *-----------------------------------------------------*/
        handle_cpic_rc(
            conversation_ID, cpic_return_code, "CMINIT");
        ret_val = 1;
    }
    return ret_val;
}
```

If the symbolic destination name that your program supplies is not configured in the local computer's CPI-C side information, your program gets a return code of CM_PARAMETER_ERROR.* Otherwise, if CPI-C has enough internal control blocks to start up the conversation, it will return the CM_OK return code.

In the *Hello* programs we showed in the first part of the book, we set the symbolic destination name with a macro; remember

```
#define SYM_DEST_NAME    "HELLO1S "    /* 8 chars, blank padded */
```

This made the programs shorter, since we didn't have to set the name from the command line with argv and argc. However, this is a poor practice. Hardcoding a symbolic destination name in a program is rotten for portability. Design your client programs for generality, and have them get their sym_dest_name from an outside source. Get it from the command line, from a file, or ask the user for it. Don't hardcode your sym_dest_name—with one exception: the all-blanks symbolic destination, which we'll discuss next.

Using an all-blank symbolic destination name

In all the examples we've looked at so far, we specified a symbolic destination name that we assumed had been set up with a corresponding entry in the local CPI-C side information. Someone must actually configure the side information with the correct values for the program to run. Often it's desirable to have your program run without requiring any external configuration. CPI-C lets your program do this by specifying a special value: all blanks.

The all-blank symbolic destination name tells CPI-C that no existing configuration information is to be used. It is up to your program to use CPI-C's *Set*

---

* On IBM's VM/ESA operating system, if an entry is not found in the side information table, the name provided in sym_dest_name will be used as the partner TP name and the return code will be CM_OK. All other conversation characteristics will be left in their default condition.

calls to provide the conversation setup information necessary to connect to the partner. We'll introduce these calls later in this chapter.

The following example shows how to use the all-blank symbolic destination name.

```
int
do_blank_sym_dest_name(unsigned char * conversation_ID)
{
    unsigned char sym_dest_name[CM_SDN_SIZE+1];

    assert(conversation_ID != NULL);

    /* Initialize the symbolic destination name to all-blanks */
    (void)strcpy((char *)sym_dest_name, "           ");

    /* Call the procedure that issues Initialize_Conversation */
    return (do_initialize_conversation(conversation_ID,
                                        sym_dest_name));
}
```

Using an all-blank symbolic destination name does not require a side information entry. The Initialize_Conversation() call using the all-blank symbolic destination name should always succeed (unless CPI-C runs out of memory or conversation IDs).* As programmers, it's fun to find out just what "runs out" really means.

Here's a little test program that calls Initialize_Conversation() in a loop, using an all-blank symbolic destination name. Run it until it stops (with a return code other than CM_OK), and you'll find out how many conversation IDs your platform actually supports. Notice that this is a stress test for CPI-C; it may cause the CPI-C software itself to abend, which will abort conversations in use by other programs as well. Remember, this is a test program; we don't recommend running it in a production environment.

```
/*------------------------------------------------------------------
 *   Stress test program. Don't run this on a production machine.
 *   (file LPINIT.C)
 *------------------------------------------------------------------*/
#include <cpic.h>            /* conversation API library   */
#include <limits.h>          /* for ULONG_MAX              */
#include <stdio.h>           /* file I/O                   */
#include <stdlib.h>          /* standard library           */
#include <string.h>          /* strings and memory         */

#include "docpic.h"          /* CPI-C do_calls             */
```

---

* The IMS and MVS platforms do not support an all-blank symbolic destination name on the Initialize_Conversation() call. An alternative technique is to create a specific symbolic destination (for example, "BLANK") for use on Initialize_Conversation() call, and to code your program to override the configuration with CPI-C *Set* calls.

```
int main(void)
{
    /*------------------------------------------------------------
     * Loop ULONG_MAX times or until CMINIT fails.
     *----------------------------------------------------------*/
    unsigned char sym_dest_name[] = "        ";     /* 8 blanks */
    unsigned long count;

    setbuf(stdout, NULL);    /* flush output immediately */
    /*------------------------------------------------------------
     * Initialize lots of conversations, until the platform
     * limit is exceeded.
     *----------------------------------------------------------*/
    for (count = 0; count < ULONG_MAX; count++) {
        CM_RETURN_CODE cpic_return_code;
        unsigned char conversation_ID[CM_CID_SIZE];

        (void)printf("cminit: %lu\r", count);
        cminit(                     /* Initialize_Conversation  */
            conversation_ID,    /* returned conversation ID  */
            sym_dest_name,      /* symbolic destination name */
            &cpic_return_code);/* return code from this call */
        if (cpic_return_code != CM_OK) {
            (void)printf("cminit: %lu\n", count);
            handle_cpic_rc(
                conversation_ID, cpic_return_code, "CMINIT");
        }
    }
    return EXIT_SUCCESS;
}
```

GETTING A SESSION

After a successful Initialize_Conversation() call and appropriate *Set* calls, your program has identified to the local CPI-C software a partner for the conversation. However, no network packets have been built and no data has left your computer. Now you're ready to connect to the server platform.

Regardless of the underlying network technology, CPI-C is *connection-oriented*. This means that once a connection is made to the partner, it continues until it is intentionally ended or until a network or platform failure occurs. When using CPI-C, this connection from the local network software to its counterpart in the partner computer is called a *session*.

The Allocate() call is used to get a session with the partner's computer—literally to get a pipe to it, through which data can be sent. If there's a free session to the partner computer, that is, an active one that's not being used, CPI-C will reserve it for your program. In this case, the Allocate() call works very quickly.

Otherwise, CPI-C sees to it that a new session is built to the partner. Here, the Allocate() call will be slower, because an acceptable path through the network must be found and the bandwidth reserved for this conversation. If there's *anything* wrong that the platform can't automatically recover from, the Allocate() call will fail, and you'll need to describe the failure to your program's user.

In addition to getting a session, an Allocate() call causes one other thing to occur: it causes CPI-C to build the first data message that will be sent on that session. This internal message is called an *Attach,* and its principal field is the TP name. You'll remember that three fields are needed in the side information for each symbolic destination name: the partner's LU name, the mode name for the session, and the TP name. Now you see how these are used: CPI-C uses the partner LU name to find the partner's computer; it uses the mode name to decide what kind of session to obtain, and it sends the TP name in the Attach so the partner computer knows which program to start.

Allocate (CMALLC)

The Allocate() call gets a session with the platform where the server program is located. This session will be used as the pipe for all data that's exchanged during the conversation. The Allocate() call also causes an Attach to be constructed. The Attach will be the first record that flows through the session. The contents of an Attach are shown in "Starting the Server Program" in Chap. 12.

Here's the function prototype for the Allocate() call.

```
CM_ENTRY                            /* Allocate               */
cmallc(unsigned char CM_PTR,        /* I: conversation_ID     */
       CM_RETURN_CODE CM_PTR);      /* O: return_code         */
```

Since all of the characteristics of the conversation have already been established (either by default or by explicit *Set* calls), the conversation ID is the only input parameter on the Allocate() call.

Here's an example of allocating a session for a conversation.

```
int
do_allocate(unsigned char * conversation_ID)
{
    /*-------------------------------------------------------------
     * Use the conversation ID from the caller to allocate a
     * session and build an Attach.
     *-------------------------------------------------------------*/

    CM_RETURN_CODE cpic_return_code;
    int            ret_val;

    assert(conversation_ID != NULL);

    /* -----------------------------------------------------------
     * Allocate a session for this conversation.
     *-----------------------------------------------------------*/
```

```
cmallc(                        /* Allocate                    */
    conversation_ID,           /* conversation ID             */
    &cpic_return_code);        /* return code from this call  */
if (cpic_return_code == CM_OK) {
    /*-------------------------------------------------------------
     * A session was successfully allocated, and an Attach
     * was built.
     *-----------------------------------------------------------*/
    ret_val = 0;
}
else if (cpic_return_code == CM_UNSUCCESSFUL) {
    /*-------------------------------------------------------------
     * This can only occur if the return_control has
     * been set to CM_IMMEDIATE. The default is
     * CM_WHEN_SESSION_ALLOCATED.
     *
     * No appropriate session was active and available, so
     * the Allocate() returned immediately, as requested.
     *-----------------------------------------------------------*/
    ret_val = 2;
}
else {
    /*-------------------------------------------------------------
     * No session could be obtained, using the partner LU
     * name and mode name that were specified. The
     * conversation ID is no longer valid.
     *-----------------------------------------------------------*/
    handle_cpic_rc(
        conversation_ID, cpic_return_code, "CMALLC");
    ret_val = 1;
}
return ret_val;
}
```

If the Allocate() call returns CM_OK, a session with the specified attributes was obtained with the server platform, and your program can proceed. The client now has the permission-to-send, that is, it's in **Send** state.

Notice that an Allocate() call only obtains an active session. Having a session means that the two computers can talk to one another, using a route through the network that satisfies the requirements of the mode name. No network packets have yet been exchanged for this conversation, and your program knows nothing about the partner program (and whether it even exists). It only knows that it can get through the network to the other computer.

If an Allocate() gets any return code other than CM_OK (or CM_UNSUCCESSFUL, which we'll discuss as part of the Set_Return_Control() call), no session could be obtained and the conversation is over. Since no connection was made, CPI-C invalidates the conversation ID; calls can no longer be issued with this conversation ID. For example, a return code you'll frequently see is CM_ALLOCATE_FAILURE_RETRY. This return code tells you that CPI-C couldn't get a session, but the reason for this may be temporary—if your program tries to allocate a session again a few seconds later, it may work. To retry the conversation, your program will need to go back to before its call to Initialize_Conversation() call, and start from there with a new conversation ID.

An Allocate() call can fail for many reasons; for newly developed and newly installed programs, the problem is usually a configuration mismatch between the two machines. For programs that have been tested and running for awhile, it's likely that a break in the network has happened somewhere between the machines. The CPI-C return code that you get from Allocate() is important in diagnosing what's wrong. Appendix A provides extensive descriptions of all the CPI-C return codes. You'll want to keep these pages handy during your early program development, and your users will want to have them handy when diagnosing network and configuration problems.

The most common nonzero return codes for Allocate() are CM_ALLOCATE_FAILURE_NO_RETRY or CM_ALLOCATE_FAILURE_RETRY. Plan now on seeing them; they indicate that there's a setup problem or a failure somewhere on the way to the partner. The network software that CPI-C uses knows a lot of details about these failures. This information can be found in a 4-byte field called SNA sense data. The sense data can be found today in system error logs or trace data. Until CPI-C 2.0, you'll need to find ways for your users to get the SNA sense data associated with these two return codes in order to diagnose the allocation failures proficiently.

One reason an Allocate() call can "fail" is if session limits have been reached and your program is waiting for a session. In this case, your program does not get a return code, but can wait indefinitely until another application frees a session. See "Set_Return_Control (CMSRC)" later in this chapter for a way to specify that the Allocate() call should not wait, but should return immediately if a session is not available.

SETTING CONVERSATION CHARACTERISTICS

You've probably noticed that when you learn new programming functions, you start with a few simple calls that work, then progressively learn about more advanced functions that let you better tune your program's operation. We've looked at the simplest way to start a conversation, which is with an Initialize_Conversation() call followed by an Allocate() call. Now, we're going to look at some of the ways we can tune the behavior of the conversation. In CPI-C, these tuning parameters are called *conversation characteristics*.

There are two categories of conversation characteristics:

1. Those that are active throughout the life of the conversation, and thus have to be set after the Initialize_Conversation() and before the Allocate(). These can only be issued by the client before a connection is made to the server.

2. Those that can be changed after the Allocate() call. These can be issued by either client or server and can be issued at any time.

We'll focus on the first category in this section. The calls in the second category are covered in the following sections at the points where we discuss the other CPI-C calls that interact with these calls.

The conversation characteristics discussed here can only be changed after the Initialize_Conversation() call because they need a valid conversation ID. They must all precede the Allocate() call because they influence the operation of that call. These conversation characteristics are either used to get the session for the conversation, used to build the Attach message, or used to influence the operation of the Allocate() call itself.

Each of the calls that changes a conversation characteristic starts with the word *Set*. We've already seen an example in "Synchronizing a Pair of Programs" in Chap. 3: Set_Sync_Level(). All conversation characteristics and their defaults are shown in Table 2 at the back of the book. All the conversation characteristics in CPI-C have default values. You need to make a Set call in your program only if you want to change from the default. In Chap. 3, we set the sync_level of the conversation to CM_CONFIRM, changing it from its default value of CM_NONE. The conversation's sync_level is part of the Attach message; when the Attach arrives at the partner computer, the attach manager software there decides whether the arriving sync_level is compatible with the sync_level in the TP definition.

Table 11.1 shows the conversation characteristics that can only be changed before the Allocate() call. This table is split into three groups: calls related to how your program operates, calls related to connecting to the server program, and calls related to security.

Of these three groups, we'll cover the first group thoroughly here (because these calls influence the operation of the Allocate() call), and then briefly intro-

TABLE 11.1   Conversation Characteristics

Program Operation Options	
Long name	Short name
Set_Conversation_Type()	cmsct()
Set_Return_Control()	cmsrc()
Set_Sync_Level()	cmssl()

Parameters Needed to Connect to the Server Program	
Long name	Short name
Set_Mode_Name()	cmsmn()
Set_Partner_LU_Name()	cmspln()
Set_TP_Name()	cmstpn()

Conversation Security Parameters	
Long name	Short name
Set_Conversation_Security_Password()	cmscsp()
Set_Conversation_Security_Type()	cmscst()
Set_Conversation_Security_User_ID()	cmscsu()

duce the other two groups. Effectively handling naming and security in your programs is tricky stuff; for this reason, we've devoted entire chapters to naming and security issues, and provided you with lots of sample code.

The three Set calls of the first group, Set_Conversation_Type(), Set_Return_Control(), and Set_Sync_Level(), share some of the same attributes:

- Issuing these calls does not permanently change the values in the local side information; no configuration files are changed. It only changes the respective characteristic for the duration of this conversation.

- The calls are quick; they just ask CPI-C to set a field in a local control block. Nothing ever flows in the network because of these, nor is the state of the conversation changed. Your program never sees the CM_DEALLO-CATED_xxxx return codes on a Set call.

We'll go through each of these calls in more detail.

Set_Conversation_Type (CMSCT)

Your choice of conversation type shows through to your programs principally in their calls to Send_Data() and Receive(). The Set_Conversation_Type() call allows you to choose whether you want to establish a mapped or a basic conversation. With mapped conversations, you send one record at a time by pointing to it and specifying its length. With basic conversations, you can put multiple records into a single data buffer, but to do this, you need to imbed the length of the records inside the data buffer.

Basic conversations are more complex to use than mapped conversations. Basic conversations let the internal construction of APPC's session packets (RUs) show through to your programs; mapped conversations work more naturally. Basic conversations are archaic and should not be used by new applications.* Because of this, all the examples we show in this book use mapped conversations.

Here's the function prototype for the Set_Conversation_Type() call and the values for the conversation_type parameter.

```
CM_ENTRY                            /* Set_Conversation_Type     */
cmsct (unsigned char CM_PTR,        /* I: conversation_ID        */
       CM_CONVERSATION_TYPE CM_PTR, /* I: conversation_type      */
       CM_RETURN_CODE CM_PTR);      /* O: return_code            */

/*  conversation_type values                                     */
/*  default is CM_MAPPED_CONVERSATION                            */

#define CM_BASIC_CONVERSATION  (CM_CONVERSATION_TYPE) 0
#define CM_MAPPED_CONVERSATION (CM_CONVERSATION_TYPE) 1
```

---

* For more information about using basic conversations, see "Basic Conversations" in Chap. 17.

Your program can set the conversation_type to one of two different values:

CM_BASIC_CONVERSATION. Establish a basic conversation with the partner.

CM_MAPPED_CONVERSATION. Establish a mapped conversation with the partner. This is the default.

Since the default conversation type in CPI-C is mapped and it is the preferred type of conversation, you should rarely have occasion to use the Set_Conversation_Type() call.

Set_Return_Control (CMSRC)

The job of the Allocate() call is to get a session. Sessions can be viewed as long-lived pipes between a pair of computers. Conversations, on the other hand, are short-lived; they are over as soon as they are deallocated. Although a conversation may be over, the session it was using hangs around, waiting to be used again.

The first thing CPI-C tries to do when an Allocate() call arrives is to reserve an active session that's not being used by any conversation. If there isn't an unused session available with the desired partner, CPI-C's default is to attempt to activate such a session. When your workstation is first powered on, for example, its Allocate() calls will each have to start sessions with each new partner it talks to. If no sessions can be activated because all the available sessions to that partner are in use, the Allocate() call will block, waiting for a session to become available.*

Although this situation is relatively rare, there may be times when you would like to have control return to your program instead of having the Allocate() call block. In these cases, use the Set_Return_Control() call to change CPI-C's default behavior.

Here's the function prototype for the Set_Return_Control() call and the values for the return_control parameter.

```
CM_ENTRY                              /* Set_Return_Control         */
cmsrc (unsigned char CM_PTR,          /* I: conversation_ID         */
       CM_RETURN_CONTROL CM_PTR,      /* I: return_control          */
       CM_RETURN_CODE CM_PTR);        /* O: return_code             */

/* return_control values                                            */
/* default is CM_WHEN_SESSION_ALLOCATED                             */

#define CM_WHEN_SESSION_ALLOCATED            (CM_RETURN_CONTROL) 0
#define CM_IMMEDIATE                         (CM_RETURN_CONTROL) 1
```

---

* Our use of the term *block* refers to situations when a call does not return for a *significant* length of time, or does not return at all.

Your program can set the return_control to one of two different values:

CM_WHEN_SESSION_ALLOCATED. If an acceptable session is active and not in use by another conversation, reserve it and return CM_OK on the Allocate() call. This is the default.

If no acceptable session is active and available, try to start one. If one can be started, reserve it and return CM_OK on the Allocate() call. If it can't be started because all available sessions with the partner are already active and in use, block, waiting until one is free.

CM_IMMEDIATE. If an acceptable session is active and not in use by another conversation, reserve it and return CM_OK on the Allocate() call.

If no acceptable session is active and available, the Allocate() call returns immediately from CPI-C. It returns with the CM_UNSUCCESSFUL return code. This return code does not invalidate the conversation ID. When your program sees this return code on Allocate(), it should report that a session wasn't available and perhaps retry the attempt later.

We've never changed the return_control value from its default in any of programs we've written, so we can't recommend a good situation to use it in. Use it if you need it; for example, if you can't afford to wait longer than a few seconds for a call to complete. If you do use it, be sure to explain to the user of your program what to do if the Allocate() call returns with CM_UNSUCCESSFUL.

Set_Sync_Level (CMSSL)

The Set_Sync_Level() call is used to change the level of synchronization services you plan to use on your conversation.

Here's the function prototype for the Set_Sync_Level() call and the values for the sync_level parameter.

```
CM_ENTRY                            /* Set_Sync_Level          */
cmssl (unsigned char CM_PTR,        /* I: conversation_ID      */
       CM_SYNC_LEVEL CM_PTR,        /* I: sync_level           */
       CM_RETURN_CODE CM_PTR);      /* O: return_code          */

/* sync_level values                                           */
/* default is CM_NONE                                          */

#define CM_NONE                             (CM_SYNC_LEVEL) 0
#define CM_CONFIRM                          (CM_SYNC_LEVEL) 1
#define CM_SYNC_POINT                       (CM_SYNC_LEVEL) 2
```

Your program can set the sync_level to one of three values:

CM_NONE. Indicates no synchronization. Neither the client nor the server program will be able to issue successful calls to Confirm() or Confirmed(), or issue the CPI-RR calls: Backout() or Commit(). This is the default setting, but you'll probably want to change it in many of your programs which require synchronization.

CM_CONFIRM. Indicates that confirmation synchronization can be used. This allows your program and its partner to choose to use the Confirm() and Confirmed() calls, and any of their variants. See "Synchronizing Programs" in Chap. 15 for more information about synchronization and how to use it. You may also hear this referred to as *sync level 1.*

CM_SYNC_POINT. Indicates that your program wants to access protected resources and use sync point's two-phase commit protocols. This is usually only used by applications accessing databases that support two-phase commit.* There's a programming interface for sync point that is a companion to CPI-C; it's named the Common Programming Interface for Resource Recovery (CPI-RR). You may hear this referred to as *sync level 2.*

Most programs you write will probably do a Confirm() somewhere, even if it's at the end of the program coupled with a Deallocate() call. So, you'll probably always want to change the sync_level from its default value of CM_NONE. Here's a short procedure that shows how to change it to CM_CONFIRM:

```
int
do_sync_level_confirm(unsigned char * conversation_ID)
{
    /*-----------------------------------------------------------
     * Use the conversation ID from the caller to set the
     * sync_level to CM_CONFIRM.
     *---------------------------------------------------------*/

    CM_RETURN_CODE cpic_return_code;
    CM_SYNC_LEVEL sync_level = CM_CONFIRM;
    int           ret_val;

    assert(conversation_ID != NULL);

    /*-----------------------------------------------------------
     * Set the sync_level to CM_CONFIRM.
     *---------------------------------------------------------*/
    cmssl (                          /* Set_Sync_Level           */
        conversation_ID,             /* conversation ID          */
        &sync_level,                 /* sync_level               */
        &cpic_return_code);          /* return code from this call */
    if (cpic_return_code == CM_OK) {
        /*-------------------------------------------------------
         * A sync_level was changed to CM_CONFIRM.
         *-----------------------------------------------------*/
        ret_val = 0;
    }
    else {
```

---

* As of this printing, only CICS and VM support a sync level of CM_SYNC_POINT, although it's soon to be delivered for the AS/400. In addition, AIX SNA Server/6000 version 2.1 provides sync point enablement capabilities for the CICS/6000 and Encina products.

```
        /*-----------------------------------------------------------
         * Set_Sync_Level() failed. The most likely reason this
         * could fail would be if it was passed a bad
         * conversation ID, or if it was issued after an
         * Allocate() or by the Accepting side.
         *----------------------------------------------------------*/
        handle_cpic_rc(
            conversation_ID, cpic_return_code, "CMSSL");
        ret_val = 1;
    }
    return ret_val;
}
```

OVERRIDING SIDE INFORMATION TABLE FIELDS

CPI-C provides three Set calls to override the key names configured in the local CPI-C side information. These calls are:

- Set_Partner_LU_Name (CMSPLN)

- Set_Mode_Name (CMSMN)

- Set_TP_Name (CMSTPN)

The most common use of these three calls is to write programs that don't require any side information configuration. Your client program puts the all-blank symbolic destination name in its Initialize_Conversation() call, and uses these calls to fill in the appropriate information.

In general, you should not use these calls if your program specifies a real symbolic destination name (other than all-blanks) on the Initialize_Conversation(). Hardcoding these values within your program can make it difficult for a user to adjust to changing requirements via external configuration; in this case, the program source code would also have to be changed. For example, the users or installers of your program might want to use a new mode name with attributes specific to their network. They could easily change the mode name by modifying the side information entry used by your program. But, if you have hardcoded a mode name into a Set_Mode_Name() call, changing the side information will have no effect on the mode name actually used by your program.

However, use these calls to make new values available to your program, via either a program configuration file or user input. In this case, you are simply providing users with different mechanisms for modifying the behavior of your program.

These three Set calls share similar attributes:

- The calls can only be successfully issued between Initialize_Conversation() and Allocate(). Thus, only the program that initiates the conversation can issue these calls.

- Issuing these calls does not permanently change the values in the local side information; no configuration files are changed. Issuing these calls only changes the respective name for the duration of this conversation.

- A pointer to a variable-length string is passed as input. This means that each call has two key parameters: a pointer to the string and a pointer to the length of that string.

- When these calls are made, CPI-C checks only the length of the string, not whether the characters in the string are valid. An invalid or unrecognized name will result in a return code of CM_PARAMETER_ERROR later on the Allocate() call.

- The calls are quick; they just ask CPI-C to set a field in a local control block. Nothing flows in the network because of these, nor is the state of the conversation changed.

Let's go through each of these calls in a little more detail.

Set_Partner_LU_Name (CMSPLN)

The Set_Partner_LU_Name() call is the one of this group that you are most likely to use. Many applications need to know only where the server application resides; the session characteristics (which are determined by the mode name) and TP name are implicit in the function that is being performed. The partner_LU_name on the call specifies the name of the computer where the server application is located. The partner_LU_name can be any name by which the local computer knows the remote computer. On most platforms, a fully qualified LU name is acceptable.

Here's the function prototype for the Set_Partner_LU_Name() call:

```
CM_ENTRY                                /* Set_Partner_LU_Name     */
cmspln(unsigned char CM_PTR,            /* I: conversation_ID      */
       unsigned char CM_PTR,            /* I: partner_LU_name      */
       CM_INT32 CM_PTR,        /* I: partner_LU_name_length max 17 */
       CM_RETURN_CODE CM_PTR);          /* O: return_code          */
```

A partner LU name is 1 to 17 bytes long. This normally consists of a two-part name: a network name (also known as the network ID or NETID) that is 1 to 8 bytes long, and a partner LU name that is 1 to 8 bytes long, separated by a period. These fully qualified LU names consist of uppercase characters, digits, and a number of special characters.

Unfortunately, there are many differences in the format of a partner LU name among platforms. For example, on OS/2 CM/2, partner LU names can either be fully qualified (as described above) or partner LU aliases, which are mixed-case and case-sensitive. On VM/ESA, the partner LU name consists of a 1- to 8-byte local gateway name and a 1- to 8-byte target LU name, separated by a space (for example, "GATEWAY LUNAME").

To make your programs more usable, we recommend that when a user specifies a partner LU name as input to your program, your program converts the partner LU name to uppercase whenever the input string contains a period, which is the separator in a fully qualified LU name.

Although your program may be aware of the partner LU name character set restrictions for your platform, we recommend that you not check the characters in the name for validity before passing the string to CPI-C. This allows your program to take advantage of more lenient naming practices on future versions of the platform.

The following procedure shows how to set the partner LU name. Its input parameters are a pointer to a conversation ID and a pointer to a null-terminated string, the partner LU name.

```c
int
do_set_partner_lu_name(unsigned char * conversation_ID,
                       unsigned char * partner_lu_name)
{
    /*------------------------------------------------------------
     * Use the conversation ID and partner LU name from the
     * caller, to set the partner LU name for the conversation.
     * The passed LU name must be a null-terminated string.
     *----------------------------------------------------------*/

    CM_RETURN_CODE cpic_return_code;
    int            ret_val;
    CM_INT32       partner_lu_name_length =
                       (CM_INT32)strlen((char*)partner_lu_name);

    assert(conversation_ID != NULL);
    assert(partner_lu_name != NULL);

    if ((partner_lu_name_length < 1) ||
        (partner_lu_name_length > CM_PLN_SIZE)) {
        handle_error(
            conversation_ID,
            "partner LU name was %ld bytes; "
            "it should be from 1 to %d bytes long",
            partner_lu_name_length,
            CM_PLN_SIZE);
    }

    /*------------------------------------------------------------
     * If there's a period in it, convert it to uppercase.
     *----------------------------------------------------------*/
    if (strchr((char*)partner_lu_name, '.') != NULL) {
        size_t i;
        for (i = 0; i < (size_t)partner_lu_name_length ; i++) {
            partner_lu_name[i] =
                (unsigned char)toupper(partner_lu_name[i]);
        }
    }

    /*------------------------------------------------------------
     * Set the partner LU name to whatever string was passed.
     *----------------------------------------------------------*/
```

```
cmspln(                         /* Set_Partner_LU_Name         */
    conversation_ID,            /* conversation ID             */
    partner_lu_name,            /* partner LU name             */
    &partner_lu_name_length,/* length of the part LU name  */
    &cpic_return_code);     /* return code from this call  */
if (cpic_return_code == CM_OK) {
    /*------------------------------------------------------
     * The partner LU name was changed.
     *----------------------------------------------------*/
    ret_val = 0;
}
else {
    /*------------------------------------------------------
     * Set_Partner_LU_Name failed.
     *----------------------------------------------------*/
    handle_cpic_rc(
        conversation_ID, cpic_return_code, "CMSPLN");
    ret_val = 1;
}
return ret_val;
}
```

Set_Mode_Name (CMSMN)

The mode name used by your program determines the kind of session it will get. Use the Set_Mode_Name() call if you want to give your users a chance to change the mode name from what's been configured in the local side information. The Set_Mode_Name() call must be used when you use an all-blank symbolic destination name on the Initialize_Conversation() call, since the mode name is necessary to establish a connection.

Here's the function prototype for the Set_Mode_Name() call:

```
CM_ENTRY                        /* Set_Mode_Name               */
cmsmn (unsigned char CM_PTR,    /* I: conversation_ID          */
       unsigned char CM_PTR,    /* I: mode_name                */
       CM_INT32 CM_PTR,         /* I: mode_name_length max 8   */
       CM_RETURN_CODE CM_PTR);  /* O: return_code              */
```

The mode name length can be from 0 to 8 bytes; this is different from other Set calls, where zero is not a legal length.

The mode name consists of the uppercase characters, digits, and three special characters. The first character cannot be a digit. Since the mode name cannot contain lowercase characters, we recommend that when a user specifies a mode name as input to your program you convert it to uppercase.

If you need to choose a mode name for your program, in the absence of user input, choose one of the five predefined mode names:

#INTER   A route appropriate for interactive data

#INTERSC   A secure route, appropriate for interactive data

#BATCH	A route appropriate for bulk data transfers
#BATCHSC	A secure route, appropriate for bulk data transfers
all blanks	The cheapest route to the partner

The following procedure shows how to set the mode name. Its input parameters are a pointer to a conversation ID and a pointer to a null-terminated string, the mode name.

```c
int
do_set_mode_name(unsigned char * conversation_ID,
                 unsigned char * mode_name)
{
    /*-------------------------------------------------------------
     *  Use the conversation ID and mode name from the caller,
     *  to set the mode name for the conversation.
     *  The passed mode name must be a null-terminated string.
     *-----------------------------------------------------------*/
    CM_RETURN_CODE cpic_return_code;
    int            ret_val;
    CM_INT32       mode_name_length =
                        (CM_INT32)strlen((char*)mode_name);

    assert(conversation_ID != NULL);
    assert(mode_name != NULL);

    if ((mode_name_length < 0) ||     /* 0 is an allowed length */
        (mode_name_length > CM_MN_SIZE)) { /* 8 is the max len */
        handle_error(
            conversation_ID,
            "Mode name was %ld bytes; "
            "it should be from 0 to 8 bytes long",
            mode_name_length);
    }

    /*-------------------------------------------------------------
     * Ensure the mode name is in uppercase.
     *-----------------------------------------------------------*/
    {
        size_t i;
        for (i = 0; i < (size_t)mode_name_length ; i++) {
            mode_name[i] =
                (unsigned char)toupper(mode_name[i]);
        }
    }

    /*-------------------------------------------------------------
     *  Set the mode name to whatever string was passed.
     *-----------------------------------------------------------*/
    cmsmn (                          /* Set_Mode_Name           */
        conversation_ID,             /* conversation ID         */
        mode_name,                   /* mode name               */
        &mode_name_length,           /* length of the mode name */
        &cpic_return_code);          /* return code from this call */
```

```
if (cpic_return_code == CM_OK) {
    /*------------------------------------------------------
     * The mode name was changed.
     *----------------------------------------------------*/
    ret_val = 0;
}
else {
    /*------------------------------------------------------
     * Set_Mode_Name() failed.
     *----------------------------------------------------*/
    handle_cpic_rc(
        conversation_ID, cpic_return_code, "CMSMN");
    ret_val = 1;
}
return ret_val;
}
```

Set_TP_Name (CMSTPN)

The TP name is a string that is sent to the partner computer in the Attach.
The partner uses the incoming string to decide which program to run. Thus,
the TP name is the most important field in an Attach (which is built whenever
an Allocate() call is successful). The attach manager software at the partner
computer uses the arriving TP name as a key into its table of TP definitions.
Presumably, the incoming TP name will match one of the TP definitions on the
server, and an executable program will be started.

The Set_TP_Name() call must always be used when you use an all-blank
symbolic destination name on the Initialize_Conversation() call. See Chap. 22
for more information about when you would use Set_TP_Name() as part of a
robust setup routine.

Here's the function prototype for the Set_TP_Name() call:

```
CM_ENTRY                          /* Set_TP_Name              */
cmstpn(unsigned char CM_PTR,      /* I: conversation_ID       */
       unsigned char CM_PTR,      /* I: TP_name               */
       CM_INT32 CM_PTR,           /* I: TP_name_length max 64 */
       CM_RETURN_CODE CM_PTR);    /* O: return_code           */
```

The TP name length must be from 1 to 64 bytes. It makes a difference whether
the characters in the TP name are uppercase or lowercase. Be sure that you
recommend to your users that they be careful in the combination of uppercase
and lowercase letters they use.

The problem won't show up for awhile if the TP name specified by the client
doesn't exactly match a TP name in the server's TP definitions. The Set_
TP_Name() call will succeed as long as you give it a validly constructed name, as
will the Allocate() call (if a session can be obtained). The mismatch won't be discovered until some CPI-C call made after the Allocate(), when the Attach message actually flows through the network and arrives at the partner computer.

The following procedure shows how to set the TP name. Its input parameters are a pointer to a conversation ID and a pointer to a null-terminated string, the TP name.

```
int
do_set_tp_name(unsigned char * conversation_ID,
               unsigned char * tp_name)
{
    /*-------------------------------------------------------------
     * Use the conversation ID and TP name from the caller,
     * to set the TP name for the conversation.
     * The passed TP name must be a null-terminated string.
     *-----------------------------------------------------------*/
    CM_RETURN_CODE cpic_return_code;
    int            ret_val;
    CM_INT32       tp_name_length =
                       (CM_INT32)strlen((char*)tp_name);
    assert(conversation_ID != NULL);
    assert(tp_name != NULL);

    if ((tp_name_length < 1) ||
        (tp_name_length > CM_TPN_SIZE)) {
        handle_error(
            conversation_ID,
            "TP name was %ld bytes; "
            "it should be from 1 to 64 bytes long",
            tp_name_length);
    }
    /*-------------------------------------------------------------
     * Set the TP name to whatever string was passed.
     *-----------------------------------------------------------*/
    cmstpn(                         /* Set_TP_Name              */
        conversation_ID,            /* conversation ID          */
        tp_name,                    /* TP name                  */
        &tp_name_length,            /* length of the TP name    */
        &cpic_return_code);         /* return code from this call */
    if (cpic_return_code == CM_OK) {
        /*-------------------------------------------------------
         * The TP name was changed.
         *-----------------------------------------------------*/
        ret_val = 0;
    }
    else {
        /*-------------------------------------------------------
         * Set_TP_Name failed.
         *-----------------------------------------------------*/
        handle_cpic_rc(
            conversation_ID, cpic_return_code, "CMSTPN");
        ret_val = 1;
    }
    return ret_val;
}
```

Getting Connected: The Server Side

We've seen that there's an asymmetry between the client and server sides in starting a conversation. Let's revisit our telephone analogy for a moment, to understand some of these concepts better.

Anyone can make a phone call to anyone else, but someone has to start the call by actually picking up the phone and dialing a number. People receiving calls don't usually know ahead of time when a call is arriving. Their participation in the conversation begins when they hear their phone ring. They drop what they're doing, pick up the ringing phone, and listen to the caller.

CPI-C operates in much the same fashion. One program decides to start a conversation with another program on another computer. It does this by issuing calls to Initialize_Conversation() and Allocate(). These calls let the client program specify where the partner program is (via the partner LU name), what kind of service it wants through the network (via the mode name), and what program it wants to talk to (via the TP name).

You can design your server program in many different ways. In one common design technique, the server program is not running when the Attach arrives. By analogy, this is how you probably work day-to-day; you don't sit by the phone waiting for calls. When a call arrives, you answer it. Similarly, the server program is started when an Attach arrives. Software resident at the partner, called the *attach manager,* handles the incoming Attach. It looks inside the Attach for the TP name, and using the TP name as a key into its table of TP definitions, decides what program to start. The attach manager's job on each platform is to know how to start programs on the native operating system. It knows about windowing, command-line parameters, multiple copies of the same program, whether a program is actually started or not, and so on.

So, all the partner program knows is that it's suddenly awake and running. Whenever this occurs, it "answers" the phone by issuing calls to accept the incoming conversation. Since it doesn't know anything about who has called, there are several CPI-C calls it can make to extract this information.

In this chapter, we'll talk in more detail about how to handle these steps in your programs. We'll first introduce the Attach, and how an attach manager handles it. We'll next discuss the Accept_Conversation() call, which is how a conversation ID is obtained on the server side. The Accept_Conversation() call waits to be paired with an incoming Attach, which is easy if the Attach has already arrived. Finally, we'll look at the group of calls used for extracting the characteristics of the newly started conversation.

If you'd like to write programs that are already running and look periodically to see if an Attach has arrived for them, use the pair of calls Initialize_For_Incoming() and Accept_Incoming(). These calls are part of the more advanced topic of nonblocking calls; we'll cover them and other related calls in Chap. 26.

STARTING THE SERVER PROGRAM

The server program can be started in either of two ways:

- by the attach manager, which was spurred to action by an incoming Attach
- by any other means that you're familiar with, such as by entering its name on the command line, or by starting it automatically when the computer is started

In the first case, the starting of the program is triggered by the arrival of an Attach, which is parsed by the attach manager. When the server program issues the call to accept the conversation, the call proceeds quickly because the Attach has already been received and processed. In the second case, the program must still issue a call to accept the Attach. If no Attach is waiting to be processed, the call can block, time-out, or return immediately to the calling program.

For every anticipated Attach, there must be a TP definition configured at the server computer. The TP definition serves two purposes: (1) it gives directions to the attach manager about what kinds of Attaches are permissible, and (2) it gives directions to the attach manager about how to start the server program and what to do if the server program's already running.

Although the Attach is crucial to setting up a conversation, it is invisible to your program—you can't actually receive one and display it on the screen. The Attach is built by CPI-C from the conversation characteristics provided at the client side, and it is processed by the attach manager software resident at the server side. Here's what's in an Attach:

Contents of an Attach

- A TP name
- Whether the conversation type is mapped or basic
- Whether the sync level is none, confirm, or sync point
- Whether the conversation is half-duplex or full-duplex (CPI-C 2.0)
- Whether any security information is present
- (Optional) conversation security user ID
- (Optional) conversation security password
- (Optional) program initialization parameters (PIP)

In Chap. 23, we talk in much more detail about the attach manager software and its operation. There's probably no code you'll have to write in order to use the attach manager on most platforms. However, it is important that users of your application are successful at setting up the TP definitions you need. Be sure to read Chap. 23, then read the manual for the platform for which you are designing your server programs. Make the setup of the TP definitions for your server programs part of your installation process, or explain clearly to the person setting them up what's involved, so they'll get them right the first time.

WAITING FOR AN INCOMING ATTACH

There are two different ways to initiate a CPI-C conversation on the server side. The traditional way is to issue an Accept_Conversation() call, which waits until it is signaled by the attach manager that an Attach has arrived for it. Starting in CPI-C version 1.2, the server initiation can be broken into a two-step process, much like the client side. These calls are Initialize_For_Incoming() and Accept_Incoming(), and conversation characteristics may optionally be changed in between these two calls.

You can use either method to accept an incoming Attach. You'll find Accept_Conversation() available on almost all platforms; we'll discuss it in this section. The trio of Initialize_For_Incoming(), Set_Processing_Mode(), and Accept_Incoming() is much newer; check to see that they're available on the platform for which you're writing your server program. For details on these three calls and how to use them, see "Nonblocking Calls" in Chap. 26.

Accept_Conversation (CMACCP)

The Accept_Conversation() call waits for the attach manager to receive an Attach for that server program. When such an Attach arrives, the Accept_Conversation() call returns with a new conversation ID, which is then used as a handle for all subsequent calls in the conversation.

Here's the function prototype for the Accept_Conversation() call.

```
CM_ENTRY                              /* Accept_Conversation      */
cmaccp(unsigned char CM_PTR,          /* O: conversation_ID       */
       CM_RETURN_CODE CM_PTR);        /* O: return_code           */
```

The Accept_Conversation() call has no input parameters and returns a conversation ID when the return code is CM_OK. The server side doesn't provide any input parameters since the connection and conversation characteristics have already been set by the client. It just accepts whatever arrives, depending upon the attach manager to filter out unacceptable partners. When the return code is CM_OK, the conversation is in **Receive** state. Here's an example procedure you can use for accepting a conversation:

```
int
do_accept_conversation(unsigned char * conversation_ID)
{
    /*------------------------------------------------------------
     * Accept the incoming conversation, returning the new
     * conversation ID into the pointed-to input parameter.
     *----------------------------------------------------------*/

    CM_RETURN_CODE cpic_return_code;
    int            ret_val;

    assert(conversation_ID != NULL);

    /*------------------------------------------------------------
     * Accept an incoming Attach, to start the conversation.
     *----------------------------------------------------------*/
    cmaccp(                        /* Accept_Conversation       */
        conversation_ID,           /* returned conversation ID  */
        &cpic_return_code);        /* return code from this call */
    if (cpic_return_code == CM_OK) {
        /*--------------------------------------------------------
         * A conversation has been successfully established
         * with the partner. The new conversation ID is
         * returned in the string pointed-to by the input
         * parameter.
         *------------------------------------------------------*/
        ret_val = 0;
    }
    else {
        /*--------------------------------------------------------
         * There was no Attach waiting and none arrived, or the
         * program was started by a user when it should have
         * been started by the Attach Manager.
         *------------------------------------------------------*/
        handle_cpic_rc(
            conversation_ID, cpic_return_code, "CMACCP");
        ret_val = 1;
    }
    return ret_val;
}
```

Users who play around with your server programs will frequently see the CM_PROGRAM_STATE_CHECK return code. It indicates that there is no incoming conversation for the server program to accept. The most likely cause of this return code is that the server program was invoked by a user, yet it was configured to be started by the attach manager. If you have the programs APING and APINGD configured on your computer, you can demonstrate this behavior by running "APINGD" from the command line.

INHERITING AND EXTRACTING CONVERSATION CHARACTERISTICS

The calls in this section can hardly be considered building blocks. We didn't use any of them in the sample programs that opened the book. These calls are most useful when used to capture information after the Accept_Conversation() call that can be used later for debugging or problem determination. Feel free to skip to the next chapter, and come back to this section when you think you're ready to use the Extract calls.

By the time an Accept_Conversation() or Accept_Incoming() call is successful, the characteristics of the conversation are already in place. The server program has little say about them; its way of influencing them is through the TP definition that is configured for it. For example, one of the fields in the TP definition is whether the type of the conversation is mapped, basic, or that it could be either. If the server program only uses mapped conversations, then the TP definition should say that. Don't configure it as "either"; by setting the TP definition to "mapped," the attach manager can do the filtering of bogus partners.

The nine Extract calls are most useful for the server program, which is why we discuss them in this chapter. They've been appearing little-by-little in CPI-C, a few new Extract calls in each CPI-C version. So, you may not find all of them on all CPI-C platforms at the time of the printing of this book.

The nine Extract calls share some of the same attributes:

- The Extract calls can be issued in any conversation state where you have a valid conversation ID. In fact, one of the calls, Extract_Maximum_Buffer_Size(), doesn't even need a conversation ID. Although Extract calls are most useful on the server side, they can be issued by either side.

TABLE 12.1   The Extract Calls, and the CPI-C Version in Which They First Appeared

Long name	Short name	CPI-C version
Extract_Conversation_Context()	cmectx()	1.2
Extract_Conversation_State()	cmecs()	1.1
Extract_Conversation_Type()	cmect()	1.0
Extract_Maximum_Buffer_Size()	cmembs()	1.2
Extract_Mode_Name()	cmemn()	1.0
Extract_Partner_LU_Name()	cmepln()	1.0
Extract_Security_User_ID()	cmesui()	1.2
Extract_Sync_Level()	cmesl()	1.0
Extract_TP_Name()	cmetpn()	1.2

- CPI-C expects pointers to the field or fields to be filled in. For example, when extracting the conversation type, a pointer to a field to hold the conversation type is the key input parameter. For the calls which extract a name, there are two key parameters: a pointer to where the string should be placed (which is at least as big as the maximum length of the returned string) and a pointer to the length of the string. The returned strings are not null-terminated by CPI-C, which is why their length is returned.

- On some platforms, CPI-C checks the validity of the field it is writing into. If the field isn't big enough, CPI-C won't process the request and returns the CM_PROGRAM_PARAMETER_CHECK return code.

- Each of these calls is quick; CPI-C just fetches a field or two from a local control block. Nothing flows in the network because of these, the partner never knows that they've been issued, and the state of the conversation never changes because of their success (or failure). Your program never sees the CM_DEALLOCATED_xxxx return codes on an Extract call.

Extract_Conversation_Context (CMECTX)

The Extract_Conversation_Context() call was added to CPI-C in version 1.2, and thus may not yet be available on some platforms.

The intent of the context ID is to allow programs to indicate for which client they perform particular actions. For example, if a server has conversations with CLIENT1 and CLIENT2, and the server creates a file, which client's user ID should own the file? The context ID allows the server to switch to the context for CLIENT1 or CLIENT2 before creating the file. The context ID is not of interest to programs which do not handle more than one client simultaneously.

The problem with context IDs today is that most operating systems do not yet have the underlying support for this concept. As platforms and interfaces evolve, the context ID can become a powerful tool for multiclient servers.

Here's the function prototype for the Extract_Conversation_Context() call.

```
CM_ENTRY                              /* Extract_Conversation_Context*/
cmectx(unsigned char CM_PTR,            /* I: conversation_ID      */
       unsigned char CM_PTR,            /* O: context_ID           */
       CM_INT32 CM_PTR,          /* O: context_ID_length max 32 */
       CM_RETURN_CODE CM_PTR);          /* O: return_code          */
```

This call requires a good conversation ID. Your program also passes a pointer to where CPI-C should return the context ID, and a pointer to where it should return the length of the context ID. The context ID that CPI-C returns is a block of binary data. Be sure that the context ID pointer points to an array that is at least 32 bytes long.

Extract_Conversation_State (CMECS)

The Extract_Conversation_State() call was added to CPI-C in version 1.1. You'll find it very handy when you're debugging a new pair of programs and get the CM_PROGRAM_STATE_CHECK return code. You should never see this return code in fully tested, production-level code, except when you're using the Wait_For_Conversation() call or you're talking to the wrong program! Otherwise, it indicates a design oversight where the two sides of the conversation aren't where they expect each other to be. This return code does not mean that the conversation is over; the two programs are still alive and you can continue processing, if necessary.

Extract_Conversation_State() can be used in two ways. Call it to find out if the conversation ID is still valid (indicated by a return code of CM_OK), and then look at the returned conversation_state value. A common misuse of this call is to issue it from a general-purpose, error-handling routine. It won't help you find the last state of a conversation that has already ended.

Following is the function prototype for the Extract_Conversation_State() call, and the possible values for conversation_state:

```
CM_ENTRY                              /* Extract_Conversation_State */
cmecs (unsigned char CM_PTR,         /* I: conversation_ID         */
       CM_CONVERSATION_STATE CM_PTR,/* 0: conversation_state      */
       CM_RETURN_CODE CM_PTR);       /* 0: return_code             */

/*  conversation_state values  */
#define CM_INITIALIZE_STATE                (CM_CONVERSATION_STATE)  2
#define CM_SEND_STATE                      (CM_CONVERSATION_STATE)  3
#define CM_RECEIVE_STATE                   (CM_CONVERSATION_STATE)  4
#define CM_SEND_PENDING_STATE              (CM_CONVERSATION_STATE)  5
#define CM_CONFIRM_STATE                   (CM_CONVERSATION_STATE)  6
#define CM_CONFIRM_SEND_STATE              (CM_CONVERSATION_STATE)  7
#define CM_CONFIRM_DEALLOCATE_STATE        (CM_CONVERSATION_STATE)  8
#define CM_DEFER_RECEIVE_STATE             (CM_CONVERSATION_STATE)  9
#define CM_DEFER_DEALLOCATE_STATE          (CM_CONVERSATION_STATE) 10
#define CM_SYNC_POINT_STATE                (CM_CONVERSATION_STATE) 11
#define CM_SYNC_POINT_SEND_STATE           (CM_CONVERSATION_STATE) 12
#define CM_SYNC_POINT_DEALLOCATE_STATE     (CM_CONVERSATION_STATE) 13
#define CM_INITIALIZE_INCOMING_STATE       (CM_CONVERSATION_STATE) 14
```

Like most of these Extract calls, this call requires a good conversation ID. Your program also passes a pointer to where CPI-C should return the conversation state.

We already looked at a comprehensive procedure that your programs can call to display the current conversation state; see Chap. 6.

Extract_Conversation_Type (CMECT)

The type of the conversation (mapped or basic) is one of the values that's always carried in an Attach. It's a field that the attach manager can thus use to filter incoming Attaches.

It's conceivable that you might someday want to design server programs that talk to a variety of different client programs with different conversation types. But we've never seen such a thing. The most likely reason for you to use basic conversations today is to connect to an older program or platform that uses basic conversations. Otherwise, always use mapped.

Here's the function prototype for the Extract_Conversation_Type() call, and the possible values for conversation_type:

```
CM_ENTRY                                /* Extract_Conversation_Type */
cmect (unsigned char CM_PTR,            /* I: conversation_ID       */
       CM_CONVERSATION_TYPE CM_PTR,     /* O: conversation_type     */
       CM_RETURN_CODE CM_PTR);          /* O: return_code           */

/*  conversation_type values  */

#define CM_BASIC_CONVERSATION            (CM_CONVERSATION_TYPE) 0
#define CM_MAPPED_CONVERSATION           (CM_CONVERSATION_TYPE) 1
```

This call requires a pointer to a good conversation ID. Your program also passes a pointer to where CPI-C should return the conversation type.

Extract_Maximum_Buffer_Size (CMEMBS)

The Extract_Maximum_Buffer_Size() call was added to CPI-C in version 1.2 and, thus, may not yet be available on some platforms.

When CPI-C was first developed, the maximum allowable buffer size on Send_Data() and Receive() was limited to a particular value in order to ensure portability of applications. The decision was made to limit buffers to 32767 bytes, which was a size supported by all APPC products at that time.

As programmers on virtual memory systems used CPI-C, they found a need for larger buffer sizes—both for program simplicity and performance. To allow platforms to increase the maximum allowable buffer size, yet still maintain portability, the Extract_Maximum_Buffer_Size() call was created.

If you want your program to use large buffer sizes on Send_Data() or Receive(), you should first call Extract_Maximum_Buffer_Size() to determine what the largest allowable buffer is. If your data buffer is smaller than the returned value, you're okay. If your buffer is larger, your program must be able to split the buffer up across multiple Send_Data() calls, or issue multiple Receive() calls into the buffer. For simplicity, avoid using data buffers larger than 32767. If you decide to use Extract_Maximum_Buffer_Size() and large buffers, always be prepared to fall back to using 32767-byte buffers.

Here's the function prototype for the Extract_Maximum_Buffer_Size() call:

```
CM_ENTRY                                /* Extract_Maximum_Buffer_Size */
cmembs(CM_INT32 CM_PTR,                 /* O: maximum_buffer_size      */
       CM_RETURN_CODE CM_PTR);          /* O: return_code              */
```

Unlike most Extract calls, this call does not require a conversation ID. Your program just passes a pointer to where CPI-C should return the maximum buffer size.

Extract_Mode_Name (CMEMN)

The Extract_Mode_Name() call can be used to find out what mode was used to construct the session that this conversation is using. This is probably most helpful for error reporting or logging. The mode name is not something that a program needs for any of its conversation calls.

If you issue Initialize_Conversation() with all blanks and issue Extract_Mode_Name(), you'll know that the mode name hasn't been set if you get a returned mode_name_length of 0.

Here's the function prototype for the Extract_Mode_Name() call:

```
CM_ENTRY                          /* Extract_Mode_Name            */
cmemn (unsigned char CM_PTR,        /* I: conversation_ID           */
       unsigned char CM_PTR,        /* O: mode_name                 */
       CM_INT32 CM_PTR,           /* O: mode_name_length max 8    */
       CM_RETURN_CODE CM_PTR);      /* O: return_code               */
```

This call requires a good conversation ID. Your program also passes a pointer to where CPI-C should return the mode name, and a pointer to where it should return the length of the mode name. The mode name that CPI-C returns is not a null-terminated string, which is why it also returns the length. Be sure that the mode name pointer points to an array that is at least 8 bytes long.

If the conversation is already over, it's a bad time to issue Extract_Mode_Name() to find out what mode was used. Issue this call just after doing an Allocate() or an Accept, and keep the returned answer for use in your error-logging code.

Extract_Partner_LU_Name (CMEPLN)

The side that is accepting an incoming Attach gets started automatically, without actually knowing which partner program sent the Attach. The Extract_Partner_LU_Name() call allows your program to find out which computer it is in session with. This can be especially helpful when an unexpected return code occurs; your program can find out who exactly it was talking to.

If you issue Initialize_Conversation() with all blanks and issue Extract_Partner_LU_Name(), you'll know that the partner LU name hasn't been set if you get a returned partner_LU_name_length of 1 and a partner_LU_name of a single blank.

Here's the function prototype for the Extract_Partner_LU_Name() call:

```
CM_ENTRY                          /* Extract_Partner_LU_Name      */
cmepln(unsigned char CM_PTR,        /* I: conversation_ID           */
       unsigned char CM_PTR,        /* O: partner_LU_name           */
       CM_INT32 CM_PTR,      /* O: partner_LU_name_length max 17 */
       CM_RETURN_CODE CM_PTR);      /* O: return_code               */
```

This call requires a good conversation ID. Your program also passes a pointer to where CPI-C should return the partner LU name, and a pointer to where it should return the length of the partner LU name. The partner LU name that CPI-C returns is not a null-terminated string, which is why it also returns the length. Be sure that the partner LU name pointer points to an array that is at least 17 bytes long; this is the maximum size of a partner LU name. Although the Set_Partner_LU_Name() call allows names in several different formats, Extract_Partner_LU_Name() returns a fully qualified partner LU name.

If the conversation is already over, it's a too late to issue Extract_Partner_LU_Name() to find out who the partner was, since the conversation ID is no longer valid. Issue this call just after doing an Allocate() or an Accept, and keep the returned answer for use in your error-logging code.

An example of using this call is shown in Chap. 4.

Extract_Security_User_ID (CMESUI)

The Extract_Security_User_ID() call was added to CPI-C in version 1.2 and, thus, may not yet be available on some platforms.

This call lets you see the user ID, if any, that was sent on the Attach that started the conversation. For security reasons, there is no corresponding call that lets you extract the password.

Here's the function prototype for the Extract_Security_User_ID() call:

```
CM_ENTRY                         /* Extract_Security_User_ID   */
cmesui(unsigned char CM_PTR,     /* I: conversation_ID         */
       unsigned char CM_PTR,     /* O: user_ID                 */
       CM_INT32 CM_PTR,          /* O: user_ID_length max 10   */
       CM_RETURN_CODE CM_PTR);   /* O: return_code             */
```

This call requires a good conversation ID. Your program also passes a pointer to where CPI-C should return the user ID name, and a pointer to where it should return the length of the user ID name. The user ID name that CPI-C returns is not a null-terminated string, which is why it also returns the length. Be sure that the user ID name pointer points to an array that is at least 10 bytes long.

If the conversation is already over, it's a bad time to issue Extract_Security_User_ID() to find out who the partner was. Issue this call just after doing an Accept, and keep the returned answer for use in your error-logging code.

A word of caution: early versions of this call existed as CPI-C extensions, and as part of the X/Open and WinCPIC specs. In these, the call was named "Extract_Conversation_Security_User_ID," and it only allowed the returned user ID to be 8 bytes long. When migrating to the Extract_Security_User_ID() call in CPI-C 1.2, make sure that you pass a 10-byte buffer and not an 8-byte one.

Extract_Sync_Level (CMESL)

The sync_level of the conversation is one of the values that's always carried in an Attach. It's a field that the attach manager can thus use to filter incoming Attaches.

Sometimes you may want to design server programs that talk to a variety of different client programs. These client programs may be using any of the three sync_level values: NONE, CONFIRM, or SYNC_POINT. By extracting the sync_level after accepting the conversation, your program can decide whether it should use program logic that issues Confirm() and Confirmed(), or even the CPI-RR calls named Backout() and Commit().

If your server program allows a variety of sync_levels from its partners, be sure to configure its TP definition to allow any incoming sync_level value.

Here's the function prototype for the Extract_Sync_Level() call, and the possible values for sync_level:

```
CM_ENTRY                          /* Extract_Sync_Level        */
cmesl (unsigned char CM_PTR,      /* I: conversation_ID        */
       CM_SYNC_LEVEL CM_PTR,      /* O: sync_level             */
       CM_RETURN_CODE CM_PTR);    /* O: return_code            */

/* sync_level values */

#define CM_NONE                              (CM_SYNC_LEVEL) 0
#define CM_CONFIRM                           (CM_SYNC_LEVEL) 1
#define CM_SYNC_POINT                        (CM_SYNC_LEVEL) 2
```

This call requires a good conversation ID. Your program also passes a pointer to where CPI-C should return the conversation's sync level.

Extract_TP_Name (CMETPN)

The Extract_TP_Name() call was added to CPI-C in version 1.2, and thus may not yet be available on some platforms. It is used by the server program to find the TP name that arrived from the partner in the Attach. This can be helpful for problem determination. If it appears that a program was started incorrectly, you can work back from its TP name to the TP definition which the attach manager used when handling the Attach.

On the client side, this call returns the TP name that was or will be sent in the Attach. Your program can use this after the Initialize_Conversation() call to check that the correct TP name was configured in the side information.

Here's the function prototype for the Extract_TP_Name() call:

```
CM_ENTRY                          /* Extract_TP_Name           */
cmetpn(unsigned char CM_PTR,      /* I: conversation_ID        */
       unsigned char CM_PTR,      /* O: TP_name                */
       CM_INT32 CM_PTR,           /* O: TP_name_length max 64  */
       CM_RETURN_CODE CM_PTR);    /* O: return_code            */
```

This call requires a good conversation ID. Your program also passes a pointer to where CPI-C should return the TP name, and a pointer to where it should return the length of the TP name. The TP name that CPI-C returns is not a null-terminated string, which is why it also returns the length. Be sure that the TP name pointer points to an array that is at least 64 bytes long.

If the conversation is already over, it's a bad time to issue Extract_ TP_Name() to find out what TP was used. Issue this call just after doing an Allocate() or an Accept, and keep the returned answer for use in your error-logging code.

Sending Data

Now that we've described the calls used on both sides to establish a conversation, we can finally get around to what you really want to accomplish: sending and receiving information. Since you can't receive data until someone has sent it, we'll start with the Send_Data() call and the calls related to it.

GETTING READY TO SEND DATA

Sending data is easy in CPI-C (we'll see in the next chapter that receiving is more challenging). You point to a place in memory containing the data to be sent, and tell CPI-C how many bytes to send.

When sending a file, you can't send directly from a file; that is, a C file I/O stream handle is not understood by CPI-C. Your program must first copy from the file to a memory block, then send that block. For best performance, malloc() one large memory block to send from. Use that memory block over and over again for every Send_Data() call, and free the memory block at the end of the program. Don't malloc() and free() for every call.

While the sending of data is easy, the structure and content of the data itself require some careful thought. You have to think about the different kinds of computers with which you'll exchange data now and in the future. For example, if you are using a C compiler in DOS, your default integer size would have been two bytes (16 bits) up until just recently. With 32-bit operating systems, the default integer size is four bytes (32 bits). Sending integers between programs with either size of integers requires conversion of the numbers.

There's a straightforward way to approach this in your programs. Assume that in the future the target program that you'll be exchanging data with will change in hardware architecture, and change in the computer language it uses. Given those assumptions, don't send integers, don't send structures, and don't even send C's special characters, like the null-terminating character ('\0') or the newline character ('\n').

The general rule is:

When sending data

Build your buffers one byte at a time.

An analogous situation exists among the standard C run-time routines for handling '\0' in your data. For example, compare the fwrite() and fprintf() routines. The fwrite() routine writes a string of bytes to a file, without regard for embedded \0 characters. The fprintf() routine, using the format %s, writes null-terminated strings, stripping off the \0. Other languages, like COBOL, don't idiomatically use null-terminating characters. Don't make the task of writing a new partner for your program too difficult.

On the other hand, if you find yourself needing to send something like the tab or newline characters in your data, it may be preferable to use C's special characters rather than to invent your own. You may still have to write code to support these characters in COBOL, but at least you'll be using standard characters rather than ones of your own invention.

Several other data conversion challenges require your attention when sending and receiving data—in particular, the conversion between different character sets (ASCII versus EBCDIC, for example) and differences between country codes (U.S. English characters versus German characters, for example). We'll delve into this in Chap. 24.

Send_Data (CMSEND)

The only way to send data from one program to another in CPI-C is with the Send_Data() call. Point to a memory location containing the data to be sent, and point to the length of the memory block you want to send. Use a separate Send_Data() call for each record to be sent.

Here's the function prototype for the Send_Data() call:

```
CM_ENTRY                                    /* Send_Data                 */
cmsend(unsigned char CM_PTR,                /* I: conversation_ID */
       unsigned char CM_PTR,                /* I: buffer          */
       CM_INT32 CM_PTR,                     /* I: send_length     */
       CM_REQUEST_TO_SEND_RECEIVED CM_PTR,  /* O: RTS_received?   */
       CM_RETURN_CODE CM_PTR);              /* O: return_code     */
```

Supply a valid conversation ID, of course. The next two parameters are a pointer to the block of data to be sent, and a pointer to the length of data to be sent. The length of data can be any value from 0 to at least 32767 bytes.* By

---

* With CPI-C 1.2, data buffer size limits larger than 32767 can be returned on the Extract_Maximum_Buffer_Size() call. However, 0 to 32767 is a range you can count on in every CPI-C platform.

adjusting the pointer to the data being sent, your program can walk through an enormous block of memory, setting a length, doing a send, then updating the pointer to the next block to be sent by adding the length that was just sent.

If you set the length to 0 bytes and issue Send_Data(), it isn't a no-op. The partner will eventually receive a record of length 0.

Here's a simple example of a Send_Data() call:

```c
int
do_send_data(unsigned char * conversation_ID,
             unsigned char * data_buffer,
             CM_INT32        send_length)
{
    /*------------------------------------------------------------
     * Use the conversation ID from the caller to send the
     * buffer that's pointed to.
     *----------------------------------------------------------*/
    CM_RETURN_CODE            cpic_return_code;
    CM_REQUEST_TO_SEND_RECEIVED rts_received;
    int                       ret_val;

    assert(conversation_ID != NULL);
    assert(data_buffer != NULL);

    cmsend(                        /* Send_Data                 */
        conversation_ID,           /* returned conversation ID  */
        data_buffer,               /* send this buffer          */
        &send_length,              /* length to send            */
        &rts_received,             /* ignore this parameter     */
        &cpic_return_code);        /* return code from this call */

    if (cpic_return_code == CM_OK) {
        /*--------------------------------------------------------
         * The data buffer has been handed to CPI-C to be sent.
         *------------------------------------------------------*/
        ret_val = 0;
    }
    else {
        /*--------------------------------------------------------
         * The Send_Data() call was not executed.
         *------------------------------------------------------*/
        handle_cpic_rc(
            conversation_ID, cpic_return_code, "CMSEND");
        ret_val = 1;
    }
    return ret_val;
}
```

There are many error return codes that can come back from Send_Data() (the *CPI-C Reference* lists 24!). Although they are many in number, they essentially involve the following cases:

- *Debug time.* Your program passed bad parameters on the call or issued Send_Data() when it didn't have the permission-to-send. These should all be caught during your testing cycle and should never occur when a customer runs your program.
- *Production time.* The conversation failed or never got started. These should be handled within your program, either with program logic or by returning them to the user for fixing.

Before we leave Send_Data(), let's talk again about data buffering. CPI-C does not immediately send your data into the network after a Send_Data() call completes. One of CPI-C's jobs is to optimize its use of the underlying network. As part of its data-buffering performance optimizations, CPI-C doesn't put a session packet into the network until one of the following conditions occurs:

- A session buffer becomes full and, thus, ready to send.
- Your program indicates that it is done sending. Your program indicates it is done sending by issuing a Receive() call, issuing a Flush() call, issuing a Prepare_To_Receive() call, or ending the conversation.

(The details of CPI-C's rules for sending session packets are covered in "Rules for Sending a Network Packet" in Chap. 9.) CPI-C's data buffering behavior will rarely be apparent to the two programs. For example, a program that is currently sending data will always get to a point where it tells CPI-C that it is done sending. During development, you may find that there are times when you write partial programs that issue Send_Data() and then wait forever. Your partner program will be expecting to receive data, but since the network packet is never delivered into the network, it too will wait forever (if using the default type of Receive(), which is CM_RECEIVE_AND_WAIT).

FLUSH (CMFLUS)

At times you may want to control when session packets get sent, rather than leaving that optimization up to CPI-C. The most frequent reason for asking for a packet to be sent right away is that you know the partner can start working on the packet as soon as it receives it. The mechanism to do this is the Flush() call, which you'll find remarkably easy to use. You can issue it any time you have the permission-to-send.

Here's the function prototype for the Flush() call:

```
CM_ENTRY                            /* Flush                    */
cmflus(unsigned char CM_PTR,        /* I: conversation_ID       */
       CM_RETURN_CODE CM_PTR);      /* O: return_code           */
```

Flush() is so easy to use, you might want to rush out and put it throughout your CPI-C programs—don't. We've seen programs by beginners with a Flush() call after every Send_Data(), to make sure the data was sent. This isn't

necessary, since all of the data will eventually be sent by CPI-C. The Flush()
call is a tool you use for performance optimization.

The best way to improve the combined performance of a pair of programs is
to increase their amount of processing overlap. If one program is idle, waiting
to receive something from its partner, their processing doesn't overlap. They're
serialized, one waiting on the other. You'd prefer that both sides are fully occupied, taking advantage of the fact that two or more computers or processes are
working together on the same problem. Flush() is a way for the sending program, knowing that it is going to stay in **Send** state, to get records it has sent
to the partner right away.

The partner program can never tell that the local program has issued a
Flush() call; there isn't any signal buried in the session packets. Because of
this, there's a straightforward way to decide where to put Flush() calls in your
programs. Get your whole application up and running, and debugged. Then, in
the late stages of testing, go back and add Flush() calls on the send side, whenever the receiving side is idle and waiting for data.

Only the program that currently has the permission-to-send—that is, the
program that is in **Send** state—can issue a Flush() call. Your program will get
a state check if it issues Flush() in any other state.

Unlike some of the other conversation calls in CPI-C, there is no such thing
as a *flush_type* conversation characteristic to set or extract. We'll see in the
next section that some of the other CPI-C calls, like Send_Data() and Deallo-
cate(), can have a Flush() coupled with them in the same call.

Set_Send_Type (CMSST)

The Set_Send_Type() call is a performance optimization. It allows you to bundle several CPI-C calls together, and issue them together, as part of a single
Send_Data() call. The reasoning behind its creation is this: if you know you're
going to issue a Send_Data() and then a Flush(), why not just have one call
that does both a Send_Data() and a Flush() together? CPI-C has to handle only
one call, instead of two (giving a small performance savings), and your program needs to handle only one set of return codes.

Here's the function prototype for the Set_Send_Type() call and the values for
the send_type parameter:

```
CM_ENTRY                                  /* Set_Send_Type               */
cmsst (unsigned char CM_PTR,              /* I: conversation_ID          */
       CM_SEND_TYPE CM_PTR,               /* I: send_type                */
       CM_RETURN_CODE CM_PTR);            /* O: return_code              */

/*   send_type values                                                    */
/*   default is CM_BUFFER_DATA                                           */

#define CM_BUFFER_DATA                             (CM_SEND_TYPE) 0
#define CM_SEND_AND_FLUSH                          (CM_SEND_TYPE) 1
#define CM_SEND_AND_CONFIRM                        (CM_SEND_TYPE) 2
#define CM_SEND_AND_PREP_TO_RECEIVE                (CM_SEND_TYPE) 3
#define CM_SEND_AND_DEALLOCATE                     (CM_SEND_TYPE) 4
```

Your program can set the send_type to one of five values:

CM_BUFFER_DATA. The default send_type is the behavior that you're familiar with. CM_BUFFER_DATA just asks CPI-C to buffer the data, and return immediately.

CM_SEND_AND_FLUSH. Asks CPI-C to issue a Send_Data(), and then to flush the currently buffered session packets.

CM_SEND_AND_CONFIRM. Asks CPI-C to issue a Send_Data(), and then to perform the Confirm() function. Like all calls to Confirm(), the session packets are first flushed, and the partner then receives a request to confirm that everything so far has been received and processed. The local program, which issued the Send_Data() with send_type(CM_SEND_AND_CONFIRM) will block, waiting for the partner to reply to the confirmation request.

CM_SEND_AND_PREP_TO_RECEIVE. Asks CPI-C to couple a Send_Data() call with a Prepare_To_Receive() call. This not only causes a record to be created and flushed, but also passes the permission-to-send to the partner program. We'll see later in this chapter that there are three prepare_to_receive_types. CPI-C uses the current prepare_to_receive_type when passing the permission-to-send to the partner.

CM_SEND_AND_DEALLOCATE. Asks CPI-C to send a record, and then to deallocate the conversation. We'll see in a later chapter that there are four deallocate_types. CPI-C uses the current deallocate_type when deallocating the conversation.

Like all the Set calls, the call itself is very fast. It just causes CPI-C to set a value in an internal control block; nothing flows in the network, and the partner never knows it was issued.

This call can be issued any time you have a good conversation ID. For example, you can change the send_type early in the conversation, right after an Initialize_Conversation() or Initialize_For_Incoming() call. However, we think this is a poor maintenance practice. The next person modifying your code may not see that the send_type is set a long way from the Send_Data() calls themselves. Since the call is almost invisibly fast, keep your Set_Send_Type() calls close to the Send_Data() calls, so what you're doing is visually obvious, and so the next programmer is less likely to make erroneous assumptions about what is going on.

GETTING READY TO RECEIVE, AFTER SENDING

The next two calls are not really building blocks, but they are performance optimizations. You can write a lot of CPI-C programs before you may ever find an opportunity to use them effectively, but when you do, it may result in a spectacular increase in processing overlap.

We'll discuss the Prepare_To_Receive() call here (along with its companion, Set_Prepare_To_Receive_Type()) because they can be issued only by the sender.

Prepare_To_Receive (CMPTR)

Sometimes after you've talked on the phone for awhile, you'll come to a pause where neither side says anything. The person at the other end might start talking if they know you are done, but they're not sure if you're really finished for now.

Prepare_To_Receive() is for that transition point where the sender has finished sending whatever it had to send, but it hasn't yet issued a Receive() call to start receiving from its partner. Until the sender causes the permission-to-send to be passed to the other side, the receiver is just stuck there, probably blocked on a Receive() call. The sender issues a Prepare_To_Receive() call because it knows it's done, but it may be a while before it actually issues a Receive() itself. In the meantime, the permission-to-send gets passed to the partner, which can start sending data, if it wants to.

Here's the function prototype for the Prepare_To_Receive() call:

```
CM_ENTRY                         /* Prepare_To_Receive        */
cmptr (unsigned char CM_PTR,     /* I: conversation_ID        */
       CM_RETURN_CODE CM_PTR);   /* O: return_code            */
```

This will sound a little like the discussion of the Flush() call because it is a similar kind of performance optimization.

The best way to improve the combined performance of a pair of programs is to increase their amount of processing overlap. If one program is idle, waiting to receive something from its partner, their processing doesn't overlap. They're serialized, one waiting on the other. You'd prefer that both sides be fully occupied, taking advantage of the fact that two or more computers or processes are working together on the same problem. Prepare_To_Receive() is a way for the sending program, which knows it has finished sending, to tell the partner that as soon as possible.

The partner program can't tell that the local program has issued a Prepare_To_Receive() call; there isn't any signal buried in the session packets. Because of this, there's a straightforward way to decide where to put Prepare_To_Receive() calls in your programs. Get your application's operation debugged and solid; then observe situations between the partners where there is a lack of processing overlap. Insert Prepare_To_Receive() calls in the sender's code where it appears that the receiving side is blocked, waiting to do a send.

Only the program that currently has the permission-to-send, that is, it is in **Send** or **Send-Pending** state, can issue a Prepare_To_Receive() call. Your program will get the CM_PROGRAM_STATE_CHECK return code if it issues Prepare_To_Receive() in any other state. The surprising situation is if Prepare_To_Receive() is issued in **Receive** state. You might think it should behave as a no-op, since the caller is trying to get to **Receive** state and it's already there. However, this too causes a state check return code; your programs must be in **Send** state to issue Prepare_To_Receive() successfully.

Set_Prepare_To_Receive_Type (CMSPTR)

There's a conversation characteristic associated with Prepare_To_Receive()
that lets you couple an additional action within a single call. This occurs during the transition period where the current sender is about to become the
receiver. When it passes the permission-to-send to the partner, should it also
issue a Confirm() call? Like the send_type characteristic, this is a performance
optimization that you can add to your programs as part of their tuning, in the
late stages of testing and debugging.

Here's the function prototype for the Set_Prepare_To_Receive_Type() call
and the values for the prepare_to_receive_type parameter:

```
CM_ENTRY                             /* Set_Prepare_To_Receive    */
cmsptr(unsigned char CM_PTR,         /* I: conversation_ID        */
       CM_PREPARE_TO_RECEIVE_TYPE CM_PTR,/* I: prep_to_rcv_type*/
       CM_RETURN_CODE CM_PTR);       /* O: return_code            */

/*  prepare_to_receive_type values                                */
/*  default is CM_PREP_TO_RECEIVE_SYNC_LEVEL                       */

#define CM_PREP_TO_RECEIVE_SYNC_LEVEL (CM_PREPARE_TO_RECEIVE_TYPE)0
#define CM_PREP_TO_RECEIVE_FLUSH      (CM_PREPARE_TO_RECEIVE_TYPE)1
#define CM_PREP_TO_RECEIVE_CONFIRM    (CM_PREPARE_TO_RECEIVE_TYPE)2
```

Your program can set the prepare_to_receive_type to one of three different
values:

CM_PREP_TO_RECEIVE_SYNC_LEVEL. This is the default value for the pre-
pare_to_receive_type characteristic. It tells CPI-C to look at the current value
for the sync_level conversation characteristic. If the sync_level is CM_NONE,
CPI-C should not add a Confirm() before the Prepare_To_Receive(). If it's
CM_CONFIRM, CPI-C should do a Confirm(). If the partner answers Yes with
Confirmed(), the permission-to-send passes to the partner. If the partner
answers No with Send_Error(), well, the partner now has the permission-to-
send anyway, since issuing Send_Error() grabs it.

CM_PREP_TO_RECEIVE_FLUSH. Tells CPI-C to pass the permission-to-send to
the partner and not do a Confirm() first.

CM_PREP_TO_RECEIVE_CONFIRM. Tells CPI-C to issue a Confirm() before passing the permission-to-send. If the partner answers Yes with Confirmed(), the
permission-to-send passes to the partner. If the partner answers No with
Send_Error(), well, the partner now has the permission-to-send anyway, since
issuing Send_Error() grabs it.

The Set_Prepare_To_Receive_Type() call can be issued any time you have a
good conversation ID. For example, you can change the send_type early in the
conversation, right after an Initialize_Conversation() or Initialize_For_Incom-
ing() call. However, we think this is a poor maintenance practice. The next person modifying your code may not see that the prepare_to_receive_type is set a
long way from the Prepare_To_Receive() calls themselves. Even more confus-

ing, by setting the send_type to CM_SEND_AND_PREP_TO_RECEIVE, a Send_Data() call can be coupled with a Prepare_To_Receive(), taking whatever behavior is indicated by the current prepare_to_receive_type.

Like all the Set calls, the call itself is very fast. It just causes CPI-C to set a value in its internal control blocks; nothing flows in the network, and the partner never knows it was issued. Since this call is fast, there isn't a good reason to be too conservative in its use. Keep your Set_Prepare_To_Receive_Type() calls close to the Prepare_To_Receive() and, optionally, Send_Data() calls, so it is more visually obvious to the next programmer what you're doing.

## Chapter 14

Receiving

In Chap. 9 we discussed the way that CPI-C buffers data. The idea of letting CPI-C hold the data you send and deliver it into the network when appropriate has a stunning result: excellent performance, through efficient use of the network bandwidth.

The Receive() call in CPI-C works a little differently than you might expect if you've done network programming with other interfaces. Notice first that the call is named simply Receive(), not "Receive_Data()," which you might expect since its complement is named Send_Data(). The reason is again for efficiency; when your program issues a Receive(), it's putting out a *listen* for whatever's around on that conversation. Not only can it receive blocks of data, but it can find out

- Whether the data is a whole record or part of one
- Whether the state of the conversation has changed (for example, your program is now the sender)
- Whether the partner has requested confirmation
- Whether the conversation has been deallocated

Thus, on any Receive() call, several kinds of information can be received, one piece at a time or many together. Because of this combinatorial complexity, the full processing of a Receive() call is the most challenging code in CPI-C. In this chapter, we'll give you some procedures to help master that complexity.

You can choose to have your receive operations work in either of two ways. They can block, waiting for information to arrive. This is the kind of receive operation we looked at in all our example programs so far. Alternatively, the receive operations can poll, getting anything that's available right now or returning quickly if there isn't anything to be received. We call the first type "Receive-and-Wait" and call the second type "Receive-Immediate." No matter which type you use, you'll find that the guidelines for using CPI-C receive operations to be the same. We'll discuss both of these receive_types in this chapter.

RECEIVING WHATEVER ARRIVES

You'll find that when you design your program logic, you'll wrap your receive operations inside a pair of loops.

In the inner loop, your program continues to receive until it has obtained a complete record. That is, the program loops while the data_received value is CM_INCOMPLETE_DATA_RECEIVED. At the end of the loop, the data_received value will be CM_COMPLETE_DATA_RECEIVED. As a piece of a record is received, it must be appended to the end of the previously received partial record.

In the outer loop, your program continues to receive records until the state of the conversation changes. It loops while the status_received value is CM_NO_STATUS_RECEIVED and the return code is CM_OK. At the end of the loop, either the return code will indicate the conversation has been deallocated, or the status_received value indicates something other than CM_NO_STATUS_RECEIVED.

Use just a single memory block as your data buffer to receive into. At the beginning of your program, malloc() a buffer to receive into; at the end of your program, free() it. Do not malloc() and free() around every Receive() call. Many CPI-C platforms internally optimize their use of data buffers by remembering a signature of each data buffer that is used for send and receive operations. By using just one or a few data buffers, you can avoid a gradual performance slowdown and the eventual consumption of all CPI-C internal buffering capabilities.

Receive (CMRCV)

Your program can issue a Receive() call whenever it needs to get information from the partner. It can be issued almost any time (except when the partner has issued a Confirm() and expects a reply from your program). If Receive() is issued while in **Send** state, your program moves to **Receive** state, passing the permission-to-send to the partner.

Here's the function prototype for the Receive() call:

```
CM_ENTRY                                /* Receive                */
cmrcv (unsigned char CM_PTR,            /* I: conversation_ID     */
       unsigned char CM_PTR,            /* O: buffer              */
       CM_INT32 CM_PTR,                 /* I: requested_length    */
       CM_DATA_RECEIVED_TYPE CM_PTR,    /* O: data_received       */
       CM_INT32 CM_PTR,                 /* O: received_length     */
       CM_STATUS_RECEIVED CM_PTR,       /* O: status_received     */
       CM_REQUEST_TO_SEND_RECEIVED CM_PTR,  /* O: RTS_received? */
       CM_RETURN_CODE CM_PTR);          /* O: return_code         */
```

As we've seen in earlier chapters, there are a lot of parameters, but you'll find they're easy to understand if you examine them one at a time.

After the conversation ID, the next two parameters are a pointer to the buffer where CPI-C should place any received data, and a pointer to the maximum length you want to receive, the requested_length. If there's data available, CPI-C will put it in the buffer your program pointed to, for a length up to what was specified in the requested_length.

For example, suppose your program calls malloc() to get a 1000-byte buffer to receive into, and sets the requested_length to 1000. If a 5000-byte record arrives, CPI-C returns the first 1000 bytes into the buffer you pointed to, and holds the rest until the next Receive(). If instead a 30-byte record arrives, CPI-C returns the 30 bytes into the buffer you pointed to. It distinguishes between these two conditions with the next parameter, data_received.

Whenever the return code is CM_OK or CM_DEALLOCATED_NORMAL, CPI-C sets the data_received parameter to tell whether data was received, and whether it was a complete record or not. There are four possible values for the returned data_received parameter:

```
#define CM_NO_DATA_RECEIVED            (CM_DATA_RECEIVED_TYPE) 0
#define CM_DATA_RECEIVED               (CM_DATA_RECEIVED_TYPE) 1
#define CM_COMPLETE_DATA_RECEIVED      (CM_DATA_RECEIVED_TYPE) 2
#define CM_INCOMPLETE_DATA_RECEIVED    (CM_DATA_RECEIVED_TYPE) 3
```

Only examine the data_received parameter when the return code is CM_OK or CM_DEALLOCATED_NORMAL.

If no record was received, CPI-C returns CM_NO_DATA_RECEIVED into the data_received field you've pointed to. How can this occur? It occurs when you issue a Receive(), and the Receive() call completes because the state of the conversation changed—which will be indicated in the status_received parameter.

If data was received and this is a full record or the end of a record, CPI-C returns CM_COMPLETE_DATA_RECEIVED. Otherwise, this is the beginning or middle of a large record, and CPI-C returns CM_INCOMPLETE_DATA_RECEIVED for data_received.* See "Viewing the Data_Received Name" in Chap. 8 for a procedure that shows your returned data_received value.

The parameter after data_received is the received_length. This is where CPI-C says how much data it actually received. This number will always be less than or equal to the requested_length.

For example, assume again that your program sets the requested_length to 1000. If a 5000-byte record arrives, CPI-C returns the first 1000 bytes into the buffer you pointed to, sets the received_length to 1000, and sets the data_received to CM_INCOMPLETE_DATA_RECEIVED. On the other hand,

---

* Looking back at the function prototype for Receive(), you can see that the names of the type-defs for data_received and status_received are slightly different. This is a programming accident that crept into the cpic.h file over its evolutionary history. CM_DATA_RECEIVED_*TYPE,* is the typedef for the data_received parameter, versus CM_STATUS_RECEIVED (without the suffix _*TYPE*) for the status_received parameter.

if a 30-byte record arrives, CPI-C returns the 30 bytes into the 1000-byte buffer you pointed to, sets the received_length to 30, and sets the data_received to CM_COMPLETE_DATA_RECEIVED.

The received_length parameter is only valid when the return_code is CM_OK or CM_DEALLOCATED_NORMAL, and the data_received value is not CM_NO_DATA_RECEIVED. In any other case, your program should not look at the received_length parameter.

Separate from these four parameters, which are related to receiving data, is the status_received parameter. This parameter is one way CPI-C communicates with your program about changes to the conversation state (the other way is via return codes). Every time that a Receive() call returns with a CM_OK return code, your program needs to check the status_received value. Here are the eight status_received values:

```
/* the conversation state hasn't changed               */
#define CM_NO_STATUS_RECEIVED           (CM_STATUS_RECEIVED) 0

/* the local program is now the sender                 */
#define CM_SEND_RECEIVED                (CM_STATUS_RECEIVED) 1

/* the partner program issued a Confirm()              */
#define CM_CONFIRM_RECEIVED             (CM_STATUS_RECEIVED) 2

/* the partner program issued Send_Data() with Confirm()  */
#define CM_CONFIRM_SEND_RECEIVED        (CM_STATUS_RECEIVED) 3

/* the partner program issued Deallocate() with Confirm() */
#define CM_CONFIRM_DEALLOC_RECEIVED     (CM_STATUS_RECEIVED) 4

/* the sync_level is CM_SYNC_POINT                      */
#define CM_TAKE_COMMIT                  (CM_STATUS_RECEIVED) 5
#define CM_TAKE_COMMIT_SEND             (CM_STATUS_RECEIVED) 6
#define CM_TAKE_COMMIT_DEALLOCATE       (CM_STATUS_RECEIVED) 7
```

Only examine the status_received parameter when the return code is CM_OK.

When you write your code to handle multiple calls to do receive operations, it should have two nested loops. The inner loop continues receiving until it has accumulated a complete record. The outer loop continues receiving until the conversation state changes. This means that as long as the return code is CM_OK, the status_received is CM_NO_STATUS_RECEIVED, and the data you're receiving is valid, your program should continue with the Receive() loop.

You'll see the status_received value of CM_SEND_RECEIVED whenever the partner has handed your program the permission-to-send. You'll see one of the three CM_CONFIRM_xxxx values when the partner is requesting synchronization. CM_CONFIRM_RECEIVED means the partner has issued a Confirm() call. CM_CONFIRM_SEND_RECEIVED means that the partner has coupled a Confirm() with passing of the permission-to-send to your program. If the local program replies with Confirmed() or Send_Error(), it will next be in **Send** state. Finally, the CM_CONFIRM_DEALLOC_RECEIVED value means that the partner program has conditionally deallocated the conversation. The partner program could have done this by issuing Deallocate() with deallocate_type(CM_CONFIRM) or by issuing deallocate_type(CM_SYNC_LEVEL), where the sync_level was CM_CONFIRM. By replying with Confirmed(), your program agrees to end the conversation. Replying with Send_Error() keeps the conversation going.

The three other values, CM_TAKE_COMMIT_xxxx, only apply when sync_level(CM_SYNC_POINT) is being used.

After using the status_received parameters for awhile, you'll find that it does an excellent job of streamlining the handling of state changes. While you're learning about its behavior, you may want to use the procedure shown in Chap. 7, p. 89. This procedure writes a text string for the current status_received value to stdout. You may also find this routine helpful during the debugging of newly designed applications.

The return code on a Receive() call is another source of received information. Whenever the return code is CM_OK, be sure to examine the status_received parameter. Whenever the return code is either CM_OK or CM_DEALLO-CATED_NORMAL, be sure to examine the data_received value. If data_received is anything other than CM_NO_DATA_RECEIVED, then retrieve the data using the received_length and the data buffer. We'll discuss another interesting return code, CM_UNSUCCESSFUL, when we discuss Receive-Immediate in the next section.

Juggling these five returned parameters, like all juggling routines, takes some practice. After we discuss Receive-Immediate, we'll explore a general-purpose procedure for using the CPI-C Receive() call.

RECEIVE-IMMEDIATE

All of the examples of the Receive() call we've shown thus far will wait to hear from the partner. They block on the Receive() call until data is received, the status changes, the partner issues Send_Error(), or the conversation is deallo-cated. However, some applications may choose a different design philosophy. They may choose to check whether something has arrived for them. If nothing has arrived, they want to continue on with what they were doing.

To handle these different kinds of designs, there are two different ways to set the receive_type conversation characteristic. The default value, CM_RECEIVE_AND_WAIT, is the behavior we're most familiar with. The other value for the receive_type is CM_RECEIVE_IMMEDIATE, which tells CPI-C to return immediately to the calling program with whatever it has or with nothing. The only new wrinkle in using this receive_type is a new return code: CM_UNSUCCESSFUL. This return code means that there was nothing to receive and the state of the conversation hasn't changed.

Set_Receive_Type (CMSRT)

The *receive_type* conversation characteristic lets you decide whether the Receive() call should block (that is, wait indefinitely for information to arrive) or return immediately to your program.

Here's the function prototype for the Set_Receive_Type() call and the values for the receive_type parameter:

```
CM_ENTRY                          /* Set_Receive_Type         */
cmsrt (unsigned char CM_PTR,      /* I: conversation_ID       */
       CM_RECEIVE_TYPE CM_PTR,    /* I: receive_type          */
       CM_RETURN_CODE CM_PTR);    /* O: return_code           */

/*  receive_type values                                       */
/*  default is CM_RECEIVE_AND_WAIT                            */

#define CM_RECEIVE_AND_WAIT                 (CM_RECEIVE_TYPE) 0
#define CM_RECEIVE_IMMEDIATE                (CM_RECEIVE_TYPE) 1
```

Your program can set the receive_type to one of two values:

CM_RECEIVE_AND_WAIT. This is the default value. It tells CPI-C to wait until one of the following occurs:

- A full record arrives, or enough data arrives to complete a record or fill the size in the requested_length.
- The status_received value changes.
- The return_code returns a value other than CM_OK.

CM_RECEIVE_IMMEDIATE. Tells CPI-C to return to the caller whatever is available at the time of the call. If there's only a partial record in its internal buffer, CPI-C returns as much as it has now and sets the data_received to CM_INCOMPLETE_DATA_RECEIVED.

With its receive_type set to CM_RECEIVE_IMMEDIATE, a program can poll for data on a conversation. You may find this technique useful when you have many concurrent conversations active within one program and non-blocking calls aren't available. The local program doesn't get stuck on any one conversation; it can go from conversation to conversation, looking to see if something's arrived.

The Set_Receive_Type() call can be issued any time you have a good conversation ID. For example, you can change the receive_type early in the conversation, right after an Initialize_Conversation() or Initialize_For_Incoming() call. As with the other Set calls, we think this is a poor maintenance practice. The next person modifying your code may not see that the receive_type is set many pages or files away from the Receive() calls themselves.

Like all the Set calls, the call itself is very fast. It just causes CPI-C to set a value in its internal control blocks; nothing flows in the network, and the partner never knows it was issued. Since this call is fast, there isn't a good reason to be too conservative in its use. Keep your Set_Receive_Type() calls close to the Receive() call loops.

A GENERAL-PURPOSE RECEIVE() ROUTINE

The routine that follows handles the five returned values from a Receive() call, assuming that every result is possible. It loops forever, until the conversation state changes or until an error is encountered. This routine assumes that the caller is responsible for calling the routine that sends data, reports an error, and cleans up after the conversation is over. You can easily modify this procedure to make those calls.

Since the source code for the general-purpose Receive() loop is fairly long, we'll first show the pseudocode for the algorithm it uses:

```
begin
    set completion_code = TIME_TO_RECEIVE
    do while completion_code = TIME_TO_RECEIVE
        Receive()
        if return_code = OK or return_code = DEALLOCATED_NORMAL
            switch on DATA_RECEIVED
            case INCOMPLETE_DATA_RECEIVED
                do process_incomplete_data
                if process_failed
                    set completion_code = TIME_TO_REPORT_ERROR
                endif
            case COMPLETE_DATA_RECEIVED
                do process_complete_data
                if process_failed
                    set completion_code = TIME_TO_REPORT_ERROR
                endif
            endcase

            if completion_code = TIME_TO_RECEIVE and
                return_code = OK
                switch on STATUS_RECEIVED
                case CONFIRM_RECEIVED
                case CONFIRM_SEND_RECEIVED
                case CONFIRM_DEALLOC_RECEIVED
                    do confirm_processing
                    if process_failed
                        set completion_code=TIME_TO_REPORT_ERROR
                    endif
                endcase
                if completion_code = TIME_TO_RECEIVE
                    switch on STATUS_RECEIVED
                    case SEND_RECEIVED
                    case CONFIRM_SEND_RECEIVED
                        set completion_code = TIME_TO_SEND
                    case CONFIRM_DEALLOC_RECEIVED
                        set completion_code = TIME_TO_CLEANUP
                    endcase
                endif
            endif
            if completion_code = TIME_TO_RECEIVE
                if return_code = DEALLOCATED_NORMAL
                    set completion_code = TIME_TO_CLEANUP
            endif
```

```
          else if return_code = UNSUCCESSFUL
              do pause_for_retrying
          endif
          else
              do unexpected_return_code_processing
              set completion_code = TIME_TO_REPORT_ERROR
          endif
      enddo
      return completion_code
  end
```

This routine will loop as long as there is something to receive. In your application, you may want to keep the loop logic inside your own program.

In most cases, your application design will preclude certain results. To modify the routine so that it rejects unexpected results, find where the unwanted result is handled, set the completion_code to TIME_TO_REPORT_ERROR, and capture information about the cause of the error.

If your application is designed to process a specific number of records, process_complete_data() should detect the error when too many records are received. The confirm_processing(), get_ready_to_send(), and get_ready_to_end() routines should detect the error when too few records are received.

The following source code implements the algorithm we've just shown. Its central procedure is named do_receive_generic(), which expects a valid conversation ID as it input parameter. It calls two procedures that you will need to rewrite to suit the purposes of your particular application. Procedure process_data() is called whenever there's a data record that's been received. You'll need to decide what to do with that data (for example, write it to a file or use it as a key into a database). You only need procedure pause_for_retrying() if you're using Receive-Immediate; use this procedure to avoid a tight loop of Receive() calls.

```
/*------------------------------------------------------------------
 * The larger a receive size you can afford, the faster your
 * overall performance. The RECEIVE_SIZE constant here is
 * smaller than the memory buffer size, to show the coding
 * needed when data_received is CM_INCOMPLETE_DATA_RECEIVED.
 * You can even set it to 1 byte, if you choose (i.e., receive
 * one byte on each Receive() call).
 *----------------------------------------------------------------*/
#define RECEIVE_SIZE (1000)      /* size of each Receive()    */
#define BUFFER_SIZE (32767)      /* largest possible record   */

typedef enum {
    TIME_TO_RECEIVE,
    TIME_TO_SEND,
    TIME_TO_REPORT_ERROR,
    TIME_TO_CLEANUP
} COMPLETION_CODE;
```

```
void
pause_before_retrying(void)
{
    /*-------------------------------------------------------------
     * Replace this procedure with your own code for waiting
     * briefly during a loop of Receive-Immediate calls.
     *------------------------------------------------------------*/
    (void)printf("Pausing, before retrying Receive-Immediate\n");
}

int
process_data(
    unsigned char          * data_buffer,
    CM_INT32                 data_length,
    CM_DATA_RECEIVED_TYPE data_received)
{
    /*-------------------------------------------------------------
     * Replace this procedure with your own code for processing
     * received data records. We've put trivial code here that
     * doesn't really do anything but show what happened.
     *------------------------------------------------------------*/
    (void)printf("processing %ld bytes\n", (long)data_length);
    switch (data_received) {
        case CM_INCOMPLETE_DATA_RECEIVED:
            (void)printf("Partial data record received\n");
            (void)fwrite((void *)data_buffer,
                         1, (size_t)data_length, stdout);
            break;
        case CM_COMPLETE_DATA_RECEIVED:
            (void)printf("Complete data record received\n");
            (void)fwrite((void *)data_buffer,
                         1, (size_t)data_length, stdout);
            break;
        default:
            show_data_received(data_received);
            break;
    }
    return 0;   /* return 0 if data was successfully processed */
}

void
do_receive_generic(
    unsigned char * conversation_ID)
{
    CM_RETURN_CODE   cpic_return_code;
    CM_INT32         received_length;
    CM_INT32         requested_length = RECEIVE_SIZE;
    CM_INT32         data_length;     /* bytes to be processed */
    CM_INT32         total_received;  /* amount from this loop */
    size_t           offset = 0; /* receive data buffer offset */
    unsigned char * data_buffer;
```

```
COMPLETION_CODE completion_code = TIME_TO_RECEIVE;
BOOL            process_incomplete_records = FALSE;

assert(conversation_ID != NULL);

/*------------------------------------------------------------
 * Get enough memory for the local buffer into which
 * you'll receive.
 *----------------------------------------------------------*/
data_buffer = (unsigned char *)malloc((size_t)BUFFER_SIZE);
if (data_buffer == NULL) {
    handle_error(conversation_ID,
        "Can't allocate %ld bytes for data_buffer",
        (long)BUFFER_SIZE);
}

while (completion_code == TIME_TO_RECEIVE) {
    CM_DATA_RECEIVED_TYPE      data_received;
    CM_STATUS_RECEIVED         status_received;
    CM_REQUEST_TO_SEND_RECEIVED rts_received;
    cmrcv (                    /* Receive                    */
        conversation_ID,       /* conversation ID            */
        &data_buffer[offset],  /* put received data here     */
        &requested_length,     /* maximum length to receive  */
        &data_received,        /* returned data_rcvd value   */
        &received_length,      /* length of received data    */
        &status_received,      /* returned status_rcvd value */
        &rts_received,         /* ignore this parameter      */
        &cpic_return_code);    /* return code from this call */

    if ((cpic_return_code == CM_OK) ||
        (cpic_return_code == CM_DEALLOCATED_NORMAL)) {

        /*----------------------------------------------------
         * First, check the data_received parameter.
         *--------------------------------------------------*/
        switch (data_received) {
            case CM_INCOMPLETE_DATA_RECEIVED:
                data_length    += received_length;
                total_received += received_length;

                if (process_incomplete_records == TRUE) {
                    if (!process_data(data_buffer,
                                      data_length,
                                      data_received)) {
                        /*------------------------------------
                         * Get ready to receive the next
                         * portion of a data record.
                         *----------------------------------*/
                        offset = 0;
                        data_length = 0;
```

```
                }
                else {
                    completion_code =
                        TIME_TO_REPORT_ERROR;
                }
            }
            else {
                /* update the offset, to receive more */
                offset += received_length;
                if (offset == BUFFER_SIZE) {
                    /*-----------------------------------
                     * We're at the end of the buffer,
                     * yet there's still more. Give up!
                     *---------------------------------*/
                    completion_code =
                        TIME_TO_REPORT_ERROR;
                    handle_error(conversation_ID,
                        "Too much data was sent");
                }
            }

            /* don't ask for more than we can hold */
            requested_length = (CM_INT32)
                min(RECEIVE_SIZE, BUFFER_SIZE - offset);
            break;

        case CM_COMPLETE_DATA_RECEIVED:
            /*---------------------------------------------
             * We've received one full data record.
             * Go process that record (e.g., write it
             * to a file). For this example, we're
             * passing it to process_data().
             *-------------------------------------------*/
            requested_length = RECEIVE_SIZE;
            data_length    += received_length;
            total_received += received_length;
            if (!process_data(data_buffer,
                              total_received,
                              data_received)) {
                /*-----------------------------------------
                 * Get ready to receive the next
                 * data record.
                 *---------------------------------------*/
                offset = 0;
                data_length = 0;
            }
            else {
                completion_code = TIME_TO_REPORT_ERROR;
            }
            break;
```

```
            default:
                /* other values are ignored */
                break;
    }   /* end of data_received switch */
/*-----------------------------------------------------
 * Next, check the status_received parameter.
 *---------------------------------------------------*/
if ((completion_code == TIME_TO_RECEIVE) &&
    (cpic_return_code == CM_OK)) {
    /*-----------------------------------------------------
     * Check for the CONFIRM status_received values.
     *---------------------------------------------------*/
    switch (status_received) {
        case CM_CONFIRM_RECEIVED:
        case CM_CONFIRM_SEND_RECEIVED:
        case CM_CONFIRM_DEALLOC_RECEIVED:
            cmcfmd(                     /* Confirmed    */
                conversation_ID,
                &cpic_return_code);
            if (cpic_return_code != CM_OK) {
                completion_code =
                    TIME_TO_REPORT_ERROR;
                handle_cpic_rc(conversation_ID,
                    cpic_return_code, "CMCFMD");
            }
        default:
            /* Only looking for CONFIRM values  */
            break;
    }   /* end of status_received switch */
    /*-----------------------------------------------------
     * Now examine other status_received values.
     *---------------------------------------------------*/
    if (TIME_TO_RECEIVE == completion_code) {
        switch (status_received) {
            case CM_SEND_RECEIVED:
            case CM_CONFIRM_SEND_RECEIVED:
                completion_code = TIME_TO_SEND;
                break;
            case CM_CONFIRM_DEALLOC_RECEIVED:
                completion_code = TIME_TO_CLEANUP;
                break;
            default:
                /* Other values have examined. */
                break;
        }   /* end of status_received switch */
    }
}
if ((completion_code == TIME_TO_RECEIVE) &&
    (cpic_return_code == CM_DEALLOCATED_NORMAL)) {
```

```
                    completion_code = TIME_TO_CLEANUP;
            }
        }
        else {
            if (cpic_return_code == CM_UNSUCCESSFUL) {
                /* No data on this Receive-Immediate */
                pause_before_retrying();
            }
            else {
                /* this isn't a return code we expected */
                completion_code = TIME_TO_REPORT_ERROR;
                handle_cpic_rc(conversation_ID,
                    cpic_return_code, "CMRCV");
            }
        }
        /* show the progress of the transfer so far */
        (void)printf("Amount received: %ld bytes\r",
                    (long)total_received);

    } /* end of while TIME_TO_RECEIVE loop */

    /* the last one needs a newline */
    (void)printf("Amount received: %ld bytes\n",
                (long)total_received);
}
```

REUSABLE RECEIVE WRAPPERS

When you design both sides of your application, you generally use only a limited set of combinations of calls. It is rare that your application would actually expect to see all of the cases covered in our general-purpose receive routine.

Usually, your program expects only one particular combination of return codes and status_received values to accompany the incoming data. So, in addition to the general-purpose receive routine we just showed, we have provided three routines that cover some common combinations of receive operations.

These three routines each receive just a single data buffer, then ensure that the expected return code and status_received values have arrived. Remember that the data, status_received, and return codes you expect don't always necessarily arrive on the same Receive() call, due to delays in the network and software. Of these, the data will always arrive first. So, if the return code or status_received information does not arrive on the first Receive(), a second Receive() is issued (with a requested_length of zero), in case the change of status did not arrive with the data.*

---

* On the second Receive() call, we've passed a pointer to a valid, 1-byte data buffer. We don't expect to receive anything in it since we've set the requested_length to 0, so we probably could have passed a NULL pointer to the data buffer. However, we're not sure what all the CPI-C platforms do when they see a NULL data buffer pointer and a zero requested_length, so to be safe, we passed a NULL pointer.

The names of these routines correspond to some of the "classic" transactions that we cover in detail in Chapter 18. Here is a list of the three receive routines and the information they expect:

do_receive_pipe()	Expects to receive one complete data record, then to see the conversation normally deallocated.
do_receive_credit()	Expects to receive one data record, followed by a status_received value of CM_CONFIRM_DEALLOC_RECEIVED. This means that if the caller replies with Confirmed(), the conversation will be over. Otherwise, if the caller replies by issuing Send_Error(), the conversation will remain active.
do_receive_inquiry()	Expects to receive one data record, followed by a status_received value of CM_SEND_RECEIVED. This means that the caller now has the permission-to-send.

All three routines expect the same parameters from their callers: a pointer to a valid conversation ID, a pointer to the data buffer where the data should be returned, the size of data buffer, and a pointer to the integer where the number of bytes actually received will be returned. We make a simplifying assumption in these procedures: we don't expect to see the data_received value of CM_INCOMPLETE_DATA_RECEIVED. To avoid this, always pass in a pointer to a data buffer that's at least 32,767 bytes long, set the buffer size to 32,767, and assure that the receive_type is set to CM_RECEIVE_AND_WAIT.

Procedure do_receive_pipe()

This procedure expects to receive one complete record and the return code CM_DEALLOCATED_NORMAL. If it sees this, it returns 0 to its caller. Otherwise, it prints what it sees, and returns 1.

```
BOOL                    /* returns FALSE if it worked as designed */
do_receive_pipe(
    unsigned char * conversation_ID,   /* I: current conv ID  */
    unsigned char * data_buffer,       /* O: where data goes  */
    CM_INT32        buffer_size,       /* I: size to receive  */
    CM_INT32      * bytes_received)    /* O: amount received  */
{
    /*------------------------------------------------------------
     * This procedure expects to receive one data record, then
     * see that the conversation has been deallocated normally.
     * If this is true, it returns the data and its length, and
     * returns a value of 0. Otherwise, it prints the problem
     * and returns a non-zero value.
     *------------------------------------------------------------*/

    BOOL                   found_error = FALSE;
    CM_RETURN_CODE         cpic_return_code;
    CM_DATA_RECEIVED_TYPE  data_received;
    CM_STATUS_RECEIVED     status_received;
    CM_REQUEST_TO_SEND_RECEIVED rts_received;
```

```
assert (conversation_ID != NULL);
assert (data_buffer    != NULL);
assert (bytes_received != NULL);

*bytes_received = 0;

cmrcv (                      /* Receive                  */
    conversation_ID,         /* conversation ID          */
    data_buffer,             /* put received data here   */
    &buffer_size,            /* maximum length to receive */
    &data_received,          /* returned data_rcvd value */
    bytes_received,          /* length of received data  */
    &status_received,        /* returned status_rcvd value */
    &rts_received,           /* ignore this parameter    */
    &cpic_return_code);      /* return code from this call */
if ((cpic_return_code == CM_OK) || /* expected return codes*/
    (cpic_return_code == CM_DEALLOCATED_NORMAL)) {
    /*-------------------------------------------------------
     *  First, check the data_received parameter.
     *-----------------------------------------------------*/
    switch (data_received) {
        case CM_COMPLETE_DATA_RECEIVED:
            /* we expect one complete record */
            break;
        default:
            handle_receive_error(
                conversation_ID,
                (unsigned char *)
                    "Unexpected data_received value",
                cpic_return_code,
                data_received, status_received);
            break;
    } /* end of data_receive switch */

    /*-------------------------------------------------------
     * Next, check the return code.
     *-----------------------------------------------------*/
    if (CM_DEALLOCATED_NORMAL == cpic_return_code) {
        /* This is what we want; the conversation is over. */
    }
    else {                         /* the return code is CM_OK */
        /* we don't expect a status_received value */
        if (CM_NO_STATUS_RECEIVED != status_received) {
            /* partner unexpectedly changed the status */
            found_error = TRUE;
            handle_receive_error(conversation_ID,
                (unsigned char *)
                    "Unexpected status_received value",
                cpic_return_code,
                data_received, status_received);
        }
```

```
            }
        }
        else {              /* This isn't a return code we expect. */
            found_error = TRUE;
            handle_cpic_rc(
                conversation_ID, cpic_return_code, "CMRCV");
        }

        if ((found_error == FALSE) &&
            (cpic_return_code != CM_DEALLOCATED_NORMAL)) {
            /* Did the data and return code arrive separately?    */

            CM_INT32 local_buffer_size = 0;
            unsigned char local_buffer[1];

            cmrcv (                      /* Receive                 */
                conversation_ID,     /* conversation ID         */
                local_buffer,        /* put received data here   */
                &local_buffer_size,  /* maximum length to receive */
                &data_received,      /* returned data_rcvd value  */
                bytes_received,      /* length of received data  */
                &status_received,    /* returned status_rcvd value */
                &rts_received,       /* ignore this parameter    */
                &cpic_return_code);  /* return code from this call */
            if (!(((cpic_return_code == CM_DEALLOCATED_NORMAL) &&
                (data_received == CM_NO_DATA_RECEIVED)))) {
                found_error = TRUE;
                handle_receive_error(conversation_ID,
                    (unsigned char *)
                        "Unexpected return code on 2nd Receive()",
                    cpic_return_code,
                    data_received, status_received);
            }
        }
        return found_error;
    }
```

Procedure do_receive_credit()

This procedure expects to receive one complete data record, followed by a status_received value of CM_CONFIRM_DEALLOC_RECEIVED. The partner expects the local program to receive and process the record; if it's okay, the caller of do_receive_credit() should issue a Confirmed() call, which will end the conversation. Otherwise, it should issue Send_Error().

```
BOOL                    /* returns FALSE if it worked as designed */
do_receive_credit(
    unsigned char * conversation_ID,    /* I: current conv ID   */
    unsigned char * data_buffer,        /* O: where data goes   */
    CM_INT32        buffer_size,        /* I: size to receive   */
    CM_INT32      * bytes_received)     /* O: amount received   */
```

```
{
    /*-----------------------------------------------------------
     * This procedure expects to receive one data record, then
     * see that it must confirm what the partner has sent.
     * If this is true, it returns the data and its length, and
     * returns a value of 0. Otherwise, it prints the problem
     * and returns a non-zero value.
     *-----------------------------------------------------------*/
    BOOL                     found_error = FALSE;
    CM_RETURN_CODE           cpic_return_code;
    CM_DATA_RECEIVED_TYPE    data_received;
    CM_STATUS_RECEIVED       status_received;
    CM_REQUEST_TO_SEND_RECEIVED rts_received;

    assert (conversation_ID != NULL);
    assert (data_buffer     != NULL);
    assert (bytes_received   != NULL);

    *bytes_received = 0;

    cmrcv (                            /* Receive                  */
        conversation_ID,               /* conversation ID          */
        data_buffer,                   /* put received data here    */
        &buffer_size,                  /* maximum length to receive */
        &data_received,                /* returned data_rcvd value  */
        bytes_received,                /* length of received data   */
        &status_received,              /* returned status_rcvd value */
        &rts_received,                 /* ignore this parameter     */
        &cpic_return_code);            /* return code from this call */
    if (cpic_return_code == CM_OK) { /* expected return code?   */

        /*-------------------------------------------------------
         * First, check the data_received parameter.
         *-------------------------------------------------------*/
        switch (data_received) {
            case CM_COMPLETE_DATA_RECEIVED:
                /* we expect one complete record */
                break;
            default:
                handle_receive_error(conversation_ID,
                    (unsigned char *)
                        "Unexpected data_received value",
                    cpic_return_code,
                    data_received, status_received);
                break;
        } /* end of data_receive switch */

        /*-------------------------------------------------------
         * Next, check the status_received parameter.
         *-------------------------------------------------------*/
        if (status_received != CM_CONFIRM_DEALLOC_RECEIVED) {
            found_error = TRUE;
```

```
                    handle_receive_error(conversation_ID,
                        (unsigned char *)
                            "Unexpected status_received value",
                        cpic_return_code,
                        data_received, status_received);
                }
            }
            else {                  /* This isn't a return code we expect. */
                found_error = TRUE;
                handle_cpic_rc(
                    conversation_ID, cpic_return_code, "CMRCV");
            }

            if ((found_error == FALSE) &&
                (status_received != CM_CONFIRM_DEALLOC_RECEIVED)) {
                /* Did the data and status_received arrive separately? */

                CM_INT32 local_buffer_size = 0;
                unsigned char local_buffer[1];

                cmrcv (                     /* Receive                    */
                    conversation_ID,    /* conversation ID            */
                    local_buffer,       /* put received data here      */
                    &local_buffer_size, /* maximum length to receive   */
                    &data_received,     /* returned data_rcvd value    */
                    bytes_received,     /* length of received data     */
                    &status_received,   /* returned status_rcvd value  */
                    &rts_received,      /* ignore this parameter       */
                    &cpic_return_code); /* return code from this call  */
                if (!((cpic_return_code == CM_OK) &&
                    (data_received == CM_NO_DATA_RECEIVED) &&
                    (status_received == CM_CONFIRM_DEALLOC_RECEIVED))){
                    found_error = TRUE;
                    handle_receive_error(conversation_ID,
                        (unsigned char *)
                            "Unexpected return code on 2nd Receive()",
                        cpic_return_code,
                        data_received, status_received);
                }
            }
        }
        return found_error;
    }
```

Procedure do_receive_inquiry()

This procedure expects to receive one complete record from the partner, then notification that it has the permission-to-send. If it sees these, it returns 0 to its caller.

```
    BOOL                    /* returns FALSE if it worked as designed */
    do_receive_inquiry(
```

```
    unsigned char * conversation_ID,   /* I: current conv ID  */
    unsigned char * data_buffer,       /* O: where data goes  */
    CM_INT32        buffer_size,       /* I: size to receive  */
    CM_INT32      * bytes_received)     /* O: amount received  */
{

    /*-----------------------------------------------------------
     * This procedure expects to receive one data record, then
     * see that it has the permission-to-send (Send state).
     * If this is true, it returns the data and its length, and
     * returns a value of 0.  Otherwise, it prints the problem
     * and returns a non-zero value.
     *----------------------------------------------------------*/

    BOOL                   found_error = FALSE;
    CM_RETURN_CODE         cpic_return_code;
    CM_DATA_RECEIVED_TYPE  data_received;
    CM_STATUS_RECEIVED     status_received;
    CM_REQUEST_TO_SEND_RECEIVED rts_received;

    assert (conversation_ID != NULL);
    assert (data_buffer     != NULL);
    assert (bytes_received  != NULL);

    *bytes_received = 0;

    cmrcv (                     /* Receive                  */
        conversation_ID,        /* conversation ID          */
        data_buffer,            /* put received data here   */
        &buffer_size,           /* maximum length to receive */
        &data_received,         /* returned data_rcvd value  */
        bytes_received,         /* length of received data   */
        &status_received,       /* returned status_rcvd value */
        &rts_received,          /* ignore this parameter     */
        &cpic_return_code);     /* return code from this call */
    if (cpic_return_code == CM_OK) {  /* expected return code? */

        /*-----------------------------------------------------
         * First, check the data_received parameter.
         *----------------------------------------------------*/
        switch (data_received) {
            case CM_COMPLETE_DATA_RECEIVED:
                /* we expect one complete record */
                break;
            default:
                handle_receive_error(conversation_ID,
                    (unsigned char *)
                        "Unexpected data_received value",
                    cpic_return_code,
                    data_received, status_received);
                break;
        } /* end of data_receive switch */
```

```
            /*-----------------------------------------------------
             *  Next, check the status_received parameter.
             *---------------------------------------------------*/
            if (status_received != CM_SEND_RECEIVED) {
                found_error = TRUE;
                handle_receive_error(conversation_ID,
                    (unsigned char *)
                        "Unexpected status_received value",
                    cpic_return_code,
                    data_received, status_received);
            }
            else {
                /* What we expect.  Fall to the bottom and return. */
            }
        }
        else {                  /* This isn't a return code we expect. */
            found_error = TRUE;
            handle_cpic_rc(
                conversation_ID, cpic_return_code, "CMRCV");
        }

        if ((found_error == FALSE) &&
            (status_received != CM_SEND_RECEIVED)) {
            /* Did the data and status_received arrive separately? */

            CM_INT32 local_buffer_size = 0;
            unsigned char local_buffer[1];

            cmrcv (                 /* Receive                      */
                conversation_ID,    /* conversation ID              */
                local_buffer,       /* put received data here       */
                &local_buffer_size, /* maximum length to receive    */
                &data_received,     /* returned data_rcvd value     */
                bytes_received,     /* length of received data      */
                &status_received,   /* returned status_rcvd value   */
                &rts_received,      /* ignore this parameter        */
                &cpic_return_code); /* return code from this call   */
            if (!(((cpic_return_code == CM_OK) &&
                (data_received == CM_NO_DATA_RECEIVED) &&
                (status_received == CM_SEND_RECEIVED)))) {
                found_error = TRUE;
                handle_receive_error(conversation_ID,
                    (unsigned char *)
                        "Unexpected information on 2nd Receive()",
                    cpic_return_code,
                    data_received, status_received);
            }
        }
    return found_error;
}
```

Exchanging Synchronization and Error Reports with Your Partner

In this chapter, we'll discuss a set of calls that differentiate CPI-C from other programming interfaces. These calls, Confirm(), Confirmed(), and Send_ Error(), let programs talk to each other about application-level problems, without inventing and imbedding special characters in their data records.

New users to CPI-C are always confused by the Send_Error() call. Many presume that when something's wrong with the network, that's when they should call Send_Error(). That's the wrong time to use it; if something's wrong with the network, you'll find out about it through return codes. Send_Error() is used when a program itself finds something wrong, especially in the following kinds of areas:

- With the data it has received from the partner
- With the data it is about to send
- With the operating system and what it knows about (for example, out of disk space)
- With programming bugs (for example, unexpected state check)

Many things can happen to a pair of communicating programs that have nothing to do with the network between them. The programs need a way to stay synchronized in their operation. For example, the receiving program may be out of disk space and is, thus, unable to write to disk the records it is receiving. Another example is when the sender finds a corrupt database record that it knows it shouldn't send to its partner. The program with the problem in both of these examples will want to interrupt the data transfer and "negotiate" with the partner program what to do next. The calls we'll discuss here are tools that let your programs step out of what they're doing, make sure they're still synchronized with one another, and decide how to handle problems that arise.

The Confirm() and Confirmed() calls we discuss in this chapter can only be used when your program has changed the sync_level of the conversation to a value other than the default of CM_NONE. Only the client side of the conversation can change the sync_level, and it has to do that before issuing its Allocate() call. The server side inherits whatever sync_level the client decided to use. For details of the Set_Sync_Level() call, see "Set_Sync_Level (CMSSL)" in Chap. 11.

SYNCHRONIZING PROGRAMS

Two programs in a conversation never know perfectly what the other is doing. They only know about each other when they issue calls which return information about what has arrived. Even then, the laws of physics tell us that the information is a little old; one partner or the other has moved on with its work. The tremendous buffering functions of CPI-C "damp" a lot of the network considerations from the programs, making them even further removed. This is a wonderful environment in which to create and run communicating programs; but every once in awhile, the two programs may need to "sync up."

Some types of applications make this critical. For example, if you withdraw cash from an automated teller machine, the program at your bank really wants to know whether the machine delivered money into your hand. If not, it has a whole series of recovery actions it needs to take.

Confirm (CMCFM)

To make the synchronization of programs easy to do, CPI-C provides the Confirm() call. If you issue a Confirm() call, it asks the partner to stop everything and make sure everything up to this point has been received and processed. If so, the partner replies Yes by issuing Confirmed(). If not, it replies No by issuing Send_Error().

Here's the function prototype for the Confirm() call:

```
CM_ENTRY                               /* Confirm                    */
cmcfm (unsigned char CM_PTR,           /* I: conversation_ID         */
       CM_REQUEST_TO_SEND_RECEIVED CM_PTR, /* O: RTS_received? */
       CM_RETURN_CODE CM_PTR);         /* O: return_code             */
```

This call is as easy to code as the Flush() call. In fact, one of the things it does is a flush. This makes sense, since you want all the buffered data to arrive at the partner before the question of whether it has been received or not. Like Flush(), you must have the permission to send, that is, you must be in **Send** state, to issue it. Unlike Flush(), your program blocks on this call. Your program will hang, potentially forever, waiting for the partner to reply. The partner has only three ways it can respond: by issuing Confirmed(), by issuing Send_Error(), or by ending the conversation abnormally (by exiting the program or by issuing Deallocate-Abend or Cancel_Conversation()).

Unlike some of the other conversation calls in CPI-C, there is no *confirm_ type* conversation characteristic to set or extract. However, CPI-C can internally couple Confirm() with other calls, to save a call and related return code checking. See the Set_Send_Type(), Set_Prepare_To_Receive_Type(), and Set_Deallocate_Type() calls for more information.

What your partner sees when you issue Confirm()

The partner finds out that your program has issued Confirm()* *only* via the returned status_received parameter of a Receive() call.

```
/*  status_received values that indicate Confirm() */

#define CM_CONFIRM_RECEIVED              (CM_STATUS_RECEIVED) 2
#define CM_CONFIRM_SEND_RECEIVED         (CM_STATUS_RECEIVED) 3
#define CM_CONFIRM_DEALLOC_RECEIVED      (CM_STATUS_RECEIVED) 4
```

The first of these, CM_CONFIRM_RECEIVED, tells the partner that if it answers with Confirmed(), it will remain in **Receive** state. CM_CONFIRM_SEND_RECEIVED says that if the partner answers with Confirmed(), it will move to **Send** state. CM_CONFIRM_DEALLOC_RECEIVED tells the partner that if it answers with Confirmed(), the conversation will be over.

These are the only three ways the partner can find out that Confirm() was issued. There's nothing hidden in the return codes or data_received parameters.

Confirmed (CMCFMD)

When the sending side of the conversation issues Confirm(), the receiving side can answer Yes or No, or end the conversation. It answers, "Yes, everything since the last time we synchronized has been received and processed" by issuing Confirmed().

Here's the function prototype for the Confirmed() call:

```
CM_ENTRY                          /* Confirmed               */
cmcfmd(unsigned char CM_PTR,      /* I: conversation_ID      */
       CM_RETURN_CODE CM_PTR);    /* O: return_code          */
```

The program that answers with Confirmed() remains in **Receive** state. It should keep track of where it was when it confirmed; if this is a long-running

---

* Or any of the variants that you could have used: Send-Confirm, Prepare_To_Receive-Confirm, or Confirm-Deallocate.

conversation, this is the place where the two programs have most recently synchronized with each other.

When you successfully issue Confirmed(), CPI-C sends your acknowledgment back to your partner, using the fastest message in APPC. Remember, the partner program is blocked, waiting to hear back from you. CPI-C makes haste in getting the reply back, so both sides can continue what they're doing.

REPORTING ERRORS

CPI-C was designed to allow the construction of robust conversations for commercial applications. When a program in one of those applications finds a problem, it may need to tell its partner about it. Imbedding special codes in the records it sends creates a messy design and maintenance challenge. Your program should be able to interrupt the current data exchange to signal to its partner that there's a problem. The Send_Error() call was created to do this.

Let's start off with a qualifier: this call has nothing to do with network failures. If the partner or a part of the network goes down, the conversation's over. The Send_Error() call is used when you want to report a problem to your partner and keep the conversation going. Use Send_Error() when your program detects something wrong with itself or with the data being sent or received—that is, something that will prevent the current piece of data from being processed.

Issuing a Send_Error() call causes CPI-C to send an error notification to the partner, after flushing any unsent data. Either program in a transaction can issue Send_Error() at any time, even in **Receive** state. The program successfully issuing the Send_Error() call enters **Send** state; its partner is forced into **Receive** state.

Send_Error (CMSERR)

The Send_Error() call is used for two different things:

- To reply No, when the partner has issued Confirm(), but the received data could not be processed successfully

- To report any kind of abnormal condition that the partner needs to know about. The local program should thus issue Send_Error() when it encounters one of these conditions:

  It is the sender, and it cannot build a record to send.

  It is the receiver, and it cannot parse or process an arriving record.

  It diagnoses an operating system problem or application-level bug.

Your program can issue Send_Error() any time after Allocate (on the client side) or after Accept (on the server side). Whenever a Send_Error() call is successful, the program that issued it gains the permission-to-send.

Here's the function prototype for the Send_Error() call:

```
CM_ENTRY                          /* Send_Error                */
cmserr(unsigned char CM_PTR,      /* I: conversation_ID        */
       CM_REQUEST_TO_SEND_RECEIVED CM_PTR, /* O: RTS_received? */
       CM_RETURN_CODE CM_PTR);     /* O: return_code           */
```

Having issued a Send_Error() call, what does your local program do next? It needs to exchange with its partner information about what the error was. The partner needs to return information about what to do next. These two pieces of information—error descriptions and replies—are things that you must design for your applications.

What the issuer of Send_Error() does next is:

- Issue Send_Data() and Flush(): send a record containing an error description to the partner.
- Issue Receive(): wait for a record containing an error reply from the partner.
- Use the received error reply to decide whether to proceed or not.

And the partner, after receiving one of the return codes which indicates Send_Error(), should:

- Issue Receive(): receive the record containing the incoming error description.
- Issue Send_Data(): send a record containing an error reply to partner, describing what to do next.

Here is a picture of these guidelines:

```
Failure in local program          Partner Side
-----------------------           -----------------------------
     |
Send_Error()
     ------------------------->
                                  gets PROGRAM_ERROR return code
Send_Data()                        |
   (with the error description) Receive-And-Wait
     ------------------------->   .
Receive-And-Wait                  .
     .                            .
     .                            Send_Data w/Prepare_To_Receive
     .                               (with the error reply)
     <-------------------------
                                  Receive (and wait)
```

To do this exchange, you'll need to implement a set of error descriptions and replies. These are specific to the application, for each nontrivial recovery action:

- Error description: what occurred, when and where
- Error reply: where I was, what we should do next

What your partner sees when you issue Send_Error()

We've talked about how the program detecting a problem issues a Send_Error() call. What does the partner see? It sees one of the following return codes that capture what happened:

```
#define CM_PROGRAM_ERROR_NO_TRUNC        (CM_RETURN_CODE) 21
#define CM_PROGRAM_ERROR_PURGING         (CM_RETURN_CODE) 22

/*  You'll see this only if the conversation_type is CM_BASIC */
#define CM_PROGRAM_ERROR_TRUNC           (CM_RETURN_CODE) 23

/* You'll see these only if the partner is not using CPI-C */
#define CM_SVC_ERROR_NO_TRUNC            (CM_RETURN_CODE) 32
#define CM_SVC_ERROR_PURGING             (CM_RETURN_CODE) 33
#define CM_SVC_ERROR_TRUNC               (CM_RETURN_CODE) 34
```

One of these return codes, CM_PROGRAM_ERROR_TRUNC, applies only to basic conversations, so you shouldn't have to plan on handling it. The three return codes that start with CM_SVC_ERROR_ can only be returned when the partner is using a native APPC API, not CPI-C, so you'll know when you design your application if these can occur. So, there are generally two return codes that the partner needs to handle:

CM_PROGRAM_ERROR_NO_TRUNC.   The partner was the sender when it issued Send_Error(). It may have failed while building a record to send. The NO_TRUNC refers to the fact that there were no records truncated or purged.

CM_PROGRAM_ERROR_PURGING.   The partner was the receiver when it issued Send_Error(). It may have failed while parsing or processing a received record. The PURGING refers to the fact that any data not yet received by the partner has been discarded by the CPI-C.

Whenever your program gets any of these return codes, it is in **Receive** state. The current sender can find that the permission to send has been pulled away unexpectedly.

Set_Error_Direction (CMSED)

You'll remember that we discussed two common conditions where a program would issue a Send_Error() call:

- The sender cannot build a record to send.
- The receiver cannot parse or process an arriving record.

There's a small opportunity for ambiguity here. Let's say that your program has been the receiver, but it has just gotten the permission to send. If your program now issues a Send_Error() call, the partner program isn't sure exactly what's wrong. Does it mean you had a problem with the last record you received, or with the record you're about to send? There's a way to resolve this, with the Set_Error_Direction() call.

Here's the function prototype for the Set_Error_Direction() call:

```
CM_ENTRY                          /* Set_Error_Direction        */
cmsed (unsigned char CM_PTR,      /* I: conversation_ID         */
       CM_ERROR_DIRECTION CM_PTR, /* I: error_direction         */
       CM_RETURN_CODE CM_PTR);    /* O: return_code             */

/*  error_direction values                                      */
/*  default is CM_RECEIVE_ERROR                                 */

#define CM_RECEIVE_ERROR                  (CM_ERROR_DIRECTION) 0
#define CM_SEND_ERROR                     (CM_ERROR_DIRECTION) 1
```

The default value is what you use when there's a problem with the last received record. When the error_direction is CM_RECEIVE_ERROR and a Send_Error() call is issued, the partner finds out about it via the CM_PROG_ERROR_PURGING return code. If you change the error direction to CM_SEND_ERROR, it means you found a problem with a record you were about to send. In this case, the partner will see the CM_PROG_ERROR_NO_TRUNC return code.

We are reluctant to consider the Set_Error_Direction() call a true "building block." Most programs don't ponder much over the difference between the two different return codes it might see because its partner issued Send_Error(). If you're in that category, don't worry about ever setting the error_direction. However, if your application is of the nature that it's very careful about how it's using Send_Error(), then be sure to set the error_direction correctly when you find a problem in that ambiguous timing window of going from **Receive** state to **Send** state.

USING SEND_ERROR() VERSUS SEND_DATA()

You might have noticed a possible trade-off here. When should your application use Send_Error() to report errors and when should it just send an error report with a Send_Data() call? Here is a useful guideline.

If data-related errors are frequent, use Send_Data(). Work out efficient handling with the partner program. And what, you might ask, is frequent? Use a 90-10 rule: If errors occur in more than 10 percent of the times you parse data, use Send_Data().

Any data related to user input can be considered "frequent" and, thus, a poor candidate for Send_Error(). For example, users frequently type in invalid account numbers. A program receiving an invalid account number should expect to respond to its partner using Send_Data() describing what's wrong. On the other hand, if a program is reading data from a database that should contain validated records and encounters invalid characters (like ASCII "smiley faces"), this is an exceptional condition, where Send_Error() is an appropriate call to issue.

## Chapter 16

Ending Conversations and Programs

When you end a telephone conversation, you generally say good-bye before you hang up. Sometimes you wait for the person to whom you're talking to say good-bye also; sometimes you pick up the conversation again because the other person's not finished. Other times, you just say good-bye and slam down the phone. These kinds of behavior are available when ending your CPI-C conversations, as well. The way to say good-bye in CPI-C is by issuing the Deallocate() call.

When one program issues a successful call to Deallocate(), the conversation is over. Notice that just one of the partners needs to deallocate; if one side ends a conversation, the conversation IDs in both programs are invalidated. The other side finds out about the end of a conversation in the return code of a subsequent call. That's why finding about the unconditional end of a conversation is always a return code value. In any subsequent CPI-C calls, the programs get the return code that indicates that the conversation ID is invalid: CM_PROGRAM_PARAMETER_CHECK.

There are four flavors of the Deallocate() call, known as the *deallocate_type*: Sync_Level, Flush, Confirm, and Abend. The first three of these imply an orderly takedown; they require your program to be the sender (that is, it is in **Send** state) in order to issue them. The deallocate_type of Abend trashes the conversation right away; it can be issued by any program in any state, as long as it has a valid conversation ID (and if it doesn't, the conversation's over anyway). The *deallocate_type* can be changed at any time in a conversation, using the Set_Deallocate_Type() call.

We've ended many of the example programs we've looked at so far by simply ending, or by calling C's exit() routine. While this works in most cases, it's not very good form. We really should try to cleanly deallocate the conversation before calling exit(). The analogy here is with C's file I/O, where exit() generally will close all files—but it's not guaranteed on all platforms. We've shown a simple cleanup routine in the samples we've looked at so far. In this chapter, we'll show you code for a robust cleanup routine.

USING THE DEALLOCATE() CALL

The Deallocate() call comes in a variety of flavors. The flavor you get when you issue a Deallocate() call depends on two conversation characteristics: deallocate_type and sync_level. The default behavior of Deallocate() is to look at the sync_level of the conversation. If the sync_level is CM_NONE, the buffers are flushed and the conversation is ended. If the sync_level is CM_CONFIRM, CPI-C issues a Confirm() first. If the partner replies Yes, via Confirmed(), the conversation is taken down; otherwise, the conversation keeps going. There are three other deallocate_types that allow you to modify this behavior.

Deallocate (CMDEAL)

Use the Deallocate() call to end an active conversation. Your program can issue a Deallocate() call any time it has a good conversation ID, but there are a few caveats to this rule.

There are four deallocate_types. Three of these four deallocate_types can only be issued if you have the permission-to-send. Only Deallocate() with de-allocate_type(CM_DEALLOCATE_ABEND) can be issued in any state. So, if you're the receiver, you can't just issue a normal Deallocate() and hope to take down the conversation. We'll see in a procedure later in this chapter that the preferred way to do this in an emergency is to issue Send_Error() first (to become the sender), and then to issue a Deallocate() call.

Here's the function prototype for the Deallocate() call:

```
CM_ENTRY                        /* Deallocate              */
cmdeal(unsigned char CM_PTR,    /* I: conversation_ID      */
       CM_RETURN_CODE CM_PTR);  /* O: return_code          */
```

When a Deallocate() call is successful, CPI-C returns the CM_OK return code. This means that the conversation is over, and the conversation ID is no longer valid. Any other CPI-C calls that are issued after deallocating a conversation will get the CM_PROGRAM_PARAMETER_CHECK return code.

Set_Deallocate_Type (CMSDT)

The default value for *deallocate_type* is CM_DEALLOCATE_SYNC_LEVEL.

Use the Set_Deallocate_Type() call to change the behavior of a Deallocate() call. The default behavior of a Deallocate() call is to deallocate the conversation with whatever the conversation's sync_level is. For example, if the sync_level is CM_CONFIRM, then as part of a Deallocate() call, CPI-C will issue a Confirm() call internally, and wait to see a Confirmed() before it actually takes down the conversation.

The deallocate_type can be set to one of four values: CM_DEALLOCATE_ SYNC_LEVEL, CM_DEALLOCATE_FLUSH, CM_DEALLOCATE_CONFIRM, or CM_DEALLOCATE_ABEND.

The deallocate_type affects only how the conversation is deallocated when the Deallocate() call is issued by the local program.

This call can be issued any time you have a good conversation ID, including right after an Initialize call. Here's the function prototype for the Set_Deallocate_Type() call and the values for the deallocate_type parameter:

```
CM_ENTRY                          /* Set_Deallocate_Type        */
cmsdt (unsigned char CM_PTR,      /* I: conversation_ID         */
       CM_DEALLOCATE_TYPE CM_PTR, /* I: deallocate_type         */
       CM_RETURN_CODE CM_PTR);    /* O: return_code             */

/*  deallocate_type values                                      */
/*  default is CM_DEALLOCATE_SYNC_LEVEL                          */

#define CM_DEALLOCATE_SYNC_LEVEL          (CM_DEALLOCATE_TYPE) 0
#define CM_DEALLOCATE_FLUSH               (CM_DEALLOCATE_TYPE) 1
#define CM_DEALLOCATE_CONFIRM             (CM_DEALLOCATE_TYPE) 2
#define CM_DEALLOCATE_ABEND               (CM_DEALLOCATE_TYPE) 3
```

The first of the deallocate_types, CM_DEALLOCATE_SYNC_LEVEL, tells CPI-C to go back and look at the conversation characteristic named *sync_level*. Sync_level was one of the handful of conversation characteristics that is set between the Initialize_Conversation() call and the Allocate(). If the sync_level is CM_NONE (the default), then the Deallocate() just flushes the data and the conversation is over. If the sync_level has been changed to CM_CONFIRM, the Deallocate() internally calls Confirm() before proceeding. If the partner responds with Confirmed(), the conversation is deallocated; otherwise, the partner must have responded with Send_Error(), and the conversation is kept alive. This is called a conditional deallocation of the conversation. Alternatively, if the sync_level is CM_SYNC_POINT, the deallocation is again conditional, this time hinging on the successful completion of the syncpoint logic among all involved transaction parties.

The next two values are easy. A deallocate_type of CM_DEALLOCATE_ FLUSH behaves like CM_DEALLOCATE_SYNC_LEVEL, when the sync_ level has been set to CM_NONE; it simply flushes any data that's in CPI-C's internal buffers, and ends the conversation. A deallocate_type of CM_DE-ALLOCATE_CONFIRM behaves just like CM_DEALLOCATE_SYNC_LEVEL, when the sync_level has been set to CM_CONFIRM. Both of these deallocate_types require your program to be the sender to use them.

The fourth value, CM_DEALLOCATE_ABEND, is a powerful tool for invalidating a conversation ID at any time, in any state. Initialize_Conversation(), Initialize_For_Incoming(), and Accept_Conversation() all give us unique conversation IDs. If we run these calls in a loop, we can eventually consume all the conversation IDs available on the platform we were using. So how do we "give back" conversation IDs? With the Deallocate() call and deallocate_type (CM_DEALLOCATE_ABEND) (which we'll abbreviate "Deallocate-Abend"). We can run the following simple program forever, getting conversation IDs via Initialize_For_Incoming() and giving them back via Deallocate-Abend.

```c
/*-------------------------------------------------------------
 *  Stress test program.  Don't run this on a production machine.
 *  (file LPINIDEA.C)
 *------------------------------------------------------------*/
#include <cpic.h>               /* conversation API library   */
#include <limits.h>             /* variable arguments         */
#include <stdarg.h>             /* variable arguments         */
#include <stdio.h>              /* file I/O                   */
#include <stdlib.h>             /* standard library           */
#include <string.h>             /* strings and memory         */

#include "docpic.h"             /* CPI-C do_ calls            */

int main(void)
{
    /*-------------------------------------------------------
     *  Looping test program -- should run until any call fails
     *  (which shouldn't occur) or until the loop count reaches
     *  ULONG_MAX.
     *------------------------------------------------------*/
    unsigned long count;       /* total number of loop iterations */

    setbuf(stdout, NULL);      /* flush output immediately */

    /*-------------------------------------------------------
     *  Initialize, then deallocate conversations, until the
     *  limit is reached.  The return code should ALWAYS be
     *  CM_OK.
     *------------------------------------------------------*/
    for (count = 0; count < ULONG_MAX; count++) {
        CM_RETURN_CODE cpic_return_code;
        CM_DEALLOCATE_TYPE deallocate_type = CM_DEALLOCATE_ABEND;
        unsigned char  conversation_ID[CM_CID_SIZE];
        (void)printf("loop count: %lu\r", count);

        /*---------------------------------------------------
         * You can use either Initialize_Conversation() or
         * Initialize_For_Incoming() to get the conversation IDs.
         * If you use Initialize_Conversation(), you'll need to
         * set its symbolic destination name to all blanks.
         *--------------------------------------------------*/
        cminic(                    /* Initialize_For_Incoming    */
            conversation_ID,       /* returned conversation ID   */
            &cpic_return_code);    /* return code from this call */
        if (cpic_return_code != CM_OK) {
```

```
            (void)printf("loop count:  %lu\n", count);
            handle_cpic_rc(
                conversation_ID, cpic_return_code, "CMINIC");
        }

        cmsdt(                     /* Set_Deallocate_Type      */
            conversation_ID,       /* conversation ID          */
            &deallocate_type,      /* deallocate_type (ABEND)  */
            &cpic_return_code); /* return code from this call  */
        if (cpic_return_code != CM_OK) {
            (void)printf("loop count:  %lu\n", count);
            handle_cpic_rc(
                conversation_ID, cpic_return_code, "CMSDT");
        }

        cmdeal(                    /* Deallocate               */
            conversation_ID,       /* conversation ID          */
            &cpic_return_code); /* return code from this call  */
        if (cpic_return_code != CM_OK) {
            (void)printf("loop count:  %lu\n", count);
            handle_cpic_rc(
                conversation_ID, cpic_return_code, "CMDEAL");
        }
    }
    return EXIT_SUCCESS;
}
```

What your partner sees when you issue Deallocate()

If the local program successfully issues a Deallocate(), what does the partner program see? The answer depends on the deallocate_type.

First is the easy case, where the Deallocate() just did a Flush() and ended the conversation. Your program can do this with either deallocate_type(CM_DEALLOCATE_SYNC_LEVEL) where the sync_level is CM_NONE, or deallocate_type(CM_DEALLOCATE_FLUSH). For these, the partner program sees the return code CM_DEALLOCATED_NORMAL on the Receive() call it issues for the last record.

Second is the case where the deallocate_type is CM_DEALLOCATE_ABEND. For these, the partner program sees the return code CM_DEALLOCATED_ABEND on the next call it issues after CPI-C finds out about it. It sees CM_DEALLOCATED_ABEND if the local program or process exits without explicitly deallocating. For example, if the local DOS or OS/2 user presses Ctrl+Break to end a CPI-C program, or if the local program calls the C exit() routine without first calling Deallocate(), the partner will see CM_DEALLOCATED_ABEND.

Third is the case of the conditional deallocation. CPI-C issues a Confirm() because your deallocate_type is CM_DEALLOCATE_SYNC_LEVEL (and the conversation sync_level is CM_CONFIRM) or the deallocate_type is CM_DEALLOCATE_CONFIRM. This can only be used when the local program has the permission-to-send, which means the partner is issuing Receive() calls. The partner finds out about the Confirm-Deallocate from the status_received parameter of its Receive() call: CM_CONFIRM_DEALLOC_RECEIVED.

If you look at the list of CPI-C return codes, you'll see eight return codes related to discovering that the conversation has been deallocated. All but the two we've just discussed don't apply to most programs you write.

```
#define CM_DEALLOCATED_NORMAL            (CM_RETURN_CODE) 18
#define CM_DEALLOCATED_ABEND             (CM_RETURN_CODE) 17

/* You'll see these only if the partner is not using CPI-C */
#define CM_DEALLOCATED_ABEND_SVC         (CM_RETURN_CODE) 30
#define CM_DEALLOCATED_ABEND_TIMER       (CM_RETURN_CODE) 31

/* You'll see these only if sync_level is CM_SYNC_POINT */
#define CM_DEALLOCATED_ABEND_BO          (CM_RETURN_CODE) 130
#define CM_DEALLOCATED_NORMAL_BO         (CM_RETURN_CODE) 135
#define CM_DEALLOCATED_ABEND_SVC_BO      (CM_RETURN_CODE) 131
#define CM_DEALLOCATED_ABEND_TIMER_BO    (CM_RETURN_CODE) 132
```

The four return codes that end in ABEND_SVC_xxx or ABEND_TIMER_xxx can be returned only if you have a basic conversation and your partner is using a native APPC programming interface, not CPI-C. The four return codes that end in _BO apply only when you're using sync_level(CM_SYNC_POINT). The _BO stands for *backout*.

CLEANING UP A CONVERSATION

When choosing to end a CPI-C program because of an unrecoverable error, do it gracefully. In general, issue Send_Error(), Send_Data(), then Deallocate-Flush. This sequence identifies an unrecoverable error to the partner: the Send_Error() distinguishes program-controlled errors from operating-system-induced errors, the Send_Data() reports details about the error, and the Deallocate() wraps it all up.

Use just Deallocate-Abend, instead of the three-call sequence mentioned above, when your program needs to leave quickly, and it is not the sender. Use it when your program finds a catastrophic problem, and thinks that it has only enough CPU cycles left to get out one last message. For example, a thousand machines may have discovered that there has been a power failure, and the battery backup will go down in five seconds. Don't dawdle, leave.

Also, use Deallocate-Abend to avoid error recursion. How many times have you seen error-handling code that itself encounters a problem? What does it do? It calls the same error-handling code, resulting in a recursive loop! If your program gets a failure while in its error-handling code, it should quit, using Deallocate-Abend.

In the following do_error_cleanup() procedure, we improve on the simple-minded procedure we showed in Chap. 7. We first issue the Deallocate() call to try to end the conversation. If it fails, it is most likely that we aren't in **Send** state. In this case, we issue Send_Error() to steal the permission-to-send and notify our partner that we have encountered an error. If the Send_Error() succeeds, then we are in **Send** state and can Deallocate-Flush. If it fails, we must resort to using Deallocate-Abend.

```
void
do_error_cleanup(unsigned char * conversation_ID)
{
    /*-------------------------------------------------------------
     *  Clean up, as appropriate for this program, platform,
     *  and operating system.
     *-----------------------------------------------------------*/
    CM_RETURN_CODE cpic_return_code;

    assert(conversation_ID != NULL);

    /*-------------------------------------------------------------
     *  First, try to Deallocate the conversation with the
     *  current deallocate_type.
     *-----------------------------------------------------------*/
    cmdeal(                        /* Deallocate                  */
        conversation_ID,           /* conversation ID             */
        &cpic_return_code);        /* return code from this call  */

    if (cpic_return_code == CM_OK) {
        /* the conversation was successfully deallocated */
    }
    else if (cpic_return_code == CM_PROGRAM_PARAMETER_CHECK) {
        /* the conversation was previously deallocated */
    }
    else {
        /*-------------------------------------------------------
         * The Deallocate() call failed, probably because we're
         * not in Send state.  Issue Send_Error().  If that
         * succeeds, we'll do a Deallocate-Flush.  If that fails,
         * it's time to do a Deallocate-Abend.
         *-----------------------------------------------------*/
        CM_REQUEST_TO_SEND_RECEIVED RTS_received;
        CM_DEALLOCATE_TYPE          deallocate_type;

        cmserr(                    /* Send_Error                  */
            conversation_ID,       /* conversation ID             */
            &RTS_received,         /* ignore the RTS_received     */
            &cpic_return_code);    /* return code from this call  */

        if (cpic_return_code == CM_OK) {
            deallocate_type = CM_DEALLOCATE_FLUSH;
        }
        else {
            deallocate_type = CM_DEALLOCATE_ABEND;
        }
```

```
        cmsdt(                    /* Set_Deallocate_Type        */
            conversation_ID,      /* conversation ID            */
            &deallocate_type,     /* deallocate_type            */
            &cpic_return_code);   /* ignore this return code    */

        cmdeal(                   /* Deallocate                 */
            conversation_ID,      /* conversation ID            */
            &cpic_return_code);   /* ignore this return code    */
    }

    exit(EXIT_FAILURE);          /* operating system cleanup    */
}
```

In summary, always issue Deallocate() explicitly to clean up a conversation, if at all possible. Issuing C's exit() call or simply exiting a running program will generally cause the conversation to be cleaned up, but the partner won't know what happened. It will just see the CM_DEALLOCATED_ABEND return code.

## Chapter 17

Rarely Used Techniques

This chapter covers some CPI-C calls that aren't of immediate use to most CPI-C programmers. We cover two rarely used topics here: signalling with the request-to-send signal and using basic conversations. We don't show these in any of the sample programs, since we don't think they have a place in most CPI-C applications. However, take the time to read through this material some day; you may find situations where these techniques are just what you need.

BEGGING AND SIGNALING

The CPI-C conversational interface exercises strong control on its conversations. It's important to know which side of the conversation is responsible for recovery. When your program is the receiver, it's essentially stuck there. The sender (that is, the side with the permission-to-send) rules the conversation. There are only two ways to force your way out of this situation: via Send_Error() or Deallocate-Abend (which is pretty drastic). You shouldn't design your applications so that one side needs to steal the permission-to-send from the other. There should be a natural back and forth dialog, as one side sends data, then waits to receive a reply from its partner.

There may be situations, however, where the receiving side would like to become the sender. CPI-C has a call that lets the receiver "beg" to send. It's still up to the sending side to hand off the permission-to-send, but at least it can be designed to check whether the partner is begging or not.

The CPI-C call that lets the receiver beg is named Request_To_Send(). The sending side can check whether the receiver is begging by issuing the Test_Request_To_Send_Received() call. It can also check the returned request_to_send_received parameter on the Send(), Send_Error(), Confirm(), and Receive() calls.

Begging, with the request-to-send signal

There's a classic scenario for using Request_To_Send(). One program is receiving data from its partner. Occasionally, some local event requires this program to send data to its partner, so it must first obtain the permission-to-send. By design, the receiving program issues Request_To_Send(); the sending program (its partner) observes a request-to-send signal and grants the partner the permission-to-send (for example, by using a Receive() call). Eventually, the receiving program observes the CM_SEND_RECEIVED value on the status_received parameter of one of its Receive() calls. The programs have now switched roles.

However, there are a number of programming dilemmas that you must confront when you decide to use Request_To_Send() in a CPI-C application. Each involves some type of race between packets of data through the network.

The first race involves the program that is receiving. There is a race between the local event and data arriving from the partner. If the receiving program issues a Receive-And-Wait, it is suspended until data arrives from the partner. If the local event which caused us to want to send in the first place occurs while the receiving program is suspended, it can't act until its Receive() call is satisfied. If data is guaranteed to arrive fast enough, this is not a problem, but typically there is no such guarantee.

One way around this is to use Receive-Immediate calls in a delay loop. The receiving program issues a Receive-Immediate call to check for data, then it checks for the local event, then it delays a bit and repeats the loop. If data arrives or if the local event occurs, it breaks out of the loop and proceeds as outlined previously.

There are other alternatives. Some platforms allow multiple threads of execution within the same conversation. In this case, a thread detecting the local event can cancel the Receive-and-Wait in the conversation thread, so the conversation thread could wake up and use Request_To_Send().

The bottom line is this: If you're going to use Request_To_Send(), don't let your program get indefinitely suspended in a conversation receive operation.

Now let's take a look at the sending program. Here there is a race between the request-to-send signal coming from the partner and the construction of a record to be sent to the partner. To see this signal, the program must issue one of the four CPI-C calls that returns request_to_send_received (for example, Send_Data()). But if the program is busy building or waiting for the next record, it won't issue a call and therefore won't notice that a request-to-send signal has arrived.

The classic alternative here is for the sending program to issue a Test_Request_To_Send_Received() call occasionally while it is waiting for a record to send. This gives CPI-C a chance to check its internal queues, find the request_to_send_received signal that came from the receiving program, and report it to the sending program. If the Test_Request_To_Send_Received() call returns with CM_OK, the program starts a receive operation to give the partner permission-to-send. If the Test_Request_To_Send_Received() call returns with CM_UNSUCCESSFUL, the program checks to see if it is ready to send a record. If a record is ready, it sends it; otherwise the loop is repeated.

Again, the bottom line is this: If your partner is going to use Request_To_Send() and if your program is not guaranteed to send data fast enough, it must not ignore the conversation while building the next record to send. It must occasionally issue a call and give CPI-C a chance to detect the signal.

Before we go on to the next race, consider this: there is a request_to_send_received parameter on the CPI-C Receive() call. Have you ever wondered why? If your program is receiving, the partner obviously has the permission-to-send! Right? No, wrong!

There are two cases and both involve races.

The first case is simple: It is a race between the permission-to-send "baton" and the partner's local event. In this case, your program sent its last record and then started to receive. But, before the permission-to-send baton arrives at the partner, the local event occurs and the partner program issues its Request_To_Send() call. The request-to-send signal and the permission-to-send baton pass each other in the network.

"So," you say to yourself, "in this case the partner is asking for the permission-to-send when my program has already granted it permission-to-send. I can ignore the request-to-send signal returned on a receive operation. Right?" No, wrong! There is one more nasty race condition.

The final race is between a request-to-send signal and the permission-to-send baton flowing in the same direction. In this scenario, your program sends its last record and issues a Receive() call. The partner program observes the permission-to-send baton, sends some data and then issues its own Receive() call, granting your program the permission-to-send. Then, before your program has a chance to find out it has the permission-to-send, the local event occurs. The partner program issues Request_To_Send() and the request-to-send signal (which is expedited through the network) passes the permission-to-send baton in the network and your program observes the request-to-send signal before it even knows it has the permission-to-send.

This race is particularly nasty because when your program observes the request-to-send signal on a receive operation it cannot tell which case occurred. It might be a request that has already been granted, in which case it can be safely ignored; or it might be a request for the future, in which case it must be remembered and processed the next time your program has the permission-to-send.

You can design your application so that this race never happens. Just make a rule: No program can issue a Request_To_Send() call until it has received at least one record. This will guarantee that a request-to-send signal observed on a receive operation can be safely ignored. Unfortunately, not all applications can live with this rule.

If you can't use the rule that eliminates the nasty race, you must design your applications properly. An application that observes a request-to-send signal on a receive operation must always assume that the nasty race has occurred, remember that the signal has arrived, and process it the next time it has the permission-to-send. If it was not the nasty race that caused the observed signal, the partner will be given the permission-to-send when it does not need it. It must be written to handle this case and recover. Typically, the program recovers by simply starting another receive operation which grants the permission-to-send without sending any data.

After all that, just remember this: If you design your applications so that they never issue a Request_To_Send() call, they never need to look at the request_to_send_received parameters. No examples in this book use Request_To_Send().

Request_To_Send (CMRTS)

The Request_To_Send() call lets a program send a request-to-send signal to its partner. A program can make this call any time after a conversation is allocated. It can issue it in any state, except in the state where it must reply to Confirm(). It does not affect any buffered packets that CPI-C is handling for this conversation, packets not sent or received yet. It does not do the function of a Flush() call.

This call is probably named wrong. It should have been called "Signal_Your_Partner." No matter whether your program is currently the sender or the receiver, this call lets you send an expedited signal through the network to your partner. The partner can decide whether to look for incoming signals, and what it wants to do when it sees one.

Here's the function prototype for the Request_To_Send() call:

```
CM_ENTRY                              /* Request_To_Send            */
cmrts (unsigned char CM_PTR,          /* I: conversation_ID         */
       CM_RETURN_CODE CM_PTR);        /* O: return_code             */
```

This call is fast, since it doesn't wait for any network traffic or buffering. The most likely return code is CM_OK, which means that CPI-C will send a request-to-send signal to the partner program. CM_OK doesn't mean the signal has actually left the local computer or arrived at the partner; it just means that CPI-C will send the signal as soon as it can.

Test_Request_To_Send_Received (CMTRTS)

There are four calls with the request_to_send_received parameter, which tells whether a request-to-send signal has arrived: Send(), Send_Error(), Confirm(), and Receive(). There's another call your programs can issue if they want to see whether this signal has arrived, but don't want to call one of these other four functions: Test_Request_To_Send_Received().

Here's the function prototype for the Test_Request_To_Send_Received() call:

```
CM_ENTRY                          /* Test_Request_To_Send_Received */
cmtrts(unsigned char CM_PTR,         /* I: conversation_ID       */
       CM_REQUEST_TO_SEND_RECEIVED CM_PTR, /* O: RTS_received? */
       CM_RETURN_CODE CM_PTR);       /* O: return_code           */

/* request_to_send_received values */
#define CM_REQ_TO_SEND_NOT_RECEIVED (CM_REQUEST_TO_SEND_RECEIVED)0
#define CM_REQ_TO_SEND_RECEIVED     (CM_REQUEST_TO_SEND_RECEIVED)1
```

This call is fast, since it just checks a local variable that CPI-C is holding. If the request-to-send signal has arrived since the last time the local program checked, CPI-C returns the return code CM_OK and sets the CM_REQ_TO_SEND_RECEIVED value.

BASIC CONVERSATIONS

APPC offers two types of conversations: mapped and basic. Mapped conversations are optimized for the typical transaction programmer. Basic conversations have some additional features that can be valuable for programs that provide a service layer for other programs. A distributed file system is an example of a service layer.

Basic conversations let you do two things that you can't do in mapped conversations. First, you can put more than one logical record inside the data buffer of a Send_Data() call. For example, you can put ten 100-byte records inside a single 1000-byte data buffer, and issue one Send_Data() call. The partner can receive these a record at a time, with ten Receive() calls, or it can get the whole block at once, and break it into its parts. Second, you can have CPI-C write a record to your system's error log file when you issue Send_Error() or Deallocate-Abend. It's the first of these two things that is potentially the most important, but it will involve some extra work to create the logical records and put them into the data buffer.

Our rule of thumb is simple: use mapped conversations. Most applications do not require the use of the extra features of basic conversations. Even many service-layer programs use mapped conversations to achieve the same effect.

The best reason we can think of for using basic conversations is where you have an existing APPC program that's already written using basic conversations. Also, there are two key platforms that still offer only a native APPC programming interface, and offer only basic conversations: base VTAM and the APPC router in the DOS PC Support product. You'll need to set your conversation_type to basic to talk with programs that use these platforms.

Building an LL field

When you're using mapped conversations, it's easy to send data. You just point to the place in memory where you want to begin sending, and say how much you want to send. When you use basic conversations, it's a little more complex—by two bytes. Inside the data you want to send, you need to put a two-byte length field, called the *logical length* (LL). The LL field goes at the beginning of each record, and its length includes its own two bytes.

For example, if you want to send a 100-byte record to your partner, you point to a 102-byte memory block, where the first two bytes are the LL field and contain the value 102. You can put multiple records inside one data buffer, and send them all with one Send_Data() call. To send ten 100-byte records, you'll need a memory block at least 1020 bytes long (10 times 102). You put the 102-byte blocks one after another, with an LL field at the beginning of each record.

Here's the catch, though. The LL field must be in "big endian" format in the data buffer. This means the highest-order byte of the two-byte field is first, followed by the lowest-order byte. Why is this important? Well, if you're used to programming in DOS, Windows, OS/2, or UNIX, you're used to using "little endian" format, where the order of the bytes is reversed. You can't just stick a two-byte integer in the LL field; you have to assure that the number you put in there is in big endian format.

To build an LL field, first assure that your integer has the typedef of unsigned short, a 16-bit integer. The top bit of the LL field has a special meaning, so the length of any individual record can be no more than 32,767 bytes. Actually, since you need to include the LL length itself, the longest data record is only 32,765 bytes.

Here's a portable procedure for creating an LL field. It takes an unsigned short integer as input, and puts the value in big-endian format into a two-byte buffer you've pointed to. If the integer is already in big-endian format, it doesn't change the ordering of the bytes.

```
void
do_build_an_ll(
    const unsigned short integer,
    unsigned char        * buffer,
    const int    continued_record)
{
    assert(buffer != NULL);

    /*------------------------------------------------------------
     * Put the high-order 8 bits in the upper byte.
     *----------------------------------------------------------*/
    buffer[0] = (unsigned char) (integer/256);

    /*------------------------------------------------------------
     * Put the low-order 8 bits in the lower byte.
     *----------------------------------------------------------*/
    buffer[1] = (unsigned char) (integer%256);

    if (continued_record != 0) {
        /*------------------------------------------------------
         * There is more to go on this record.
         * Mask off the top bit of the first byte.
         *----------------------------------------------------*/
```

```
        buffer[0] &= 0x80;
    }
}
```

Set_Fill (CMSF)

You have two choices about how you want to receive data buffers when you're using basic conversations. There can be only one record in a data buffer in mapped conversations. In mapped conversations, when you issue a Receive(), you get back all or part of a single record. In basic conversations, there can be one or many records inside a data buffer. You have the choice of getting all or part of a single record (just like in mapped), or you can ask that the data buffer your program provides be filled. The conversation characteristic used to make this decision is called the *fill;* it takes two values: CM_FILL_LL or CM_FILL_BUFFER.

Let's continue the discussion we started a few paragraphs ago. The sending program is going to send ten 100-byte records with one Send_Data(). It should point to a buffer that is 1020 bytes in length, and assemble all ten records in the buffer, each separated by a 2-byte LL field with the number 102 in it. On the receiving side, let's say we have a 200-byte receive buffer. We'll issue Receive() calls where the requested_length is 200 bytes.

If the fill characteristic is set to CM_FILL_LL, we'll have to issue ten Receive() calls. After each call, we'll get a single record. The received_length will be 102 bytes. The data_received value will say CM_COMPLETE_DATA_RECEIVED.

If fill is set to CM_FILL_BUFFER, it will take only six Receive() calls to receive the entire 1020 bytes. On the first Receive() call, we'll get the first 102-byte record, and 98 bytes of the next one. The data_received value is one that only applies to basic conversations: CM_DATA_RECEIVED.

Here's the function prototype for the Set_Fill() call:

```
CM_ENTRY                              /* Set_Fill              */
cmsf  (unsigned char CM_PTR,          /* I: conversation_ID    */
       CM_FILL CM_PTR,                /* I: fill               */
       CM_RETURN_CODE CM_PTR);        /* O: return_code        */

/*   fill values                                               */
/*   default is CM_FILL_LL                                     */

#define CM_FILL_LL                             (CM_FILL) 0
#define CM_FILL_BUFFER                         (CM_FILL) 1
```

Your program can set the conversation_type to one of two different values:

CM_FILL_LL.   Receive only one record at a time, including its 2-byte LL field. This is the only way Receive() calls work in mapped conversations. This is the default value.

CM_FILL_BUFFER.   Receive as much data as is currently available, up to the requested_length.

Set_Log_Data (CMSLD)

Basic conversations were intended for programs that provide SNA services to other programs. For example, you may have heard about how APPN makes it much easier to set up computers, since it lets the network dynamically find your partner LU across the network. To make this work, APPN internally uses APPC programs to pass the necessary directories and tables among the computers in the network. These programs use basic conversations.

One of the attributes of these programs is that they usually aren't installed by users. They're already set up when APPN is installed. So, what happens when one of these programs encounters an error, since most users never know they're there? When one of these programs has a problem such that it needs to issue Send_Error() or Deallocate-Abend, it logs its problem to both computers' system-error logs. It does this by first setting the log_data conversation characteristic.

If you're writing basic conversations for computers that may be unattended, you may also want to use log_data to track problem determination information.

Here's the function prototype for the Set_Log_Data() call:

```
CM_ENTRY                            /* Set_Log_Data                 */
cmsld (unsigned char CM_PTR,        /* I: conversation_ID           */
       unsigned char CM_PTR,        /* I: log_data                  */
       CM_INT32 CM_PTR,             /* I: log_data_length max 512 */
       CM_RETURN_CODE CM_PTR);      /* O: return_code               */
```

For a description of the format and content of log data, see the "GDS Variables" section of the *SNA Formats* reference, listed in App. D. We've never used log_data in our programs, since we always recommend using mapped conversations.

Building Robust Applications

Five Classic Transactions

You've learned that CPI-C is a conversational programming interface. It was designed so you can readily build a pair of programs that appear to be in conversation with one another.

The conversational model is important since it lets you build *transactions* easily. You are already quite familiar with the concept of a transaction from your personal life. A transaction is simply a "deal" completed by two or more parties. We've left the term "deal" intentionally vague. If we consider computer applications, a deal can be as simple as a message exchange or as complicated as the program interaction needed for a space shuttle launch. Transactions are the reason most commercial applications are written. Transactions are at the heart of all client/server applications.

Communicating programs inevitably exchange more than just data. They also exchange information about the status of the transaction, such as:

- This is a new transaction.
- This transaction is complete.
- This program gives its partner the permission to send.
- This program wants confirmation that all the data sent so far has been received and processed successfully by its partner.
- This program confirms its success. The transaction programs are now synchronized.
- This program wants to report an error and negotiate the recovery.

CPI-C makes it easy to exchange this type of information, as well as data. All the code necessary to manage this information (for example, resource assignment, special record formatting, protocol handling, race resolution, and buffer management) is hidden from your program by CPI-C, rather than being duplicated in every transaction program. This leaves you free to focus on the specific code necessary to complete your transaction.

We looked at several simple transactions in the early chapters of this book. Surprisingly, most of the transactions that do real work can be condensed to the five examples described in this chapter. You will frequently see these classic transactions, alone or in combination, when you look at distributed applications. Lots of programmers are writing transactions like these, even programmers not using CPI-C.

The first transaction, the *pipeline transaction,* sends data from one program to its partner, without waiting to verify that it arrived. The *credit check transaction* builds on the pipeline transaction by acknowledging that the data was received and processed successfully. In the *inquiry transaction,* data is sent, to which the partner replies. The last two transactions are really elaborations on the first three. The *file transfer transaction* looks like an extended form of the credit check, generalized to send bulk data. Finally, the *database update transaction* combines the inquiry and credit check transactions to allow the client to update a database record.

We'll show full source code for each of these transaction pairs. To make the programs shorter, easier to read, and easier to maintain, we'll use many of the "do_" calls we introduced in the previous part of the book. The function prototypes for these calls, as well as the "handle_" calls, are brought in by including file "docpic.h" at the top of these source files.

THE PIPELINE TRANSACTION (DATAGRAM)

The pipeline transaction is typically used to send small messages between applications. This transaction is the simplest to show, yet the hardest to debug and probably the least useful.

The client sends a block of data and then deallocates the conversation; there is no positive acknowledgment of the data. The two programs must find a way to correlate their requests and replies because there is no guarantee that the server completely processed the incoming record. Consider using this transaction in your applications only when the client or server is severely limited in its resources.

The pipeline transaction is often used when a large number of independent units of work need to be done, but it is impossible to allocate enough conversations and sessions so that they can run in parallel. That is, the arrival rate is too large to be handled by the network resources or the server. This can occur when a node contains insufficient storage or when an impossibly large number of transactions must be run in parallel.

In this situation, consider designing your application to use two conversations: one conversation to send data and one conversation to receive data. The application builds a correlator into each data record sent to identify the unit of work it belongs to. The partner returns the correlator in related data records so that the application can correlate the data to the correct unit of work. Effectively, the application is building its own "conversations" on top of the CPI-C conversation pair.

Other common examples of when you might use this kind of transaction involve situations where losing data isn't a problem. For example, you might have one program that regularly sends the current time to other programs. If one of these messages is lost, it's okay, since another will soon follow. Another example involves ongoing status information, such as an application that simulates a stock ticker-tape. You may have even heard this transaction called a "datagram" on some systems.

In Fig. 18.1 we sketch out both sides of the transaction.

We've created two source code files for the pipeline transaction: PIPE.C (the client side) and PIPED.C (the server side). The client side is shown first. You'll see that the source code for the client side is about half the size of the server side (this ratio isn't uncommon).

PIPE.C consists of a main() procedure, which calls many of the procedures we introduced earlier in the book. For example, it calls handle_cpic_rc() and handle_error(), two procedures for doing some simple reporting of unexpected conditions.

The handle_error() procedure, shown in "Simple Error-Handling Procedures" in Chap. 7, uses variable arguments to call vprintf(), flushing its reports to stderr.

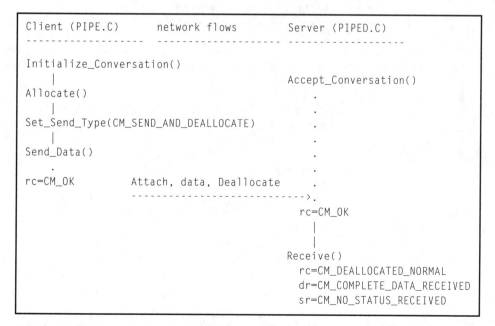

```
Client (PIPE.C)        network flows        Server (PIPED.C)
------------------     --------------------  -------------------

Initialize_Conversation()
    |                                         Accept_Conversation()
Allocate()                                    .
    |                                         .
Set_Send_Type(CM_SEND_AND_DEALLOCATE)         .
    |                                         .
Send_Data()                                   .
    .                                         .
rc=CM_OK        Attach, data, Deallocate      .
                ---------------------------->.
                                         rc=CM_OK
                                             |
                                             |
                                         Receive()
                                         rc=CM_DEALLOCATED_NORMAL
                                         dr=CM_COMPLETE_DATA_RECEIVED
                                         sr=CM_NO_STATUS_RECEIVED
```

Figure 18.1 Pipeline (One-Way Bracket) transaction model.

The getchar() call is used to assure that you see the report. The handle_error() procedure then calls the exit() function, which terminates the entire program. You may choose to add more sophisticated error handling and reporting. If you choose to omit the calls to getchar() and exit(), your program will continue on through its mainline code. Unless you add code to recover from previous errors, your program will likely encounter errors on subsequent CPI-C calls.

Here is the pipeline transaction, client program, file PIPE.C:

```
/*----------------------------------------------------
 *  Pipeline transaction, client side.
 *  (file PIPE.C)
 *------------------------------------------------------*/
#include <cpic.h>              /* conversation API library    */
#include <stdarg.h>            /* variable arguments          */
#include <stdio.h>             /* file I/O                    */
#include <stdlib.h>            /* standard library            */
#include <string.h>            /* strings and memory          */

#include "docpic.h"            /* CPI-C do_ calls             */

int main(int argc, char *argv[])
{
    /*----------------------------------------------------
     *  This side sends a single mapped record, followed by a
     *  Deallocate Flush.
     *------------------------------------------------------*/
    CM_RETURN_CODE  cpic_return_code;
    unsigned char   conversation_ID[CM_CID_SIZE];

    /*----------------------------------------------------
     *  Get the symbolic destination from the command line and
     *  initialize a conversation.
     *------------------------------------------------------*/
    if (argc > 1) { /* is there at least one argument? */
        do_initialize_conversation(conversation_ID, argv[1]);
    }
    else {
        handle_error(
            conversation_ID,
            "A symbolic destination name must be provided");
    }

    /*----------------------------------------------------
     *  Allocate a session for this conversation.
     *------------------------------------------------------*/
    do_allocate(conversation_ID);

    /*----------------------------------------------------
     *  Couple a Deallocate Flush with this single Send_Data(),
```

```
 *    using a Set_Send_Type() call.
 *--------------------------------------------------------------*/
{
    CM_SEND_TYPE send_type = CM_SEND_AND_DEALLOCATE;

    cmsst(                      /* Set_Send_Type              */
        conversation_ID,        /* conversation ID            */
        &send_type,             /* set the send type          */
        &cpic_return_code);     /* return code from this call */
    if (cpic_return_code != CM_OK) {
        handle_cpic_rc(
            conversation_ID,
            cpic_return_code,
            "CMSST");
    }
}


/*--------------------------------------------------------------
 *   This is where your program prepares the data record
 *   that should be sent on this pipeline transaction.
 *--------------------------------------------------------------*/
{
    unsigned char *data_buffer =
        "Test of the Pipeline transaction";
    CM_INT32 send_length = (CM_INT32)strlen(data_buffer);

    do_send_data(
        conversation_ID,    /* conversation ID            */
        data_buffer,        /* send this buffer           */
        send_length);       /* length to send             */
}

    return EXIT_SUCCESS;        /* program was successful     */
}
```

The main() procedure expects the symbolic destination name to be passed as the first command line parameter; thus, if present, the symbolic destination name should be found in argv[1] and argc should be at least 2. The call to do_initialize_conversation() assures that the symbolic destination name is copied correctly and padded on the right with blanks, if it's shorter than 8 bytes. It also gets a conversation ID and commits to using the symbolic destination name. The do_allocate() call obtains a session to be used for a conversation. If the CPI-C return code is anything but CM_OK, do_allocate() calls procedure handle_cpic_rc() to display the unexpected return code and exit the program.

The most interesting call in the client is the single call to do_send_data(), which in turn issues Send_Data(). By its nature, the pipeline transaction is designed to send a single, mapped data record and then end the conversation. Since we know that the next call will be Deallocate(), we can couple this function on the Send_Data() call by setting the send_type to CM_SEND_AND_ DEALLOCATE.

The client program points to the data it wants to send, and sets the send_length parameter with the length of that data block. In this example, we've sent a short string to the partner, so we can see whether the transaction works when we test it.

When you run PIPE, you'll see that it runs quickly, since there is not even an acknowledgment that the partner program exists. The operation of this transaction is truly pipelined. So, while the client side runs fine, the server side may never even get started. This is not a good pair of programs for casually testing whether a pair of machines is set up right, since you can't tell from the client side whether the server's TP definition is correct. Be sure to watch both sides carefully the first few times you try this program in any new configuration. Here's the pipeline transaction, server program, file PIPED.C:

```
/*---------------------------------------------------------------
 *  Pipeline transaction, server side.
 *  (file PIPED.C)
 *-------------------------------------------------------------*/
#include <cpic.h>              /* conversation API library   */
#include <limits.h>            /* integer bounds             */
#include <stdio.h>             /* file I/O                   */
#include <stdlib.h>            /* standard library           */
#include <string.h>            /* strings and memory         */

#include "docpic.h"            /* CPI C do_ calls, BOOL      */


/*---------------------------------------------------------------
 *  The larger a receive size you can afford, the faster your
 *  overall performance.
 *-------------------------------------------------------------*/
#define BUFFER_SIZE  (32767)    /* largest possible record    */

int main(void)
{
    /*---------------------------------------------------------
     *  The client side should have sent a single record,
     *  followed by a Deallocate Flush.
     *
     *  We've arbitrarily bounded the size of the incoming
     *  record to 32767 bytes.
     *-------------------------------------------------------*/
    unsigned char   conversation_ID[CM_CID_SIZE];

    CM_INT32        received_length;
    unsigned char * data_buffer;

    /*---------------------------------------------------------
     *  Accept a new conversation from the client.
```

```
 *
 *  We assume (without explicitly checking) that the
 *  conversation_type is MAPPED and the sync_level is NONE.
 *  The TP definition should restrict these values, which
 *  will then be verified by the attach manager.
 *------------------------------------------------------------*/
do_accept_conversation(conversation_ID);

/*------------------------------------------------------------
 *  Allocate enough memory for whatever you expect to
 *  receive from the partner.
 *------------------------------------------------------------*/
data_buffer - (unsigned char *)malloc((size_t)BUFFER_SIZE);
if (NULL == data_buffer) {
    handle_error(
        conversation_ID,
        "Can't get %u bytes of memory for a data_buffer",
        (unsigned)BUFFER_SIZE);
}

/*------------------------------------------------------------
 *  Call do_receive_pipe(), which expects a single
 *  data record followed by a return code of
 *  CM_DEALLOCATED_NORMAL.
 *------------------------------------------------------------*/
do_receive_pipe(
    conversation_ID,
    data_buffer,
    BUFFER_SIZE,            /* buffer size              */
    &received_length);      /* bytes received           */

/*------------------------------------------------------------
 *  This is where your program processes the received data.
 *  For this example, we just display it, using fwrite().
 *------------------------------------------------------------*/
if (received_length > 0) {
    (void)fwrite((void *)data_buffer, 1,
            (size_t)received_length, stdout);
}
else {
    handle_error(
        conversation_ID,
        "No data was sent");
}

(void)printf("\nPress Enter to end the program\n");
(void)getchar();

return EXIT_SUCCESS;           /* program was successful    */
}
```

On the server side, no command line parameters are required. The first call in the main() procedure is to accept the conversation. This call "blocks," that is, it waits until it connects with a conversation started by the client. If PIPED was started by the attach manager because of an incoming Attach, the Accept_Conversation() call returns almost immediately.

The important work on the server side is done within the do_receive_pipe() call, which we introduced in "Procedure do_receive_pipe()" in Chap. 14. This procedure expects its partner to send a single record and then to deallocate the conversation. If any other data or information is received, do_receive_pipe() handles it as an error condition. This frees the PIPED program from checking the return values itself; PIPED just processes the data buffer returned by do_receive_pipe().

THE CREDIT CHECK TRANSACTION (CONFIRMED DELIVERY)

In the credit check transaction, you send a piece of data to a partner, and wait for an acknowledgment. The acknowledgment consists of a simple Yes or No. This transaction is the quickest way to find out whether the partner thinks a piece of data is good or not.

The credit check transaction can be used when a client program wants to perform a specified function, and the probability that the server will grant permission is much higher than the probability that the server will not grant permission. No data is returned by the server; the server just acknowledges that the data sent by the client program was successfully received and processed.

This transaction was named for its most common usage: doing credit checks. The client program builds a credit check record, sends the record to the credit check server, and requests a confirmation. If the credit check is okay (the usual case), no reply is necessary; the server needs only to grant the confirmation. If the credit check is not successful (a rare case), the server rejects the confirmation by reporting an error and sending an error record that explains why the credit check failed. Notice that, in the usual case, only a confirmation returns to the client.

The server does not have to send an explicit reply if the transaction can be processed successfully. Because a reply does not have to be formatted, sent, or received, the overhead and turnaround time is minimized. On the other hand, the error case creates an additional flow in addition to the reply. This is an acceptable trade-off if the error case is rare enough. If the normal case occurs frequently enough (a rule of thumb is 90 percent of the time or better), the credit check transaction performs better than the inquiry transaction.

This type of transaction is also good for the following situations:

- *Confirmed delivery.* A client program needs to send information to the server and needs a guarantee that the information has been successfully received and processed. An excellent example of confirmed delivery is an e-mail program. When your local program sends the message, your program

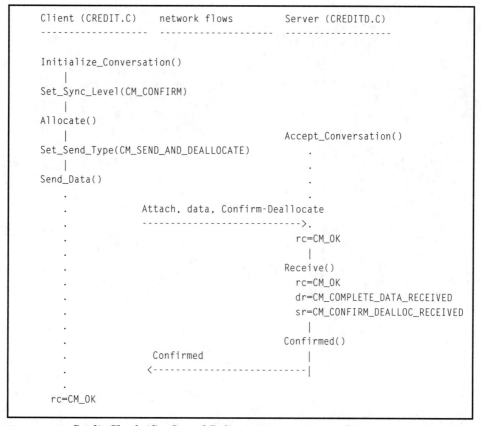

```
Client (CREDIT.C)     network flows        Server (CREDITD.C)
-------------------   --------------------  -------------------


Initialize_Conversation()
   |
Set_Sync_Level(CM_CONFIRM)
   |
Allocate()
   |                                        Accept_Conversation()
Set_Send_Type(CM_SEND_AND_DEALLOCATE)       .
   |                                        .
Send_Data()                                 .
   .                                        .
   .        Attach, data, Confirm-Deallocate
   .        ---------------------------->.
   .                                       rc=CM_OK
   .                                          |
   .                                       Receive()
   .                                         rc=CM_OK
   .                                         dr=CM_COMPLETE_DATA_RECEIVED
   .                                         sr=CM_CONFIRM_DEALLOC_RECEIVED
   .                                          |
   .                                       Confirmed()
   .              Confirmed                   |
   .        <---------------------------|
   .
  rc=CM_OK
```

Figure 18.2 Credit Check (Confirmed Delivery) transaction model.

waits until the message has been saved (that is, written to the disk) of the e-mail server, which then confirms its delivery.*

- *Permission.*   A client program needs permission from a controlling server before it can continue.

- *Polls.*   This is used for applications wanting to know simply "Are you there?" The reply shows "Yes, I am here."

In Fig. 18.2 we sketch out both sides of the transaction.

There are two source code files for the credit check transaction: CREDIT.C (the client side) and CREDITD.C (the server side). The client side is shown first, on the following page.

---

* Many e-mail programs let you send your message and continue working even though the receipt of the message has not been confirmed. Usually, the e-mail program is still waiting for an acknowledgment that the message was successfully delivered to the destination mailbox.

```
/*-------------------------------------------------------------
 *  Credit check transaction, client side.
 *  (file CREDIT.C)
 *-----------------------------------------------------------*/
#include <cpic.h>               /* conversation API library   */
#include <stdarg.h>             /* variable arguments         */
#include <stdio.h>              /* file I/O                   */
#include <stdlib.h>             /* standard library           */
#include <string.h>             /* strings and memory         */

#include "docpic.h"             /* CPI-C do_ calls            */

int main(int argc, char *argv[])
{
    /*-----------------------------------------------------------
     *  This side sends a single mapped record, followed by a
     *  Confirm-Deallocate, to assure it was received.
     *---------------------------------------------------------*/
    CM_RETURN_CODE  cpic_return_code;
    unsigned char   conversation_ID[CM_CID_SIZE];

    /*-----------------------------------------------------------
     *  Get the symbolic destination from the command line and
     *  initialize a conversation.
     *---------------------------------------------------------*/
    if (argc > 1) { /* is there at least one argument? */
        do_initialize_conversation(conversation_ID, argv[1]);
    }
    else {
        handle_error(
            conversation_ID,
            "A symbolic destination name must be provided");
    }

    /*-----------------------------------------------------------
     *  Set the sync_level to CONFIRM.
     *---------------------------------------------------------*/
    do_sync_level_confirm(conversation_ID);

    /*-----------------------------------------------------------
     *  Allocate a session for this conversation.
     *---------------------------------------------------------*/
    do_allocate(conversation_ID);

    /*-----------------------------------------------------------
     *  Couple a Confirm-Deallocate with this single Send_Data(),
     *  using a Set_Send_Type() call.
     *---------------------------------------------------------*/
    {
        CM_SEND_TYPE send_type = CM_SEND_AND_DEALLOCATE;
```

```
    cmsst(                      /* Set_Send_Type               */
        conversation_ID,        /* conversation ID             */
        &send_type,             /* set the send type           */
        &cpic_return_code);     /* return code from this call  */
    if (cpic_return_code != CM_OK) {
        handle_cpic_rc(
            conversation_ID, cpic_return_code, "CMSST");
    }
}


/*-------------------------------------------------------------
 *  This is where your program prepares the data record
 *  that should be sent on this transaction.
 *-----------------------------------------------------------*/
{
    unsigned char *data_buffer =
        "Test of the Credit Check transaction";
    CM_INT32 send_length = (CM_INT32)strlen(data_buffer);

    do_send_data(
        conversation_ID,        /* conversation ID             */
        data_buffer,            /* send this buffer            */
        send_length);           /* length to send              */
}


/*-------------------------------------------------------------
 *  Two return codes are expected:
 *  - CM_OK (indicating that the partner received and
 *      processed the data successfully), or
 *  - CM_PROGRAM_ERROR_PURGING (indicating that the partner
 *      did NOT receive and process the data successfully)
 *-----------------------------------------------------------*/
switch (cpic_return_code) {
  case CM_OK:
    /*-------------------------------------------------------
     *  The partner is happy and the conversation has
     *  been deallocated.
     *-----------------------------------------------------*/
    break;

  case CM_PROGRAM_ERROR_PURGING:
    /*-------------------------------------------------------
     *  The partner is not happy with the data, and
     *  replied with a Send_Error.  Issue a Receive() to
     *  get the expected DEALLOCATED_NORMAL return code.
     *-----------------------------------------------------*/
    (void)fprintf(stderr,
        "The partner encountered a problem "
        "and issued Send_Error.\n");

    {
```

```
            CM_INT32         zero_length = (CM_INT32)0;
            CM_INT32         received_length;
            CM_STATUS_RECEIVED status_received;
            CM_DATA_RECEIVED_TYPE data_received;
            CM_REQUEST_TO_SEND_RECEIVED rts_received;

            cmrcv (                        /* Receive              */
                conversation_ID,  /* conversation ID      */
                NULL,             /* no data is expected  */
                &zero_length,     /* maximum receive length */
                &data_received,   /* returned data_rcvd   */
                &received_length, /* received data length */
                &status_received, /* returned status_rcvd */
                &rts_received,    /* did partner RTS?     */
                &cpic_return_code); /* return code        */
            if (CM_DEALLOCATED_NORMAL != cpic_return_code) {
                handle_cpic_rc(
                    conversation_ID, cpic_return_code, "CMRCV");
            }
        }
        break;

    default:
      handle_cpic_rc(
          conversation_ID, cpic_return_code, "CMDEAL");
      break;
    }
    return EXIT_SUCCESS;           /* program was successful    */
}
```

This program starts like PIPE.C, but adds a call to set the sync_level of the conversation to CONFIRM. The Set_Send_Type() call causes CPI-C to combine the functions of a confirmation and a conditional deallocate with the Send_Data() call. Thus, when the do_send_data() procedure issues Send_Data(), the client side blocks, waiting for a response from its partner. If the server successfully receives and processes the data, it issues Confirmed(). The client side sees a CM_OK return code and the conversation is over.

Otherwise, the server issues a Send_Error() call, which is reflected in the client by a CM_PROGRAM_ERROR_PURGING return code. The final call to Receive() in this program is there to get the CM_DEALLOCATED_NORMAL return code. Since it's not looking for any data, the requested_length is set to 0, which means the pointer to the data_buffer is ignored; so we've set it to NULL. Here's the credit check transaction, server program, file CREDITD.C:

```
/*------------------------------------------------------------
 * Credit check transaction, server side.
 * (file CREDITD.C)
 *----------------------------------------------------------*/
```

```
#include <cpic.h>              /* conversation API library  */
#include <stdio.h>             /* file I/O                  */
#include <stdlib.h>            /* standard library          */
#include <time.h>              /* time                      */

#include "docpic.h"            /* CPI-C do_ calls, BOOL     */

/*---------------------------------------------------------------
 *  The larger a receive size you can afford, the faster your
 *  overall performance.
 *-------------------------------------------------------------*/
#define BUFFER_SIZE (32767)    /* largest possible record   */

int main(void)
{
    /*-----------------------------------------------------------
     *  The client side should have sent a single record,
     *  followed by a Deallocate-Confirm.
     *
     *  We've arbitrarily bounded the size of the incoming
     *  record to 32767 bytes.
     *---------------------------------------------------------*/
    unsigned char   conversation_ID[CM_CID_SIZE];
    CM_RETURN_CODE  cpic_return_code;

    CM_INT32        received_length;
    int             ok_to_confirm;
    unsigned char * data_buffer;

    /*-----------------------------------------------------------
     *  Accept a new conversation from the client.
     *
     *  We assume (without explicitly checking) that the
     *  conversation_type is MAPPED, and the
     *  sync_level is CONFIRM.
     *  The TP definition should restrict these values, which
     *  will then be verified by the attach manager.
     *---------------------------------------------------------*/
    do_accept_conversation(conversation_ID);

    /*-----------------------------------------------------------
     *  Allocate enough memory for whatever you expect to
     *  receive from the partner...
     *---------------------------------------------------------*/
    data_buffer = (unsigned char *)malloc((size_t)BUFFER_SIZE);
    if (NULL == data_buffer) {
    handle_error(
            conversation_ID,
            "Can't allocate %lu bytes for data_buffer",
            (unsigned long)BUFFER_SIZE);
    }
```

```
/*-------------------------------------------------------------
 *  Call do_receive_credit(), which expects a single
 *  data record followed by a status_received value
 *  CM_CONFIRM_DEALLOC_RECEIVED.
 *-------------------------------------------------------------*/
do_receive_credit(
    conversation_ID,
    data_buffer,
    BUFFER_SIZE,              /* buffer size                   */
    &received_length);        /* bytes received                */


/*-------------------------------------------------------------
 *  When we get here, we should be in Confirm-Deallocate
 *  state.
 *
 *  This is where your program processes the received data.
 *  For this example, we randomly decide if it's good or
 *  not, and display the result of the decision.
 *-------------------------------------------------------------*/
srand((unsigned int)time(NULL));
ok_to_confirm = rand() % 4;

if (ok_to_confirm) {
    fwrite((void *)data_buffer, (size_t)1,
        (size_t)received_length, stdout);
    (void)printf("\nPress Enter to issue Confirmed\n");
}
else {
    (void)printf("Credit Check transaction failed randomly");
    (void)printf("\nPress Enter to issue Send_Error\n");
}

(void)getchar();

/*-------------------------------------------------------------
 *  Decide whether to Confirm or not.
 *-------------------------------------------------------------*/
if (ok_to_confirm) {
    /*-------------------------------------------------------------
     *  The data that was sent has been successfully received
     *  and processed.  Replying with Confirmed() will cause
     *  the conversation to be deallocated.
     *-------------------------------------------------------------*/
    do_confirmed(conversation_ID);
}
else {
    /*-------------------------------------------------------------
     *  The data that was sent was NOT successfully received
     *  and processed.  Replying with Send_Error() notifies
```

```
    *  the client that there was a problem, and gives us
    *  the permission to send.  The conversation is not
    *  automatically deallocated.
    *-------------------------------------------------------*/
   do_send_error(conversation_ID);


   /*-----------------------------------------------------------
    *  Do a Deallocate-Flush of the conversation.
    *  We have to set the deallocate_type first, since the
    *  default type is SYNC_LEVEL, and the sync_level of
    *  this conversation is CONFIRM, not NONE.
    *-------------------------------------------------------*/
   {
       CM_DEALLOCATE_TYPE deallocate_type =
           CM_DEALLOCATE_FLUSH;

       cmsdt(                       /* Set Deallocate Type    */
           conversation_ID,         /* conversation ID        */
           &deallocate_type,        /* deallocate type        */
           &cpic_return_code);      /* return code            */
       if (cpic_return_code != CM_OK) {
           handle_cpic_rc(
               conversation_ID, cpic_return_code, "CMSDT");
       }
   }

       cmdeal(                      /* Deallocate             */
           conversation_ID,         /* conversation ID        */
           &cpic_return_code);      /* return code            */
       if (cpic_return_code != CM_OK) {
           handle_cpic_rc(
               conversation_ID, cpic_return_code, "CMDEAL");
       }
   }
   return EXIT_SUCCESS;             /* program was successful  */
}
```

The server side of the credit check transaction uses the do_receive_credit()
procedure we saw earlier in "Procedure do_receive_credit()" in Chap. 14. In the
credit check transaction, the deallocation of the conversation is conditional upon
the confirmation by the server. The do_receive_credit() procedure expects a data
record and a status_received value of CM_CONFIRM_DEALLOC_RECEIVED.

At this point, the client has declared that it has sent everything it has to
send, and the server must decide whether it has successfully received and processed what was sent—and reply with Yes or No.

To simulate these two conditions in this example, we've constructed a call to
C's rand() function, with a modulo of 4 (arbitrarily picked). If the returned
value is 0, we decide the processing has failed; otherwise it's okay to confirm.

If it is okay, the server issues Confirmed() and the conversation is over. If not, it issues Send_Error(), which overrides the client's conditional deallocation of the conversation and gives the server permission to send. In a more robust application, it would send a record describing why it issued the Send_Error() call.

In this transaction, the server simply deallocates the conversation, with deallocate_type of FLUSH. The deallocate_type needs to be explicitly set to CM_DEALLOCATE_FLUSH, since the default deallocate_type for any conversation is SYNC_LEVEL. The sync_level conversation characteristic, which was received from the client program in the Attach, is CONFIRM.

THE INQUIRY TRANSACTION (REQUEST AND REPLY)

The inquiry transaction is typically used by the client to request information from a server. Here, in contrast to the credit check transaction, we're looking to receive more information than just Yes or No. This transaction is also known as "request and reply," because the entire conversation is made up of one request and one reply. A client sends a request to a server, which computes the answer and replies.

Inquiry transactions are frequently used by banks and retailers. For example, it is used to create the transaction "How much is in my account, given my account number?" This type of transaction is also good for the following situations:

- *Remote procedure calls.*   A client program sends a subroutine call request to a server program. The server program performs the subroutine and returns the result.

- *Database applications.*   A client program sends a set of keys to the database server, which then returns the data records selected.

- *Status queries.*   A client program wants to know "Are you there, and what is your status?"

In Fig. 18.3 we illustrate both sides of the transaction. Several parameters for these calls are not shown (such as the buffer parameters), to emphasize the parameters that express the essence of the transaction.

Two source code files comprise the inquiry transaction: INQUIRY.C (the client side) and INQUIRYD.C (the server side). The client side is shown first. Here's the inquiry transaction, client program, file INQUIRY.C:

```
/*---------------------------------------------------------------
 *  Inquiry transaction, client side.
 *  (file INQUIRY.C)
 *-------------------------------------------------------------*/
#include <cpic.h>          /* conversation API library   */
#include <stdarg.h>        /* variable arguments         */
```

```
   Client (INQUIRY.C)   network flows    Server (INQUIRYD.C)
   ------------------    ---------------   -------------------


   Initialize_Conversation()
       |
   Allocate()
       |                                  Accept_Conversation()
   Send_Data()                              .
       |                                    .
   Receive()                                .
       .          Attach, data, Send        .
       .       -------------------------->.
       .                           rc=CM_OK
       .                               |
       .                           Receive()
       .                             rc=CM_OK
       .                             dr=CM_COMPLETE_DATA_RECEIVED
       .                             sr=CM_SEND_RECEIVED
       .                               |
       .                           Set_Send_Type(CM_SEND_AND_DEALLOCATE)
       .                               |
       .                           Send_Data()
       .                               |
       .          data, Deallocate      |
       .        <-------------------------|
   rc=CM_DEALLOCATED_NORMAL
   dr=CM_COMPLETE_DATA_RECEIVED
   sr=CM_NO_STATUS_RECEIVED
```

Figure 18.3 Inquiry (Request and Reply) transaction model.

```
#include <stdio.h>              /* file I/O               */
#include <stdlib.h>             /* standard library       */
#include <string.h>             /* strings and memory     */

#include "docpic.h"             /* CPI-C do_ calls, BOOL   */

/*------------------------------------------------------------------
 *  The larger a receive size you can afford, the faster your
 *  overall performance.
 *------------------------------------------------------------------*/
#define BUFFER_SIZE  (32767)    /* largest possible record */

int main(int argc, char *argv[])
{
```

```
/*------------------------------------------------------------
 *  This side sends a single mapped record, then waits to
 *  receive a single mapped record and Deallocate-Normal
 *  from its partner.
 *
 *  We've arbitrarily bounded the size of the incoming
 *  record to 32767 bytes.
 *------------------------------------------------------------*/
unsigned char   conversation_ID[CM_CID_SIZE];

CM_INT32        received_length;
unsigned char * data_buffer;

/*------------------------------------------------------------
 *  Get the symbolic destination from the command line and
 *  initialize a conversation.
 *------------------------------------------------------------*/
if (argc > 1) { /* is there at least one argument? */
    do_initialize_conversation(conversation_ID, argv[1]);
}
else {
    handle_error(
        conversation_ID,
        "A symbolic destination name must be provided");
}

/*■■■■■■■■■■■■■■■■■
 *  Allocate a session for this conversation.
 *------------------------------------------------------------*/
do_allocate(conversation_ID);

/*------------------------------------------------------------
 *  This is where your program prepares the data record
 *  that should be sent on this transaction.
 *------------------------------------------------------------*/
{
    unsigned char *send_buffer =
            "Test of the Inquiry transaction";
    CM_INT32 send_length = (CM_INT32)strlen(send_buffer);

    do_send_data(
        conversation_ID,    /* conversation ID          */
        send_buffer,        /* send this buffer         */
        send_length);       /* length to send           */
}

/*------------------------------------------------------------
 *  Allocate enough memory for whatever you expect to
 *  receive from the partner...
 *------------------------------------------------------------*/
data_buffer = (unsigned char *)malloc((size_t)BUFFER_SIZE);
```

```
        if (NULL == data_buffer) {
            handle_error(
                conversation_ID,
                "Can't allocate %lu bytes for data_buffer",
                (unsigned long)BUFFER_SIZE);
        }

        /*------------------------------------------------------------
         * The receiving the reply looks like the server side
         * of the PIPE transaction; we receive a record
         * and DEALLOCATED_NORMAL.
         *----------------------------------------------------------*/
        do_receive_pipe(
            conversation_ID,
            data_buffer,
            BUFFER_SIZE,              /* buffer size              */
            &received_length);       /* bytes received           */

        /*------------------------------------------------------------
         * This is where your program processes the received data.
         * For this example, we just display it, using fwrite().
         *----------------------------------------------------------*/
        (void)fwrite((void *)data_buffer, (size_t)1,
                (size_t)received_length, stdout);
        (void)printf("\nPress Enter to end the program\n");
        (void)getchar();

        return EXIT_SUCCESS;         /* program was successful    */
    }
```

Constructing the code for the inquiry transaction was easy; it consists of the code from the client side of the pipeline transaction followed by the code from its server side. At the point that the pipeline client ends by issuing a Deallocate() call, the inquiry client executes the logic for a receive loop—in fact, it's the same code as in the server side of the pipeline transaction. The change from sending to receiving causes the permission-to-send to be handed from the client to the server. Here's the inquiry transaction, server program, file INQUIRYD.C:

```
    /*------------------------------------------------------------
     * Inquiry transaction, server side.
     * (file INQUIRYD.C)
     *----------------------------------------------------------*/
    #include <cpic.h>                /* conversation API library  */
    #include <stdio.h>               /* file I/O                  */
    #include <stdlib.h>              /* standard library          */
    #include <string.h>              /* strings and memory        */

    #include "docpic.h"              /* CPI-C do_ calls, BOOL     */
```

```
/*-------------------------------------------------------------
 *  The larger a receive size you can afford, the faster your
 *  overall performance.
 *-----------------------------------------------------------*/
#define BUFFER_SIZE  (32767)     /* largest possible record    */

int main(void)
{
    /*-------------------------------------------------------------
     *  The client side should have sent a single record, and
     *  then be waiting for a record in reply and Deallocate.
     *
     *  We've arbitrarily bounded the size of the incoming
     *  record to 32767 bytes.
     *-----------------------------------------------------------*/
    unsigned char   conversation_ID[CM_CID_SIZE];
    CM_RETURN_CODE  cpic_return_code;

    CM_INT32        received_length;
    unsigned char * data_buffer;

    /*-------------------------------------------------------------
     *  Accept a new conversation from the client.
     *
     *  We assume (without explicitly checking) that the
     *  conversation_type is MAPPED and the sync_level is NONE.
     *  The TP definition should restrict these values, which
     *  will then be verified by the attach manager.
     *-----------------------------------------------------------*/
    do_accept_conversation(conversation_ID);

    /*-------------------------------------------------------------
     *  Allocate enough memory for whatever you expect to
     *  receive from the partner...
     *-----------------------------------------------------------*/
    data_buffer = (unsigned char *)malloc((size_t)BUFFER_SIZE);
    if (NULL == data_buffer) {
        handle_error(
            conversation_ID,
            "Can't allocate %lu bytes for data_buffer",
            (unsigned long)BUFFER_SIZE);
    }

    /*-------------------------------------------------------------
     *  Call do_receive_inquiry(), which expects a single
     *  data record followed by a status_received value of
     *  CM_SEND_RECEIVED.
     *-----------------------------------------------------------*/
    do_receive_inquiry(
        conversation_ID,
```

```
            data_buffer,
            BUFFER_SIZE,            /* buffer size                   */
            &received_length);     /* bytes received                */

/*--------------------------------------------------------------
 *  When we get here, we should be in Send state.
 *------------------------------------------------------------*/
if (received_length > 0) {
    (void)fwrite((void *)data_buffer, 1,
              (size_t)received_length, stdout);
}
else {
    handle_error(
        conversation_ID,
        "No data was sent");
}
(void)printf("\nPress Enter to reply and deallocate\n");

(void)getchar();

/*--------------------------------------------------------------
 *  Couple a Deallocate Flush with this single Send_Data(),
 *  using a Set_Send_Type() call.
 *------------------------------------------------------------*/
{
    CM_SEND_TYPE send_type = CM_SEND_AND_DEALLOCATE;

    cmsst(                     /* Set_Send_Type                 */
        conversation_ID,       /* conversation ID               */
        &send_type,            /* set the send type             */
        &cpic_return_code);    /* return code from this call    */
    if (cpic_return_code != CM_OK) {
        handle_cpic_rc(
            conversation_ID,
            cpic_return_code,
            "CMSST");
    }
}

/*--------------------------------------------------------------
 *  This is where your program prepares the data reply
 *  that should be sent on this inquiry transaction.
 *------------------------------------------------------------*/
{
    unsigned char *send_buffer =
        "Reply to the Inquiry transaction";
    CM_INT32 send_length = (CM_INT32)strlen(send_buffer);

    do_send_data(
        conversation_ID,     /* conversation ID               */
```

```
                    data_buffer,          /* send this buffer        */
                    send_length);         /* length to send          */
        }

    return EXIT_SUCCESS;      /* program was successful   */
    }
```

The server side of the inquiry is similarly easy to construct; it consists of the server side of the pipeline transaction followed by its client side. The do_receive_inquiry() that starts this side looks for the change to **Send** state (in the status_received parameter), instead of looking for a return code of CM_DEALLOCATED_NORMAL. After completing do_receive_inquiry(), it executes the code to send a reply and Deallocate-Flush, ending the conversation.

THE FILE TRANSFER (BATCH SEND)

This transaction is an extended version of the credit check transaction. As discussed in Chap. 9, your programs do not need to be concerned about record sizes to optimize links and transmission speeds. The client and server simply send and receive records; buffer sizes for each side of the application don't have to be matched at all.

The file transfer transaction is typically used to send large amounts of data from one location to another. It is used in situations where several related data records need to be moved. For example, applications that do software distribution use this type of transaction to distribute files.

In this transaction, the client uses one or more Send_Data() calls to transfer the contents of a file. When all records have been sent, the client issues a Confirm(), to assure all have been successfully received and processed. The server receives data with a loop of Receive() calls until it is clear that there is no more data to receive. It then confirms that it received and processed everything successfully.

This is a good place to illustrate how your application can determine the kind of session it gets. The transactions we've shown so far use the mode name that was set up for them in the local side information. Presumably the side information has been set up to use the mode named #INTER, to obtain a session suitable for interactive traffic. A file transfer application doesn't necessarily need quick response time; it can use a session that is suitable for batch traffic. The client program guides the underlying network software in obtaining a session for batch traffic by choosing the mode named #BATCH.

In Figure 18.4 we show both sides of the transaction.

Two programs, FILEX.C and FILEXD.C, constitute the client and server sides of the transaction, respectively. The client side is shown first, beginning on p. 234.

```
    Client (FILEX.C)    network flows        Server (FILEXD.C)
    -----------------   --------------------  -------------------


    Initialize_Conversation()
        |
    Set_Sync_Level(CM_CONFIRM)
        |
    Set_Mode_Name("#BATCH")
        |
    Allocate()
        |                                      Accept_Conversation()
    DO UNTIL all data is sent or               .
            an error is encountered            .
        |                                      .
      Send_Data()                              .
        |           Attach, data               .
        |           -------------------------->.
        |                         rc=CM_OK
        |                             |
        |                         DO ---
        |                             |
        |                         Receive()
        |                                      .
        |           data                       .
        |           -------------------------->.
        |                                      .
    ENDDO                                      .
        |                                      .
    Deallocate()                               .
        .           data, Confirm-Deallocate   .
        .           ------------------------->
        .                         WHILE (rc=CM_OK and
        .                             sr=CM_NO_STATUS_RECEIVED)
        .                                      .
        .                         rc=CM_OK
        .                         sr=CM_CONFIRM_DEALLOC_RECEIVED
        .                             |
        .                         Confirmed()
        .           Confirmed                  |
        .           <-------------------------|
        .
      rc=CM_OK
```

Figure 18.4 File Transfer (Batch Send) transaction model.

```
/*--------------------------------------------------------------
 *  File transfer transaction, client side.
 *  (file FILEX.C)
 *--------------------------------------------------------------*/
#include <cpic.h>              /* conversation API library   */
#include <stdarg.h>            /* variable arguments         */
#include <stdio.h>             /* file I/O                   */
#include <stdlib.h>            /* standard library           */
#include <string.h>            /* strings and memory         */

#include "docpic.h"            /* CPI-C do_ calls            */

#define DEFAULT_SEND_SIZE    (1000000)
#define SEND_BUFFER_SIZE     ((size_t)(32763))

int main(int argc, char *argv[])
{
    /*----------------------------------------------------------
     *  This side sends some number of bytes, followed by
     *  Confirm-Deallocate, to ensure they were received.
     *----------------------------------------------------------*/
    unsigned char    conversation_ID[CM_CID_SIZE];
    CM_RETURN_CODE   cpic_return_code;

    long             amount_to_send;
    long             offset;
    unsigned char *  send_buffer;

    /*----------------------------------------------------------
     *  Get the symbolic destination from the command line and
     *  initialize a conversation.
     *----------------------------------------------------------*/
    if (argc > 1) { /* is there at least one argument? */
        do_initialize_conversation(conversation_ID, argv[1]);
    }
    else {
        handle_error(
            conversation_ID,
            "A symbolic destination name must be provided");
    }

    /*----------------------------------------------------------
     *  Get a length to send from the command line, or use the
     *  default value.
     *----------------------------------------------------------*/
    if (argc > 2) { /* is there at least two arguments? */
        amount_to_send = atol(argv[2]);
    }
    else {
        amount_to_send = DEFAULT_SEND_SIZE;
```

```
}
setbuf(stdout, NULL);                      /* don't buffer I/O */

/*-------------------------------------------------------------
 *  Set the sync_level to CONFIRM.
 *-----------------------------------------------------------*/
do_sync_level_confirm(conversation_ID);

/*-------------------------------------------------------------
 *  Set the mode_name to #BATCH, for batch traffic.
 *-----------------------------------------------------------*/
do_set_mode_name(conversation_ID, "#BATCH");

/*-------------------------------------------------------------
 *  Allocate a session for this conversation.
 *-----------------------------------------------------------*/
do_allocate(conversation_ID);

/*-------------------------------------------------------------
 *  Get memory for the send buffer.
 *-----------------------------------------------------------*/
send_buffer = (unsigned char *)malloc(SEND_BUFFER_SIZE);
if (send_buffer != NULL) {
    /* set the buffer to all q's, just so there's something*/
    memset((void *)send_buffer, (int)'q', SEND_BUFFER_SIZE);
}
else {
    handle_error(conversation_ID,
        "Can't allocate %u bytes for send_buffer",
        (unsigned)SEND_BUFFER_SIZE);
}

for (offset = 0; offset < amount_to_send; ) {

    CM_REQUEST_TO_SEND_RECEIVED rts_received;
    CM_INT32 send_length = min((CM_INT32)SEND_BUFFER_SIZE,
                        (CM_INT32)(amount_to_send - offset));

    /*-------------------------------------------------------------
     *  Here's where your program should fill the send_buffer
     *  with data to be sent, up to send_length.
     *-----------------------------------------------------------*/


    /*-------------------------------------------------------------
     *  Call do_send_data(), which calls Send_Data and
     *  checks the result.
     *-----------------------------------------------------------*/
    do_send_data(
        conversation_ID,    /* conversation ID        */
```

```
                    send_buffer,          /* send this buffer           */
                    send_length);         /* length to send             */

            /* show the progress so far */
            (void)printf("Amount sent:  %lu bytes\r",
                        offset += send_length);
        }

    /* the last one needs a newline */
    (void)printf("Amount sent:  %lu bytes\n", offset);

    /*-------------------------------------------------------------
     *  This following Deallocate() call uses the default
     *  deallocate_type, which is CM_DEALLOCATE_SYNC_LEVEL.
     *  The conversation's sync_level is CM_CONFIRM, which was
     *  set at the top of the program.
     *-------------------------------------------------------------*/
    cmdeal(                              /* Deallocate                 */
        conversation_ID,                 /* conversation ID            */
        &cpic_return_code);              /* return code                */

    /*-------------------------------------------------------------
     *  Two return codes are expected:
     *  - CM_OK (indicating that the partner received and
     *      processed the data successfully), or
     *  - CM_PROGRAM_ERROR_PURGING (indicating that the partner
     *      did NOT receive and process the data successfully)
     *-------------------------------------------------------------*/
    switch (cpic_return_code) {
      case CM_OK:
        /*-------------------------------------------------------------
         *  The partner is happy and the conversation has
         *  been deallocated.
         *-------------------------------------------------------------*/
        break;

      case CM_PROGRAM_ERROR_PURGING:
        /*-------------------------------------------------------------
         *  The partner is not happy with the data, and
         *  replied with a Send_Error.  Issue a Receive() to
         *  get the expected DEALLOCATED_NORMAL return code.
         *-------------------------------------------------------------*/

        (void)fprintf(stderr,
            "The partner encountered a problem "
            "and issued Send_Error.\n");

        {
            CM_INT32        zero_length = (CM_INT32)0;
            CM_INT32        received_length;
```

```
            CM_STATUS_RECEIVED status_received;
            CM_DATA_RECEIVED_TYPE data_received;
            CM_REQUEST_TO_SEND_RECEIVED rts_received;

            cmrcv (                      /* Receive                */
                conversation_ID,        /* conversation ID        */
                NULL,                   /* no data is expected     */
                &zero_length,           /* maximum receive length  */
                &data_received,         /* returned data_rcvd      */
                &received_length,       /* received data length    */
                &status_received,       /* returned status_rcvd    */
                &rts_received,          /* did partner RTS?        */
                &cpic_return_code);     /* return code             */
            if (cpic_return_code != CM_DEALLOCATED_NORMAL) {
                handle_cpic_rc(
                    conversation_ID,
                    cpic_return_code,
                    "CMRCV");
            }
        }
        break;

    default:
        handle_cpic_rc(
            conversation_ID, cpic_return_code, "CMDEAL");
        break;
    }
    return EXIT_SUCCESS;          /* program was successful      */
}
```

In this example, the client program doesn't actually transfer a file. Robustly transferring a file adds a lot more complexity related to file I/O—file naming, security and access control, text and binary data, and so on—that aren't essential to the skeleton transactions we're showing here. So, the client simply transfers a number of bytes to the server, who receives them (and throws them away).

The client program retrieves two items from the command line: the symbolic destination name of the server, and the size of the transfer. If no size is provided, the client transfers, by default, a total of 1 million bytes.

As with the credit check transaction, the client conversation starts by setting the sync_level to CONFIRM, to allow the later Deallocate() call to confirm that the server is happy with what it has received. The data is sent by a loop of Send_Data() calls, where the size of the data_buffer is subtracted from the number of bytes remaining in each trip through the loop.

The send buffer size of 32,763 was chosen because of its good performance characteristics. All CPI-C platforms can send mapped data of length 32,767, but there is an underlying overhead of 4 bytes (2 bytes of length and 2 bytes indicating that this is mapped data). If you send more than 32,763 bytes, it gets split into at least two underlying logical records.

A call to printf() inside the loop shows the progress of the transfer; it uses the carriage-return character ('\r') to rewrite the same line repeatedly. At the end of the loop, the total amount sent is printed with a newline ('\n') character. This technique works well on workstations, but may not work well on some hosts which wait for a newline before writing anything to the screen.

A Confirm-Deallocate follows, because the conversation uses the default deallocate_type—which is to use the sync_level of the conversation. The return code from the Deallocate() call is handled the same way as in the credit check transaction. If the return code is CM_OK, the conversation is over. A return code of CM_PROGRAM_ERROR_PURGING indicates that the server was unable to process the data, and issued a Send_Error() call. The client issues a call to Receive() to get the indication that the conversation has been deallocated by the server. Here's the file transfer transaction, server program, file FILEXD.C:

```
/*-------------------------------------------------------------
 *   File transfer transaction, server side.
 *   (file FILEXD.C)
 *-------------------------------------------------------------*/
#include <cpic.h>                /* conversation API library    */
#include <stdio.h>               /* file I/O                     */
#include <stdlib.h>              /* standard library             */
#include <time.h>                /* time                         */

#include "docpic.h"              /* CPI-C do_ calls, BOOL        */

/*-------------------------------------------------------------
 *   The larger a receive size you can afford, the faster your
 *   overall performance.  The RECEIVE_SIZE constant here is
 *   smaller than the memory buffer size, to show the coding
 *   needed when data_received is CM_INCOMPLETE_DATA_RECEIVED.
 *   You can even set it to 1 byte, if you choose (i.e., receive
 *   one byte on each Receive() call).
 *-------------------------------------------------------------*/
#define RECEIVE_SIZE (1000)      /* size of each Receive()       */
#define BUFFER_SIZE  (32767)     /* largest possible record      */

int main(void)
{
    /*-------------------------------------------------------------
     *   The client side should send the target filename, then
     *   the file, followed by a Confirm-Deallocate.
     *
     *   We've arbitrarily bounded the size of the incoming
     *   records to 32767 bytes.
     *-------------------------------------------------------------*/
    unsigned char    conversation_ID[CM_CID_SIZE];
    CM_RETURN_CODE   cpic_return_code;
```

```
BOOL           done;
CM_INT32       received_length;
CM_INT32       requested_length;
int            ok_to_confirm;
size_t         offset;
unsigned char * data_buffer;
unsigned long  total_received;


CM_DATA_RECEIVED_TYPE data_received;
CM_STATUS_RECEIVED    status_received;


/*-------------------------------------------------------------
 *  Accept a new conversation from the client.
 *
 *  We assume (without explicitly checking) that the
 *  conversation_type is MAPPED, and the
 *  sync_level is CONFIRM.
 *  The TP definition should restrict these values, which
 *  will then be verified by the attach manager.
 *-------------------------------------------------------------*/
do_accept_conversation(conversation_ID);


/*-------------------------------------------------------------
 *  Allocate enough memory for the local buffer into which
 *  you'll receive.
 *-------------------------------------------------------------*/
data_buffer = (unsigned char *)malloc((size_t)BUFFER_SIZE);
if (NULL == data_buffer) {
    handle_error(
        conversation_ID,
        "Can't allocate %lu bytes for data_buffer",
        (unsigned long)BUFFER_SIZE);
}


/*-------------------------------------------------------------
 *  The following loop receives mapped data records until
 *  Confirm-Deallocate is returned in the status_received
 *  parameter.
 *  It receives directly into the data buffer, with a
 *  requested length that's less than or equal to the size
 *  of the buffer.  It diagnoses the following conditions:
 *  - a record sent by the partner was too large
 *  - any unexpected return_code.
 *-------------------------------------------------------------*/
done = FALSE;       /* this flag control the loop */
total_received = 0; /* total bytes received so far */
offset = 0;         /* offset into the receive data buffer */
requested_length = RECEIVE_SIZE;
```

```
              do {            /* continue while there's more to receive */
          CM_REQUEST_TO_SEND_RECEIVED rts_received;

          cmrcv (                  /* Receive                    */
              conversation_ID,     /* conversation ID            */
              &data_buffer[offset], /* put received data here    */
              &requested_length,   /* maximum length to receive  */
              &data_received,      /* returned data_rcvd value    */
              &received_length,    /* length of received data     */
              &status_received,    /* returned status_rcvd value  */
              &rts_received,       /* ignore this parameter       */
              &cpic_return_code);  /* return code from this call  */


          /*---------------------------------------------------------
           * CM_OK is the only return code we expect.  The
           * indication of Confirm-Deallocate arrives in the
           * status_received parameter, not in the return code.
           *-------------------------------------------------------*/
          if (CM_OK == cpic_return_code) {

              /*---------------------------------------------------------
               *  The data_received value is very important!
               *-------------------------------------------------------*/
              switch (data_received) {
                  case CM_INCOMPLETE_DATA_RECEIVED:
                      total_received += received_length;
                      /* update the offset, to receive more */
                      offset += received_length;
                      if (BUFFER_SIZE == offset) {
                          /* We're at the end of the buffer, yet
                             there's still more.  Give up! */
                          done = TRUE;
                          handle_error(
                              conversation_ID,
                              "Too much data was sent");
                      }

                      /* don't ask for more than we can hold */
                      requested_length = (CM_INT32)
                          min(RECEIVE_SIZE, BUFFER_SIZE - offset);
                      break;

                  case CM_COMPLETE_DATA_RECEIVED:
                      /*---------------------------------------------
                       *  We've received one full data record.
                       *  Go process that record (e.g., write it
                       *  to a file).  For this example, we're
                       *  throwing it away.
                       *-------------------------------------------*/
                      offset = 0; /* ignore the received data */
```

```
                    requested_length = RECEIVE_SIZE;
                    total_received += received_length;
                    break;

                default:
                    /* other values are ignored */
                    break;

            } /* end of switch */

            /*-------------------------------------------------------
             *  The status_received value is very important!
             *------------------------------------------------------*/
            if (CM_CONFIRM_DEALLOC_RECEIVED == status_received) {
                done = TRUE;     /* the transfer is complete */
            }
        }
        else {  /* this isn't a return code we expected */
            done = TRUE;
            /* the last one needs a newline */
            (void)printf("Amount received:  %lu bytes\n",
                        total_received);
            handle_cpic_rc(
                conversation_ID,
                cpic_return_code,
                "CMRCV");
        }

        /* show the progressof the transfer so far */
        (void)printf("Amount received:  %lu bytes\r",
                    total_received);

} while (FALSE == done);

/* the last one needs a newline */
(void)printf("Amount received:  %lu bytes\n",total_received);

/*-------------------------------------------------------------
 *  When we get here, we should be in Confirm-Deallocate
 *  state.
 *
 *  This is where your program processes the received data.
 *  For this example, we randomly decide if it's good or
 *  not, and display the result of the decision.
 *-------------------------------------------------------------*/
srand((unsigned int)time(NULL));
ok_to_confirm = rand() % 4;      /* fail 1/4th of the time */

if (ok_to_confirm) {
    (void)printf("\nPress Enter to issue Confirmed\n");
```

```
        }
        else {
           (void)printf("File transfer transaction failed randomly");
           (void)printf("\nPress Enter to issue Send_Error\n");
        }

        (void)getchar();

        /*-------------------------------------------------------------
         *  Decide whether to Confirm or not.
         *-----------------------------------------------------------*/
        if (ok_to_confirm) {
           /*----------------------------------------------------------
            *  The data that was sent has been successfully received
            *  and processed.  Replying with Confirmed will cause
            *  the conversation to be deallocated.
            *-------------------------------------------------------*/
           do_confirmed(conversation_ID);
        }
        else {
           /*----------------------------------------------------------
            *  The data that was sent was NOT successfully received
            *  and processed.  Replying with Send_Error notifies
            *  the client that there was a problem, and gives us
            *  the permission to send.  The conversation is not
            *  yet deallocated.
            *-------------------------------------------------------*/
           do_send_error(conversation_ID);

           /*----------------------------------------------------------
            *  Do a Deallocate-Flush of the conversation.
            *  First, we have to set the deallocate_type, since the
            *  default type is SYNC_LEVEL, and the sync_level of
            *  this conversation is CONFIRM, not NONE.
            *-------------------------------------------------------*/
           {
               CM_DEALLOCATE_TYPE deallocate_type =
                   CM_DEALLOCATE_FLUSH;

               cmsdt(                    /* Set_Deallocate_Type     */
                   conversation_ID,      /* conversation ID         */
                   &deallocate_type,     /* deallocate type         */
                   &cpic_return_code);   /* return code             */
               if (cpic_return_code != CM_OK) {
                   handle_cpic_rc(
                       conversation_ID,
                       cpic_return_code,
                       "CMSDT");
               }
           }

           cmdeal(                       /* Deallocate              */
               conversation_ID,          /* conversation ID         */
               &cpic_return_code);       /* return code             */
```

```
        if (cpic_return_code != CM_OK) {
            handle_cpic_rc(
                conversation_ID,
                cpic_return_code,
                "CMDEAL");
        }
    }
    return EXIT_SUCCESS;         /* program was successful     */
}
```

The important work on the server side is done by the Receive() call, which returns four kinds of useful information each time it is called. The two partners are otherwise loosely coupled; for example, the amount of data requested on each Receive() doesn't need to match the size of the data that the partner sent. The Receive() call is inside a do-while loop, which loops until the received data is complete and confirmation has been requested.

The fact that confirmation has been requested is discovered in the status_received parameter of the Receive(). The fact that all the data has been received is discovered with the data_received parameter. The data_received value is invalid unless the return_code is CM_OK or CM_DEALLO-CATED_NORMAL. If there is valid data, it is placed in the large data buffer at the next available position.

The Receive() call is imbedded in an extended loop that looks a little long. This loop illustrates how to handle the data_received value of CM_INCOM-PLETE_DATA_RECEIVED, which means that the requested_length is smaller than the record that was sent. It also illustrates error diagnosis for a few of the many situations that can arise if this program is called by the wrong client (or the client is designed wrong). For example, it checks that CM_COM-PLETE_DATA_RECEIVED is received only once. It assures that memory isn't overrun by the incoming data. It also allows the CM_CONFIRM_DEALLOC_RECEIVED status_received value to arrive separately after the data. This isn't the all-purpose receive loop to handle any bizarre situation, but it is reasonable for the size of this program.

In this example, we discard the data, and go back to the beginning of the same data buffer. In a real file transfer, this is where your program would write a complete data record to a file.

As we did in the credit check transaction, we demonstrate a little technique for executing both branches of code. At the time the confirmation request is encountered, we randomly decide if the entire transfer was successful or not. If so, the program issues Confirmed() and the conversation is over. If not, the program issues Send_Error(), followed by Deallocate-Flush to end the conversation.

THE DATABASE UPDATE TRANSACTION (CONVERSATIONAL REPLY)

The database update transaction is typically used to update information managed by a partner program. It is used in database applications where a client

```
    Client (UPDATE.C)    network flows         Server (UPDATED.C)
    ------------------   ---------------------  --------------------


    Initialize_Conversation()
        |
    Set_Sync_Level(CM_CONFIRM)
        |
    Allocate()
        |                                       Accept_Conversation()
    Send_Data()                                     .
        |                                           .
    Receive()                                       .
        .          Attach, data, Send state         .
        .          ---------------------------->.
        .                                       rc=CM_OK
        .                                           |
        .                                       Receive()
        .                                       rc=CM_OK
        .                                       dr=CM_COMPLETE_DATA_RECEIVED
        .                                       sr=CM_SEND_RECEIVED
        .                                           |
        .                                   At this point, the server should freeze
        .                                   the database entry until further notice.
        .                                           |
        .                                       Send_Data()
        .                                           |
        .                                       Receive()
        .          data, Send state                .
        .          <---------------------------.
      rc=CM_OK                                      .
      dr=CM_COMPLETE_DATA_RECEIVED                  .
      sr=CM_SEND_RECEIVED                           .
        |                                           .
    Set_Send_Type(CM_SEND_AND_DEALLOCATE)          .
        |                                           .
    Send_Data()                                     .
        .          data, Confirm-Deallocate         .
        .          ---------------------------->.
        .                                       rc=CM_OK
        .                                       dr=CM_COMPLETE_DATA_RECEIVED
        .                                       sr=CM_CONFIRM_DEALLOC_RECEIVED
        .                                           |
        .                                   At this point, the server can record in
        .                                   its audit trail that this is committed.
        .                                           |
        .          Confirmed              Confirmed()
        .          <---------------------------|
      rc=CM_OK
```

Figure 18.5 Database Update (Conversational Reply) transaction model.

program requests information from the database server, updates the information, and returns the update to the server to be set into the database.

A common example of this transaction is a change of mailing address. The client program sends a name or account number to the server. It replies with the current address that corresponds to the name or number. The user of the client program gets back the old address, types the new address over it, and sends it back to the server, which updates its database.

This transaction is really an inquiry transaction followed by a credit check transaction performed on the same conversation. A single conversation is necessary to control the work being performed. If separate conversations are used, transactions from other clients could race between the first and second conversations, resulting in lost updates and transactions performed with invalid data.

The database update transaction may be used when a client requests information from a server and the server, in turn, requests information (usually for accounting or auditing purposes) from the client. In this case, the server appends the new request to the reply sent to the original request, and the result is returned in another record. In this environment, this transaction is called a "conversational reply" because the reply solicits an additional reply from the originator.

In Fig. 18.5 we sketch out both sides of the transaction.

There are two source code files for the database update transaction: UPDATE.C (the client side) and UPDATED.C (the server side). The client side is shown first. Here's the database update transaction, client program, file UPDATE.C:

```c
/*------------------------------------------------------------------
 *  Database update transaction, client side.
 *  (file UPDATE.C)
 *----------------------------------------------------------------*/
#include <cpic.h>          /* conversation API library   */
#include <stdarg.h>        /* variable arguments         */
#include <stdio.h>         /* file I/O                   */
#include <stdlib.h>        /* standard library           */
#include <string.h>        /* strings and memory         */

#include "docpic.h"        /* CPI-C do_ calls, BOOL      */

/*------------------------------------------------------------------
 *  The larger a receive size you can afford, the faster your
 *  overall performance.
#define BUFFER_SIZE (32767)    /* largest possible record    */

int main(int argc, char *argv[])
{
    /*------------------------------------------------------------
     *  This side sends a single mapped record, then waits to
     *  receive a single mapped record and Deallocate-Normal
```

```
 *   from its partner.
 *
 *   We've arbitrarily bounded the size of one incoming
 *   logical record to the value of BUFFER_SIZE.
 *-----------------------------------------------------------*/
unsigned char   conversation_ID[CM_CID_SIZE];
CM_RETURN_CODE  cpic_return_code;


CM_INT32        received_length;
unsigned char * data_buffer;


/*-----------------------------------------------------------
 *   Get the symbolic destination from the command line and
 *   initialize a conversation.
 *-----------------------------------------------------------*/
if (argc > 1) { /* is there at least one argument? */
    do_initialize_conversation(conversation_ID, argv[1]);
}
else {
    handle_error(
        conversation_ID,
        "A symbolic destination name must be provided");
}


/*-----------------------------------------------------------
 *   Set the sync_level to CONFIRM.
 *-----------------------------------------------------------*/
do_sync_level_confirm(conversation_ID);


/*-----------------------------------------------------------
 *   Allocate a session for this conversation.
 *-----------------------------------------------------------*/
do_allocate(conversation_ID);


/*-----------------------------------------------------------
 *   This is where your program prepares the data record
 *   that should be sent on this transaction.
 *-----------------------------------------------------------*/
{
    unsigned char *send_buffer =
        "Test of the Database Update transaction";
    CM_INT32 send_length = (CM_INT32)strlen(send_buffer);

    do_send_data(
        conversation_ID,    /* conversation ID      */
        send_buffer,        /* send this buffer     */
        send_length);       /* length to send       */
}
```

```
/*---------------------------------------------------------------
 *   Allocate enough memory for whatever you expect to
 *   receive from the partner...
 *-------------------------------------------------------------*/
data_buffer = (unsigned char *)malloc((size_t)BUFFER_SIZE);
if (NULL == data_buffer) {
    handle_error(
        conversation_ID,
        "Can't allocate %lu bytes for data_buffer",
        (unsigned long)BUFFER_SIZE);
}




/*---------------------------------------------------------------
 *   Since we're expecting our partner to send us a record
 *   and give us send permission, we'll use its equivalent;
 *   the receive code from the INQUIRY transaction.
 *-------------------------------------------------------------*/
do_receive_inquiry(
    conversation_ID,
    data_buffer,
    BUFFER_SIZE,            /* buffer size                 */
    &received_length);      /* bytes received              */

/*---------------------------------------------------------------
 *   This is where your program processes the received data.
 *   For this example, we just display it, using fwrite().
 *-------------------------------------------------------------*/
(void)fwrite((void *)data_buffer, (size_t)1,
        (size_t)received_length, stdout);
(void)printf("\n");

/*---------------------------------------------------------------
 *   Couple a Confirm-Deallocate with this single Send_Data(),
 *   using a Set_Send_Type() call.
 *-------------------------------------------------------------*/
{
    CM_SEND_TYPE send_type = CM_SEND_AND_DEALLOCATE;

    cmsst(                  /* Set Send Type               */
        conversation_ID,    /* conversation ID             */
        &send_type,         /* set the send type           */
        &cpic_return_code); /* return code from this call  */
    if (cpic_return_code != CM_OK) {
        handle_cpic_rc(
            conversation_ID, cpic_return_code, "CMSST");
    }
}
```

```
/*-------------------------------------------------------------
 *  This is where your program modifies the received data,
 *  before returning it to the partner.
 *-----------------------------------------------------------*/
{
    unsigned char *send_buffer =
        "Modification of reply record";
    CM_INT32 send_length = (CM_INT32)strlen(send_buffer);
    CM_REQUEST_TO_SEND_RECEIVED rts_received;   /* ignored */

    cmsend(                     /* Send_Data                 */
        conversation_ID,    /* conversation ID           */
        send_buffer,        /* send this buffer          */
        &send_length,       /* length to send            */
        &rts_received,      /* did partner RTS?          */
        &cpic_return_code); /* return code from this call */
}


/*-------------------------------------------------------------
 *  Two return codes are expected:
 *  - CM_OK (indicating that the partner received and
 *      processed the data successfully), or
 *  - CM_PROGRAM_ERROR_PURGING (indicating that the partner
 *      did NOT receive and process the data successfully)
 *-----------------------------------------------------------*/
switch (cpic_return_code) {
  case CM_OK:
    /*-------------------------------------------------
     * The partner is happy and the conversation has
     * been deallocated.
     *-----------------------------------------------*/
    break;

  case CM_PROGRAM_ERROR_PURGING:
    /*-------------------------------------------------------
     * The partner is not happy with the data, and
     * replied with a Send_Error.  Issue a Receive() to
     * get the expected DEALLOCATED_NORMAL return code.
     *-----------------------------------------------------*/
    (void)fprintf(stderr,
        "The partner encountered a problem "
        "and issued Send_Error.\n");

    {
        CM_INT32            zero_length = (CM_INT32)0;
        CM_INT32            received_length;
        CM_STATUS_RECEIVED status_received;
        CM_DATA_RECEIVED_TYPE data_received;
        CM_REQUEST_TO_SEND_RECEIVED rts_received;
```

```
            cmrcv (                    /* Receive                  */
                conversation_ID,       /* conversation ID          */
                NULL,                  /* no data is expected      */
                &zero_length,          /* maximum receive length   */
                &data_received,        /* returned data_rcvd       */
                &received_length,      /* received data length     */
                &status_received,      /* returned status_rcvd     */
                &rts_received,         /* did partner RTS?         */
                &cpic_return_code);    /* return code              */
            if (cpic_return_code != CM_DEALLOCATED_NORMAL) {
                handle_cpic_rc(
                    conversation_ID, cpic_return_code, "CMRCV");
            }
        }
        break;

    default:
        handle_cpic_rc(
            conversation_ID, cpic_return_code, "CMSEND");
        break;
    }

    return EXIT_SUCCESS;          /* program was successful     */
}
```

The client side of the database update transaction is constructed from the client sides of two previous transactions. It consists of an inquiry transaction, followed by a credit check transaction. A record is sent to the server (presumably a key to a database), who replies with another record. The client takes this reply, modifies it, and returns it to the server, requesting confirmation before deallocating the conversation. If the server replies with Send_Error(), the client enters a Receive() loop, and exits upon the arrival of a CM_DEALLOCATED_NORMAL return code. Here's the database update transaction, server program, file UPDATED.C:

```
/*---------------------------------------------------------------
 * Database update transaction, server side.
 * (file UPDATED.C)
 *-------------------------------------------------------------*/
#include <cpic.h>            /* conversation API library   */
#include <stdio.h>           /* file I/O                   */
#include <stdlib.h>          /* standard library           */
#include <string.h>          /* strings and memory         */
#include <time.h>            /* time                       */
#include "docpic.h"          /* CPI-C do_ calls. BOOL      */


/*---------------------------------------------------------------
 * The larger a receive size you can afford, the faster your
 * overall performance.
 *-------------------------------------------------------------*/
```

```
#define BUFFER_SIZE  (32767)    /* largest possible record    */

int main(void)
{
    /*-------------------------------------------------------------
     *  The client side should have sent a single record, and
     *  then be waiting for a record in reply.  It should
     *  modify that reply, and return it for confirmation.
     *
     *  We've arbitrarily bounded the size of the incoming
     *  record to 32767 bytes.
     *-------------------------------------------------------------*/
    unsigned char   conversation_ID[CM_CID_SIZE];
    CM_RETURN_CODE  cpic_return_code;

    CM_INT32        received_length;
    int             ok_to_confirm;
    unsigned char * data_buffer;

    /*-------------------------------------------------------------
     *  Accept a new conversation from the client.
     *
     *  We assume (without explicitly checking) that the
     *  conversation_type is MAPPED, and the
     *  sync_level is CONFIRM.
     *  The TP definition should restrict these values, which
     *  will then be verified by the attach manager.
     *-------------------------------------------------------------*/
    do_accept_conversation(conversation_ID);

    /*-------------------------------------------------------------
     *  Allocate enough memory for whatever you expect to
     *  receive from the partner...
     *-------------------------------------------------------------*/
    data_buffer = (unsigned char *)malloc((size_t)BUFFER_SIZE);
    if (NULL == data_buffer) {
        handle_error(
            conversation_ID,
            "Can't allocate %lu bytes for data_buffer",
            (unsigned long)BUFFER_SIZE);
    }

    /*-------------------------------------------------------------
     *  The first part of the UPDATE transaction looks like
     *  an INQUIRY; the client requests a record.
     *-------------------------------------------------------------*/
    do_receive_inquiry(
        conversation_ID,
        data_buffer,
        BUFFER_SIZE,            /* buffer size        */
        &received_length);      /* bytes received     */
```

```
/*------------------------------------------------------------
 *  When we get here, we should be in Send state.  Process
 *  the incoming record and reply.
 *
 *  Your program should use the information in the incoming
 *  record (presumably the key into a database), to find
 *  the record requested by the partner.
 *------------------------------------------------------------*/
if (received_length > 0) {
    fwrite((void *)data_buffer, (size_t)1,
        (size_t)received_length, stdout);
    (void)printf("\n");
}
else {
    handle_error(
        conversation_ID,
        "No data was sent");
}

/*------------------------------------------------------------
 *  This is where your program prepares its reply to
 *  the client.
 *
 *  Send back the record requested by the client.  If that
 *  record is in a database, lock that record at this point.
 *------------------------------------------------------------*/
{
    unsigned char *send_buffer =
        "Reply record, Database Update transaction";
    CM_INT32 send_length = (CM_INT32)strlen(send_buffer);

    do_send_data(
        conversation_ID,    /* conversation ID            */
        send_buffer,        /* send this buffer           */
        send_length);       /* length to send             */
}

/*------------------------------------------------------------
 *  The first part of the UPDATE transaction looks like
 *  a CREDIT_CHECK; the client sends the updated record
 *  to be stored.
 *------------------------------------------------------------*/
do_receive_credit(
    conversation_ID,
    data_buffer,
    BUFFER_SIZE,            /* buffer size                */
    &received_length);      /* bytes received             */

/*------------------------------------------------------------
 *  When we get here, we should be in Confirm-Deallocate
 *  state.
```

```
 *
 *  This is where your program processes the received data.
 *  For this example, we randomly decide if it's good or
 *  not, and display the result of the decision.
 *-----------------------------------------------------------*/
srand((unsigned int)time(NULL));
ok_to_confirm = rand() % 4;

if (ok_to_confirm) {
    fwrite((void *)data_buffer, (size_t)1,
        (size_t)received_length, stdout);
    (void)printf("\nPress Enter to issue Confirmed\n");
}
else {
    (void)printf("Database update failed randomly");
    (void)printf("\nPress Enter to issue Send_Error\n");
}
(void)getchar();


/*-----------------------------------------------------------
 *  Decide whether to Confirm or not.
 *-----------------------------------------------------------*/
if (ok_to_confirm) {
    /*-------------------------------------------------------
     *  The data that was sent has been successfully received
     *  and processed.  Replying with Confirmed will cause
     *  the conversation to be deallocated.
     *-----------------------------------------------------*/
    do_confirmed(conversation_ID);
}
else {
    /*-------------------------------------------------------
     *  The data that was sent was NOT successfully received
     *  and processed.  Replying with Send_Error notifies
     *  the client that there was a problem, and gives us
     *  the permission to send.  The conversation is not
     *  automatically deallocated.
     *-----------------------------------------------------*/
    do_send_error(conversation_ID);

    /*-------------------------------------------------------
     *  Do a Deallocate-Flush of the conversation.
     *  We have to set the deallocate_type first, since the
     *  default type is SYNC_LEVEL, and the sync_level of
     *  this conversation is CONFIRM, not NONE.
     *-----------------------------------------------------*/
    {
        CM_DEALLOCATE_TYPE deallocate_type =
            CM_DEALLOCATE_FLUSH;
```

```
        cmsdt(                      /* Set Deallocate Type    */
            conversation_ID,    /* conversation ID        */
            &deallocate_type,   /* deallocate type        */
            &cpic_return_code); /* return code            */
        if (cpic_return_code != CM_OK) {
            handle_cpic_rc(
                conversation_ID, cpic_return_code, "CMSDT");
        }
    }

    cmdeal(                      /* Deallocate             */
        conversation_ID,        /* conversation ID        */
        &cpic_return_code);     /* return code            */
    if (cpic_return_code != CM_OK) {
        handle_cpic_rc(
            conversation_ID, cpic_return_code, "CMDEAL");
    }
    }
    return EXIT_SUCCESS;         /* program was successful  */
}
```

The database update transaction was designed assuming that the server side has access to a database. The client is requesting records from the database, which it will modify and return. The server side looks like the server side of an inquiry transaction followed by the server side of a credit check transaction. It receives a record from the client, and replies with a record that corresponds to the incoming one. It locks that record in its database before replying. The server then calls do_receive_credit(), waiting for a modified version of that record to return from the client. If the modification is okay, it updates the database with the modified record, unlocks that record, and issues a Confirmed() call. If it is not okay, it issues Send_Error(), followed by a Deallocate-Flush to end the conversation.

Improving Performance

In this chapter, we discuss guidelines to improve the performance of your CPI-C applications. We start with a set of general guidelines related to hardware and network tuning. These guidelines often have the greatest effect on performance, but they're generally the items over which you have the least control.

The other guidelines in this chapter are sets of tips and techniques which you can apply to your programs as their designer and coder. These can have dramatic effect when the application is well understood and the amount of work done by the two programs is not balanced (that is, one side is spending a lot of time waiting while the other side is working). Otherwise, the effects of these suggestions will be overshadowed by the changes that can be made by using fast hardware and network components.

GENERAL GUIDELINES

The coding techniques in the remaining sections of this chapter won't generally improve your application's performance by orders of magnitude. The performance changes made by implementing the coding techniques are often dwarfed by other, more influential performance considerations. Before we look at the coding techniques in more detail, let's survey some general aspects of performance that can affect your application.

- *Send only the data that really needs to be sent.* Your programs should transfer only the data that is actually required to make a transaction work. For example, if your program is modifying 100 bytes in a large database, don't retrieve the entire database, modify the 100 bytes, and then send it back.

- *Use appropriate algorithms.* The algorithm analysis techniques you learned for stand-alone application programming apply to distributed applications as well. No amount of excellent CPI-C programming is going to help the distributed equivalent of a bubble sort (a poor algorithm) run faster than a quick sort (a better algorithm).

- *Invest in your network transports and computing power.* Your application's performance will often be limited by the speed of the network links over which you send data. In some cases, the easiest and cheapest way to improve performance is to invest in additional or faster network links that are capable of handling the amounts of data that your program is sending. Similarly, you'll need appropriate computing horsepower to accomplish your task. Remind your application users of this obvious fact.

- *Tune your APPC configuration.* Performance problems on high-speed links (LANs and faster) can often be attributed to a poorly tuned APPC configuration. Depending upon how badly configured things are, you can sometimes get performance improvements of two to ten times.

  We discussed in Chap. 5 the lower-layer connections that must occur before a conversation can be started. The most important tuning parameters are related to these connections: links and the sessions that go over them. Links are created based on DLC definitions. Sessions are created based on mode definitions. For both of these, overall performance is improved by having large frames and large windows (the number of frames that are buffered). The trade-off for using large frames and buffers is that they consume commensurate amounts of memory. Our explicit recommendations are:

  Use large DLC frame sizes.

  Use large DLC window sizes.

  Use mode RU sizes that fit into DLC frames (this avoids segmenting).

  Use large mode pacing windows.

CPI-C CODING TIPS AND TECHNIQUES

After you have considered the nonprogramming items that can affect performance, you're ready to move on to the CPI-C coding techniques. The coding techniques we discuss fall into six broad categories. We'll spend several pages talking about each of these in the remainder of this chapter:

1. *Improving processing overlap.* When you're writing a distributed application, you have at least two computers at your disposal to perform work for you. There are techniques you can use in your CPI-C conversation to decrease the idle time of each program and thus make the best use of both computers.

2. *Using your conversation as an optimized pipe.* Many applications encounter situations where they have to move a lot of data among comput-

ers. To move a lot of data as quickly and efficiently as possible, treat the conversation as a pipe. Turning the conversation around is costly; it stops the pipe for the time required to a one-way trip across the network.

3. *Reducing data flows.*   In most applications, reducing the number of network flows is the best way to improve your application's performance. Your application achieves the same result while requiring less network resources and processing. There are a number of good techniques to consider, as well as a few pitfalls to avoid.

4. *Reducing the number of Send_Data() and Receive() calls.*   The CPI-C calls that actually send and receive data are relatively expensive to execute compared to other CPI-C calls. An application that processes its data in large chunks will perform better than a similar application that processes its data one byte at a time.

5. *Reducing call overhead.*   Each communications call your program issues incurs processor overhead. CPI-C has to acknowledge each call, process the parameters, and return. There are some simple techniques you can use to reduce the number of CPI-C calls your program needs to issue to perform a task. Reducing the call overhead can have a large effect for small transactions that are done frequently.

6. *Making the most of underlying APPC sessions.*   In most situations, it's okay to share APPC sessions serially with other applications. However, there will be times when your applications will need to be "greedy" and keep a conversation active for as long as you might possibly need it.

IMPROVING PROCESSING OVERLAP

One way to get better performance in your distributed application is to take advantage of the fact that you have two computers that can do work for you. Think about how you can turn your application into a parallel processing application by getting both application sides doing work at the same time. The more that two programs can overlap their processing, the better the overall performance. This section discusses several techniques for improving processing overlap. Many of these techniques can be applied to the programs when they are in the final phases of testing and debugging.

Use Flush() to allow timely processing of data

Your program can use the Flush() call during a series of Send_Data() calls to ensure that the partner program has data to work on while your local program prepares more data to send. This can be especially helpful when your program requires extra time to build the next record to be sent.

To illustrate using Flush(), consider an application that is sending a file from a client to a server. The server has to create a new file after it receives the file header information from the client. For purposes of illustration we will say that creating the new file takes a significant amount of time. Ordinarily, we would write this application like this:

```
Time   Client                        Server
----   --------------------          --------------------
  1    Send_Data(file_header)
  2    open file
  3    .
  4      .
  5      . long delay
  6    Send_Data(record)
  7    Send_Data(record)             Receive(file_header)
  8    Send_Data(record)             create file
  9    Confirm()                       .
 10                                    .
 11                                    . long delay
 12                                  Receive(record)
 13                                  Receive(record)
 14                                  Receive(record)
 15                                  Confirmed()
```

In this example, at Time-1 we send the file_header of the file to be opened on the server. It then takes a long time before we can open the file locally and send the first data record from the file. While we are opening the file, our server doesn't have anything to do, since CPI-C hasn't actually sent the file_header on the wire. After we begin sending data records, the file_header is finally sent on the wire to the server at Time-6. We then continue sending the file, requesting confirmation of a successful file transfer.

By using Flush(), our application would look like this:

```
Time   Client                        Server
----   --------------------          --------------------
  1    Send_Data(file_header)
  2    Flush()
  3    open file                     Receive(file_header)
  4    .                             create file
  5      .                             .
  6      . long delay                  .
  7    Send_Data(record)               . long delay
  8    Send_Data(record)             Receive(record)
  9    Send_Data(record)             Receive(record)
 10    Confirm()                     Receive(record)
 11                                  Confirmed()
```

In this example, we use Flush() to ask CPI-C to send the file_header at Time-2. The server is therefore able to start opening the file at the same time the client continues to open its file. Both sides are working at the same time.

When adding Flush() into your application, make sure to do so only when the advantages of processing overlap are greater than the overhead of extra network traffic and possibility of extra Receive() calls. There is rarely an advantage to adding Flush() calls after every Send_Data(record). The time between Send_Data() calls isn't long enough to overcome the extra network and CPU overhead of processing each record in a separate network data flow.

Use Prepare_To_Receive()

You can use Prepare_To_Receive() in a similar fashion to increase processing overlap. Prepare_To_Receive() should be used after you have sent your last record, but there will be a delay before you are ready to receive a record from your partner.

Let's look at our file transfer application again, this time receiving a file instead of sending it:

```
Time  Client                          Server
----  -----------------------         -------------------
 1    Send_Data(file_request)
 2    create file (open it for write)
 3    .
 4     .
 5     . long delay
 6    Receive()                  file_request
 7    |                          --------->
 8    |                                      Receive(file_header)
 9    |                                      open file for read
10    |                                      .
11    |                                       .
12    |                                        . long delay
13    returns with record       <---------    Send_Data(record)
14    Receive(record)           <---------    Send_Data(record)
15    Receive(record)           <---------    Send_Data(record)
16    Confirmed()               <--------->    Confirm()
```

This example is similar to the Flush() example. In this case, after the client sends the file_request, there is a long delay while the client creates the file. When the client finally gets around to issuing its first Receive() call, the file_request record is sent to the server.

Now, let's look at how to improve the processing overlap in this transaction. If we were to use a Flush() after sending the file_request, the server would start opening the file sooner. But Flush() would cause one network flow to send the file_request and another network flow when the client issues the Receive() call. In addition, the server would have to Receive() the file_request and issue a second Receive() to get permission to send.

By using Prepare_To_Receive(), we can get the file_request record and the permission to send to the server in one network flow.

Now let's look at the same application using Prepare_To_Receive:

```
Time  Client                                      Server
----  --------------------                        --------------------
 1    Send_Data(file_request)
 2    Prepare_To_Receive()      file_request
 3    create file               --------->        Receive(file_header)
 4    .                                           open file for read
 5    .                                               .
 6      . long delay                                  .
 7    Receive()                                     . long delay
 8    returns with record       <---------        Send_Data(record)
 9    Receive(record)           <---------        Send_Data(record)
10    Receive(record)           <---------        Send_Data(record)
11    Confirmed()               <--------->       Confirm()
```

As in our Flush() example, by using Prepare_To_Receive() both the client and server are doing work at the same time. We have increased the parallel processing of our distributed transaction, while maintaining the original design.

USING YOUR CONVERSATION AS AN OPTIMIZED PIPE

When you are trying to get a lot of data from one application side to the other, your programs need to treat their CPI-C conversation as a pipe. If there is time during which your program isn't sending data, you aren't fully utilizing your pipe. When your program is sending data, send as much as possible before interrupting yourself. This provides CPI-C the best opportunity to optimize the pipe and make your application run faster.

When you are trying to apply the following guidelines to your applications, think about what would happen if the propagation delay is huge. Consider that it can take minutes for a packet to reach your partner and for the response to return. If you design your application to make the best use of your conversation pipe, the Jupiter astronauts who use your program will appreciate your design skills.

Don't turn the line around when you don't need to. Going from **Send** state to **Receive** state, and back to Send state again is a clean way to design many types of transactions, but it doesn't yield the ultimate in performance.

Use the Confirm() call appropriately

Every time your program issues a Confirm() call, it temporarily shuts down the pipe and waits for the partner program to respond. There will be a delay while your partner program receives all of the data your program has sent, a delay while your partner processes the data, and another delay waiting for the Confirmed() response to get back to your program.

Since Confirm() disrupts your pipe, you should use it only when your application needs to know that all data sent has been received and processed successfully. Confirm() should be used only when you really can't do anything else before verifying that everything previously sent was processed successfully.

One common pitfall that CPI-C programmers fall into is using Confirm() between Send_Data() calls that are related. For example, if you are sending a large file, issuing Confirm() after every file record you send can drastically reduce your program's throughput. Your program should continue sending all of the data records in the file. After it sends the last record, it should ask for confirmation of the entire file.

In a sophisticated file transfer program, you can take this one step further. If you are transferring a set of files, you can send all the files through the pipe and hold off confirmation until you have sent the last record of the last file. This increases your use of the conversation pipe and improves your file transfer performance.

There's a trade-off to consider here between the loss of performance incurred by doing a Confirm() and the time it takes to recover if a problem is uncovered. You can see this behavior in the transfer of multiple files we discussed in the previous paragraph. If it takes an inordinate amount of time to recover if one of the files in the middle of the transfer is bad (for example, that file and the files after it have to be sent again), then certainly confirm after the delivery of each file.

Use implicit confirmation instead of Confirm()

If your application has sent a data record that should be confirmed, but your application also wants to go into **Receive** state, skip the explicit call to Confirm(). Just go directly into your Receive code. If there is a problem with the data you sent, your partner will notify your application and it will find out on the Receive() call.

REDUCING DATA FLOWS

APPC and CPI-C, by their design, try to reduce the number of network flows for your application. But there are CPI-C calls which can cause extra and often unnecessary network flows. Examine your use of the following calls:

- Flush()
- Send_Error()
- Deallocate-Abend

Use Flush() judiciously

The Flush() call is used to tell CPI-C to send all of its buffers as soon as possible. This will often result in more network buffers being used than would otherwise be necessary. In addition to the extra overhead this causes on the network, your application may actually run slower because of the extra time required to process the extra network buffers.

In general, don't use the Flush() call unless there will be a significant delay between your Send_Data() call and your next call to CPI-C. See "Use Flush() to Allow Timely Processing of Data" earlier in this chapter for an illustration of when using Flush() can help improve your performance.

Minimize use of Send_Error()

Send_Error() should never be called as part of the mainline Send-Receive path of your program. Use it only when either partner detects a real error situation. Even in real error situations, Send_Error() should only be used if you must interrupt your partner, who is still sending data to your program. Information sent by the partner, but not yet received, will be purged.

Send_Error() causes two internal message exchanges to occur between your platform and your partner's platform. In addition, the underlying platform software may write an entry to a log file each time Send_Error() is called. For example, OS/2 Communications Manager writes such an entry to disk each time Send_Error() is issued.

Avoid using Deallocate-Abend

In general, you should use Deallocate with deallocate_type(CM_DEALLO-CATE_FLUSH) rather than Deallocate with deallocate_type(CM_DEALLO-CATE_ABEND). The Deallocate-Abend is handled similarly to the Send_Error() call; CPI-C generates two internal message exchanges, and on some platforms, CPI-C writes a log file entry to disk.

Design your applications so that the program that should deallocate the conversation has the permission to send (that is, it's in **Send** state) at that time and can use Deallocate-Flush.

REDUCING THE NUMBER OF SEND_DATA() AND RECEIVE() CALLS

With any programming interface, the fewer calls your program issues to complete a task, the more efficient it will be. For example, if your program is reading data from a file, it should read data in large blocks rather than a single byte at a time.

Similarly, your programs are more efficient when they use large buffers on CPI-C's Send_Data() and Receive() calls.

Using shared data buffers on OS/2 Communications Manager

When using the OS/2 Communications Manager, your data transfer performance can be greatly improved if you use OS/2 shared data buffers on your

Send_Data() and Receive() calls. By using a shared data buffer, you eliminate a data copy from your buffer into the special buffers that Communications Manager uses. If you don't use a shared data buffer, you pay a large performance penalty for this extra data copy. Tests with APING indicate throughput that is up to 2.5 times faster when using shared data buffers than when using buffers obtained using malloc().

Here is a routine you can use in place of malloc() to get a buffer for use on Send_Data() and Receive():

```c
#include <cpic.h>
#include <stdlib.h>

#if   defined( CM_OS2 )

/* include the definitions and prototype for DosAlloc call */
#define   INCL_BASE
#include <os2.h>

#endif


/*
 * alloc_cpic_buffer()
 *        OS/2 can optimize performance if a special shared memory
 *        buffer is used as the data buffer on calls to CMSEND and
 *        CMRCV.  To hide this special case from the calling
 *        program, this procedure should be called to allocate all
 *        CPI-C data buffers.
 *
 *    if you're compiling with a 16-bit OS/2 compiler:
 *        Returns a shared memory buffer allocated with
 *        DosAllocSeg().
 *
 *    if you're compiling with a 32-bit OS/2 compiler:
 *        Returns a shared memory buffer allocated with
 *        DosAllocSharedMem().
 *
 *    default:
 *        Returns a memory buffer allocated with the C run-time
 *        malloc() call.
 */

unsigned char CM_PTR
alloc_cpic_buffer(unsigned int size)
{
#if   defined( CM_OS2 )

#   if (__IBMC__ >= 100) || __BORLANDC__
    /* using an OS/2 32-bit compiler */
```

```
        PVOID address;
        ULONG dos_rc;

        dos_rc = DosAllocSharedMem(&address, NULL, size, fALLOCSHR);
        if (dos_rc == 0) {
            return(address);
        }
        else {
            /*
             * DosAllocSharedMem() failed, but we may still be able
             * to get a buffer from malloc().
             */
            return malloc(size);
        }

#   elif (_MSC_VER >= 600) || __IBMC__
    /* using an OS/2 16-bit compiler */
    USHORT selector;            /* selector from DosAllocSeg     */
    USHORT dos_rc;
    unsigned char far *memory_pointer;

    dos_rc = DosAllocSeg((unsigned)size,
                         (PSEL)&selector,
                         (unsigned)1);/*shared, unnamed segment*/
    if (dos_rc == 0) {
        SELECTOROF(memory_pointer) = selector;
        OFFSETOF(memory_pointer) = 0; /* set the offset to 0    */
        return(memory_pointer);
    } else {
        /*
         * DosAllocSeg() failed, but we may still be able to get
         * a buffer from malloc().
         */
        return malloc(size);
    }

#   else
    /* using an OS/2 compiler we haven't checked for */
    return malloc(size);
#   endif

#else
    /* not on OS/2 */
    return malloc(size);

#endif
}
```

This routine allocates a shared buffer with 16- and 32-bit OS/2 compilers. If you are compiling on another platform, it simply calls malloc() and returns the result.

Send as much data as possible on each Send_Data()

If you are writing data to a file, your program will be more efficient if it writes data in large blocks rather than one byte at a time. Similarly, you will get better data throughput if you use large buffer sizes on your Send_Data() and Receive() calls. Choosing an appropriate buffer size can have a significant impact on the performance of your program.

Send as much data as possible on each Send_Data() call. For example, if you are transferring a file, send large blocks of data instead of sending the file one byte at a time. When processing files, it is also helpful to use a multiple of the file system's block size. For example, in DOS, Windows, and OS/2, we suggest using a buffer size of 28,672, which is seven times the block size of 4096.

You should avoid using a buffer size greater than 32,763, since this results in two APPC packets being sent in the network (which may result in two Receive() calls on the partner side).*

You will often be faced with a situation where your program has two pieces of data that need to be sent that are not in a contiguous data buffer. Your program can either issue two Send_Data() calls or copy both pieces of data into one buffer and issue one Send_Data() call. In general, building the data buffer in your program and issuing one Send_Data() call is slightly more efficient; it also means only a single Receive() call on your partner's side.

Receive as much data as possible with each Receive() call

When your program receives data, avoid multiple Receive() calls by using data buffers large enough to receive the entire record being sent. By doing so, you also avoid the code necessary to handle the CM_INCOMPLETE_DATA_RECEIVED value on the data_received parameter. We suggest allocating a data buffer of 32,767 bytes, which is the largest receive_buffer size in CPI-C versions before 1.2. Starting in CPI-C 1.2, the Extract_Maximum_Buffer_Size() call lets your program determine if it can use buffers larger than the old maximum size.

To avoid incurring the overhead of memory management, get your buffer with malloc() once at the beginning of your programs and release it using free() at the end, before exiting.

Even more dire consequences occur with the OS/2 Communications Manager. If you use shared buffers, as described previously, it tracks every shared data_buffer that it sees, clearing its table when the process is exited. Calls to DosFreeXXX do not actually free memory that has been used as a data_buffer. A loop of DosAllocXXX, Receive(), and DosFreeXXX will eventually consume all the memory available in OS/2.

---

* Although most platforms will handle this as one Receive() call, we have observed some host platforms (for example, IBM's VM/ESA CMS) that handle this as two Receive() calls.

REDUCING CALL OVERHEAD

Each time your application issues a CPI-C call, it incurs some API overhead. For most calls, the overhead is slight. For calls that create or process data flows, the overhead of just making the API call becomes significant.

CPI-C call overhead is usually only significant when the call is issued many times. Using four calls instead of five within a tight data processing loop may result in improved performance.

In addition to the number of calls your application makes, you must also consider how often your application will be run. If you are writing an airline reservation transaction to be called 3000 times per minute, every API call that you can eliminate will result in higher transaction rates!

The methods for reducing the number of CPI-C calls your program makes are:

- Performing other functions while calling Send_Data()
- Extracting from CPI-C only the information you need
- Setting conversation characteristics only when necessary

Combine functions on Send_Data()

You can reduce the number of data flow calls by combining operations on the Send_Data() call. By using the Set_Send_Type() call which we discussed in "Set_Send_Type (CMSST)" in Chap. 13, you can tell CPI-C to execute any of the following operations after each Send_Data() call:

- Flush()
- Confirm()
- Prepare_To_Receive()
- Deallocate()

Wherever you would normally follow a Send_Data() call with one of the previous calls, you can instead combine them on a single Send_Data() call. In order to take advantage of combined functions, your program must:

1. Recognize when it is possible to combine functions.
2. Set the send_type appropriately.
3. Know what happens after the Send_Data() completes.

For example, your program can issue separate calls to confirm that the partner has received and processed the data it just sent:

```
Send_Data()
Confirm()
```

It can couple the two operations in a single Send_Data() call by first setting the send_type:

```
Set_Send_Type(CM_SEND_AND_CONFIRM)
Send_Data()
```

Although in this example there are the same number of calls, the overhead of Set_Send_Type() is much less than the overhead for Confirm().

The partner application program cannot tell the difference between using combined functions and issuing each call individually.

If your program uses combined functions, it has to change the value of the send_type conversation characteristic. The send_type is a sticky value; it will retain the same value until you issue a Set_Send_Type() to change it. A potential problem exists if different portions of your code issue Send_Data() with different intentions.

To avoid using the wrong send_type you should do one of the following:

- Always set the send_type before starting to issue Send_Data() calls.
- Always reset the send_type to the default value after changing it.

Minimize the number of required Set calls

You can potentially reduce two classes of Set calls in your programs. The first class is those Set calls which are redundant because they are simply resetting CPI-C defaults. For example, calling Set_Conversation_Type() and passing CM_MAPPED_CONVERSATION is unnecessary since a mapped conversation is the default.

The second class deals with the conversation characteristics that affect the behavior of other CPI-C calls. These include:

- Set_Deallocate_Type()
- Set_Fill()
- Set_Prepare_To_Receive_Type()
- Set_Receive_Type()
- Set_Send_Type()

This problem was addressed previously, in the context of combined functions on Send_Data() and the use of Set_Send_Type(). Depending upon how your code is structured, you can reduce the number of Set calls issued by choosing one of the following alternatives:

- Always set the value before starting to use its associated call.
- Always reset the value to the default value after using an altered value.

Don't toil too much on the Set calls, however. They're the fastest calls in CPI-C. The time you can save in improved maintainability will probably exceed the accumulated microseconds saved over the lifetime of your application!

Remember the information obtained from Extract calls

The information provided by CPI-C's Extract calls is usually either known by your application or not of any real use anyway. If you do need some information, extract it once and save it in local program variables for possible later use.

The Extract calls may prove to be helpful on error paths, so do not omit them entirely. For example, if a return code indicates that a call was issued in the wrong conversation state (CM_PROGRAM_STATE_CHECK), the Extract_Conversation_State() call can be issued to find the current state of the conversation.

MAKING THE MOST OF UNDERLYING APPC SESSIONS

Most applications don't run in isolation. There will probably be other transaction programs running at the same time on your client and server platforms. There may, in fact, be other applications running between the same pairs of computers.

These applications share a need for the same set of resources: sessions and conversations. There are two costs associated with sessions and conversations that we need to worry about minimizing:

- Sessions use up memory throughout the network.

    Each session requires buffer storage (memory) on both partner platforms as well as on the intermediate nodes in the network.

- Sessions take time and CPU cycles to start.

Unfortunately, reducing both costs simultaneously is not possible. If we free up memory, by deallocating sessions, we will later incur the overhead of starting the sessions when we need them again.

In the rest of this section, we will describe two ways to reduce the costs of sessions and how to strike a balance between them.

Have multiple conversations serially reuse a session

To reduce the costs of having many active sessions, you can have many applications share the same set of sessions. This technique relies on the observation that a pair of transaction programs do not spend all of their time sending data back and forth. In a typical program, there will be relatively long periods of "silence" when neither side is sending data.

The key is to deallocate a conversation when it will not be used for a significant length of time. The session previously in use by that conversation is then available for another program to use. This technique is known as short conversations. In "Using Short Conversations" in Chap. 27 we discuss short conversations and how to break up long conversations into shorter ones.

To understand how short conversations reduce session overhead, consider the following example. If we run four applications from our client to the server, each application requires a session for its conversation. But if we code our transactions using short conversations, perhaps only one or two of the programs would need a session at any given instant. Thus, we would only need two sessions between our client and server. Although this example uses only a small number of sessions, the number of sessions in use in production environments may be much greater. You must also consider the session overhead at the server platform; each client creates a certain number of sessions and there may be thousands of clients.

Keep conversations active when using APPC frequently

Every time your program activates a session or a conversation, there is overhead involved. Depending upon the work your programs perform, this overhead may or may not be significant. For example, if your program is transferring a 1-gigabyte file, there is very little chance you'll notice conversation start-up costs. On the other hand, if your program is sending the results of each individual stock sale on the New York Stock Exchange, conversation start-up costs may visibly impact your application's performance.

Consider the following when deciding whether to deallocate a conversation:

- Do not deallocate a conversation that is still being used frequently.

    For example, the aforementioned stock sale program may have small periods of idle time (seconds) but it is still used frequently. But when the stock market closes and traffic subsides, it would be wise to deallocate the conversation, freeing the session.

- The conversation start-up time should be small compared to the conversation duration.

    If the start-up time is significant compared to the work performed, consider accumulating a number of tasks together and complete them during a single conversation.

UNDERSTANDING THE SPEED OF INDIVIDUAL CALLS

We've shown you some general guidelines for improving the performance of your programs. Unfortunately, we can't anticipate every circumstance or application scenario.

To help you investigate other ways to improve performance, we've provided an analysis of the performance characteristics of each CPI-C call. Table 19.1 shows for each call or class of call the following characteristics:

Speed.   How long does it usually take for the call to complete? Many calls return quickly after little processing, some require CPI-C to do extensive processing, and some must wait for the network to process things and, thus, take longer.

Line flows.   Knowing whether a call generates a line flow can be important. The calls that do not generate line flows usually take the same amount of

TABLE 19.1   Relative Performance of CPI-C Calls

CPI-C call	Speed	Line flows	Can it block?
Set_, Extract_, Specify_, and Release_calls	very fast	none	no
Initialize_Conversation	fast (may require loading of side information)	none	no
Initialize_For_Incoming	very fast	none	no
Allocate	seconds	Bind and Bind(RSP), if session must be started; always sends an Attach	yes, if return_control is CM_WHEN_SESSION_ALLOCATED; no, if return_control is CM_IMMEDIATE
Accept_Conversation, Accept_Incoming	fast, if Attach has arrived	none	may wait for an arriving Attach, depending on TP definition
Confirm	waits for a reply	tiny	always; waits for partner to issue Confirmed or Send_Error
Confirmed	fast	tiny	may block for pacing
Flush	fast	none (line flows are the result of previous calls)	no
Prepare_To_Receive	fast	small	may block for pacing
Receive-And-Wait	waits for information	none	waits for data or status change
Receive-Immediate	medium or fast	none	no
Request_To_Send	fast	small	no
Send_Data	medium	data buffer	may block for pacing
Send_Error	medium	2 small flows	yes
Test_RTS_Received	very fast	none	no
Deallocate-Flush	fast	tiny	yes
Deallocate-Abend	fast	2 small flows	yes
Wait_For_Conversation	waits for a previously incomplete call to complete	none	waits for a previously incomplete call to complete

time to complete. Calls that do generate line flows are subject to the performance characteristics of the underlying network. If you are on a slow network with a large propagation delay, you should minimize the number of calls you issue that generate line flows.

Can it block?   Some CPI-C calls can wait indefinitely before returning control to your program. This is important, for example, in graphical user interface programs, which are expected to return control to the operating system within a certain time. If your program is waiting on a blocked CPI-C call, you can lock up the entire system.

By knowing the blocking calls, you can decide where you have to add special processing to handle the wait conditions.

Handling Errors

Making a distributed application robust is much harder than making a stand-alone application robust. Why? Because the flow of computing is split between two or more computers. Failures can occur in the local computer, the remote computer, or anywhere in between. When something fails, at least one of the computers will be "the last to know," and it probably will have continued on in the meantime. Compared to stand-alone applications, there are many more ways that failures can occur: race and timing conditions, version mismatches, setup problems, and combinations of errors. There are more places to report to, as well—principally, to any human who can fix the problem. A further challenge is that one side or the other of a distributed application is often unattended.

With distributed applications, excellent error handling and reporting will often "make the sale." That is, good problem management is a big selling factor to whomever uses the CPI-C applications you write.

This chapter introduces error-handling concepts, and techniques to handle an error once it has occurred. The next chapter covers the reporting of errors (because sometimes there is nothing to do but report the problem to the closest person) and techniques to use to avoid encountering problems in the first place.

EXPECTING THE UNEXPECTED

The failures encountered by distributed application failures fall into two broad categories. One category consists of the errors introduced because you've split an application into two parts across a network. The second category consists of traditional application failures, such as "out of memory" or "disk full," whose reporting and recovery are exacerbated by the application's split.

The first category encompasses the kinds of problems introduced when an application is split among computers and processes. Most commonly, one side or the other—or both—are not set up correctly. Finding the cause of these kinds of problems is knowledge-intensive and time-consuming. It's almost like a courtroom case: one side or the other is lying, and you have to figure out what the truth is! Other problems occur because something in the middle of the network is set up incorrectly, broken, or overloaded. The computers running the application and the programs themselves are both okay, yet the application still doesn't run right. Often the programs must diagnose the network's illness and report it to a human. Last, the programs, computers, and network can be set up correctly, but the programs are simply at different release levels among computers.

The second category consists of problems that are already well known to most programmers, but become magnified because the application is distributed. For example, invalid user input might not be diagnosed until it is parsed by a remote partner program, which then has to report back to the original program, which, in turn, reports back to the user. Similarly, corrupted data in a file or database might not be detected until a partner program reads something that it deems unacceptable. Operating system and hardware illnesses must be conveyed to a partner, which can be challenging. If your side is out of memory, how does it get enough memory to report the condition to its partner? Additionally, distributed applications can cause complex timing and race conditions that aren't a problem for applications running on a single computer.

Finally, it's usually not acceptable for a remote program to terminate when it encounters an internal error. When a stand-alone program ends with "file write failed," it's easy for a DOS user to issue a CHKDSK or DIR command and see that the disk is full. If the file write fails on the remote side of a distributed application, however, the remote side must provide information back to its local partner, diagnosing the situation itself.

LEARNING OF FAILURES

So, how do users find out about any of these failures? Users usually find out from their programs, since these are normally the reason that the computer is running. The programs themselves learn of failures from several types of returned or exchanged indicators.

One way a program learns of problems is through return codes. As a programmer, you see return codes returned from calls to communications software like CPI-C, from operating system calls, from supervisor calls or calls to library functions, or from other program procedures. If the return code at any point is not one expected by the normal program logic, special code must be executed to recover from the error to report it.

Distributed applications constantly exchange data and status to understand where they are. Yet another way a CPI-C program finds out about defects is through an unexpected status_received or data_received value. An unexpected status_received or data_received value suggests a bug in the program's logic or mismatched program versions.

Programs can also reveal failures through some kind of gauge or threshold that lets them keep track of their performance. If performance gets too poor, the application can inform its users that something is wrong. CPI-C also offers the Send_Error() call to let a partner program know something is wrong with the data or program logic. Receiving invalid data (from the partner, from a database, or from a human user) is also a sure sign that something is wrong.

In all these cases, it is the logic in a program that first discovers something is amiss. Each program should be designed so that it first tries to correct or work around problems, if possible, to avoid human intervention.

So, how exactly do human users learn of problems? They commonly see messages issued by the application they are running. Alternatively, they sense something wrong when they experience long periods of silence, or some repeated or looping situation. And sometimes, they only know something's really wrong when they smell smoke! Confounding the difficulty for the application programmer is that it's not application users who can generally do much to fix a problem, let alone do any significant diagnosis. They often need outside help from someone not directly associated with the running program.

Network administrators aren't the ones normally running the end-user applications, but they are the ones who will be called upon to fix failures. Irate users let them know quickly about problems. Administrators would prefer to learn about problems well ahead of those irate calls (for example, from alert reports in their network management system). They also learn about failures by visiting end users' computers and by reviewing their message logs and error logs. All of these are mechanisms to let those who can fix and diagnose problems find out about them.

DEALING WITH CPI-C RETURN CODES

All CPI-C calls have a *return_code* parameter. CPI-C passes a return code value back to your programs at the completion of a call. The return code can indicate a problem with the local program or computer, with the partner program or computer, or with the network between them.

Some of the CPI-C return codes indicate the results of the local processing of a call. These return codes are returned on the call that invoked the local processing. An example is the CM_PROGRAM_PARAMETER_CHECK return code, which reports on an error in one of the passed parameters.

Other return codes indicate results of processing done at the remote end of the conversation. Depending on the call, these return codes can be returned on the call that invoked the remote processing or on some subsequent call. An example is the CM_TPN_NOT_RECOGNIZED return code, which is caused when the attach manager at the server side realizes it has no TP definition that matches an arriving TP name. This return code is never returned on the

Allocate() call which caused the TP name to be sent, but on a later call, after the Attach has arrived at the partner.

Still other return codes report on events or calls that originate at the remote end of the conversation. An example is the CM_PROGRAM_ERROR_NO_TRUNC return code, which indicates that the partner program issued a Send_Error() call.

No matter the cause of a return code, it serves one of three different purposes for your programs:

- To control the flow and execution of a program
- To aid application developers and testers, when your programs are in a debug environment
- To help the users of your programs, when human intervention is required in a production environment

Notice the difference here between production-level code and debug-level code. For example, in production-level code, a state check return code probably means you're talking to the wrong program. In debug-level code, however, where you know you've set up the programs right in your lab, a state check means you've probably found a bug in your application design.

You should exhaustively test the pairs of programs you write. Correct the programs if they supply invalid parameters or result in invalid conversation states. Users of your programs should not encounter these types of errors in a production environment. We'll talk more about testing in "Testing Your CPI-C Programs" at the end of this chapter.

Assume the users of your programs know nothing about data communications. Your users thus have two tasks: to get your application configured and running correctly the first time, and to get it running again if it fails. Never assume that a user can fix or debug the programs, or reconnect a cable without the appropriate amount of guidance. It is your job to make this guidance information useful to the user and to the person who must debug the real problem.

Categories of return codes

In App. A we provide our guide to the CPI-C return codes. We've developed this guide after years of using the descriptions in the CPI-C reference manuals, and being frustrated that they didn't tell us plainly enough what was wrong and how to fix the problem. Share this guide with the users of your programs, if your programs let CPI-C return codes show through your applications' installers and users.

While it looks like there are a lot of return codes, only a subset of these really makes sense on most of your CPI-C calls. To manage the complexity, we recommend establishing the following seven groups of return codes that can be handled similarly. The groups are as follows:

Group 1: Normal program operation.   For each CPI-C call, your program has one or more return codes that it expects to see. CM_OK and CM_DEALLO-

CATED_NORMAL are the return codes that you'll plan to see on most CPI-C calls. Return codes for normal program operation include:

```
  0  CM_OK
 18  CM_DEALLOCATED_NORMAL
100  CM_TAKE_BACKOUT
135  CM_DEALLOCATED_NORMAL_BO
```

For most other return codes, your program must divert from its mainline, high-performance path.

Group 2: Recoverable by the program. The local program or its partner should handle the situation, since it is reasonable to expect it to occur some percentage of the time. The programs should take the appropriate recovery action and continue. The following is a list of return codes that are recoverable by the program. Many of them apply only to specific CPI-C calls:

```
21  CM_PROGRAM_ERROR_NO_TRUNC
22  CM_PROGRAM_ERROR_PURGING
23  CM_PROGRAM_ERROR_TRUNC
28  CM_UNSUCCESSFUL
32  CM_SVC_ERROR_NO_TRUNC
33  CM_SVC_ERROR_PURGING
34  CM_SVC_ERROR_TRUNC
```

Group 3: Human intervention may help. Because your program generally cannot fix the way CPI-C or APPC are set up on both computers, or the network components between them, human intervention may be needed to allow it to run successfully. Users of your programs should expect to see these return codes, which indicate common setup problems. As the program developer, you should translate each of these into useful directions that an unskilled user can follow to correct the situation. Examples of this type of return code are:

```
 1  CM_ALLOCATE_FAILURE_NO_RETRY
 3  CM_CONVERSATION_TYPE_MISMATCH
 5  CM_PIP_NOT_SPECIFIED_CORRECTLY
 7  CM_SYNC_LVL_NOT_SUPPORTED_LU
 8  CM_SYNC_LVL_NOT_SUPPORTED_PGM
 9  CM_TPN_NOT_RECOGNIZED
10  CM_TP_NOT_AVAILABLE_NO_RETRY
19  CM_PARAMETER_ERROR
```

Group 4: Recoverable by the program with user help. Your program can recover from a conversation security failure by changing the security type and/or by prompting the user for a valid user ID and password.

```
 6  CM_SECURITY_NOT_VALID
```

Your program will need to start the conversation again from the beginning.

Group 5: Recoverable by the program by retrying the conversation.   Several pairs of CPI-C return codes have the suffix RETRY or NO_RETRY in their name:

RETRY.   Means that the condition indicated by the return code may not be permanent, and the program can try to allocate a session again. Whether or not the retry attempt succeeds depends on the duration of the condition. Your program should limit the number of times it attempts to retry without success. Your program should *always* retry at least once, however. There are many conditions where the first failure triggers the network components to take action, and the condition is fixed a millisecond later.

NO_RETRY.   Means that the condition is probably permanent. A program should not attempt to allocate a session again until the condition is corrected.

Your program should handle these situations by retrying the conversation and repeating the transaction that was interrupted. This allows your programs the opportunity to recover automatically from network failures by re-establishing a new conversation over a different network route.

```
  2   CM_ALLOCATE_FAILURE_RETRY
 11   CM_TP_NOT_AVAILABLE_RETRY
 26   CM_RESOURCE_FAILURE_NO_RETRY
 27   CM_RESOURCE_FAILURE_RETRY
133   CM_RESOURCE_FAIL_NO_RETRY_BO
134   CM_RESOURCE_FAILURE_RETRY_BO
```

If the conversation can't be started or restarted after several tries, your program needs to take the same steps it takes for the return codes in Group 3. Human intervention is probably required to fix the problem.

Group 6: Unexpected errors.   Users of your program shouldn't expect to see these errors. Recovery from unexpected errors requires a fix to your programs, the environment they're running in, or both. You may see these return codes frequently during program development and testing; they probably indicate a bug in these situations. In a production-level environment, the three return codes probably indicate some operational or setup problem. The following return codes are unexpected in most programs:

```
20   CM_PRODUCT_SPECIFIC_ERROR
24   CM_PROGRAM_PARAMETER_CHECK
25   CM_PROGRAM_STATE_CHECK
```

In a production environment, CM_PRODUCT_SPECIFIC_ERROR probably means that the underlying network software is not installed or is not active. CM_PROGRAM_STATE_CHECK is an expected return code on the Wait_For_Conversation() call. Otherwise, CM_PROGRAM_STATE_CHECK probably means that you're talking to the wrong program altogether; either the TP name sent by the client or the TP definition on the server side is wrong. You'll probably find these kinds of problems on the first few calls of your program.

Whether in a debug or production environment, you have a problem that needs to be reported and fixed. Your program should produce a detailed log entry for the problem. The log entry (either a message log, error log, or both) should contain enough information to allow a reader of the entry to discern if the error is a bug (that is, a genuine program defect that should be fixed) or a user error. You should tell the user that the program or its setup has a defect. Provide sufficient information in the log entry to allow someone to do problem determination (for example, the module name, function name, failing line of code, and type of error). After creating a log entry, the program should end. The conversation in error should terminate. See "Cleaning Up a Conversation" in Chap. 16 for a general procedure to clean up the conversation.

Group 7: Conversation is unexpectedly over.   Last, there are a set of return codes that indicate that the partner abruptly ended the conversation. Most likely, the partner program was stopped while it was running. If this return code is preceded by a return code that indicated a Send_Error() was issued, the program probably encountered an unrecoverable error.

```
 17   CM_DEALLOCATED_ABEND
 30   CM_DEALLOCATED_ABEND_SVC
 31   CM_DEALLOCATED_ABEND_TIMER
130   CM_DEALLOCATED_ABEND_BO
131   CM_DEALLOCATED_ABEND_SVC_BO
132   CM_DEALLOCATED_ABEND_TIMER_BO
```

Explain to your user that the partner program has ended unexpectedly. The user may need to phone or visit the partner to see why this occurred.

Additional diagnostic information

On many platforms that support CPI-C, additional platform-specific diagnostic information accompanies return codes. The most useful of these is SNA sense data. You may also find error log entries and alerts generated because of the condition identified by a CPI-C return code.

SNA sense data.   Four-byte SNA sense data can provide pinpoint detail on the exact cause of a network failure. (An example of a sense code is X'081C0013'.) These are particularly valuable for the CM_ALLOCATE_FAILURE_(RETRY or NO_RETRY) return codes, the return codes which indicate that a session could not be established for some reason.

For example, whenever the OS/2 Communications Manager returns one of these two return codes on an Allocate verb (using the native APPC API), it also returns the sense data in the verb control block. SNA sense data can often be found within traces, messages, and error logs, depending on the platform and type of error. It will be part of the CPI-C secondary return code information in CPI-C 2.0, but that's of little help to your users today. Find a way to get your users to the associated sense data whenever they get an allocation failure.

We've put our collection of SNA sense data descriptions for APPC and APPN problems on the diskette that accompanies this book. Consider shipping this with your applications. A set of architectural descriptions for each sense data value is listed in *SNA Formats,* but these descriptions contain little diagnostic assistance or recommendations.

Error log entries.   On many platforms, additional information about hardware and software failures, such as adapter card problems, is automatically logged in an operating-system-specific error log file. For example, the OS/2 Communications Manager and OS/400 automatically log such communications errors.

Alerts.   Some failures are caused by errors encountered in the lower layers of the underlying network software. This software may automatically generate its own report when it finds a problem. This report is called an *alert.* It is an internal message that finds its own way through the network to a network management help desk. If this occurs, the central network manager can highlight the problem, and potentially do some diagnostics on the failure.

The types of failures associated with alerts are generally hardware failures, ID mismatches of various types, and overflow of counters. Your CPI-C application has no direct control of these automatic alerts, but your users may be happy to know that someone at a help desk knows about their problem even before they pick up the telephone.

HANDLING OTHER UNEXPECTED RETURNED VALUES

On some calls, the return code is not the only source of information about what happened during the call. For example, on a Receive() call, the values of the *data_received* and *status_received* parameters should also be checked.

Data_received

The most likely reason for an unexpected data_received value in a production environment is that your programs are mismatched. The wrong TP name was sent, or the wrong executable program name was encoded in the TP definition. If this occurs, tell your user and exit the program.

Your programs can encounter an unexpected CM_INCOMPLETE_DATA_ RECEIVED value if their receive buffer is too small. Always use a receive buffer that's as large as possible, nominally 32,767 bytes. Make sure the requested_length value is correct on your Receive() call. If your partner program's design has changed so that it no longer matches the design of the local program, the partner may now be sending records larger than the local program was designed to receive. For example, starting with CPI-C 1.2, the partner can send records larger than 32,767 bytes. If the local program can't accommodate these, there's obviously a version mismatch between the programs. They should be exchanging version numbers right after the Allocate() call, not encountering this problem later in their code.

Finally, at the time of this printing, VM/ESA has a bug that is in evidence when you send it a record larger than 32,763 bytes—for example, 32,767 bytes. Even if your requested_length and receive buffer is 32,767 bytes long, if your local program is running on VM/ESA, it will receive the incoming record as two partial records. This means your program will see CM_INCOM-PLETE_DATA_RECEIVED on the first of the Receive() calls.

Status_received

Like the data_received value, the most likely reason for an unexpected status_received value in a production environment is that your programs are mismatched. The wrong TP name was sent or the wrong executable program name was encoded in the TP definition. If this occurs, tell your user and exit the program.

The data_received and status_received value can arrive together—on one Receive() call, or separately, on two calls. If your program sees a status_received value of CM_NO_STATUS_RECEIVED when it expects to see a status change, it should issue another Receive() call. The expected status change should be returned on that next call.

CHOOSING THE RIGHT MECHANISM FOR HANDLING ERRORS

Despite the steps you have taken to make your application and its configuration bulletproof, it will still fail. Can you help the application recover without human intervention? Depending on the return code, indicator, and CPI-C call, there is a hierarchy of techniques to consider in recovering from an error.

- *Retry the last CPI-C call.* This is done when the return code, data_received, or status_received indicator reports that the communications call was unsuccessful, but may work if tried again. For example: the CM_UNSUC-CESSFUL return code on Receive-Immediate.

- *Skip data record(s) and continue on.* A syntactic or semantic error in the data should be detected by the sender or receiver of the data. Either partner can choose to skip this record (or more) and continue with the transaction. Consider what reporting techniques you need to implement when records are skipped.

- *Go back to the last checkpoint.* Similarly, they can choose to go back to the last place where they knew everything was okay. They can choose this because of data errors, or because of a conversation failure. They start the conversation again where they last successfully confirmed.

- *Retry this conversation.* Sometimes it is easier just to restart the entire conversation. If so, be sure that any complete or partial transactions can be re-run multiple times without requiring additional recovery.

- *Rerun the whole program.*   A single program may consist of many conversations, in parallel or in sequence. The least appealing action for a user is to require a program be rerun from the beginning.

Thus, there are three primary tools to use when an error has been encountered in a distributed application.

1. Issue Send_Error(), to report to the partner, and continue to the next agreed-upon record. This is used for two types of errors:

   - Errors in parsing bad data
   - Errors discovered by the program

2. Deallocate the conversation and leave as soon as possible. This action should be saved for the following catastrophes:

   - Operating system and hardware: shortages, complex interactions, faults
   - Latent bugs in the application logic
   - Can't recover without human intervention

3. Retry the last call or restart the conversation. This is a common recovery action, used for the following:

   - Configuration and setup mistakes (or mismatches)
   - Network outages and slowdowns

RETRYING CONVERSATIONS

The first thing that must occur in order for a pair of programs to communicate is that they must successfully establish a connection between the two computers. You know now that this connection is called a session; a session is established between the logical units used by the two communicating programs.

An underlying session is necessary for each conversation between two programs. A session is set aside for a conversation by issuing the Allocate() call. If the local LU is unable to allocate the session it needs, the Allocate() call will fail with one of two return codes: CM_ALLOCATE_FAILURE_NO_RETRY or CM_ALLOCATE_FAILURE_RETRY. These return codes are seen frequently by application programs that use CPI-C; your application must plan ahead on how to handle them—they will occur!

CM_ALLOCATE_FAILURE_NO_RETRY.   This return code says that the local communications software (that is, the local LU) finds that there is "no hope" a session with its partner can be established without human intervention. For example, there is no communications adapter card in this computer.

CM_ALLOCATE_FAILURE_RETRY.   This return code indicates that there is "some hope"; the local LU is unable to tell for sure what is wrong, so there is hope that it may get better by itself. For example, some piece of wire in the middle of the network has been cut. At other times, however, the failure is due to an error in the network setup, which must be manually corrected.

Your application should plan to call its retry procedure (retry guidelines will be introduced below). No data has flowed to the partner application yet; the retry of this conversation is simple. If the retry fails, report this condition to the application user.

The most likely problem, for both these return codes, is a configuration mismatch or error on one or both computers. This type of configuration problem is the type that you want to catch with the sanity-check program, APING, mentioned earlier. Try to assure that all obvious setup and configuration problems have been solved before an application user has to suffer through this type of problem late at night—when a user sees one of these return codes in an actual production environment, it should only be because of a real network fault.

If the configuration and setup are correct, the other likely cause is the failure of a network component. The major network component categories are listed as follows, but your search for the network fault will rarely include all six. Often, symptoms collected before you get to this point will rule out certain component categories.

- Local computer
- Network adapter
- Wiring concentrator and cable
- Partner computer (server or host)
- Interconnection devices (bridges, routers, gateways, APPN network nodes)
- Protocol stacks (networking and application software)

Handling other retry return codes

There are two other pairs of return codes where one member of the pair indicates a retry condition, and the other indicates no retry. Each of these return codes indicates that the current conversation ID is no longer valid.

CM_TP_NOT_AVAILABLE_RETRY and **NO_RETRY.** These return codes indicate that a session was established with the partner, but the attach manager (or similar software) on the target computer signals that the executable program could not be started. For example, CM_TP_NOT_AVAILABLE_NO_RETRY is returned when the program corresponding to the received TP name cannot be found on the partner computer. In contrast, the CM_TP_NOT_AVAILABLE_RETRY return code can indicate, for example, that the program is present on the partner computer and could ordinarily be started, but the operating system on the partner computer had no more processes available in which to start it.

These return codes are not returned on the Allocate() call; they are returned after the Attach arrives at the target. Since no data was received by the target, if retry is indicated, the conversation can be restarted from the beginning.

CM_RESOURCE_FAILURE_RETRY and **NO_RETRY.** The historic SNA name for a conversation is "resource." A conversation (and hence, its underlying session) was up and running, but that active conversation went away for some reason. This can occur any time after the conversation is allocated. If the return code indicates retry, it may be necessary for your application to return to the point where data was last received and acknowledged by the partner program.

Deciding how often to retry

If the return code indicates a retry condition, how often should the conversation be retried? The answer depends on the application user's patience and on the application's needs.

- Is a user waiting? Is the program attended by a human?
- How critical is response time for the user? For the application?
- Should the application tell the user that it is retrying?
- How critical is this conversation?
- Retry forever?

You can envision a number of different retry guidelines; here are some all-purpose retry guidelines, based on solid principles of network traffic and cognitive psychology:

Retry guidelines

1. Retry continuously for the first 10 seconds—then report to the user that there is a problem and that the program is retrying. (Use your judgment in retrying continuously; on some platforms, a hard retry loop may tie up the CPU and all available resources. Consider yielding or sleeping briefly between retries.) If the user does not (or cannot) interrupt the program's operation, then
2. Retry every second for the first minute, then
3. Retry every minute forever.

Lowering the impact of retrying a conversation

Design your applications to minimize the amount of data that needs to be resent after a successful recovery. For example, the CM_RESOURCE_FAILURE_RETRY return code can indicate an aborted data exchange with the partner.

The first step is to assure a good conversation before sending (or resending) any data. Force any CM_ALLOCATE_FAILURE_ or CM_TP_NOT_AVAILABLE_ return codes, using an Allocate() call followed by Confirm() call. Assure the right versions of the programs are conversing, by exchanging version numbers.

Next, if agreement of the data between the two programs is important, break the data exchanges into small chunks. Follow each of these with a Confirm-Confirmed exchange, and be prepared to return to the point of the last successful Confirm on both sides should the conversation fail.

If necessary, keep an audit trail suited to the application. For example, when transferring multiple files, your programs can synchronize after each file (that is, the program sending the file issues Confirm(), and the program receiving the file replies with a Confirmed() or Send_Error() call) or they can exchange a count of the number of files transferred so far.

TESTING YOUR CPI-C PROGRAMS

Extensive testing of your new CPI-C applications is somewhat beyond the scope of this book, but we'll offer a few of our favorite suggestions.

It's easy to write and use test driver programs that talk with either side of your CPI-C application. The side information (on the client side) and TP definition (on the server side) decouple your programs from their "regular partners." Let's say you write a client test program that you use to test the server side of your application. To talk to your server program, all you have to do is make sure the right TP name gets used, the one that the server is already expecting to see. When the TP name arrives at the server, the attach manager will find the existing TP definition for your server program, and start it. Similarly, you can put any program you want on the server side, by just changing the name of the executable filename in the server's TP definition.

We'll illustrate this situation with two small test programs. Program SERROR.C initializes a conversation and allocates a session, then issues Send_Error() calls forever in a loop. Does your server program handle the repeated return codes correctly? Here's the source code for program SERROR.C:

```
/*----------------------------------------------------------------
 *  Send_Error test, client side.
 *  (file SERROR.C)
 *--------------------------------------------------------------*/
#include <cpic.h>               /* conversation API library    */
#include <stdarg.h>             /* variable arguments          */
#include <stdio.h>              /* file I/O                    */
#include <stdlib.h>             /* standard library            */
#include <string.h>             /* strings and memory          */

#include "serrloop.h"           /* Send_Error loop             */

#include "docpic.h"             /* CPI-C do_ calls             */

int main(int argc, char *argv[])
{
```

```
/*------------------------------------------------------------
 * Issue Send_Error calls forever (client side)
 *----------------------------------------------------------*/
CM_RETURN_CODE   cpic_return_code;
unsigned char    conversation_ID[CM_CID_SIZE];

for ( ; ; ) {
    /*------------------------------------------------------------
     * Get the symbolic destination from the command line and
     * initialize a conversation.
     *----------------------------------------------------------*/
    if (argc > 1) { /* is there at least one argument? */
        do_initialize_conversation(conversation_ID, argv[1]);
    }
    else {
        handle_error(
            conversation_ID,
            "A symbolic destination name must be provided");
    }

    /*------------------------------------------------------------
     * Allocate a session for this conversation.
     *----------------------------------------------------------*/
    do_allocate(conversation_ID);

    cpic_return_code = send_error_loop(conversation_ID);

    if ((cpic_return_code != CM_DEALLOCATED_NORMAL) &&
        (cpic_return_code != CM_DEALLOCATED_ABEND)) {
        handle_cpic_rc(
            conversation_ID, cpic_return_code, "CMSERR");
    }
}

return EXIT_SUCCESS;          /* program was successful      */
}
```

Both the client and the server side of these two test drivers use the same procedure to loop forever doing Send_Error() calls: send_error_loop(). Here's the code for that procedure:

```
/*------------------------------------------------------------
 * Send_Error() loop.
 * (file SERRLOOP.C)
 *----------------------------------------------------------*/
#include <cpic.h>                 /* conversation API library   */
#include <stdio.h>                /* file I/O                   */

CM_RETURN_CODE
send_error_loop(unsigned char * conversation_ID)
```

```
{
    /*-------------------------------------------------------------
     *  Issue Send_Error() while the return_codes are expected.
     *-----------------------------------------------------------*/
    unsigned long send_error_count = 0;
    unsigned long cm_ok_count = 0;

    for ( ; ; send_error_count++) {
        CM_REQUEST_TO_SEND_RECEIVED rts_received;
        CM_RETURN_CODE              cpic_return_code;

        (void)printf(
            "\rSend_Error count = %lu, CM_OK count = %lu",
            send_error_count, cm_ok_count);

        cmserr(                     /* Send_Error                */
            conversation_ID,        /* conversation ID           */
            &rts_received,          /* ignore partner's RTS      */
            &cpic_return_code);     /* return code               */

        if (cpic_return_code == CM_OK) {
            cm_ok_count++;          /* count when it's not a race */
        }

        if ((cpic_return_code != CM_OK) &&
            (cpic_return_code != CM_PROGRAM_ERROR_PURGING)) {
            /* we got an unexpected return code */
            (void)printf("\n");
            return cpic_return_code;
        }
    }
}
```

A test driver for the server side is now simple to create. Program SERRORD.C accepts an incoming conversation, then issues Send_Error() calls forever in a loop. Do your client programs handle the repeated return codes correctly? Here's the source code for program SERRORD.C.

```
/*-------------------------------------------------------------
 *  Send_Error test, server side.
 *  (file SERRORD.C)
 *-----------------------------------------------------------*/
#include <cpic.h>               /* conversation API library  */
#include <limits.h>             /* integer bounds            */
#include <stdio.h>              /* file I/O                  */
#include <stdlib.h>             /* standard library          */
#include <string.h>             /* strings and memory        */

#include "serrloop.h"           /* Send_Error loop           */
```

```
#include "docpic.h"              /* CPI-C do_ calls           */

int main(void)
{
    /*--------------------------------------------------------------
     *  Issue Send_Error calls forever (server side)
     *------------------------------------------------------------*/
    unsigned char   conversation_ID[CM_CID_SIZE];
    CM_RETURN_CODE  cpic_return_code;

    /*--------------------------------------------------------------
     *  Accept a new conversation from the client.
     *
     *  We assume (without explicitly checking) that the
     *  conversation_type is MAPPED and the sync_level is NONE.
     *  The TP definition should restrict these values, which
     *  will then be verified by the attach manager.
     *------------------------------------------------------------*/
    do_accept_conversation(conversation_ID);

    cpic_return_code = send_error_loop(conversation_ID);

    handle_cpic_rc(
        conversation_ID, cpic_return_code, "CMSERR");

    return EXIT_SUCCESS;          /* program was successful     */
}
```

For fun, you can connect these two programs to one another. You'll get to see examples of the classic Send_Error() race condition. If two programs issue Send_Error() at the same time, the side with the current permission-to-send wins the race and the other side gets CM_PROGRAM_ERROR_PURGING. Otherwise, the permission-to-send gets passed to whatever side issues a successful Send_Error() call.

Now that you have the idea, you might want to mix up the combination of calls that are issued in the test drivers. You'll probably want to force your application to execute its Deallocate-Abend logic (both on the sending and on the receiving side) at random intervals. Deallocate-Abend processing can also be tested by getting the application running, then terminating one of the programs.

How about writing a test driver program that does nothing but loop forever, sending large records? If the partner ever grabs the permission-to-send, it can always get it back by issuing a Send_Error() call.

We also recommend testing the retry logic in your application well. Get your application programs running in a loop, then unplug the cable between the computers. Plug the cable back in, and see what happens. Then repeat the process. Often, a program will navigate its error-handling logic once but cause some side effects along the way, and not be able to execute that same code a second time.

Without explicitly creating a test-driver program, here's a simple test shell that loops forever. This is the DOS version, but you can build a similar program easily for most operating systems we know. In DOS, the string "%1 %2 %3 . . ." simply takes the first thing from the command line, then the second, then the third, up to the ninth.

```
@echo off
:LABEL
call %1 %2 %3 %4 %5 %6 %7 %8 %9
GOTO :LABEL
```

Save this program as file LOOP.BAT. To use it, just type LOOP, followed by the command you want to execute and its parameters. For example, to run the credit-check transaction client over and over again (which will keep the server quite busy), enter the following:

```
LOOP CREDIT your-sym-dest-name
```

This creates a continual stream of traffic, and makes it easy to find different random ways to terminate either program or anything in the network between them. You can create a heavier load on your server program and platform by starting lots of copies of this program at the same time!

Reporting (and Avoiding) Failures

A problem in a network or in a distributed application shows up first as an unexpected return code on a communications call, or as an unexpected status_received or data_received value on a Receive() call. We've discussed techniques that applications can use to try to recover from unexpected errors. However, for many errors, human intervention is required to correct the problem. It is the responsibility of your application, the place where a failure is first encountered, to get every piece of available information about the error into the hands of the right people. And you'll find that many people are often involved.

Three persons or groups need to know about errors encountered by an application:

1. The person who needs to know first

2. The person who can give the quickest solution

3. The person who can fix the problem permanently

The person who needs to know first is often an end user, someone running an application. This person may know nothing about computers and networking, but is nonetheless the person sitting in front of a display watching the screen. This person needs to know that something is wrong, because, depending on what his or her application does, it may be time to start changing their schedule of appointments for the day.

To avoid disrupting a user's day too much, someone should rush to assist him or her and get the program back up and running again. Often, this is a "quick fix," to work around the problem in the fastest way. The person doing this may be a member of the local support staff. He or she may be the person who installed or configured the application, the operating system, the computer, or its network connection. The fix may be given over the telephone, consisting of explicit, but simple, directions for the end user to follow.

Many of the failures that users of your application may encounter will require a permanent fix somewhere. If components in the network are failing, a central network management staff will need to know about the problem. If there is a defect in the application itself, the owner or vendor of the application needs to be contacted with a problem report.

We've identified three different groups of people who may need to know about a problem. These groups have different skills, and need different degrees of detailed information. But we're familiar with real life: In a world of personal computers, home computers, notebook computers, and late office hours, it may be only the end user who's there, helpless, trying to get some work done! Your application needs to provide as much overview and introductory information as possible for users in this situation.

CAPTURING NETWORK AND APPLICATION INFORMATION

So, let's start with what your application should do upon encountering its first unexpected, unrecoverable situation. Assume the error cannot be recreated— assume this is the first time any program has seen this situation—assume you get $1000 for each unique error your application finds. Capture everything you can before the first failure.

Capture this information in a *footprint* of the error, capturing as many aspects of the problem as are applicable. Write the footprint information to a unique file, either creating a new file for each occurrence or appending to an existing file.

This information comes in several classes. First is information related to the communications problem: the CPI-C call being executed, the CPI-C return code, the status_received and data_received values from a Receive() call, the supplied and returned parameters on the call, the conversation state, and any related SNA sense data (if available). Next is information related to the application: the application's name, version, module name, and the current location in the source code. Other programs on the same computer may have influenced the problem; what other programs were running? What version of the operating system and communications code were running? And, of course, capture the date, time, and location of the computer.

In addition to capturing as much as possible about the application, the computer, and its setting, capture relevant information about the current network setup. In APPC, this information includes the following:

- Local and partner logical unit (LU) names
- Name of the local control point (CP)
- Name of the mode being used

- Mode's session limits
- TP names that were sent or received
- User ID
- Validity of the password (don't record the password itself)
- Type of data link control (DLC) being used
- Local and remote DLC addresses
- Current network topology (if available from an APPN network node)

In addition, capture hardware information about the local computer: its machine type and serial number, and the adapter cards being used.

Not all of this information is available to applications on every platform, so capture what your application can. CPI-C offers the group of Extract calls, which are of some help in collecting CPI-C–related names and status. These CPI-C calls require an active conversation ID, so calling them after an error has caused a conversation failure is no help.

You will generally have to include some platform-specific calls in your footprint-capture routines. For example, platforms like the OS/2 Communications Manager and CICS provide DISPLAY verbs, offering lots of detailed SNA information. The DISPLAY_APPN verb in the OS/2 Communications Manager can be used to obtain the contents of local APPN directories and topology databases. These verbs do not require active conversations.

Error information and information about the environment the application is running in are computer-dependent (and will be for a long time). Segregate your error-reporting code from your mainline, production code. Have it be separately loaded, if allowed by your operating system and linker. Structure it so that it is easy to port among platforms.

REPORTING FAILURES: LOCALLY

Having done "first failure data capture" of the error footprint information, what do you show to the human users of the application? Answer: Use your judgment about what you show your users, depending on who your expected users are.

In general, start with some sort of pop-up message for the application's user or installer. Describe the problem briefly "in plain English." Refer to the detailed documentation that will be necessary for problem determination. Point to the footprint information captured by the program. Provide a course of action for likely solutions. You can often give some easy pointers on what to do about common setup errors, common network failures, and data or application errors.

However, you are never guaranteed that there is a person who is sitting and watching the application. This is especially important for server, background, and unattended programs. Thus, the error-reporting routines must also write their information to a problem log, which points to the footprint information. On some platforms, such as OS/400 and the OS/2 Communications Manager, system-supplied logs exist that applications can choose to write to. On other platforms, the preferred behavior is to write error information to an application-defined problem log.

Return code text

Where should your program get the text and help for the error messages it shows to users and installers? First, clearly show the type of return code. An application program can deal with many types of return codes—you've certainly seen these kinds of error messages yourself where you get something that is labeled a return code but have no idea what it relates to. Return codes can come from operating system calls, library routines, communications calls, and even application-specific procedures. Point to more details about the code: refer to system and common on-line help if possible. Point to files that contain softcopies of diagnostic information. Name the exact reference book containing the first level of additional information. Supply a reference to a telephone number where human help can be obtained (from anywhere in the world).

The full text for the extended help for the hundreds of possible return codes can take megabytes. Don't bundle this with every application you ship, but find a way to get the user to such information in the shortest possible time.

Separate error text from code

A classic axiom of good programming is "If the application you build is successful, you will want to port it to another platform." You understand the value of CPI-C for porting communications calls, but everything discussed so far about local error reporting involves screen I/O and file I/O—which is still not too portable. Recognize this ahead of time, and do everything you can to group this code together; plan to port it someday soon.

Another reminder: in a world of international users, assume that there will someday be international translation of your application. Never bury error messages (or any text strings, for that matter) in the middle of your code. Use message files or resource files, if available, on the platform you're writing to. These are available with Windows, OS/2, OS/400, and VM. Alternatively, put message text in separately compilable files. This lets you isolate all translation to separate files, which can then be recompiled and relinked.

REPORTING FAILURES: REMOTELY

Once your application has successfully captured everything it can on the local computer, and reported to any user who might be sitting there, where else should it report problems it finds? If possible, report it to the partner application, using the Send_Error() or Send_Data() protocols discussed earlier.

Report the problem to the central network management authority. The management services facilities available in SNA are one of its competitive strengths. Many platforms support automatic reporting of errors detected in communications adapters or in the APPC kernel code itself. In addition, they support programming interfaces that allow the reports to be initiated by an application program.

Finally, certain problems need to be reported directly to the application's vendor. In a world of inexpensive modems, why not have an application diagnose its own failures, then call directly to a vendor's report center and automatically report what is wrong? An example of an application error that needs to be reported to its vendor is the CPI-C return code CM_PROGRAM_PARAM-ETER_CHECK in a production-level program.

REDUCING THE OPPORTUNITY FOR FAILURE

You can avoid the frequency with which your programs report failures if you simply cut down on the opportunities for problems. You know as a programmer that there are two kinds of problems: those you have thought about and have written code to handle, and the bizarre ones you have not encountered and never expected. Gain as much experience in the early life of your application on how to handle both classes of problems smoothly.

It has been said many times before, but here it is again: write your error-handling and reporting code as early as possible, so it gets as much exercise as you can give it. Many unusual errors occur during program development and testing—build your error-handling code so that it guides you through these problems. If your error-reporting code is not helpful and accurate enough to speed your own debugging during the development process, then make the time to improve that code as early as possible.

Do everything you can to minimize the opportunity for user mistakes. You know that users must set up your application to run it. Make your application installation and network setup as foolproof as possible. We'll spend a whole chapter discussing the things you can do in your client program, in Chap. 22. This helps with half the problem, but your users still need to get the TP definition right on the server side. Describe the setup of the TP definition and its interaction with the attach manager in ways that don't allow the application installer to take any missteps.

Distributed applications can fail in many more ways than stand-alone programs. Test your applications extensively and with gusto. Test them as widely as possible before you ship them. Do as large a beta test as you can, for as long as you can. During the testing, have your tracing hooks enabled so you can make problem determination as simple as possible. Finally, provide excellent response to those early users—treat your beta testers like gold.

Avoiding user interaction during installation

Millions of people of all ages are able to "install and run" TV video computer games. TV video games are a good model to use when considering how easy your application is to set up and use. As much as possible, make your application setup "plug and play."

Parts of the CPI-C setup for an application cannot be made plug-and-play on some existing platforms. Try to automate and simplify the network configuration required by those applications. Here are some ways to do that:

- *Use a programmed interface for setup verbs.*   The OS/2 Communications Manager is an example of a platform where you can run a network setup program. You can write programs that issue verbs to set up the CPI-C or APPC environments needed to run an application. For example, use the DEFINE_TP verb when appropriate to avoid additional TP definitions.

- *Provide ready-to-run configuration files.*   Ship a ready-to-run network configuration file, ready to be merged with a user's existing configuration, or to be used as a model for making changes throughout the network.

- *Ship prebuilt configuration templates.*   Build a template of what the configuration should be. Show each of the network configuration parameters; for example, what fields should always be set to particular values, and which fields a user must set.

- *Supply EXECs, batch, or command files.*   Sometimes, it comes down to manual changes that need to be made. Can these be combined into a command-level program? Perhaps the name of the local LU can be provided as a parameter to a command program, which makes changes to a number of files throughout the system.

Preparing for the worst

Murphy's Law suggests that you still have work to do after having made the setup and configuration of your distributed application as foolproof as possible. Assume that the person who installs your application has no experience with computers, software, or networks. Let's face it: someday, somewhere, somebody will forget to run something, or they'll turn off the computer in the middle of setup, or they'll delete a required file, or something else.

Thoroughly document the network configuration. Use lots of diverse examples. Do market research on the most common combinations of computers, links, and configurations; be sure to show the configuration of these explicitly. Use lots of pictures, including pictures of the exact screens that must be changed—or must be verified for correctness. If things must be done manually, list every keystroke, and provide lots of checkpoints: "Does the screen look like this after you did that?" If it doesn't look like you show, describe how the installer can get back on track again.

While you're automating the application's network setup, make sure there is an easy way to back out of the installation. We've seen the recent development of software packages designed to back out the installation of other Windows applications. While the installation may be foolproof for fools, expert users often need more flexibility; your installation and setup procedures must address multiple audiences.

Additionally, remember that you are setting up a distributed application. All computers involved must be correctly set up and be at the right level. Is the required hardware present? Is the operating system at the right release level? Have any required fixes been installed? Assure that you have provided ways to find out not only that the application is installed correctly on one computer, but that it is installed at the right level on every computer involved.

Ship a sanity-check program with your application (mainframe programmers may know of this as an *installation verification procedure;* LAN programmers may know of this as a *Ping* program). Use the portable APING application, now available on most CPI-C platforms. Have the application's installer run it to assure correct network setup for the computers running your application. If your application will be used in a production environment, encourage the installer and administrative staff to run it frequently for preventive maintenance; whenever something in the middle of the network changes, run APING to assure a path between the partners in your application.

Checking for a good connection

There are times when you want to design your application so that it knows it has a good connection to its partner before it goes any further. This can be handled with the set of calls shown in Fig. 21.1. This sequence forms the core of the sanity-check program mentioned previously (APING), and should be used when testing the application before it ships. The sanity-check application also exchanges release and version numbers with its partner. You don't necessarily want to include these calls at the beginning of every possible conversation; they have a small performance penalty.

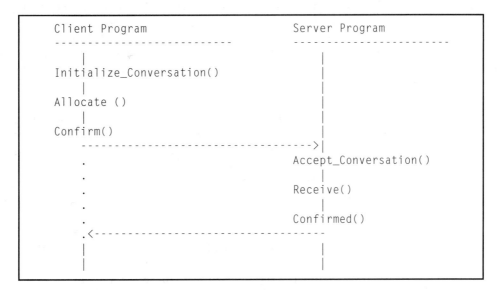

Figure 21.1 Assuring the Attach is successful.

- This sequence is good for the first conversation of a sequence or group, or for long-running conversations.

- This sequence is good for detecting conversation security failures, before progressing too far into the application.

- On the contrary, placing this sequence at the beginning of every conversation is not great for performance in a repetitious production environment.

Better yet, the preferred exchange at the beginning of many applications is a coordination of versions and releases. Put program version and release numbers in the initial conversation flows for all your important conversations. Distributed programs must be at the same level with one another or have special code to be *upward compatible* with old releases. Write this type of information in your debugging or trace file.

Anticipating requirements and tracing

Another way to avoid problems later in a conversation is to ensure that your application has the resources it needs when it begins. This can reduce the kinds of problems that have to be recovered from. The recommendations introduced here are part of a larger topic, known as deadlock detection and avoidance. Carefully evaluate the complexity of situations that can arise with your distributed application. In particular, anticipate the operating system demands of your applications.

Does your application lock files? Can those files be locked early in the application, so your application doesn't complete partially, and then find it can't get the files it needs?

Similarly, how much disk space is necessary? Can its size be anticipated and set aside? How about memory? Can anticipated memory be reserved early, to avoid a partial conversation? Are there program stack requirements that can be anticipated? Don't go overboard on this, however. You can probably think of piggish programs that take a long time to load, going around gobbling up all the resources they might ever need.

As your distributed application is designed, coded, and tested, always assume that someday, somewhere, the application will inexplicably fail. When that occurs, how are you, the programmer, going to diagnose the problem and fix it? Build debugging hooks or tracing facilities into the application. Make command-line parameters (or another mechanism) available so that these hooks can be activated when the program starts. Write tracing information to an incorruptible file, one that can be written to and retrieved even when the application fails catastrophically. Write the debugging and tracing information in a compact, yet easily printable format; don't assume that you'll do debugging from a diskette or other softcopy. We've received large traces via fax, and one colleague has told the story of a long phone call where a desperate user read an entire network trace aloud in hex digits!

The trace facilities built into most CPI-C platforms allow you lots of control over the tracing of CPI-C calls and the frames that actually flow over the network. This is good for some types of problems, but you'll often find that you want to know exactly what procedures and what lines of code were executed in your own program, and in what order. To do this, you'll need to add some kind of application-level tracing.

The following is a set of routines that you can call from your programs to do this kind of tracing. These routines have nothing to do with CPI-C, so feel free to use them anywhere you have C code. Procedure trace_set_filename() lets you specify where you want the trace records written. Procedure trace_set_level() lets you set a threshold for what kinds of data go into the trace file. You can filter out some of your trace records from run to run, if you choose. Finally, procedure trace_log() writes whatever string you want to the trace file.

These trace routines may not exactly meet the requirements of your application, but you'll find them a good starting point for your modification. To use them, compile and link file TRACE.C, and include the header file, TRACE.H, in the top of the files where you want to do tracing. Call trace_set_filename() and trace_set_level() before making any calls to trace_log(). Here's file TRACE.C:

```
/*------------------------------------------------------------
 *   Application-level tracing routines
 *   (TRACE.C)
 *------------------------------------------------------------*/
#include <stdio.h>
#include <string.h>
#include <time.h>

#include "trace.h"


/*
 *   There are three calls that your program can use to set up and
 *   use application-level tracing:
 *
 *   1.   trace_set_filename(FILE *);
 *            to name the file where trace records are written
 *         Example:
 *            trace_set_filename("WHATSUP.TXT");
 *                to send trace records to file WHATSUP.TXT
 *
 *   2.   trace_set_level(unsigned);
 *            to set your threshold tracing level
 *         Example:
 *            trace_set_level(30);
 *                to trace everything with level 30 and lower.
```

```
 *
 *   3.   trace_log(unsigned, (TS, args...));
 *            called whenever you want a trace record written
 *          Example:
 *            trace_log(0, (TS, "%s, code = %lu", "CMINIT",
 *                cpic_return_code));
 *
 *                to send this string (via fprintf) to the trace
 *                file, following the source filename, line number,
 *                and time
 *
 *   "trace_log" is a macro; it is ignored unless the constant
 *   DEBUG is defined.
 */

/* three global vaiables */
FILE *trace_stream;
char trace_filename[255] = {'\0'};
/* by setting trace_level to zero, if trace_set_level() isn't
   called, no tracing occurs */
unsigned trace_level = 0;


void
trace_set_filename(char *filename)
{
    if (strlen(filename) < sizeof(trace_filename)) {
        (void)strcpy(trace_filename, filename);
    }
    else {
        *trace_filename = '\0';
    }
}

void
trace_set_level(unsigned level)
{
    trace_level = level;
}

void
trace_init(unsigned level, char *filename, unsigned line)
{
    /* this procedure called as part of the trace_log macro */
    time_t t = time(NULL);

    /* open the file for appending */
    if (NULL == (trace_stream = fopen(trace_filename,"a"))) {
        trace_stream = stderr;
    }
```

```
            (void)fprintf(trace_stream,
                "==== %s, line: %u, level: %u, %s",
                filename, line, level, ctime(&t));
    }

    void
    trace_close(void)
    {
        /* this procedure called as part of the trace_log macro */
        (void)fprintf(trace_stream, "\n");
        if (stderr != trace_stream) {
            (void)fclose(trace_stream);
        }
    }
```

File TRACE.H is the header file to include when using the procedures listed in file TRACE.C. Here's file TRACE.H:

```
    /*----------------------------------------------------------------
     *  Macros and function prototypes for application-level
     *  tracing routines (TRACE.H)
     *----------------------------------------------------------------*/
    #ifndef _TRACE_H_INCLUDED
    #define _TRACE_H_INCLUDED

    #define TS trace_stream

    /* these show through in the macro trace_log */
    extern FILE *trace_stream;
    extern unsigned trace_level;
    void trace_init(unsigned level, char *file, unsigned line);
    void trace_close(void);

    /* external function prototypes */
    void trace_set_level(unsigned level);   /* set the trace level */
    void trace_set_filename(char *file);    /* name the trace file */

    #ifdef TRACE

    /* in this macro the magic occurs */
    #define trace_log(level,args)                            \
        if(level<=trace_level)                               \
        {trace_init(level,__FILE__,__LINE__);fprintf args; \
        trace_close();}else

    #else
    /* define 'em away, if DEBUG is not defined */
    #define trace_log(l,args)
    #endif
```

```
#define LVL_FAILURES        (10)
#define LVL_API             (20)
#define LVL_MODULE          (30)
#define LVL_FUNCTION        (40)
#define LVL_IO_OPEN_CLOSE   (50)
#define LVL_LINE_FLOW       (100)
#define LVL_IO_READ_WRITE   (110)
#define LVL_STATUS_DUMP     (120)
#define LVL_VARIABLE        (130)
#define LVL_LOCATION        (140)
#define LVL_LOOPLOC         (200)     /* You may loop here often */

#endif
```

To show you how to use these trace routines, we've added them to one of our friends from the first part of the book, program HELLO3.C. You can see that it is easy to add these without adding much to your source code:

```
/*----------------------------------------------------------------
 *  CPI-C "Hello, world" program, waiting for a reply, with trace
 *  Client side (file HELLO3T.C)
 *--------------------------------------------------------------*/
#include <cpic.h>                /* conversation API library   */
#include <stdio.h>               /* file I/O                    */
#include <string.h>              /* strings and memory          */
#include <stdlib.h>              /* standard library            */

#include "trace.h"               /* trace calls                 */

/* this hardcoded sym_dest_name is 8 chars long & blank padded */
#define SYM_DEST_NAME   (unsigned char*)"HELLO3S "

/* this is the string we're sending to the partner             */
#define SEND_THIS       (unsigned char*)"Hello, world"

int main(void)
{
    unsigned char   conversation_ID[CM_CID_SIZE];
    unsigned char   data_buffer[100+1];
    CM_INT32        send_length;
    CM_INT32        requested_length =
                        (CM_INT32)sizeof(data_buffer)-1;
    CM_INT32        received_length;
    CM_RETURN_CODE  cpic_return_code;

    CM_DATA_RECEIVED_TYPE data_received;
    CM_STATUS_RECEIVED    status_received;
    CM_REQUEST_TO_SEND_RECEIVED rts_received;

    trace_set_filename("hello3t.trc"); /* send trace data here */
```

```
trace_set_level(100);    /* don't capture anything over 100 */

trace_log(10, (TS, "Using sym_dest of %s\n", SYM_DEST_NAME));

cminit(                     /* Initialize_Conversation      */
    conversation_ID,        /*  O: returned conversation ID  */
    SYM_DEST_NAME,          /*  I: symbolic destination name */
    &cpic_return_code);     /*  O: return code from this call */

trace_log(10, (TS, "CMINIT RC = %ld\n", cpic_return_code));

trace_log(200, (TS, "This won't be traced!\n"));

cmallc(                     /* Allocate                     */
    conversation_ID,        /*  I: conversation ID           */
    &cpic_return_code);     /*  O: return code from this call */

trace_log(10, (TS, "CMALLC RC = %ld\n", cpic_return_code));

(void)strcpy(data_buffer, SEND_THIS);
send_length = (CM_INT32)strlen(SEND_THIS);
cmsend(                     /* Send_Data                    */
    conversation_ID,        /*  I: conversation ID           */
    data_buffer,            /*  I: send this buffer          */
    &send_length,           /*  I: length to send            */
    &rts_received,          /*  O: was RTS received?         */
    &cpic_return_code);     /*  O: return code from this call */

trace_log(10, (TS, "CMSEND RC = %ld\n", cpic_return_code));

cmrcv(                      /* Receive                      */
    conversation_ID,        /*  I: conversation ID           */
    data_buffer,            /*  I: where to put received data */
    &requested_length,      /*  I: maximum length to receive */
    &data_received,         /*  O: data complete or not?     */
    &received_length,       /*  O: length of received data   */
    &status_received,       /*  O: has status changed?       */
    &rts_received,          /*  O: was RTS received?         */
    &cpic_return_code);     /*  O: return code from this call */

trace_log(10,
    (TS, "CMRCV RC = %ld, data_recv = %ld stat_recv = %ld\n",
      cpic_return_code, data_received, status_received));

data_buffer[received_length] = '\0';    /* insert the null */
(void)printf("%s\n", data_buffer);

return(EXIT_SUCCESS);

}
```

Configuration

Client Side: Building a Robust, Reusable Setup Routine

In the "Hello, world" programs earlier in the book, we showed the client programs using hard-coded symbolic destination names, like `"HELLO1S"`. Compiling the symbolic destination name as a text string makes the program easy to write, but it has an unfortunate side effect; someone has to configure the `"HELLO1S"` symbolic destination name in the local side information before our program can successfully run.

Every setup step required by your program is a burden on those installing and administering your application. You should strive to make it as easy as possible to install your application on the computers in a network. For example, rather than requiring a symbolic destination name to be configured, you can use the all-blank symbolic destination name and set up the three required names within your program. This lets you create programs that don't require updating of the local CPI-C side information.

Unfortunately, we can't use the all-blank symbolic destination name in all circumstances. Consider these cases:

- Some platforms do not support the all-blank symbolic destination name.*

- There may be occasions when a user has already configured a symbolic destination name and wants to reuse that definition for your application.

- On some platforms, symbolic destination names are easier to configure and to remember than partner LU names.

---

* MVS and IMS do not support the all-blank symbolic destination name.

Deciding how to direct your users to set up their symbolic destination name, and to get the right partner LU name, mode name, and TP name is not always straightforward. Don't despair! We have developed generic conversation setup routines with the following attributes:

- They allow your users to specify either a symbolic destination name or a partner LU name—without needing to know which of these two it is.
- They free the person installing your application from configuring symbolic destination names in the local CPI-C side information.
- They provide a way for your program to provide application-specific defaults for all CPI-C conversation characteristics.
- They allow your users to specify or override any CPI-C conversation characteristic.
- They utilize any existing side information.
- They are portable across all CPI-C platforms.

The rest of this chapter describes the source for our generic conversation setup routines, as well as the reasoning we used in creating them.

Getting a valid conversation ID

The most important step in conversation setup is getting a valid conversation ID from the Initialize_Conversation() call. There are three ways for your program to coerce Initialize_Conversation() into giving it a valid conversation ID.

- Hardcode a symbolic destination name.
- Obtain a symbolic destination name as input to your program.
- Use the all-blank symbolic destination name.

Before showing you how we've integrated all of these techniques into a single setup procedure, we'll show you the mechanics of each technique as well as the advantages and disadvantages of each.

HARDCODING THE SYMBOLIC DESTINATION NAME

The easiest way to set up a conversation is to require the configuration of a particular symbolic destination name in the side information:

```
{
    unsigned char conversation_ID[CM_CID_SIZE];
    CM_RETURN_CODE cpic_return_code;

    cminit(                      /* Initialize_Conversation    */
        conversation_ID,         /* returned conversation ID   */
        "HELLO1S ",              /* symbolic destination name  */
        &cpic_return_code);      /* return code from this call */
}
```

Advantage of this simple technique:

- It doesn't require any interaction with the user when the program is run.

Disadvantages:

- Someone must configure the symbolic destination name in the side information of the client computer.
- The symbolic destination name you choose may conflict with another application's choice.
- Your client program can only connect to a single server. If a compatible server program resides on other computers in your network, your program can't access them without a change to the local CPI-C side information.

Obtaining a symbolic destination name

To avoid tying your client program to a particular symbolic destination name and, thus, to a single server, you can obtain a symbolic destination name as an input parameter to your program.

Here is a source code example showing how to use an input parameter as a symbolic destination name:

```
int main(int argc, char *argv[])
{
    /*-------------------------------------------------------------
     *  This side sends some number of bytes, followed by
     *  Confirm-Deallocate, to assure they were received.
     *-----------------------------------------------------------*/
    unsigned char   conversation_ID[CM_CID_SIZE];
    unsigned char   sym_dest_name[CM_SDN_SIZE+1];
    CM_RETURN_CODE cpic_return_code;

    /*-------------------------------------------------------------
     *  Get the symbolic destination from the command line and
     *  initialize a conversation.
     *-----------------------------------------------------------*/
    if (argc > 1) { /* is there at least one argument? */
        /* first, set it to 8 blanks, then copy the name */
        (void)strcpy(sym_dest_name, "        ");
        (void)memcpy(sym_dest_name, argv[1],
            min(strlen(argv[1]), sizeof(sym_dest_name) - 1));
    }
     lse {
        handle_error(
            "A symbolic destination name must be provided");
    }

    cminit(                        /* Initialize_Conversation     */
```

```
            conversation_ID,     /* returned conversation ID   */
            sym_dest_name,       /* symbolic destination name  */
            &cpic_return_code); /* return code from this call  */
    }
```

Advantage of getting the symbolic destination name when the program starts is

■ The server program can reside on any number of computers in the network.

Disadvantages:

■ Each server program your user wants to connect to must be configured with a unique symbolic destination name in the local side information. The different server program may require different partner LU names, mode names, and TP names. This can grow to be a large number of required definitions.

■ If the user only knows the partner's LU name, he or she must look up the correct symbolic destination name and specify that instead.

Using the all-blank symbolic destination name

You can avoid configuration entirely by using the all-blank symbolic destination name:

```
{
    unsigned char conversation_ID[CM_CID_SIZE];
    CM_RETURN_CODE cpic_return_code;
    cminit(                         /* Initialize_Conversation  */
        conversation_ID,            /* returned conversation ID  */
        "        ",                 /* symbolic destination name */
        &cpic_return_code);         /* return code from this call */
}
```

However, your program must now set the required conversation characteristics explicitly by using the Set calls, namely Set_Mode_Name(), Set_Partner_LU_Name(), and Set_TP_Name().

Advantages of using all-blanks:

■ The server program can reside on any number of computers in the network.

■ No configuration of symbolic destination names is required.

Disadvantages:

■ Your program must specify the three conversation characteristics. These can come from user input or from strings hardcoded into your program.

■ Platform-specific conversation characteristics ordinarily hidden in the side information must be specified by the program. Some characteristics may not be accessible through a Set call. For example:

OS/2 Communications Manager allows you to specify that the arriving TP name is an SNA Service TP name. This is a special hexadecimal name, up to 4 bytes in length, which is used by internal SNA components in their conversations.

The operating system on AS/400 allows you to specify which local LU to use for the conversation.

IMPLEMENTING THE SETUP CONVERSATION TECHNIQUE

We've seen that each method of getting a valid conversation ID has its advantages and disadvantages. We can be both flexible and usable if we're prepared to use all of these methods together. Here's the design of our scheme to set up conversations. The steps we'll take are as follows:

1. Define the input variables.

2. Get a conversation ID.

3. Set any user-provided or required conversation characteristics.

The input variables are gathered into a structure named SET_UP_CONV, which, as we'll see in a few pages, holds seven variables.

```
void
set_up_conversation(
    unsigned char * conversation_ID,    /* new conversation ID */
    SET_UP_CONV    * set_up_conv)       /* 7 input variables   */
{
    /* Do what's necessary to get a good conversation ID       */
    get_conversation_ID(
        conversation_ID,
        set_up_conv);

    /* Set the partner LU name, if necessary.                  */
    set_up_partner_LU_name(
        conversation_ID,
        set_up_conv);

    /* Set the mode name, if necessary.                        */
    set_up_mode_name(
        conversation_ID,
        set_up_conv);

    /* Set the TP name, if necessary.                          */
    set_up_tp_name(
        conversation_ID,
        set_up_conv);
}
```

This set_up_conversation() procedure file SETUP.C, gets a conversation ID and sets up the conversation characteristics.

Defining the input variables

There are three input variables that we'll need for an Allocate() call to work. We'll let the program's user specify any or all three of these, on the command line or in the side information. We'll also hold default values for all three, for use when they aren't otherwise supplied.

The way that a user gets these variables to your client program differs from application to application. For example, you may choose to have your program get the input from the command line, with argv and argc. You may choose to read the information from a program setup file, an .INI file, or an environment variable. You might also choose to offer dialog boxes or prompts for this information. How your program accepts input from the user is up to you. We recommend that you remain consistent with the rest of your program's input techniques.

user_destination.   Either a symbolic destination name or a partner LU name. The set_up_conversation() code dynamically figures out what type of name the user_destination is and uses it accordingly. This allows users to specify whichever type of name they are more familiar with.

user_mode_name.   Overrides the client program's default_mode_name as well as any mode name set through the side information.

user_tp_name.   Overrides the client program's default_tp_name as well as any TP name set through side information. In general, users should never need to specify a TP name. You may consider omitting this variable and not allowing your users to specify a TP name.

For our set_up_conversation() technique, the client program must also supply the following hardcoded values:

default_sym_dest_name.   Used whenever a user_destination is not specified. This allows the program to run successfully without any user input. Usually, this parameter should be the same as the server program name. This makes it easier to match the side information entry to the application that uses it. For example, APING's default_sym_dest_name is APINGD, which is the same as the server TP name.

default_mode_name.   Used whenever the mode name is not initialized. This can occur when the all-blank symbolic destination name is used or when the side information entry does not have a mode name specified. If a user_mode_name is specified, it is used in place of this default parameter.

default_tp_name.   Used for every conversation. This allows programs to share symbolic destination names, since each application specifies its own TP name to override the value configured in side information. If a user_tp_name is specified, it is used in place of this default parameter.

To make it easier to keep track of all of these parameters, we've created a C structure, SET_UP_CONV, so we can keep them all in one place:

```
typedef struct set_up_conv_s {
    char user_destination[CM_PLN_SIZE+1];
    char user_mode_name[CM_MN_SIZE+1];
    char user_tp_name[CM_TPN_SIZE+1];
    char default_sym_dest_name[CM_SDN_SIZE+1];
    char default_mode_name[CM_MN_SIZE+1];
    char default_tp_name[CM_TPN_SIZE+1];
    BOOL destination_is_plu;
} SET_UP_CONV;
```

GETTING A CONVERSATION ID

In our attempt to get a valid conversation ID, we end up employing all three methods of getting a conversation ID described previously.

Here's the pseudocode for getting a conversation ID:

```
if the user_destination is set
    cminit(user_destination)
    if rc == CM_PROGRAM_PARAMETER_CHECK or
        conv_partner_lu_name_isn't_set()
        if rc != CM_OK
            destination_is_plu = TRUE
            cminit(default_sym_dest_name)
            if rc == CM_PROGRAM_PARAMETER_CHECK
                cminit(all-blanks)

        else
            free the conv_id (Deallocate-Abend)

else
    cminit(default_sym_dest_name)
```

The first thing we check is whether the user_destination is set. If there is no user_destination, the only chance we have of getting a conversation ID with a valid partner LU name is to use the default symbolic destination name hard-coded in the application.

If the user_destination is set, we try to use it as a symbolic destination name on Initialize_Conversation(). You'll remember that the user_destination could be either a symbolic destination name or a partner LU name. We can discover that the user_destination isn't a symbolic destination name and should be used as a partner LU name when

- The return code on Initialize_Conversation() is CM_PROGRAM_PARAME-TER_CHECK, which indicates the user_destination was not found in the local CPI-C side information.

- The partner LU name conversation characteristic is not set. This can occur if there is no partner LU name defined in the side information for this symbolic destination name. It can also occur on some CPI-C platforms which return CM_OK even if the symbolic destination name is not configured (for example, VM/CMS).

In this case, be sure to clean up the valid conversation ID, since we know it will not be used. As we discussed in "Set_Deallocate_Type (CMSDT)" in Chap. 16, valid conversation IDs can be cleaned up using Deallocate-Abend.

If we've found that we can't use the user_destination as a symbolic destination name, we'll set a flag indicating that the user_destination should be used as a partner LU name. We'll check this flag later when we're setting the conversation characteristics.

If we determine that the user_destination wasn't a symbolic destination name, our next step is to attempt to use the default_sym_dest_name in a call to Initialize_Conversation(). If we get a return code indicating the default symbolic destination name is not configured, we'll try our last option: using the all-blank symbolic destination name. The reason we use the default_sym_dest_name before the all-blank name is that:

■ A configured symbolic destination name can specify conversation characteristics that are not accessible by set calls from the program.

■ Some platforms, like MVS and IMS, do not support the all-blank symbolic destination name.

If using the all-blank symbolic destination name on Initialize_Conversation() gives a return code that isn't CM_OK, we have to give up, having exhausted all of the possible ways to get a valid conversation ID.

Here's the C source for getting a conversation ID:

```
void
copy_sym_dest_name(
    unsigned char * sym_dest_name,
    char *          input_string);

BOOL
is_partner_lu_name_valid(
    unsigned char *conversation_ID);

BOOL
is_mode_name_valid(
    unsigned char *conversation_ID);

void
get_conversation_ID(
    unsigned char   *conversation_ID,
    SET_UP_CONV     *set_up_conv)
{
    unsigned char    sym_dest_name[CM_SDN_SIZE+1];
    CM_INT32         user_destination_length;
    CM_RETURN_CODE   cpic_return_code;
```

```
BOOL            user_dest_too_long = FALSE;

sym_dest_name[sizeof(sym_dest_name)-1] = '\0';

user_destination_length =
    (CM_INT32)strlen(set_up_conv->user_destination);

/*-----------------------------------------------------------
 * Check to see if the user_destination was set.
 * It's set if it has a non-zero length.
 *----------------------------------------------------------*/
if (user_destination_length != 0) {
    if (user_destination_length < sizeof(sym_dest_name)) {
        copy_sym_dest_name(
            sym_dest_name,
            set_up_conv->user_destination);
        cminit(                /* Initialize_Conversation   */
            conversation_ID,
            sym_dest_name,
            &cpic_return_code);
    }
    else {
        /*
         * The user_destination was too long.
         */
        user_dest_too_long = TRUE;
    }
    if (CM_PROGRAM_PARAMETER_CHECK == cpic_return_code ||
        TRUE == user_dest_too_long ||
        !is_partner_lu_name_valid(conversation_ID)) {
        if (CM_OK == cpic_return_code) {
            /*
             * Free the old conversation ID
             */
            cmdeal(
                conversation_ID,
                &cpic_return_code);
        }
        set_up_conv->destination_is_plu = TRUE;
        copy_sym_dest_name(
            sym_dest_name,
            set_up_conv->default_sym_dest_name);
        cminit(
            conversation_ID,
            sym_dest_name,
            &cpic_return_code);

        if (CM_PROGRAM_PARAMETER_CHECK ==
            cpic_return_code) {
            (void)memset(sym_dest_name,
```

```
                                        ' ',
                                  CM_SDN_SIZE);
                    cminit(
                        conversation_ID,
                        sym_dest_name,
                        &cpic_return_code);
                }
            }
        }
        else {
            copy_sym_dest_name(
                sym_dest_name,
                set_up_conv->default_sym_dest_name);
            cminit(                        /* Initialize_Conversation   */
                conversation_ID,     /* conversation ID           */
                sym_dest_name,       /* symbolic destination name */
                &cpic_return_code); /* return code from this call */
        }

#ifdef DEBUG
        fprintf(stderr, "RC was %lu\n", cpic_return_code);
        fprintf(stderr,
            "Used a sym dest name of \"%s\"\n", sym_dest_name);
#endif

        if (CM_OK != cpic_return_code) {
            handle_cpic_rc(
                conversation_ID, cpic_return_code, "CMINIT");
        }

}


void
copy_sym_dest_name(
    unsigned char * sym_dest_name,
    char          * input_string)
{
    size_t i;
    /* copy in the symbolic destination name */
    (void)memset(sym_dest_name, ' ', CM_SDN_SIZE);
    (void)memcpy(sym_dest_name, input_string,
                 min(strlen(input_string), CM_SDN_SIZE));
    /* convert the sym_dest_name to uppercase */
    for (i=0; i < CM_SDN_SIZE ; i++) {
        sym_dest_name[i] =
            (unsigned char)toupper(sym_dest_name[i]);
    }
    strupr(sym_dest_name);
}
```

```
BOOL
is_partner_lu_name_valid(
    unsigned char * conversation_ID)
{
    unsigned char  destination[CM_PLN_SIZE+1];

    CM_INT32       partner_LU_name_length = 0;
    CM_RETURN_CODE cpic_return_code;
    BOOL           name_is_valid;

    cmepln(                           /* Extract_Partner_LU_Name    */
        conversation_ID,              /* conversation ID            */
        destination,                  /* partner LU name            */
        &partner_LU_name_length,/* length of the part LU name  */
        &cpic_return_code);           /* return code from this call */

    if ((cpic_return_code != CM_OK) ||
        ((partner_LU_name_length == 1) &&
        (destination[0] == ' '))) {
        /* there isn't a current partner LU name */
        name_is_valid = FALSE;
    } else {
        /* there is a current partner LU name */
        name_is_valid = TRUE;
    }

    return name_is_valid;
}
```

This get_conversation_ID() procedure, in file SETUP.C, uses the default program information and provided user information to get a valid conversation ID.

Setting conversation characteristics

With our valid conversation ID, we now need to ensure that the conversation characteristics are set properly. If we used a nonblank symbolic destination name, chances are the conversation characteristics have been set, but we have no guarantee.* If we used the all-blank symbolic destination name, none of the conversation characteristics will have been set.

We are able to ensure that the conversation characteristics are set properly without having to keep track of what symbolic destination name was used to get a conversation ID.

Now let's look at the three procedures we'll use to set up the conversation characteristics: set_up_partner_LU_name(), set_up_mode_name(), and set_up_tp_name().

---

* On some platforms, not all of the CPI-C conversation characteristics must be configured. In fact, on VM/CMS they are all optional.

set_up_partner_LU_name().   The only time we need to set a partner LU name is if the user_destination was set and it wasn't used as a symbolic destination name. Whether the user_destination could be a partner LU name has already been captured in our "destination_is_plu" flag, so we'll test that here:

```
void
set_up_partner_LU_name(
    unsigned char  *conversation_ID,
    SET_UP_CONV    *set_up_conv)
{
    CM_INT32 length;
    CM_RETURN_CODE  cpic_return_code;

    if (TRUE == set_up_conv->destination_is_plu) {
        length = (CM_INT32)strlen(set_up_conv->user_destination);

        if (strchr((char*)set_up_conv->user_destination, '.') !=
                NULL) {
            /* if there was a period, map to uppercase */
            size_t i;
            unsigned char * string =
                set_up_conv->user_destination;
            for (i=0; i < (size_t)length ; i++) {
                set_up_conv->user_destination[i] =
                    (unsigned char)toupper(
                            set_up_conv->user_destination[i]);
            }
        }

#ifdef DEBUG
        fprintf(stderr, "Setting partner LU name to \"%s\"\n",
            set_up_conv->user_destination);
#endif
        cmspln(                        /* Set Partner LU Name       */
            conversation_ID,
            (unsigned char *)set_up_conv->user_destination,
            &length,
            &cpic_return_code);

        if (CM_OK != cpic_return_code) {
            handle_cpic_rc(conversation_ID, cpic_return_code,
                "CMSPLN");
        }
    }
}
```

set_up_mode_name().   If the user_mode_name was set, we use it to set the mode name conversation characteristic. If no user_mode_name was set, we use the default_mode_name only if the mode name conversation characteristic is not already set from side information.

```
void
set_up_mode_name(
    unsigned char * conversation_ID,
    SET_UP_CONV   * set_up_conv)
{
    CM_INT32        mode_name_length;
    CM_RETURN_CODE  cpic_return_code;
    size_t i;

    assert (conversation_ID != NULL);
    assert (set_up_conv != NULL);

    mode_name_length =
        (CM_INT32)strlen(set_up_conv->user_mode_name);
    if (mode_name_length != 0) {
        /*--------------------------------------------------------
         *  Ensure the mode name is in uppercase.
         *------------------------------------------------------*/
        for (i=0; i < (size_t)mode_name_length ; i++) {
            set_up_conv->user_mode_name[i] =
                (unsigned char)toupper(
                            set_up_conv->user_mode_name[i]);
        }
#ifdef DEBUG
        fprintf(stderr,
            "Setting user mode name to \"%s\"\n",
            set_up_conv->user_mode_name);
#endif
        cmsmn(
            conversation_ID,
            (unsigned char *)set_up_conv->user_mode_name,
            &mode_name_length,
            &cpic_return_code);
        if (CM_OK != cpic_return_code) {
            handle_cpic_rc(
                conversation_ID, cpic_return_code, "CMSMN");
        }
    }
    else {
        if (!is_mode_name_valid(conversation_ID)) {
            mode_name_length =
                (CM_INT32)strlen(set_up_conv->default_mode_name);
            /*--------------------------------------------------------
             *  Ensure the mode name is in uppercase.
             *------------------------------------------------------*/
```

```
                    for (i=0; i < (size_t)mode_name_length ; i++) {
                        set_up_conv->default_mode_name[i] =
                            (unsigned char)toupper(
                                    set_up_conv->default_mode_name[i]);
                    }
#ifdef DEBUG
                    fprintf(stderr,
                        "Setting default mode name to \"%s\"\n",
                        set_up_conv->default_mode_name);
#endif
                    cmsmn(
                        conversation_ID,
                        (unsigned char *)set_up_conv->default_mode_name,
                        &mode_name_length,
                        &cpic_return_code);
                    if (CM_OK != cpic_return_code) {
                        handle_cpic_rc(
                            conversation_ID, cpic_return_code, "CMSMN");
                    }
                }
            }
        }


BOOL
is_mode_name_valid(
    unsigned char * conversation_ID)
{
    unsigned char   mode_name[CM_MN_SIZE+1];
    CM_INT32        mode_name_length = 0;
    CM_RETURN_CODE cpic_return_code;
    BOOL            rc;

    cmemn(conversation_ID, mode_name, &mode_name_length,
        &cpic_return_code);

    if (cpic_return_code != CM_OK || (mode_name_length == 0)) {
        rc = FALSE;
    }
    else {
        rc = TRUE;
    }

    return rc;
}
```

set_up_tp_name().   To let many programs share and reuse symbolic destination names, we always set the TP name. In contrast to how we handle the mode name characteristic, we cannot check if the TP name is already valid, even if we wanted to.* If the user_tp_name was set, we use that. If not, we use the default_tp_ name that was hardcoded by the application.

```
void
set_up_tp_name(
    unsigned char * conversation_ID,
    SET_UP_CONV   * set_up_conv)
{

    CM_INT32       tp_name_length;
    CM_RETURN_CODE cpic_return_code;

    assert (conversation_ID != NULL);
    assert (set_up_conv != NULL);

    tp_name_length =
        (CM_INT32)strlen(set_up_conv->user_tp_name);
    if (tp_name_length != 0) {
#ifdef DEBUG
        fprintf(stderr,
            "Setting user TP name to \"%s\"\n",
            set_up_conv->user_tp_name);
#endif
        cmstpn(
            conversation_ID,
            (unsigned char *)set_up_conv->user_tp_name,
            &tp_name_length,
            &cpic_return_code);
        if (CM_OK != cpic_return_code) {
            handle_cpic_rc(
                conversation_ID, cpic_return_code, "CMSTPN");
        }
    }
    else {
#ifdef DEBUG
        fprintf(stderr, "Setting default TP name to \"%s\"\n",
            set_up_conv->default_tp_name);
#endif
        tp_name_length =
            (CM_INT32)strlen(set_up_conv->default_tp_name);

        cmstpn(
            conversation_ID,
            (unsigned char *)set_up_conv->default_tp_name,
            &tp_name_length,
```

---

* As we described in Chap. 12, CPI-C 1.2 now provides an Extract_TP_Name() call which allows us to retrieve the TP name.

```
                        &cpic_return_code);
              if (CM_OK != cpic_return_code) {
                 handle_cpic_rc(
                    conversation_ID, cpic_return_code, "CMSTPN");
              }
          }
       }
```

At this point, we're just about done setting up our conversation characteristics. If there are any other conversation characteristics that need to be set, they should be taken care of at this point. Examples are

- Conversation security (see "Coding Your Client Program" in Chap. 25 for more information)
- Sync_level (see "Set_Sync_Level (CMSSL)" in Chap. 11 for more information)
- Return_control (see "Set_Return_Control (CMSRC)" in Chap. 11 for more information)
- Conversation type (see "Set_Conversation_Type (CMSCT)" in Chap. 11 for more information)

USING SET_UP_CONVERSATION()

Here is an example of how you could use the set_up_conversation() routines in your programs. This example is designed to talk to the server side of the APING application, APINGD. Its defaults are to use the mode name #BATCH to obtain a session, and to send the string APINGD as the TP name. The users of this client program will need either to configure an entry in their side information table for whatever partner LU they want to talk to, or respond to the prompting from the program, which reads its input from stdin.

Getting your client programs to talk to APINGD is an excellent practice. The program APINGD should be configured on all the computers you plan to talk to. You can choose to ignore whatever APINGD sends back to your samples; you'll at least know your programs are set up correctly, and the underlying links and sessions are established.

```
/*-------------------------------------------------------------
 *  Set up the partner LU name, mode name, and TP name
 *  (file TSTSETUP.C)
 *-------------------------------------------------------------*/
#include <cpic.h>                    /* conversation API library  */
#include <stdarg.h>                  /* variable arguments        */
#include <stdio.h>                   /* file I/O                  */
#include <stdlib.h>                  /* standard library          */
#include <string.h>                  /* strings and memory        */

#include "docpic.h"                  /* CPI-C do_ calls, BOOL     */
#include "setup.h"                   /* set_up_conv_ calls        */
```

```
int main(int argc, char *argv[])
{
    /*------------------------------------------------------------
     * Set up a conversation
     *----------------------------------------------------------*/
    unsigned char    conversation_ID[CM_CID_SIZE];
    SET_UP_CONV      set_up_conv;



    /*------------------------------------------------------------
     * Set the seven fields in the SET_UP_CONV structure
     *----------------------------------------------------------*/
    strcpy(set_up_conv.default_sym_dest_name, "SETUPRR");
    strcpy(set_up_conv.default_mode_name,     "#BATCH");
    strcpy(set_up_conv.default_tp_name,       "APINGD");

    *set_up_conv.user_destination = '\0';
    *set_up_conv.user_mode_name = '\0';
    *set_up_conv.user_tp_name = '\0';
    set_up_conv.destination_is_plu = FALSE;

    /*------------------------------------------------------------
     * Prompt the user for three names
     *----------------------------------------------------------*/
    printf("Enter a destination: ");
    fgets(
        set_up_conv.user_destination,
        sizeof(set_up_conv.user_destination),
        stdin);
    set_up_conv.user_destination[
        strlen(set_up_conv.user_destination)-1] = '\0';

    printf("Enter a mode name: ");
    fgets(
        set_up_conv.user_mode_name,
        sizeof(set_up_conv.user_mode_name),
        stdin);
    set_up_conv.user_mode_name[
        strlen(set_up_conv.user_mode_name)-1] = '\0';
    strupr(set_up_conv.user_mode_name);

    printf("Enter a TP name: ");
    fgets(
        set_up_conv.user_tp_name,
        sizeof(set_up_conv.user_tp_name),
        stdin);
    set_up_conv.user_tp_name[
        strlen(set_up_conv.user_tp_name)-1] = '\0';
```

```
/*-------------------------------------------------------------
 * Print out the six names in SET_UP_CONV
 *-----------------------------------------------------------*/
printf("****** Setup Conversation Parameters ******\n");
(void)printf("User destination is \"%s\"\n",
    set_up_conv.user_destination);
(void)printf("User mode name is \"%s\"\n",
    set_up_conv.user_mode_name);
(void)printf("User TP name is \"%s\"\n",
    set_up_conv.user_tp_name);
(void)printf("Default sym_dest_name is \"%s\"\n",
    set_up_conv.default_sym_dest_name);
(void)printf("Default mode name is \"%s\"\n",
    set_up_conv.default_mode_name);
(void)printf("Default TP name is \"%s\"\n",
    set_up_conv.default_tp_name);
printf("*******************************************\n");

/*-------------------------------------------------------------
 * Get a good conversation ID
 *-----------------------------------------------------------*/
set_up_conversation(conversation_ID, &set_up_conv);

/*-------------------------------------------------------------
 * Allocate a session
 *-----------------------------------------------------------*/
do_allocate(conversation_ID);

/*-------------------------------------------------------------
 * Deallocate the conversation; the sync_level is NONE
 *-----------------------------------------------------------*/
do_deallocate(conversation_ID);

return EXIT_SUCCESS;         /* program was successful      */
}
```

Server Side: Taking Advantage of an Attach Manager

This chapter takes the viewpoint of the server program, which is started at the request of a client program. As a user or the administrator of the computer where the server program is located, you will want to maintain control over which programs in that computer can be remotely started. Clearly, you don't want a user at a remote computer to be able to start programs that destroy data or use up computer memory at critical times. CPI-C depends upon software, resident at the computer where the server program is located, to perform the duties of "gatekeeper." This software is called the *attach manager,* and we'll cover its operation thoroughly in this chapter.

We introduced the attach manager in Chap. 12. You'll remember that the attach manager gets its name from the internal SNA message that flows between the pair of computers; this message is known as an *Attach.* CPI-C builds an Attach whenever a client program successfully issues an Allocate() call. The Attach contains all the information necessary to construct a conversation between the client program and the server program. Whenever the APPC software in the server computer receives an Attach, it hands the Attach to its attach manager for processing. The contents of an Attach are shown in "Starting the Server Program" in Chap. 12.

SETTING UP THE TP NAME

A key piece of information in an incoming Attach is the name used by the attach manager to decide what program to start in the server computer. This is

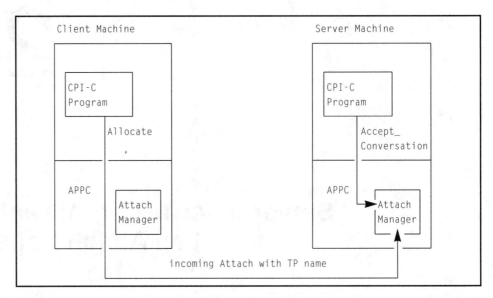

Figure 23.1 The attach manager function. For a given pair of programs, the attach manager is only necessary in the machine receiving Attaches.

called the *TP name,* which stands for "Transaction Program name." This name must be agreed upon by the users and administrators at both computers.

Client specifies the TP name

At the client computer, the TP name is either configured as part of an entry in the CPI-C side information, or it is supplied as a parameter to a Set_TP_Name() call. In either case, the client program commits to using a TP name when it issues its Allocate() call.

See "Implementing the Setup Conversation Technique" in Chap. 22 for examples of how the client program can specify the TP name.

Server configures a list of TP names

On the server, the attach manager keeps an internal table of allowable TP names and other information associated with each TP name. If an Attach arrives and its TP name matches one in the Attach Manager's internal table, the attach manager reads information from the table to begin performing its gatekeeper functions. Otherwise, the Attach is rejected; that is, the client program is notified that no program could be started. If the TP name is not recognized, the client program sees the CM_TPN_NOT_RECOGNIZED return code.

The attach manager's table of TP names is constructed as part of configuring the CPI-C software on the computer where the server program runs. For each unique TP name to be accepted, a *TP definition* must be created. This TP definition serves as a container for the information associated with the TP name in the attach manager's table. Similarly, a table of security information (allowable passwords and user IDs) is also maintained, either by the attach manager or by a different security product.

UNDERSTANDING TP DEFINITION VERSUS TP NAME VERSUS TP FILESPEC

The configuration of a TP employs three levels of naming to identify the server program:

- The definition that describes all the attributes and parameters of the server program to be started (the TP definition)
- The identifier of the server program as known by the client program (the TP name)
- The file name of the executable server program to be started (the TP filespec)

These three concepts allow "late-binding" (in computer science terminology); they make it easy to create or to change how programs are started, which increases the flexibility and portability of your CPI-C programs among different operating systems.

TP definition.   You configure the description of the server program to be started and its start-up attributes in a TP definition. A TP definition serves as a container for all the information about a given program, and how the attach manager should handle an incoming Attach destined for that program.

TP name.   There is one-to-one correspondence between TP names and TP definitions in a given configuration. In database terms, the TP name is a key that provides quick lookup access into the TP definition database. The TP name is the name that flows over the communications line from the client transaction program to the attach manager in the server computer.

TP filespec.   This specifies the name of the actual program to be started on the server. It may specify a file name, or a path and file name of an executable program. This character string varies widely in format from one operating system to another. For example, on DOS, Windows, or OS/2, the TP filespec consists of the drive, path, file name, and file extension of the executable program.

Here's an example of a TP definition on the OS/2 Communications Manager. It shows the setup for the server side of the APING application.

```
DEFINE_TP TP_NAME(APINGD)
          DESCRIPTION(APING: server side)
          FILESPEC(c:\aping\apingd.exe)
```

```
CONVERSATION_TYPE(EITHER)
CONV_SECURITY_RQD(NO)
SYNC_LEVEL(EITHER)
TP_OPERATION(NONQUEUED_AM_STARTED)
PROGRAM_TYPE(VIO_WINDOWABLE)
RECEIVE_ALLOCATE_TIMEOUT(INFINITE);
```

CHECKING CONVERSATION ATTRIBUTES FIRST

The conversation attributes known as sync level, conversation type, and conversation security do not directly influence how the attach manager starts a program. However, they are used by the attach manager to decide whether to reject an incoming Attach before ever queuing it or checking for corresponding Accept_Conversation() calls.

Sync level

When you configure the sync level, you specify whether your server program will support the calls and parameters dealing with confirmation processing. The calls in question are Confirm and Confirmed; additionally, certain parameters on the Deallocate and Prepare_To_Receive calls deal with confirmation processing.

An incoming Attach includes a field that says whether the client program issues confirmation processing calls or parameters. The attach manager checks the field on the incoming Attach against the configured value in its TP definition. The possible configuration choices are as follows:

None.   This server program does not issue any call relating to confirmation processing in any of its conversations.

Confirm.   This server program can perform confirmation processing on its conversations. The server program can issue calls and recognize returned values relating to confirmation. If the server program is written with the calls listed above, you should configure Confirm here to guarantee a compatible session.

Sync_point.   This server program can perform confirmation processing using either Confirm() and Confirmed() or the sync point resource recovery calls.

Any.   This server program can participate in conversations whether the partner program ever issues any confirmation calls or not.

When configuring a program on a platform that allows these or similar options, you'll need to give your installers and users guidance on when to specify a particular sync level and when to indicate that any value is acceptable. We recommend you follow these guidelines:

■ When advising users on how to install your server programs, tell them which particular sync level your program uses. This eliminates any potential problems caused by an inadvertent mismatch between your client program and your server program.

- When configuring a server program and you don't know the sync level it uses, specify *any* or *either*. This avoids potential setup problems caused when you don't know the program's actual sync level. You can rely on the correctness of the programs to avoid potential sync level mismatches.

If the client sends an Attach which specifies a sync level not supported by the server (as specified in its TP definition), the client program sees the CM_SYNC_LEVEL_NOT_SUPPORTED_PGM return code.

Conversation type

The conversation type specifies whether the program to be started supports basic or mapped records when it sends and receives data. Whether basic or mapped calls are used by a server program is checked by the attach manager, which looks at the conversation type configured for the program.

In CPI-C, the default conversation is mapped. As you may remember from "Basic Conversations" in Chap. 17, we strongly recommend using mapped conversations in your applications because it simplifies their programming and maintenance. When configuring the conversation type, there are usually three options available:

Basic.   Only basic conversation calls will be issued by this server program for its conversations.

Mapped.   Only mapped conversation calls will be issued by this server program for its conversations.

Either.   Either basic or mapped conversation calls, depending on what arrives on the incoming Attach.

When configuring a server program on a platform that allows these or similar options, you'll need to decide when to specify a particular conversation type and when to indicate that any value is acceptable. We recommend you follow guidelines similar to those we talked about for sync_level.

If the client sends an Attach which specifies a conversation type not supported by the server (as specified in its TP definition), the client program sees the CM_CONVERSATION_TYPE_MISMATCH return code.

Conversation security

When configuring a TP, you can specify that a password and user ID must be supplied on the incoming Attach. Both the password and user ID are optional parameters when the client starts the conversation. If conversation security is specified in the server's TP definition, the attach manager will validate the password and user ID of an incoming Attach, and reject the Attach if they aren't present or if they don't match a valid combination in its table of passwords and user IDs. If no password and user ID are present, the attach manager will reject the Attach.

Checking user IDs and passwords

Even if you configure for no conversation security on the server side, the attach manager always checks an incoming password and user ID, if these are present in the incoming Attach. The Attach will be rejected if they don't match a valid configured security combination. Thus, if a password or user ID arrives in an Attach, they are never ignored.

If the attach manager decides it doesn't like an incoming Attach for any reason related to conversation security, the client program sees the CM_SECURITY_NOT_VALID return code on one of the calls after its Allocate().

MATCHING ATTACHES WITH PROGRAMS

After an incoming Attach has passed the checks for the conversation attributes, the attach manager must determine how to match up the Attach with a server program. The decision that must be made is whether to start a new program instance or to give the Attach to an already-running program.

On most platforms, this decision is controlled by a configuration parameter in the TP definition. Thus, some servers could have all clients handled by the same program instance and some servers could always start a new program instance. Even if the attach manager is configured to give Attaches to an already running program, the attach manager is smart enough to load a new server program if there isn't one already running.

In this section, we first look at what happens when the attach manager starts a new program. We then examine how the attach manager gives an Attach to an already-running program.

When the attach manager starts a new program

When the attach manager starts a program in the server computer, it reads the fields in its table of TP definitions to decide exactly how the program should be run in the server operating system. The configuration parameters and their values vary widely from platform to platform.

On the OS/2 Communications Manager, for example, the attach manager knows about the different ways that the server program can appear on the display. It can run in its own character-based screen, it can run in its own window, or it can run in the background, doing no screen I/O. Running in the background may give the best performance, but is obviously the hardest to debug since you can't see what's going on.

Different operating systems have different ways that they can start programs. The TP definition for your server program should direct the attach manager on how to start your program for its best behavior.

Occasionally the attach manager just can't start the server program. One example is when no more memory is available from the operating system to start another process. When the attach manager sees that it cannot start the program, it rejects the incoming Attach. Depending upon the type of failure that occurred, the client program sees either CM_TP_NOT_AVAIL_RETRY or CM_TP_NOT_AVAIL_NO_RETRY return code on one of the calls following its Allocate().

When connecting an Attach to an existing application

When a TP definition specifies that the attach manager should give incoming Attaches to already-running programs, those programs are often referred to as queued programs. This is due to the way that the attach manager has to handle Attaches without programs and programs without Attaches.

For each queued TP name in its TP table, the attach manager maintains two queues: one for incoming Attaches and one for Accept calls. For example, when an incoming Attach arrives, the attach manager starts the corresponding server program or sends a message to the operator. The incoming Attach sits on the queue until a matching Accept call is issued by the program just started by the attach manager (or until a timeout occurs). Other Attaches may arrive for that TP or for some other TP; they sit on their respective queues until a matching Accept call is issued.

Server programs might issue Accept calls before any matching Attach arrives. The Accept is held on its respective queue, waiting for an Attach to arrive from a client computer. Associated with each queue is a timeout value, specifying how long something can sit on a queue before it "expires." The attach manager rejects queued Attaches whose timeout has expired. Similarly, queued Accept calls are returned to their associated programs with a return code indicating what happened. The timeout for Accept calls can be defined as zero; this lets a program check to see if an Attach is queued for it and, if not, to continue with other processing.

On the OS/2 Communications Manager, the attach manager saves the OS/2 process ID whenever a queued program issues a valid Accept call for a TP. When the OS/2 process ends, the attach manager examines the queue of Attaches for that TP. If the queue is not empty, the attach manager will start a new copy of the program (or send a new message to the operator). For each TP, you define the maximum size of the queue for incoming Attaches.

ESTIMATING CONVERSATION START-UP OVERHEAD

While we're looking at how the server program gets started by the attach manager, let's also look at the steps that occur when the client connects to the server, and how long each step takes. The overhead of starting a conversation greatly impacts performance, especially when the conversation duration is short.

We'll assume the following sequence of calls on the client and server that we saw back in Chap. 21:

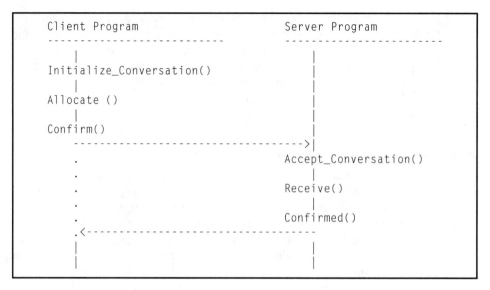

```
   Client Program                          Server Program
   --------------------------              ------------------------

       |                                       |
   Initialize_Conversation()                   |
       |                                       |
   Allocate ()                                 |
       |                                       |
   Confirm()                                   |
       --------------------------------------->|
       .                                   Accept_Conversation()
       .                                       |
       .                                   Receive()
       .                                       |
       .                                   Confirmed()
       .<----------------------------------
       |                                       |
       |                                       |
```

Figure 21.1 Assuring the Attach is successful.

All the client has done to this point is to get a conversation established and to verify that the server program is running.

Let's see what APPC does "under the covers" and see where our time gets spent. In this example, the elapsed times we discuss assume a LAN transport and, thus, a short propagation delay.

The client's Initialize_Conversation() call pulls the necessary CPI-C parameters from a side information table. This is usually stored in memory while CPI-C is running and, therefore, is a very fast operation, usually on the order of tens of milliseconds.

The client's Allocate() call does a number of things. The first duty performed by the Allocate() call is to make sure there is a session available for use. After a session is available, a conversation is "allocated" to it for use by the client program.

If there is no session currently available, a session will need to be activated. Session activation usually takes on the order of hundreds of milliseconds to complete. But, since sessions may be reused (serially, not simultaneously), it is not always necessary to activate a session. In this case, the only overhead of the Allocate() call is the matching of a conversation to an active session, which takes on the order of tens of milliseconds.

The last thing that the Allocate() call does is put an Attach into APPC's buffers to be sent to the server platform. The Attach contains all of the program start-up and security information for the conversation.

The Confirm() call flushes the Attach and sends it to the server platform along with the confirmation request.

On the server platform, the processing of the Attach header itself is usually a simple matter, taking only about 20 ms. If the server program is already running, the Accept_Conversation() gets the conversation ID and we're off and running. If the server program is not already running, the server platform will have to start the program. The overhead to start a program varies among platforms, but a good rule of thumb is that program start-up takes on the order of seconds to complete, usually between 1 and 10 seconds.

The Receive() and Confirmed() calls take about another 10 ms to complete.

So, let's summarize where we've spent our time:

```
Initialize                 < 10ms
Session Activation         100-1500ms
Conversation Allocation    < 10ms
Attach                     about 20ms
Program Startup            about 1-10 seconds
```

The two places we should look to make improvements are in the session activation and program start-up.

Let's tackle session activation first. Most programs are not concerned with session activation and have little control over it. Session activation is not normally a source of performance problems since it is usually done only once. The first time you Allocate() your conversation, session activation is performed, but subsequent Allocate() requests can reuse that session. There are also many configuration options that can be used to ensure that there is always an active session available for use by your program.

We're left with program start-up as the last major element of start-up overhead. As mentioned previously, the program start-up time will vary from platform to platform. On a system like CICS, which was designed for quick program start-up and takedown, program start-up is likely to be less than 10 ms. Although normal program start-up time on OS/2 is around 2 seconds, a PC/AT running OS/2 with only 3 MB of memory could take minutes!

The best mechanism you have as an application developer to limit the program start-up time is to have your server program already running when the Attach arrives from the client. What you would really like is to start one copy (or many copies) of your program and have it accept one conversation after another without ending their process. See "Using Accept Multiple in CPI-C 1.2" in Chap. 27 for more information about how to code your server to accept more than one conversation.

DEBUGGING ATTACH-MANAGER-STARTED PROGRAMS

No matter how well you develop and write your code, there comes a time when you need to do some debugging. The fact that the attach manager often starts your server program can complicate the debugging process. In this section, we will cover:

- How to figure out why your server program wasn't started
- How to load your server program under a source code debugger

Determining why the server program wasn't started

Figuring out why your server program doesn't start is a two-part battle:

1. *Find the return code!* This can often be more difficult than it seems, because return codes generated by the attach manager do not show up immediately at the client program. Since the Attach is buffered by CPI-C, the client program may not receive the failure return code until it issues a call that elicits a response from the partner program.

   In most cases, this merely means that your program won't find out about an attach-manager-related return code until later on. Some programs, though, never issue a call that elicits the return code. An example is the pipeline transaction described in "The Pipeline Transaction (Datagram)" in Chap. 18. This transaction will almost never get an attach-manager-related return code because the conversation is deallocated before the Attach ever reaches the server platform.

   In these cases, you may need to use one of the following sources of information:

   - The client platform's error log
   - The server platform's error log
   - An APPC line trace

2. *Use the return code as a guide to fixing the problem.*   There are six CPI-C return codes that are the direct result of the attach manager. These occur when the attach manager rejects an incoming Attach, either because of its contents or because the server program could not be started. The return codes are as follows:

   - CM_CONVERSATION_TYPE_MISMATCH
   - CM_PIP_NOT_SPECIFIED_CORRECTLY
   - CM_SECURITY_NOT_VALID
   - CM_SYNC_LVL_NOT_SUPPORTED_PGM
   - CM_TPN_NOT_RECOGNIZED
   - CM_TP_NOT_AVAILABLE_NO_RETRY
   - CM_TP_NOT_AVAILABLE_RETRY

For more information about the root causes of each return code, consult App. A.

LOADING YOUR SERVER PROGRAM
UNDER A SOURCE DEBUGGER

You may often find the need to load your server program under a debugger. On most platforms, the easiest way to do so is to configure the attach manager to load an intermediate command file rather than loading your program directly. For example, on OS/2 you could load a batch file which then invokes your program. When you configure a filespec on the OS/2 Communications Manager, the file extension must always be .EXE; to run batch files (which have a file extension of .CMD in OS/2), you need to start the CMD.EXE program and pass the filespec of the batch file as a parameter, as the following exemplifies.

```
DEFINE_TP TP_NAME(APINGD)
          DESCRIPTION(APING: server side as a .CMD file)
          FILESPEC(c:\os2\cmd.exe)
          PARM_STRING(/C c:\aping\apingd.cmd)
          ;
```

Under normal operation, the .CMD would simply invoke your executable file directly:

```
call c:\aping\apingd.exe
```

When you want instead to run the server program under the debugger, you can simply edit the .CMD file to start the debugger. The filespec for the server program is passed as a parameter to the debugger. The following is a sample batch file for the OS/2 Communications Manager which starts the IPMD source-code debugger, which in turn calls APINGD:

```
call ipmd c:\aping\apingd.exe
```

Advanced Topics

Converting Data Between Different Computers

CPI-C's portability across a wide variety of computer architectures and operating systems makes the porting of your program source a snap. CPI-C handles the conversion of all the names you give it, like LU names, mode names, and TP names. This relieves you of handling this part of your code differently as you move it to other computers. But while all your code may be portable, your data may not be.

In all the source code we've shown you so far, we've made a simplifying assumption. We've assumed that all data looks the same on every platform. Unfortunately, due to differences in computer architectures and national language character sets, we can't always depend on every platform to represent data in the same way.

Everyone needs to worry about data conversion. If you are writing both application sides for a single computer type or for computers that are very similar, you might think that you don't have to worry about data conversion. But building data conversion into your programs in the first release is important; when the first release of your application proves successful, you'll be ready for international distribution for your second release.

Indeed, you should pay attention to data conversion

- To expand the scope of platforms your application runs on

- To harness the power of new computer architectures

- To adapt to the needs of an ever-increasing international market

Each of these will require your application to convert data from one encoding to another one.

To address the data conversion problem, we need to change the way we handle our data. For each piece of data that we send or receive, we need to know two things:

1. The order in the buffer of the bytes of data (for example, low-to-high order or high-to-low)

2. The meaning of each byte and what it represents (for example, the character set or code page that is used)

When we examine the problem in more detail, we find that the solution is to specify exactly how our data looks in buffers and what each byte means. In most cases, this entails putting every data byte into a buffer individually and possibly converting it as we do so to change its encoding.

USING EXISTING DATA CONVERSION TOOLS

Before continuing with the nitty-gritty details of data conversion, we need to point out that there are existing standards or "libraries" that you can use to help with data conversion. By using existing data conversion tools you can

- Save yourself the time and effort of reinventing similar functions
- Inherit well-tested and robust functions

A number of data conversion tools and techniques currently exist (for example, Sun's XDR and OSI's ASN.1). If these tools are available in your environments, you may be able to use them and make your data conversion job transparent. These standards can handle any data type or combination of data types that your program can send.

Unfortunately, we must also warn you in advance that these data conversion tools are not necessarily ubiquitous. You may not find the same tools when you move your application to a new environment. Using data conversion tools can present you with a number of problems:

- Reinventing the tool yourself on a new platform which does not support the tool
- Discovering deficiencies in the tool that cannot be controlled

Most general-purpose data conversion tools require you to declare in an external file all of the data types that you will transfer. Names or identifiers are then assigned to each data type or structure. At the time your program sends its data, you simply tell the data conversion facility what kind of data is being sent and data conversion occurs automatically.

We find that the advantage of using existing standard tools is that data conversion is coded for you at little or no extra cost. The biggest problem with using these tools arises when you port to an environment that doesn't support the standard. You have to rewrite all of the standard code! The cost of rewriting a general-purpose standard will likely be higher than if you had done your own data conversion from the start. Therefore, we recommend against using external data conversion tools in your CPI-C programs until such time as they are integrated into the CPI-C architecture and products.

CONVERTING CHARACTERS

Characters and text strings present a number of problems for your programs. On the surface, handling text data is relatively simple; one character follows another in the buffer. The complexity in handling text data conversion lies in different character sets employed by the underlying hardware platforms and code pages used to represent different national language character sets.

The problems of character conversion range from the relatively simple to the extremely complex:

- *Special characters used in C and C++.* You need to be concerned about how you use C's special characters because not all computer languages treat these characters the same way that C does.

- *Different character sets.* Most workstations and personal computers use the ASCII character set. Most mainframe systems (for example, AS/400, CICS, IMS, MVS, VM/CMS) use the EBCDIC character set. Even if all the alphabetic characters get converted correctly, we don't know any C programmers who haven't discovered that their square brackets or curly braces don't always get converted correctly when they're uploading C source code to a host.

- *National language code pages.* Each national language specifies a code page used to represent its character set. When transferring data from one environment to another, your application may have to convert characters from one code page to another.

- *Double-byte character sets.* Some languages, like Chinese, have more characters in their alphabet than will fit in a byte (that is, more than 256). The double-byte character set representation uses two bytes to represent each character. To do this, they also have two special bytes, which indicate to "start interpreting" and "stop interpreting" the data as two-byte characters.

    There are other schemes gaining favor, such as Unicode, which represent characters using two bytes instead of one. As software goes global, expect this to be an area of growing interest.

Handling C's special characters

The C language defines the following set of escape sequences:

\a   alert (bell) character

\b   backspace

\f	formfeed
\n	newline
\r	carriage return
\t	horizontal tab
\v	vertical tab
\\	backslash
\?	question mark
\'	single quote
\"	double quote

You may program in C and C++ exclusively, but not everyone does. What happens when your program communicates with a program written in another computer language? For example, someday you may find a CICS programmer using COBOL trying to write a program which connects to your C program.

One option might be to "disable" the special characters so you wouldn't have to implement special handling for them in another language. Unfortunately, you would probably end up reinventing another mechanism to achieve the same results in a nonstandard way. In addition, you would have to invest in the coding effort to disable C's special handling of these characters.

We recommend limiting the number of special characters you use in your data. When you do need the character provided by an escape, use C's special characters for their intended purpose. You should document which special characters are used and ensure that programs connecting to yours interpret the characters in the same way.

Another character constant of note is '\0', which represents the null character and terminates C strings. Unfortunately, many other computer languages do not use C's null byte to terminate strings. It is difficult for a program written in another language to insert and parse the null byte, but relatively easy for a C program to handle length-delimited strings. We therefore recommend that you not send the null byte in your text strings.

Converting from ASCII-EBCDIC using CPI-C 1.2 functions

The X/Open CPI-C specification introduced a pair of data conversion calls that handle text data. X/Open CPI-C was originally intended for UNIX computers; these two calls were added to the X/Open CPI-C spec to allow UNIX computers to exchange text data with EBCDIC computers. These calls are now part of CPI-C 1.2, allowing any computer to exchange data between its native encoding and EBCDIC.

Convert_Outgoing. Allows your program to convert text data to EBCDIC. Your program issues this call before sending text to a computer that uses EBCDIC encoding.

Convert_Incoming. Allows your program to convert text data from EBCDIC. Your program issues this call after receiving text data from a computer that uses EBCDIC encoding.

The CPI-C 1.2 Convert calls solve only a small part of the whole data conversion problem; they only deal with text data and only on a limited set of characters. There is no capability to extend the conversion to handle multiple code pages or double-byte character sets.

In addition, all text data is converted to EBCDIC or converted from EBCDIC. If your program runs on an EBCDIC computer, these calls are essentially no-ops; the data isn't modified by the convert calls. But if you are on an ASCII computer, you must convert incoming and outgoing data, even if your partner is also running on an ASCII computer.

As we see CPI-C and client/server evolving, your connections are likely to be from workstation to host or workstation to workstation. When running from workstation to workstation, your text data is converted twice! Therefore, it may be to your benefit to consider text conversion methods that don't lock your programs into sending text in EBCDIC.

Convert_Outgoing (CMCNVO)

Use the Convert_Outgoing() call to translate text strings from the native encoding on your local computer to EBCDIC. You'll probably do this conversion before issuing a Send_Data(). This is one of five calls in CPI-C 1.2 that does not require a conversation ID. You can convert data any time you want, even if you don't have an active conversation.

Here's the function prototype for the Convert_Outgoing() call:

```
CM_ENTRY                              /* Convert_Outgoing   */
cmcnvo(unsigned char CM_PTR,          /* I/O: buffer        */
       CM_INT32 CM_PTR,               /* I: buffer_length   */
       CM_RETURN_CODE CM_PTR);        /* O: return_code     */
```

If CPI-C returns something other than CM_OK on Convert_Outgoing(), it's probably because your program passed a bad buffer pointer or a length parameter that is larger than the size of your buffer. The maximum size that can be converted is "implementation-specific." As we see more CPI-C 1.2 platforms, we'll start to get a better feel for how big this can be. In the meantime, we'll assume it's actually a 31-bit integer, meaning you could convert more than 2 billion bytes (if you can get a buffer that big!).

Convert_Incoming (CMCNVI)

The Convert_Incoming() call is designed to be used for translating text strings after receiving them on the Receive() call. This call does not take a conversation ID as input and can, therefore, be used even if you do not have an active conversation.

Here's the function prototype for the Convert_Incoming() call:

```
CM_ENTRY                              /* Convert_Incoming   */
cmcnvi(unsigned char CM_PTR,          /* I/O: buffer        */
```

```
CM_INT32 CM_PTR,              /* I: buffer_length    */
CM_RETURN_CODE CM_PTR);       /* O: return_code      */
```

As with Convert_Outgoing(), the only likely reason for Convert_Incoming() to fail is if you pass a bad buffer pointer or an invalid length.

Converting from ASCII-EBCDIC using tables

Convert_Outgoing() and Convert_Incoming() offer one way to convert to and from EBCDIC. You may find that your conversion needs are more sophisticated. For example, an easy way to handle ASCII to EBCDIC text translation is by using simple tables. This technique uses two tables; one for converting ASCII to EBCDIC and one for converting EBCDIC to ASCII. Each table is just a 256-byte array, mapping each byte value to a corresponding translated value.

The advantages of using tables over CPI-C's two Convert calls are:

- You can control the range of characters translated and assure consistent translation from platform to platform.

- The translation tables can be tailored.

- Performance may be better. Depending upon your CPI-C platform, a local procedure call may be much faster than a CPI-C API boundary crossing.

Here is the source code for two conversion procedures, along with the translation tables. Procedure convert_ascii_to_ebcdic_field() overlays EBCDIC characters on top of the ASCII characters that they are equivalent to. It takes a pointer to the ASCII character string and the length of the string; it doesn't depend on null-terminated strings to operate correctly. Procedure convert_ebcdic_to_ascii_field() goes in the opposite direction:

```
#include <stdio.h>
#include <assert.h>

/*-------------------------------------------------------------
 * All of the variables and parameters in this file are unsigned.
 * This avoids problems with using a signed (negative) number
 * as an array index.
 *-----------------------------------------------------------*/

extern const unsigned char ascii_to_ebcdic_table[];
extern const unsigned char ebcdic_to_ascii_table[];

void
convert_ascii_to_ebcdic_field (
    unsigned char    * ascii_field,
    const unsigned int field_size)
{
```

```
        unsigned int i;

        assert(ascii_field != NULL);

        for (i = 0; i < field_size; i++) {
            ascii_field[i] =
                ascii_to_ebcdic_table[(unsigned)ascii_field[i]];
        }
    }

    void
    convert_ebcdic_to_ascii_field(
        unsigned char    * ebcdic_field,
        const unsigned int field_size)
    {
        unsigned int i;

        assert(ebcdic_field != NULL);

        for (i = 0; i < field_size; i++) {
            ebcdic_field[i] =
                ebcdic_to_ascii_table[(unsigned)ebcdic_field[i]];
        }
    }
```

Here's the source code for C arrays, used to convert between ASCII and EBCDIC. The index into the first array by the value of an ASCII character holds the corresponding EBCDIC value. The index into the second array by the value of an EBCDIC character holds the corresponding ASCII value.

```
    /*---------------------------------------------------------------
     * ASCII to EBCDIC translation table.
     * This contains only the U.S. English character set, which is
     * known as the UGL (universal glyph list) character set.
     *-------------------------------------------------------------*/
    const unsigned char ascii_to_ebcdic_table[] = {
    /* 00-0F */
    "\x00\x01\x02\x03\x37\x2D\x2E\x2F\x16\x05\x15\x0B\x0C\x0D\x0E\x0F"
    /* 10-1F */
    "\x10\x11\x12\x13\x3C\x3D\x32\x26\x18\x19\x3F\x27\x22\x1D\x35\x1F"
    /* 20-2F */
    "\x40\x5A\x7F\x7B\x5B\x6C\x50\x7D\x4D\x5D\x5C\x4E\x6B\x60\x4B\x61"
    /* 30-3F */
    "\xF0\xF1\xF2\xF3\xF4\xF5\xF6\xF7\xF8\xF9\x7A\x5E\x4C\x7E\x6E\x6F"
    /* 40-4F */
    "\x7C\xC1\xC2\xC3\xC4\xC5\xC6\xC7\xC8\xC9\xD1\xD2\xD3\xD4\xD5\xD6"
    /* 50-5F */
    "\xD7\xD8\xD9\xE2\xE3\xE4\xE5\xE6\xE7\xE8\xE9\xAD\xE0\xBD\x5F\x6D"
    /* 60-6F */
```

```
     "\x79\x81\x82\x83\x84\x85\x86\x87\x88\x89\x91\x92\x93\x94\x95\x96"
/* 70-7F */
     "\x97\x98\x99\xA2\xA3\xA4\xA5\xA6\xA7\xA8\xA9\xC0\x4F\xD0\xA1\x07"
/* 80-8F */
     "\x43\x20\x21\x1C\x23\xEB\x24\x9B\x71\x28\x38\x49\x90\xBA\xEC\xDF"
/* 90-9F */
     "\x45\x29\x2A\x9D\x72\x2B\x8A\x9A\x67\x56\x64\x4A\x53\x68\x59\x46"
/* A0-AF */
     "\xEA\xDA\x2C\xDE\x8B\x55\x41\xFE\x58\x51\x52\x48\x69\xDB\x8E\x8D"
/* B0-BF */
     "\x73\x74\x75\xFA\x15\xB0\xB1\xB3\xB4\xB5\x6A\xB7\xB8\xB9\xCC\xBC"
/* C0-CF */
     "\xAB\x3E\x3B\x0A\xBF\x8F\x3A\x14\xA0\x17\xCB\xCA\x1A\x1B\x9C\x04"
/* D0-DF */
     "\x34\xEF\x1E\x06\x08\x09\x77\x70\xBE\xBB\xAC\x54\x63\x65\x66\x62"
/* E0-EF */
     "\x30\x42\x47\x57\xEE\x33\xB6\xE1\xCD\xED\x36\x44\xCE\xCF\x31\xAA"
/* F0-FF */
     "\xFC\x9E\xAE\x8C\xDD\xDC\x39\xFB\x80\xAF\xFD\x78\x76\xB2\x9F\xFF"
};


/*-------------------------------------------------------------
 * EBCDIC to ASCII translation table.
 * This contains only the U.S. English character set, which is
 * known as the UGL (universal glyph list) character set.
 *-------------------------------------------------------------*/
const unsigned char ebcdic_to_ascii_table[] = {
/* 00-0F */
     "\x00\x01\x02\x03\xCF\x09\xD3\x7F\xD4\xD5\xC3\x0B\x0C\x0D\x0E\x0F"
/* 10-1F */
     "\x10\x11\x12\x13\xC7\x0A\x08\xC9\x18\x19\xCC\xCD\x83\x1D\xD2\x1F"
/* 20-2F */
     "\x81\x82\x1C\x84\x86\x0A\x17\x1B\x89\x91\x92\x95\xA2\x05\x06\x07"
/* 30-3F */
     "\xE0\xEE\x16\xE5\xD0\x1E\xEA\x04\x8A\xF6\xC6\xC2\x14\x15\xC1\x1A"
/* 40-4F */
     "\x20\xA6\xE1\x80\xEB\x90\x9F\xE2\xAB\x8B\x9B\x2E\x3C\x28\x2B\x7C"
/* 50-5F */
     "\x26\xA9\xAA\x9C\xDB\xA5\x99\xE3\xA8\x9E\x21\x24\x2A\x29\x3B\x5E"
/* 60-6F */
     "\x2D\x2F\xDF\xDC\x9A\xDD\xDE\x98\x9D\xAC\xBA\x2C\x25\x5F\x3E\x3F"
/* 70-7F */
     "\xD7\x88\x94\xB0\xB1\xB2\xFC\xD6\xFB\x60\x3A\x23\x40\x27\x3D\x22"
/* 80-8F */
     "\xF8\x61\x62\x63\x64\x65\x66\x67\x68\x69\x96\xA4\xF3\xAF\xAE\xC5"
/* 90-9F */
     "\x8C\x6A\x6B\x6C\x6D\x6E\x6F\x70\x71\x72\x97\x87\xCE\x93\xF1\xFE"
/* A0-AF */
     "\xC8\x7E\x73\x74\x75\x76\x77\x78\x79\x7A\xEF\xC0\xDA\x5B\xF2\xF9"
/* B0-BF */
```

```
"\xB5\xB6\xFD\xB7\xB8\xB9\xE6\xBB\xBC\xBD\x8D\xD9\xBF\x5D\xD8\xC4"
/* C0-CF */
"\x7B\x41\x42\x43\x44\x45\x46\x47\x48\x49\xCB\xCA\xBE\xE8\xEC\xED"
/* D0-DF */
"\x7D\x4A\x4B\x4C\x4D\x4E\x4F\x50\x51\x52\xA1\xAD\xF5\xF4\xA3\x8F"
/* E0-EF */
"\x5C\xE7\x53\x54\x55\x56\x57\x58\x59\x5A\xA0\x85\x8E\xE9\xE4\xD1"
/* F0-FF */
"\x30\x31\x32\x33\x34\x35\x36\x37\x38\x39\xB3\xF7\xF0\xFA\xA7\xFF"
};
```

Rather than having every part of our source know what character set is supported by the platform, we encapsulate this within a set of macros. These macros make the conversion to and from ASCII occur on the EBCDIC computer:

```
/*
 * Test whether this is an EBCDIC character set computer.
 * Define the constant EBCDIC_HOST so it's known to the compiler.
 */

#ifdef EBCDIC_HOST

/* This should be used before sending data. */
#define convert_to_ascii(buffer, len)     \
         convert_ebcdic_to_ascii_field(buffer,len)

/* This should be used after receiving data. */
#define convert_from_ascii(buffer, len)   \
         convert_ascii_to_ebcdic_field(buffer,len)

#else

/*
 * This is an ASCII computer.  Define the macros to a no-op.
 */

/* This should be used before sending data. */
#define convert_to_ascii(buffer, len)    ((void)0)
/* This should be used after receiving data. */
#define convert_from_ascii(buffer, len)  ((void)0)

#endif
```

You should use these macros whenever you send or receive text strings. If you are on an EBCDIC computer, conversion to or from ASCII will occur. If you are on an ASCII computer, no conversion will take place.

We choose ASCII as the base encoding for our text strings, to reduce the overhead when transferring data between two ASCII workstations.

Handling national language code pages

The difference in computer hardware implementations makes the need for ASCII/EBCDIC conversion obvious. Perhaps less obvious is the reason behind the concept of code pages and the differences among them.

As native speakers of English, we generally deal with only 26 letters (uppercase and lowercase), 10 digits, and a handful of punctuation marks. If you've studied other languages, it's likely that you got a taste of the diversity of other character representations. There are a wide variety of accented characters, combinations of letters into one character, and characters different from the 26 English characters we're familiar with.

The number of different character representations across written languages is far greater than the 256 values that can be represented by an 8-bit byte. Although there are many different kinds of characters worldwide, most languages do use less than 256 distinct characters. Thus, code pages were invented.

A code page is a redefinition of the values of a byte to the characters that a particular national language uses. Some new characters are given representations and others are moved around or are no longer representable in that code page.

For example, the U.S. dollar sign ($) is encoded as X'5B' in the U.S. EBCDIC code page (037). In the U.K. EBCDIC code page (285), the U.S. dollar sign is encoded as X'4A' and the British pound sign is encoded as X'5B'. If you didn't convert from one code page to other, any monetary numbers you transferred would inadvertently be interpreted as pounds rather than dollars without the required exchange rate conversion! Problems converting characters exist throughout each pair of code pages.

Some platforms may provide system facilities to convert from one code page to another. If such calls exist, it is quickest and easiest for you to use them.

If your platform does not provide system facilities to convert from one code page to another, you may have to invent your own. You'll need a set of translation tables similar to the ones we saw earlier for ASCII and EBCDIC, but to convert from one code page to another. You can then use an adaptation of the convert_ascii_to_ebcdic_field() routine shown previously to pass in the translation table as an input parameter.

Handling double-byte character sets

Some languages require far more character representations than can fit into a single byte. For example, Japanese and traditional Chinese all use ideographic characters which number in the thousands. The Double-Byte Character Set (DBCS) was developed to handle such languages.

To handle DBCS characters and DBCS strings, your programs must provide twice the buffer space for character strings. You must also be careful not to treat your DBCS string as if it were a single-byte character string.

Covering DBCS string handling completely is beyond the scope of this book. We provide here a number of tips and considerations when enabling your applications for DBCS support:

- Your program needs to determine from the operating system whether your program is running under a DBCS code page. The technique required differs from platform to platform.

- The C language's library routines are not DBCS-enabled.

  In particular, the "search," "concatenate," and "truncate" string functions do not work properly. The strlen() call will work, but it returns the number of bytes in the string, not the number of characters.

- When searching for characters or delimiters within strings, make sure that you don't find just one byte of a 2-byte character. In particular, care should be taken when processing file path delimiters.

- Consider using the new ANSI C routines for multibyte characters. The new support includes a new data type which represents a wide (double-byte) character. The typedef for these characters is wchar_t.

  C also provides a set of routines to convert from wide character strings to and from multibyte character strings, which are a combination of single-byte and double-byte characters.

mblen()	Get the length and determine the validity of a multibyte character.
mbstowcs()	Convert a sequence of multi-byte characters to a corresponding sequence of wide characters.
mbtowc()	Convert a multibyte character to a corresponding wide character.
wcstombs()	Convert a sequence of wide characters to a corresponding sequence of multibyte characters.
wctomb()	Convert a wide character to the corresponding multibyte character.

We've listed some IBM books that you'll find helpful in planning for your DBCS support. See "Data Conversion Books" in App. D.

CONVERTING OTHER DATA TYPES

Although much of the data your applications send may be text data or binary streams of bytes, you may also have to send other data types. In particular, integers and floating-point numbers need conversion or special handling. For both integers and floating-point numbers, we need to concern ourselves with the size of the data and how the computer hardware represents the data values.

Converting integers

The size of integers can differ substantially from one computer to another. The only thing that C guarantees you is the following:

```
sizeof(char) <= sizeof(short) <= sizeof(int) <= sizeof(long)
```

We've observed that most systems have 2-byte integers and 4-byte integers. When you are sending integers as data to your partner program you need to make sure that you send the number of bytes that your partner expects.

Although you may program on a system with integer sizes other than two and four, using different sizes makes it difficult to write partner programs on "normal" platforms. We recommend limiting your programs to send only 2- or 4-byte integers.

To help ensure that you always send the correct size integers, we recommend that you typedef the integer data types that you send on conversations. For example,

```
/*-----------------------------------------------------------
 * On this sample system and compiler:
 *      sizeof(unsigned short) is 2 bytes or 16 bits
 *      sizeof(unsigned long) is 4 bytes or 32 bits
 *---------------------------------------------------------*/
typedef unsigned short int16;
typedef unsigned long int32;
```

When you port this code to another platform or compiler, you will need to verify that these typedefs result in the correct size definitions. You may consider adding

```
assert(sizeof(int16) == 2);
assert(sizeof(int32) == 4);
```

Our other concern with integers is how the computer hardware represents them in memory. When computer hardware designers sit down to work, one of their architectural decisions is how to store integers in memory. One option is to store the most significant byte of an integer first (big-endian). The other option is to store the least significant byte of the integer first (little-endian).*

To illustrate the difference between the storage of big-endian and little-endian numbers, let's consider how we would represent the number 305419896, which happens to be X'12345678' in hex notation.

```
   Big Endian       Little Endian
   *********         *********
   0  1  2  3        0  1  2  3
 -------------      -------------
 |12|34|56|78|      |78|56|34|12|
 -------------      -------------
```

Just to give you an idea of what computers fall where, here is a list of some big- and little-endian computer architectures:

---

* The term *big-endian* is from Jonathan Swift's *Gulliver's Travels,* via the paper "On Holy Wars and a Plea for Peace," by Danny Cohen, USC/ISI IEN 137, April 1, 1980.

Big-endian computers	Little-endian computers
Cray	DEC PDP-11
DEC PDP-10	DEC VAX
IBM AS/400	Intel x86 (e.g., PCs, IBM PS/2, Pentium)
IBM RISC System/6000	
IBM S/360, S/370, S/390	
Motorola 680×0 (e.g., Macintosh)	
Next	
Sun	

Let's look at how we're going to reconcile big- versus little-endian. First of all, you must choose the byte order for your integers when you send them in conversation buffers. We recommend using big-endian because:

- The data is easier to read in line traces and buffer traces.
- Should you ever write a basic conversation, the logical-length (LL) field must be encoded as a 2-byte big-endian integer. Your code will be easier to maintain if you have only one set of integer conversion routines.

Here's the code we use to convert our integers into the right format for data transmission. No where in this integer conversion code do we have to know whether our computer is big- or little-endian. The routines have been written to store the integers in big-endian format, regardless of how the computer has stored the bytes in memory.

```
#include <stdio.h>        /* file I/O           */
#include <assert.h>       /* assert macro       */
#include "inttype.h"

/*-------------------------------------------------------------
 * Store a 2-byte (16-bit) integer into a data buffer.
 *-----------------------------------------------------------*/
void
convert_store_int16_in_buffer(
    int16          integer,
    unsigned char * buffer)
{
    assert(buffer != NULL);

    /*-------------------------------------------------------
     * Mask the high byte of the integer, shift it into the
     * low-order byte, and put it into the first character of the
     * buffer.
     *-----------------------------------------------------*/
    buffer[0] = (unsigned char)
                ((int16)((int16)0xFF00 & integer) >> 8);
```

```
                /*-----------------------------------------------------------
                 * Mask the low byte of the integer and put it into the
                 * second character in the buffer.
                 *----------------------------------------------------------*/
                buffer[1] = (unsigned char)
                              (int16)((int16)0x00FF & integer);
        }


        /*-----------------------------------------------------------------
         * Get a 2-byte (16-bit) integer from a data buffer.
         *----------------------------------------------------------------*/
        void
        convert_get_int16_from_buffer(
            int16         * integer,  /* pointer to the target integer */
            unsigned char * buffer)
        {
            assert(integer != NULL);
            assert(buffer != NULL);

            /*-----------------------------------------------------------
             * Take the first buffer character, shift it to the
             * upper byte, and OR it with the second buffer character
             * (the lower byte).
             *----------------------------------------------------------*/
            *integer = (int16)
              ((int16)((int16)((int16)((unsigned char)buffer[0])) << 8)
               |
               ((unsigned char)buffer[1]));
        }


        /*-----------------------------------------------------------------
         * Store a 4-byte (32-bit) integer into a data buffer.
         *----------------------------------------------------------------*/
        void
        convert_store_int32_in_buffer(
            int32           integer,
            unsigned char * buffer)
        {
            assert(buffer != NULL);

            /*-----------------------------------------------------------
             * Mask and shift the high byte, storing it into
             * the first buffer location.
             *----------------------------------------------------------*/
            buffer[0] = (unsigned char)
                          (((int32)0xFF000000 & integer) >> 24);

            /*-----------------------------------------------------------
             * Mask and shift the second highest byte, storing it into
             * the second buffer location.
             *----------------------------------------------------------*/
```

```
    buffer[1] = (unsigned char)
                (((int32)0x00FF0000 & integer) >> 16);

    /*----------------------------------------------------------
     * Mask and shift the third highest byte, storing it into
     * the third buffer location.
     *-------------------------------------------------------*/
    buffer[2] = (unsigned char)
                (((int32)0x0000FF00 & integer) >> 8);

    /*----------------------------------------------------------
     * Mask and shift the lowest byte, storing it into
     * the fourth buffer location.
     *-------------------------------------------------------*/
    buffer[3] = (unsigned char)
                ((int32)0x000000FF & integer);
}


/*----------------------------------------------------------------
 * Get a 4-byte (32-bit) integer from a data buffer.
 *-------------------------------------------------------------*/
void
convert_get_int32_from_buffer(
    int32        * integer,  /* pointer to the target integer */
    unsigned char * buffer)
{
    assert(integer != NULL);
    assert(buffer != NULL);

    /*----------------------------------------------------------
     * Shift the byte values into their correct positions,
     * then logically OR them together.
     *-------------------------------------------------------*/
    *integer =
        (((int32)((unsigned char)buffer[0])) << 24) |
        (((int32)((unsigned char)buffer[1])) << 16) |
        (((int32)((unsigned char)buffer[2])) <<  8) |
         ((int32)((unsigned char)buffer[3]));
}
```

To give you an example of how you could use these routines in your applications, here are two code snippets: one sending a 4-byte integer and the other receiving it.

```
#include <cpic.h>          /* conversation API library   */
#include "inttype.h"       /* typedefs for int32, int16  */
#include "intconv.h"       /* conversion prototypes      */
#include "docpic.h"        /* CPI-C do_ calls            */

void
send_int32(
```

```
                unsigned char *conversation_ID,
                int32          integer)
        {
            CM_REQUEST_TO_SEND_RECEIVED rts_received;   /* ignored */
            CM_RETURN_CODE              cpic_return_code;
            unsigned char               buffer[sizeof(integer)];
            CM_INT32                    length = sizeof(integer);

            convert_store_int32_in_buffer(integer, buffer);

            cmsend(                     /* Send_Data                */
                conversation_ID,    /* conversation ID          */
                buffer,             /* send this buffer         */
                &length,            /* length to send           */
                &rts_received,      /* did partner RTS?         */
                &cpic_return_code); /* return code from this call  */
            if (CM_OK != cpic_return_code) {
                handle_cpic_rc(
                    conversation_ID, cpic_return_code, "CMSEND");
            }
        }


        int32
        receive_int32(
            unsigned char *conversation_ID)
        {
            int32                   integer;

            CM_RETURN_CODE          cpic_return_code;
            unsigned char           buffer[sizeof(integer)];
            CM_INT32                requested_length = sizeof(integer);
            CM_INT32                received_length;
            CM_DATA_RECEIVED_TYPE   data_received;
            CM_STATUS_RECEIVED      status_received;
            CM_REQUEST_TO_SEND_RECEIVED rts_received;   /* ignored */

            cmrcv (                     /* Receive               */
                conversation_ID,    /* conversation ID       */
                buffer,             /* place data here       */
                &requested_length,  /* max length to receive  */
                &data_received,     /* returned data_rcvd    */
                &received_length,   /* length of received data */
                &status_received,   /* returned status_rcvd  */
                &rts_received,      /* did partner RTS?      */
                &cpic_return_code); /* return code           */

            if (CM_OK != cpic_return_code) {
                handle_cpic_rc(
                    conversation_ID, cpic_return_code, "CMRCV ");
            }

            convert_get_int32_from_buffer(&integer, buffer);

            return integer;
        }
```

Converting floating-point numbers

C defines three different types of floating-point numbers, with a relationship similar to that of integers:

```
sizeof(float) <= sizeof(double) <= sizeof(long double)
```

On most implementations, these will all be different sizes.

The real problem with handling floating-point numbers in binary is that they are represented differently among computer architectures, compilers, and even libraries. The general definition of a floating-point number consists of a sign bit, a mantissa, and an exponent. There are two major standards for defining how many and which bits are used for each of the floating-point components: IEEE and System/370. IEEE floating point is an international standard which is used by most workstation and personal computers, as well as by larger computers. System/370 floating point is used almost exclusively by IBM mainframes.

This wouldn't be too bad if the story ended here. Although IEEE floating point is an established standard, each computer or compiler may use its own variation on the standard. In fact, the Microsoft C++ 7.00 compiler has an alternate math library that uses a nonstandard floating-point representation.

The number of different floating-point sizes and formats along with the inherent complexity of manipulating floating-point bits makes direct conversion impractical.

We recommend that when your programs send floating-point numbers, they send them as text strings. This conversion is easy, using C's sprintf() routine. In programs which receive floating-point numbers (which should now be arriving in their text representation), the receiver converts the text string back to the local floating-point format. This conversion is also easy in C, using the atof() routine.

Here are two code samples which illustrate how your programs can convert from the binary floating-point format to a text string.

```
#include <cpic.h>          /* conversation API library   */
#include <stdarg.h>        /* variable arguments         */
#include <stdio.h>         /* file I/O                   */
#include <stdlib.h>        /* standard library           */
#include <string.h>        /* strings and memory         */
#include <assert.h>        /* assert macro               */
#include <math.h>          /* floating point math        */

#include "docpic.h"        /* CPI-C do_ routines         */

void
send_double(
    unsigned char * conversation_ID,
    double          floating_point_number)
{
```

```
        unsigned char    buffer[32+1];
        CM_INT32         send_length;


        /* convert the floating point number to a text string      */
        sprintf(buffer, "%16f", floating_point_number);

        send_length = (CM_INT32)strlen(buffer);

        do_send_data(conversation_ID, buffer, send_length);
    }


double
receive_double(
    unsigned char * conversation_ID)
{
    unsigned char    data_buffer[32+1];
    CM_INT32         requested_length = sizeof(data_buffer) - 1;
    CM_INT32         received_length;

    assert(conversation_ID != NULL);

    do_receive_pipe(
        conversation_ID,
        data_buffer,
        requested_length,        /* buffer size                    */
        &received_length);       /* bytes received                 */

    /*----------------------------------------------------
     * Add the null terminator, assuming this is a good
     * floating point number.
     *--------------------------------------------------*/
    data_buffer[received_length] = '\0';
    return atof(data_buffer);
    }
```

CONVERTING RECORDS WITH MULTIPLE DATA TYPES

Many applications will never send more than one type of data in a single record. But there may be times when sending many differently typed fields in a single data record is the easiest and most efficient way to code your program.

For example, a file transfer program might want to send a file-information data structure. It seems sensible that one file-information data structure should correspond to one CPI-C data record. The file-information data structure might consist of a string representing the file name and a 4-byte integer representing the timestamp.

When programs are exchanging data with many different types, the receiver of the data has a real challenge. It has to figure out what was sent. It has to parse the data so its syntax makes sense, and it then needs to interpret what it sees correctly. The two sides have to agree on how the sequence of multiple data types will be represented. This can be done by deciding the order and size of fields ahead of time, or by including special codes in your records to identify each field.

Handling C data structures

When you are trying to send multiple data types in a single record, there is a good chance that you've already organized your data into a C data structure. At first glance, it might seem like all you would need to do is pass the data structure pointer on a Send_Data() call. For example,

```
typedef struct data_item {
    unsigned char   flag;
    unsigned long   timestamp;
    unsigned char * filename;
} DATA_ITEM;

DATA_ITEM data_item;
send_length = (CM_INT32)sizeof(data_item);

do_send_data(conversation_ID, &data_item, send_length);
```

Unfortunately, there are a number of problems with using C data structures in this fashion:

- *C compilers pad between the fields in a structure.* The C language standard allows compilers the flexibility to align structure fields on memory boundaries. This can lead to blank, or unused, space between fields. Of course, every platform and every compiler may use a different alignment of fields, so you can't send a structure on one platform and simply receive it on another.

- *Pointers don't make sense to the partner.* If your structure fields are actually pointers to other data, all you would end up sending would be the pointer value. The actual data that your program pointed to would never be sent, and the partner has no use for the pointer. For example, if you had a field like

```
unsigned char * file_name;
```

the pointer value would be sent to the partner program, but not the text string that you really wanted to send.

To send C structures, you will have to copy each field element into the data buffer individually. In this way, you can ensure that the bytes go into the buffer in the proper order and that they can be read properly by the receiving program.

Encoding data

When your programs send multiple data types in a single record, the most important concern is that the program receiving the record can understand its contents. Both programs must agree on a protocol for encoding the data types if the receiving side is to have any hope at parsing and interpreting what it receives.

There are two basic methods for encoding data fields:

- *Put the data items in a consistent, predefined order.*   Both programs must coordinate and define the order and size of each data field that is in the data buffer. This method is relatively simple and requires no extra bytes in the buffer.

    One problem with making your data items order-dependent is that there is no room for expansion if you later need to send additional data fields.

- *Precede each data item with a field identifier.*   This allows your programs to send data fields in any order, since each field is preceded by a unique identifier. It also gives your programs the flexibility to add fields or remove fields depending upon circumstances.

Although the field identifiers require additional buffer space, we recommend that you use the second method when sending complex data records that may change in the future.

Interacting with Security

Security is an important part of the distributed computing world. Although distributed security is more complex than on a stand-alone computer, the concern is the same; protecting sensitive resources.

Sometimes your application and the resources it accesses determine what level of security is required. Other times, the user environment where the application is installed requires a certain level of security. As an application programmer, you must adjust to the security concerns of your users. You cannot assume that your application will never use security or will always use security.

This chapter shows you:

- An overview of security concepts and APPC security tools

- A guide to configuring your server application for security

- A guide to using conversation security calls within your client program

INTRODUCING APPC SECURITY

The goal of security is to protect sensitive resources. But who are we protecting our resources from? To safeguard sensitive resources, APPC provides for:

- Protection against an attacker with a computer that masquerades as a valid computer

- Protection from an attacker pretending to be a valid user

- Protection from a valid user who is not authorized to access data or resources

In addition, there are other security concerns not fully addressed by APPC that you may have to consider building into your own application:

- Protection against an attacker who can capture and view data records in transit

- Protection against an attacker who captures records, modifies them and then sends them on

Security hooks are built into the heart of APPC, APPN, and CPI-C software. These provide three mechanisms that can be used separately or together to safeguard resources:

Route security.   Lets the client program request a secure route through the network to the partner computer. If no such route can be obtained, the Allocate() call fails.

Session security.   Lets the client LU software verify the identity of the partner LU software. If the client LU or the partner LU can't respond correctly, the Allocate() call fails. You may also hear this referred to as LU-LU security.

Conversation security.   Lets the server's attach manager software verify the identity of the client program by inspecting the user ID and password that arrives on an Attach. If the client program didn't supply a valid combination, the server program is never started.

Your programs only have influence on route security and conversation security; session security is strictly a setup option between a pair of LUs. Let's look further at all three mechanisms.

APPC route security

We've talked in many chapters about the mode name. It's the way your program can say what kind of session it requires. You'll remember that a session is like a pipe between the two computers that your programs are using. By picking different mode names, you can get different kinds of pipes between the computers.

In all the examples we've looked at so far, we've suggested that you use one of the five predefined mode names: #BATCH, #INTER, #BATCHSC, #INTERSC, and all blanks. Specifically, we've talked about using #BATCH and #INTER, for batch or interactive traffic, respectively. The modes named #BATCHSC and #INTERSC are their secure counterparts. If your program asks for a session that meets the criteria of the mode named #INTERSC, it is asking for a path through the network suitable for interactive traffic, that is secure from being watched.

It's up to the people who set up the network to say which links are secure. For example, cabling that passes from one computer to another through a conduit guarded from radiation is considered secure. Local area network (LAN) links normally are not described as secure, since anyone can potentially plug a network analyzer into a LAN and capture the frames that go by. However, if the entire LAN is confined to an area with physical security (for example, behind locked doors and with badge access only to authorized personnel), then the LAN can be considered secure.

Most APPC platforms do not provide for automatic encryption of data frames, but you can choose hardware or software that gives you link-level encryption for given pairs of links. You can probably trust these links to be secure. APPC does provide for automatic compression of the data on a session. Session-level compression is another characteristic of a session that can influence your choice of mode names. A session with compression shields the data it is carrying from prying eyes to some extent.* If no secure session is available, you might suggest that your users request a session with compression.

Chapter 22 showed procedures you might modify for your programs to allow your users to specify alternate mode names. The option to choose mode names that request routes with security or compression is another good reason to allow your users this flexibility.

APPC session security

You may choose to configure APPC session security in a network because it lets you protect against an attacker with a computer that masquerades as a valid computer. Session security is completely outside the scope of your CPI-C programs; it is entirely based in configuration. You should never need to add any code to your application to enable or know about session security. You should, though, be aware of what session security provides for your application and users as well as the overhead involved in using it.

Session-level security works by requiring that a password be configured as part of the LU definition on each computer. The passwords must match identically between a pair of LU definitions. The checking of the passwords occurs whenever a session is set up between a pair of LUs.

The *LU-LU passwords* themselves are never exchanged by the partners. Instead, the first LU, the one requesting the session, uses its password to encrypt a token that it sends to its potential partner. The partner LU software, when it sees an encrypted token arrive, further uses its password to encrypt a reply. If the first LU can undo the encrypted token, the session is established.

You should recommend that your users consider using APPC session security to protect resources not protected by authorization control. For example, most personal computers running DOS have no built-in restrictions on which users can use which files. Session security might also be considered for the control sessions between network nodes in an APPN network.

---

* It prevents "lazy" attackers from being able to browse data captured in a line trace. A determined attacker could still figure out how to decompress the data.

If you choose to recommend using session security, you should keep in mind the following advantages and disadvantages.

Advantages of session security:

- There are no changes required in your application programs.
- LU-LU passwords are never exposed to attackers.

Disadvantages of session security:

- A scheme must be devised for inventing, synchronizing, and setting up the passwords between each relevant pair of LUs.
- These LU-LU passwords require the kind of maintenance you need to lavish on any passwords, except they come in pairs. They must be updated regularly, aged out, and so on.

APPC conversation security

Working our way up, from securing the route to securing the computers at the ends of the route, we get to securing the programs themselves. APPC conversation security is used to protect against an attacker masquerading as a valid user. If a security manager is available, as in most multiuser systems, APPC interacts with that security manager to assure that nonauthorized access does not occur.

Conversation security is implemented in two steps. These steps must be passed in order before data access is permitted. The steps are.

1. *Authentication*
   - Is this user who he claims to be?
   - Does the user know the secret password?

2. *Authorization* (also known as access control)
   - Is this user authorized to perform the function?
   - Is the user's ID in a list of authorized users?

The primary goal of APPC conversation security is to get an authenticated user ID from the client to the server. The attach manager on the server platform has the final say; it uses the client's user ID to perform the authorization step.

The corresponding conversation characteristic is named *conversation_security_type,* and, as you might guess, a Set call lets you set the type: Set_Conversation_Security_Type(). The client program can specify three conversation security types: None, Program, and Same.

CM_SECURITY_NONE.   The Attach carries no user ID or password. The Attach will only be accepted if the TP definition for the server program has been configured not to require conversation security.

CM_SECURITY_PROGRAM. The client program specifies a user ID and password, which is carried in the Attach. The user ID and password are authenticated by the attach manager at the computer where the server program is. Note that this password is not encrypted, and it is, thus, exposed to line trace attackers.

CM_SECURITY_SAME. The client platform should copy the local security environment (from the locally logged-on user) to the server platform. This allows full security support without requiring the user to enter a user ID and password every time the client program is run. The details of how CM_SECURITY_ SAME is implemented are provided below.

Of these three types, CM_SECURITY_SAME is the most interesting for making security easy to use and administer. The sophistication of the software that underlies it has evolved over the years and encompasses a number of different security techniques. In order to know what happens when you choose CM_SECURITY_SAME, you need to know what level of security sophistication the client and server platforms support and what the server has been configured to allow.

The three methods of performing security SAME are:

Already verified
The server platform must "trust" that the client platform has properly authenticated the user. The client sends the logged on user ID to the server without any accompanying password. The server skips the authentication step and performs the authorization step.

Already verified's requirement of "trust" is difficult to come by in the computing world. Because of this, we recommend that already verified only be used in conjunction with APPC's session security feature, which gives you an assurance that the client computer is valid and thus trustable.

Requirements
- The client and server must both support already verified.
- The server must be configured to allow already verified from the client.

Persistent verification
The first time the client connects to the server, the currently logged-on user ID and password are sent to the server for authentication. On subsequent conversations, only the user ID is sent, along with an indicator reminding the server that this is an already signed-on user. This reduces the number of times the password is exposed in the clear. It also reduces the overhead of authenticating the user ID and password on each conversation.

Requirements
- The client and server must both support persistent verification.
- The server must be configured to allow persistent verification from the client.

Enhanced security SAME

The client platform sends the currently logged-on user ID and password. To the server platform, it appears as if the client was using CM_SECURITY_ PROGRAM. Although the user ID and password are always sent in the clear (the same as security PROGRAM) the client program does not have to obtain and supply the user ID and password.

Requirements

- The client must support enhanced security SAME.

- Server platform needs only to be able to authenticate a user ID and password. This is the same as security PROGRAM.

Before you can determine what actually happens when your application specifies security SAME, you need to know what is supported by the client and server platforms. We've put a table on our diskette with the conversation security support for some of the platforms we're familiar with (you may want to add additional columns for the platforms and releases you're working with). You also need to know whether the server has been configured to allow already verified or persistent verification from the client computer.

Armed with this knowledge, let's go through the steps that CPI-C goes through in handling security SAME. As soon as CPI-C finds a match and chooses a security method, the higher-numbered options are no longer considered.

1. *Already verified.* Used if the following conditions are true.

   - There is a locally logged-on user.
   - The server platform said in the Bind* that already verified is accepted. This means that the server platform supports already verified and is configured to allow it from the client.
   - The client platform supports already verified (it knows how to set already verified and extract the locally logged-on user ID).

2. *Persistent verification.* Used if the following conditions are true:

   - There is a locally logged-on user.
   - The server platform said in the Bind that persistent verification is accepted. This means that the server platform supports persistent verification and is configured to allow it from the client.
   - The client platform supports persistent verification (it knows how to use persistent verification and extract the locally logged on user ID and password).[†]

---

* The internal message that flows between a pair of LUs when a session is set up.

[†] Not all operating systems allow extracting the cleartext password. These platforms cannot support persistent verification.

3. *Enhanced security SAME.*   Used if the following are true:

- There is a locally logged-on user.
- The server platform said in the Bind that conversation security is accepted. This is the same as accepting CM_SECURITY_PROGRAM and is almost universally set.
- The client platform supports enhanced security same. This means that it knows how to extract the locally logged-on user ID and password.

4. *Downgrade to CM_SECURITY_NONE.*   If none of the previous CM_ SECURITY_SAME methods can be used, the security type is downgraded to CM_SECURITY_NONE.

Whenever the incoming conversation security type, user ID, or password don't match exactly what the attach manager at the server platform expects, the attach manager rejects the Attach. You'll see this in the client program via the CM_SECURITY_NOT_VALID return code, on one of the calls after an Allocate(). This return code is decidedly cryptic; it was designed to tell your program that something is wrong, but not to be too specific. This vagueness is supposedly more "secure" than telling you exactly what's wrong. That's okay, but it does make it challenging for a well-meaning user who's made a typing mistake to debug what's happened! See App. A for a detailed discussion of this return code.

ADDITIONAL SECURITY MEASURES

As we alluded to in "Introducing APPC Security" earlier in this chapter, there are security attacks that APPC security does not protect against. Depending upon the security requirements of your application and your users, you may need to build some features into your application to provide for:

- Protection against an attacker who can capture and view data records in transit
- Protection against an attacker who captures records, modifies them and then sends them on

An effective protection against both of these attacks is to encrypt all of the data you send. You can do this encryption and decryption in each program of an application, or you can rely on encryption hardware or software that may be available on both platforms. For example, VTAM supports automatic encryption of APPC application data between two host applications. Encryption is enabled by configuration parameters in the mode name specified by the client program.

CONFIGURING YOUR SERVER TRANSACTION PROGRAM

Before configuring your application on the server platform, you must first determine what the "proper" level of security is. The design and intended use of your application will indicate a particular minimum level of security. But the needs and concerns of the application *users* may lead to stricter or more lax security guidelines.

You need to guide your users and make recommendations to help them configure your server program appropriately. In this section, we outline some scenarios for different application environments. For each scenario, we show the kind of security that is appropriate.

Disabling security: public transaction programs

There are some applications that you want literally anyone to be able to run. For example, the APING application, which is a connectivity test tool, should be available to everyone. All users should be able to use APING to bring up a test connection to a platform. Since APING doesn't access any resources, it is relatively safe* to allow everyone access to the server program without authentication or authorization control.

Most platforms allow you to configure the server program to not require conversation security. Since some operating systems require each program to run under a valid user ID, you may have to assign your server program to run under a particular user ID. In these instances, you should set up a specific user ID like "guest" that has limited access permissions.

Handling security program

The normal setup for a server program is to require some form of authenticated user before starting the program. On most platforms, this is as simple as setting a parameter in the server program's TP definition that indicates that conversation security is required. Having done so, unless we change our configuration to allow one of the security SAME types, each Attach for this server program will require a user ID and a password.

When the user ID and password arrive at the server platform in the Attach, they are authenticated in the operating system's user database. On some systems, the CPI-C platform may supply an alternative method of configuring user ID and password pairs. This alternative database is usually checked only after the user ID and password aren't found in the operating system's user database.

Allowing persistent verification

If you are able to, you should always allow the client to use persistent verification. This feature reduces the risk of password exposure while reducing the overhead of authenticating security information multiple times. Security is not compromised, since each user is authenticated at least once whenever the first connection to the server is made.

---

* *Caveat:* We can't think of any distributed application that is perfectly safe. If we started thousands of copies of APING running against your computer, you wouldn't be happy.

Tightening security: enabling already verified

Often, your application is installed in environments where security must be maintained at all costs. Some situations require secure setups that also do not expose passwords to attack. An example is whenever data packets flow over a public network and the exposed passwords could be compromised.

Here are the steps you should take:

- Ensure physical security of your computers! No amount of distributed security will help if someone can walk up to the computer and steal information. Ensure that the client terminal is never left unattended when a user is logged on. Ensure that no one can walk up to the server computer and copy data files onto a diskette or tape!

- Use already verified. This prevents passwords from flowing in the clear.

- Use APPC session security. This ensures your LU software is talking to the right partner LU software. LU-LU passwords are not sent in the clear. Without session security, an attacker can use an untrusted computer and get access to resources through already verified.

Avoiding user mistakes

You and those installing your application need to be aware of the fact that the default configuration is often "no security required." If your application should never be run without authenticated user access, you may want to check the security settings within your server program. This can be done with the Extract_Conversation_Security_User_ID() call. If there is a user ID, then some form of user authentication was performed. If not, you may choose to deallocate the conversation and notify the installer that there is a configuration problem.

CODING YOUR CLIENT PROGRAM

This section discusses:

- The conversation security calls and how to use them
- The problems associated with each security type
- Three approaches to getting the security parameters set appropriately

  Setting the correct conversation security parameters is done with three calls:

- Set_Conversation_Security_Type()
- Set_Conversation_Security_User_ID()
- Set_Conversation_Security_Password()

To allow your server programs to determine the user ID specified from the client side, you can use the following call:

- Extract_Security_User_ID()

These four calls became part of the official CPI-C spec starting with CPI-C 1.2. Although the calls were not part of the CPI-C standard before CPI-C 1.2, they are available as extension calls on most platforms.

We discussed the Extract_Security_User_ID() call in "Extract_Security_User_ID (CMESUI)" in Chap. 12 in the discussion of all the Extract calls. Notice that there is no "Extract_Security_Password" call. Passwords are values that CPI-C keeps in confidence; there are no calls that let you look specifically at them.

Here are the three Set calls related to conversation security. These calls must be issued before the Allocate() call for a conversation, since the conversation security type, user ID, and password (if present) are carried in the Attach.

Set_Conversation_Security_Type (CMSCST)

Here's the function prototype for the Set_Conversation_Security_Type() call and the values for the conversation_security_type parameter:

```
CM_ENTRY                            /* Set_Conversation_Security_Type */
cmscst(unsigned char CM_PTR,        /* I: conversation_ID            */
       CM_CONVERSATION_TYPE CM_PTR, /* I: conv_security_type         */
       CM_RETURN_CODE CM_PTR);      /* O: return_code                */

/*  conversation_security_type values                                */
/*    default is CM_SECURITY_NONE                                    */

#define CM_SECURITY_NONE        (CM_CONVERSATION_SECURITY_TYPE) 0
#define CM_SECURITY_SAME        (CM_CONVERSATION_SECURITY_TYPE) 1
#define CM_SECURITY_PROGRAM     (CM_CONVERSATION_SECURITY_TYPE) 2
```

This call is new to CPI-C 1.2. However, it was available on many platforms as a CPI-C extension call prior to this. If you're using a CPI-C platform before CPI-C 1.2, you'll probably find the call is named XCSCST.

Set_Conversation_Security_User_ID (CMSCSU)

Here's the function prototype for the Set_Conversation_Security_User_ID() call:

```
CM_ENTRY                     /* Set_Conversation_Security_User_ID */
cmscsu(unsigned char  CM_PTR,   /* I: conversation_ID           */
       unsigned char  CM_PTR,   /* I: user_ID                   */
       CM_INT32 CM_PTR,         /* I: user_ID_length max 10     */
       CM_RETURN_CODE CM_PTR);  /* O: return_code               */
```

The user ID can be from 1 to 10 bytes in length. The characters in the user ID are case-sensitive; you can choose from any of the characters in character set 00640, which is composed of the uppercase and lowercase letters A through Z, numerals 0 through 9, and 20 special characters.

This call is new to CPI-C 1.2. However, it was available on many platforms as a CPI-C extension call prior to this. If you're using a CPI-C platform before CPI-C 1.2, you'll probably find the call is named XCSCSU. Also, note that before CPI-C 1.2, the maximum length of the user ID on most platforms was 8 bytes.

Set_Conversation_Security_Password (CMSCSP)

Here's the function prototype for the Set_Conversation_Security_Password() call:

```
CM_ENTRY                        /* Set_Conversation_Security_Password */
cmscsp(unsigned char  CM_PTR,      /* I: conversation_ID       */
       unsigned char  CM_PTR,      /* I: password              */
       CM_INT32 CM_PTR,            /* I: password_length max 10 */
       CM_RETURN_CODE CM_PTR);     /* O: return_code           */
```

Like the user ID, the password can be from 1 to 10 bytes in length. The characters in the password are case-sensitive; you can choose from any of the characters in character set 00640, which is composed of the uppercase and lowercase letters A through Z, numerals 0 through 9, and 20 special characters.

This call is new to CPI-C 1.2. However, it was available on many platforms as a CPI-C extension call prior to this. If you're using a CPI-C platform before CPI-C 1.2, you'll probably find the call is named XCSCSP. Also, note that before CPI-C 1.2, the maximum length of the password on most platforms was 8 bytes.

Setting a conversation security type

Determining which of the three conversation security types to select in your client program is difficult. Although the client may have a general idea of the kind of security that might be used, the installer on the server side makes the final decision. The client has no way to determine how the server was configured.

Let's look at the different problems we can encounter with each of the conversation security types:

CM_SECURITY_SAME

- Already verified depends upon the server being configured to allow it, and the configuration of the accompanying session security.
- Persistent verification and enhanced security SAME fail if the user does not have a user ID or has a different user ID on the server computer.
- Persistent verification and enhanced security SAME require that the user keep passwords in sync across the different computers. In some user environments, a user's password is actually required to be different on every computer.

CM_SECURITY_NONE

- Most transaction programs require security, thus security NONE will not be allowed.
- On some server platforms, an incoming user ID is required to start the server program.*
- If the user doesn't have an ID on the server platform, this may be the only available option.

CM_SECURITY_PROGRAM

- Exposes the conversation_security_password in the clear.
- Requires user intervention to supply the user ID and password to the client program.

Since there is no one security option that works in all circumstances, our programs need to be able to try all available options. We show three different approaches to coding security in your program. These options differ mostly in how much your program depends upon the client user to specify a security type. The three security coding options are

- Avoid user interaction until it is the last possible option.
- Let the user tell you what to use.
- Prompt the user for what to use.

Before we examine the three coding options in more detail, let's look at some of the code we'll need to implement these options. To use CM_SECURITY_ NONE or CM_SECURITY_SAME, you need only issue the Set_Conversation_Security_Type() call. The default security type is SAME. Here's an example of using the Set_Conversation_Security_Type() call to select security NONE.

```
#define SYM_DEST_NAME    "HELLO1S "    /* 8 chars, blank padded */

{
    unsigned char conversation_ID[CM_CID_SIZE];
    CM_RETURN_CODE cpic_return_code;
    CM_CONVERSATION_SECURITY_TYPE security_type =
        CM_SECURITY_NONE;

    cminit(                        /* Initialize_Conversation   */
        conversation_ID,           /* returned conversation ID  */
        SYM_DEST_NAME,             /* symbolic destination name */
        &cpic_return_code);        /* return code from this call */
```

---

* For example, when running to VM/CMS and using a private, nondedicated gateway.

```
       cmscst(                       /* Set_Conversation_Security_Type */
           conversation_ID,          /* conversation ID                */
           &security_type,           /* security type                  */
           &cpic_return_code);       /* return code from this call     */

       cmallc(                       /* Allocate                       */
           conversation_ID,          /* conversation ID                */
           &cpic_return_code);       /* return code from this call     */
   }
```

To properly use security PROGRAM, you need all three Set calls: Set_Conversation_Security_Type(), Set_Conversation_Security_User_ID(), and Set_Conversation_Security_Password(). Now let's look at an example of using these three calls together. To make things simpler, let's assume that the user ID and password were obtained from the user and passed into our function. We'll also assume that the Initialize_Conversation() and Allocate() calls are done elsewhere.

```
   void
   set_security_program(
       unsigned char * conversation_ID,
       unsigned char * user_ID,
       unsigned char * password)
   {
       CM_CONVERSATION_SECURITY_TYPE security_type =
           CM_SECURITY_PROGRAM;
       CM_RETURN_CODE  cpic_return_code;
       CM_INT32        length;

       cmscst(                       /* Set_Conversation_Security_Type */
           conversation_ID,          /* conversation ID                */
           &security_type,           /* security type                  */
           &cpic_return_code);       /* return code from this call     */

       length = (CM_INT32)strlen(user_ID);
       cmscsu(                       /* Set_Conversation_Security_Userid */
           conversation_ID,          /* conversation ID                */
           user_ID,                  /* user_ID                        */
           &length,                  /* user_ID_length                 */
           &cpic_return_code);       /* return_code                    */

       length = (CM_INT32)strlen(password);
       cmscsp(                       /* Set_Conversation_Security_Password */
           conversation_ID,          /* conversation ID                */
           password,                 /* password                       */
           &length,                  /* password_length                */
           &cpic_return_code);       /* return_code                    */
   }
```

Avoiding user interaction until the last possible option

To avoid user interaction, your program should try to exhaust all other options before requiring the user to enter a user ID and password. To do so, your client program should use the conversation security types in the following order:

1. Security SAME
2. Security NONE
3. Security PROGRAM, with parameters supplied by the user

Advantages of this technique are

- If at all possible, a connection is established without user intervention.
- User intervention is limited to responding to user ID/password prompt.
- Your user does not need to know about security options.

Disadvantages of this technique are

- Prompting for user ID/password causes problems in automated command scripts.
- Using security SAME (enhanced security same or persistent verification) may result in logon failures at the server. Depending upon the security environment, an excessive number of logon failures may cause the user ID to be revoked.

Here's the source code to implement this technique, making use of procedures we've seen in this chapter and in Chap. 22.

```
void
force_connection(
    unsigned char *  conversation_ID,
    CM_RETURN_CODE * cpic_return_code);

void
prompt_for_security_info(
    unsigned char * user_ID,
    unsigned char * password);

void
init_with_security(SET_UP_CONV * set_up_conv)
{
    unsigned char    conversation_ID[CM_CID_SIZE];
    CM_RETURN_CODE   cpic_return_code;
    CM_CONVERSATION_SECURITY_TYPE security_type;
    unsigned int     times_through_loop = 0;
    unsigned char    user_ID[CM_UID_SIZE+1];
    unsigned char    password[CM_PLN_SIZE+1];

    do {
```

```
            /*-------------------------------------------------------
             * Get a good conversation ID
             *-----------------------------------------------------*/
            set_up_conversation(conversation_ID, set_up_conv);

            switch (times_through_loop) {
                case 0:
                    /*
                     * This is our first time through the loop.
                     * We'll leave the security type as the default
                     * or whatever was setup in the side information
                     * table.
                     */
#ifdef DEBUG
                    printf("Using default security type.\n");
#endif
                    break;
                case 1:
#ifdef DEBUG
                    printf("Using default security NONE.\n");
#endif
                    security_type = CM_SECURITY_NONE;
                    cmscst(         /* Set_Conversation_Security_Type */
                        conversation_ID,    /* conversation ID    */
                        &security_type,     /* security type      */
                        &cpic_return_code); /* return code        */
                    break;
                case 2:
#ifdef DEBUG
                    printf("Using default security PROGRAM.\n");
#endif
                    security_type = CM_SECURITY_PROGRAM;
                    cmscst(         /* Set_Conversation_Security_Type */
                        conversation_ID,    /* conversation ID    */
                        &security_type,     /* security type      */
                        &cpic_return_code); /* return code        */

                    /*
                     * Prompt for the user_ID and password.  Since
                     * this is user interface specific, we haven't
                     * supplied this procedure.
                     */
                    prompt_for_security_info(
                        user_ID,
                        password);

                    set_security_program(
                        conversation_ID,
                        user_ID,
                        password);
                    break;
                default:
                    ;
                    /*
```

```
                             * This would be a bug.  We should never get
                             * here.
                             */
                    }

            /*----------------------------------------------------------
             * Allocate a session
             *--------------------------------------------------------*/
            do_allocate(conversation_ID);

            /*----------------------------------------------------------
             * Since the Attach hasn't yet been sent to the partner
             * platform, the security values haven't been checked
             * yet.  We'll force the issue by waiting for some form
             * of acknowledgement.
             *--------------------------------------------------------*/
            force_connection(
                conversation_ID,
                &cpic_return_code);

            times_through_loop++;

        } while (cpic_return_code == CM_SECURITY_NOT_VALID &&
                times_through_loop < 3);

#ifdef DEBUG
    if (cpic_return_code == CM_SECURITY_NOT_VALID) {
        printf(
            "SECURITY_NOT_VALID, ran out of security options\n");
    }
    else {
        printf("A security failure did not occur\n");
        show_cpic_return_code(cpic_return_code);
    }
#endif

}

/*
 * force_connection()
 *
 * This routine should be called after the Allocate() call to
 * force the Attach to flow.  The intent is to force any
 * TP start or security return codes to occur now, rather than
 * later in the conversation.  The return codes we're forcing
 * are:
 *     CM_CONVERSATION_TYPE_MISMATCH
 *     CM_PIP_NOT_SPECIFIED_CORRECTLY
 *     CM_SECURITY_NOT_VALID
 *     CM_SYNC_LVL_NOT_SUPPORTED_LU
 *     CM_SYNC_LVL_NOT_SUPPORTED_PGM
 *     CM_TPN_NOT_RECOGNIZED
 *     CM_TP_NOT_AVAILABLE_NO_RETRY
 *     CM_TP_NOT_AVAILABLE_RETRY
```

```
 */
void
force_connection(
    unsigned char  * conversation_ID,
    CM_RETURN_CODE * cpic_return_code_ptr)
{
    unsigned char data_buffer[1];
    CM_INT32       requested_length = 0;
    CM_INT32       received_length;

    CM_DATA_RECEIVED_TYPE data_received;
    CM_STATUS_RECEIVED     status_received;
    CM_REQUEST_TO_SEND_RECEIVED rts_received;

    /*-------------------------------------------------------------
     * There are two methods we could use to force the
     * connection:  Confirm() and Receive().  So that we don't
     * require the use of sync level CONFIRM, we'll use
     * Receive() here.
     *-----------------------------------------------------------*/
    cmrcv (                             /* Receive                */
        conversation_ID,                /* conversation ID        */
        data_buffer,                    /* place data here        */
        &requested_length,              /* max length to receive  */
        &data_received,                 /* returned data_rcvd     */
        &received_length,               /* length of received data */
        &status_received,               /* returned status_rcvd   */
        &rts_received,                  /* did partner RTS?       */
        cpic_return_code_ptr);          /* return code            */
}


void
prompt_for_security_info(
    unsigned char * user_ID,
    unsigned char * password)
{
    /*-------------------------------------------------------------
     * This routine prompts the user to enter a user ID and
     * password, then reads in the fields.
     *-----------------------------------------------------------*/
    size_t length;

    /* need to allow space for \n and \0 */
    char user_ID_buffer[CM_UID_SIZE+1+1];
    char password_buffer[CM_UID_SIZE+1+1];

    printf("Please enter a user ID and password.\n");
    printf("user ID: ");

    if (NULL !=
        fgets(user_ID_buffer, sizeof(user_ID_buffer), stdin) {

        length = strlen(user_ID_buffer);
        if (user_ID_buffer[length-1] == '\n') {
```

```
                user_ID_buffer[length-1] = '\0';
                strcpy(user_ID, user_ID_buffer);
            }
            else {
                fprintf(stderr, "User ID too long.\n");
                exit(EXIT_FAILURE);
            }
        }
        else {
            perror("Error reading user ID:");
        }

        printf("password: ");
        if (NULL !=
            fgets(password_buffer, sizeof(password_buffer), stdin)) {

            length = strlen(password_buffer);
            if (password_buffer[length-1] == '\n') {
                password_buffer[length-1] = '\0';
                strcpy(password, password_buffer);
            }
            else {
                fprintf(stderr, "Password too long.\n");
                exit(EXIT_FAILURE);
            }
        }
        else {
            perror("Error reading password:");
        }


    }
```

This source code for setting up security parameters, in file SECURE.C, attempts all possible options before asking for user input.

Letting users tell you what to use

The simplest and most straightforward method to use is to make the client user indicate what conversation security type to use. The user must be more aware of what security is and how it works in order to correctly choose the right security.

This method has a distinct advantage over others; the user is never prompted for information once the program is started. Because of this, it is a very useful method for command line programs which may be integrated into automated command scripts.

An example of an application that employs this method is the APING program. It has a series of command line flags that are used to specify the security type:

default. Use security SAME.

-n. Use security NONE.

-u*user_ID* -p*PASSWORD*. Use security PROGRAM with the supplied user ID and password.

After the program parses all its command line options, it knows exactly what security to use. If the conversation start-up fails because of CM_SECU-RITY_NOT_VALID, this is reported to the user, who can restart the program with different security information.

Advantage of this method:

- Works well in automated environments (never needs to prompt for new information).

Disadvantage of this method:

- The user must become aware of security type options and when to use each.

Prompting your users for what they want to use

This option involves a combination of prompting and automatic processing of security options. The user is prompted for a user ID. Based on the user's response, the client program chooses which conversation security type to use.
Here is the algorithm, based upon the user's response to the user ID prompt:

(nothing). Try security SAME. If that fails with CM_SECURITY_ NOT_ VALID, try security NONE.

"anonymous". Try security NONE. The user has indicated that no security is to be used.

any valid string. Prompt for associated password and try security PROGRAM.

Advantages of this method:

- User can access all security types without being a security expert.
- Security NONE is hidden behind the often familiar concept of an anonymous login.

Disadvantages of this method:

- User interaction is always required

Nonblocking Operation

CPI-C supports two processing modes for its calls, starting with CPI-C 1.2:

Blocking. In blocking mode, the CPI-C call must complete processing before control will be returned to your program. If the call can't complete immediately, it "blocks," and the calling program is forced to wait until the call operation finishes. While waiting, the program is unable to perform other processing or to communicate with any of its other partners.

Nonblocking. If possible, the CPI-C call completes immediately and control is returned to your program. However, if while processing the call, CPI-C determines that the call operation cannot complete immediately, control is returned to the program even though the call operation has not completed. The call operation remains in progress, and completion of the call operation occurs at a later time.

The nonblocking calls are designed to make it easy to create server programs that handle more than one client. It is unlikely that you will need to use the nonblocking calls in your client programs.

In addition to CPI-C 1.2, nonblocking mode is also part of the Windows CPI-C 1.0 (WinCPIC) specification. WinCPIC adds six additional calls to handle single-threaded systems, and to have better uniformity across the other calls in the Windows SNA (WinSNA) specification.

The CPI-C nonblocking calls are the subject of the first half of the chapter; the additional calls added for WinCPIC comprise the second half.

NONBLOCKING CALLS

CPI-C 1.2 added a new conversation characteristic, the *processing_mode,* which can be set at any time in a conversation, like many of the other Set calls. The default value for the processing_mode is CM_BLOCKING, which means that CPI-C uses the blocking mode on its conversation calls. In all the code we've shown so far, we've used blocking mode. The processing_mode of your program is a local-only option; your partner program can't tell a difference if you use blocking or nonblocking.

You can use nonblocking operations in your programs by setting the processing_mode conversation characteristic to CM_NON_BLOCKING. When the processing_mode is set to CM_NON_BLOCKING for a conversation and a call cannot complete immediately, CPI-C returns control to your program with a return code of CM_OPERATION_INCOMPLETE. Your program can do other processing while the previous CPI-C call operation remains in progress. The following calls can return the CM_OPERATION_INCOMPLETE return code when the processing_mode is CM_NON_BLOCKING.

- Accept_Incoming()
- Allocate()
- Confirm()
- Confirmed()
- Deallocate()
- Flush()
- Prepare_To_Receive()
- Receive()
- Request_To_Send()
- Send_Data()
- Send_Error()

When your program sees the CM_OPERATION_INCOMPLETE return code on one of these calls, the operation remains in progress as an *outstanding operation.* Your program must issue a Wait_For_Conversation() call to determine when an outstanding operation is completed and to retrieve the return code for that operation. CPI-C keeps track of all conversations with outstanding operations. It responds to a subsequent Wait_For_Conversation() call with the conversation identifier of one of those conversations when the operation on it completes.

CPI-C allows only one outstanding operation per conversation. The only valid calls on a conversation with an outstanding operation are Wait_For_Conversation() and Cancel_Conversation(). Any other CPI-C call with that conversation ID will get the CM_OPERATION_NOT_ACCEPTED return code.

A conversation's state does not change when a call on that conversation gets the CM_OPERATION_INCOMPLETE return code. If there's a state change to make, it occurs when a subsequent Wait_For_Conversation() call completes and indicates that an operation completed for that conversation. The conversation enters the state called for by a combination of the operation that completed, the return code for that operation (the *conversation_return_code* value returned on the Wait_For_Conversation() call), and the other factors that determine state transitions (like the status_received value on a Receive() call).

Your programs can use the Cancel_Conversation() call to end a conversation and any outstanding operation on that conversation. This has the same effect as issuing a Deallocate-Abend for the conversation.

Programs that use nonblocking mode are much more complex to design, code, and test than programs that use blocking mode. Your program must maintain state information as well as call parameters for each incomplete call. If you use nonblocking mode, be sure you don't put the call parameters in the automatic variables of a procedure—and then return from the procedure before the operation is completed. When you come back to wait on the call, the parameters will be in a different scope. Nonblocking mode should be used only when necessary and not by the faint of heart.

Set_Processing_Mode (CMSPM)

The Set_Processing_Mode() call is the mechanism that allows your program to switch between blocking and nonblocking.

The processing_mode can be changed many times during a conversation. So, you can always use one processing_mode, or switch from one to the other, depending upon what your program is doing at the time.

Here's the function prototype for the Set_Processing_Mode() call:

```
CM_ENTRY                               /* Set_Processing_Mode     */
cmspm (unsigned char CM_PTR,           /* I: conversation_ID      */
       CM_PROCESSING_MODE CM_PTR,      /* I: processing_mode      */
       CM_RETURN_CODE CM_PTR);         /* O: return_code          */

/*   processing_mode values                                       */
/*   default is CM_BLOCKING                                       */

#define CM_BLOCKING                    (CM_PROCESSING_MODE) 0
#define CM_NON_BLOCKING                (CM_PROCESSING_MODE) 1
```

Your program can set the processing_mode to one of two different values:

CM_BLOCKING. Calls using this conversation ID will complete before returning control to the calling program. This is the default value.

CM_NON_BLOCKING. If possible, calls using this conversation ID will complete immediately. When a call operation cannot complete immediately, CPI-C returns control to the program with the CM_OPERATION_INCOMPLETE return code.

Cancel_Conversation (CMCANC)

Use the Cancel_Conversation() call to end any conversation immediately. Cancel_Conversation() can be issued in blocking or nonblocking mode, and regardless of whether there is an outstanding operation on the conversation. To the partner program, it appears that your program issued a Deallocate-Abend.

Cancel_Conversation() results in the immediate termination of any outstanding operation on the specified conversation. No guarantees are given on the results of the outstanding operation. For example, if a Cancel_Conversation() call is issued while a nonblocking Send_Data() call is outstanding, no statement may be made about how much data was actually placed into the network.

Here's the function prototype for the Cancel_Conversation() call:

```
CM_ENTRY                           /* Cancel Conversation     */
cmcanc(unsigned char CM_PTR,       /* I: conversation_ID      */
       CM_RETURN_CODE CM_PTR);     /* O: return_code          */
```

Although this call works for either processing mode, it's most useful in nonblocking mode when there is an outstanding call operation. For example, if a Receive-and-Wait operation has been issued in nonblocking mode and your program decides it wants to exit abruptly without waiting for the call to complete, your program can issue Cancel_Conversation() to deallocate the conversation. In blocking mode, it would still have to wait for the Receive() to return, where it could just as easily issue Deallocate-Abend instead.

Wait_For_Conversation (CMWAIT)

This is the magical call for making nonblocking operations work. The Wait_For_Conversation() call waits for previously incomplete calls to finish. When any incomplete call completes processing, Wait_For_Conversation() returns the conversation ID and return code of the completed call. CPI-C also returns the return code for the Wait_For_Conversation() call itself. Thus, all the parameters are returned parameters.

Here's the function prototype for the Wait_For_Conversation() call:

```
CM_ENTRY                           /* Wait_For_Conversation   */
cmwait(unsigned char CM_PTR,       /* O: conversation_ID      */
       CM_RETURN_CODE CM_PTR,      /* O: conv_return_code     */
       CM_RETURN_CODE CM_PTR);     /* O: return_code          */
```

The Wait_For_Conversation() call accepts no input parameters. This call returns the conversation ID of a *single* call that has completed. The first return code parameter, *conversation_return_code,* is the return code of the conversation call that completed. The second return code parameter is the return code of the Wait_For_Conversation() call itself. Unless it's CM_OK, the other two parameter values can be ignored.

CPI-C assumes your program is keeping a table of the conversation IDs for conversations with outstanding calls. After calling Wait_For_Conversation(), your program must correlate the returned conversation ID with the completed call and its parameters.

One technique you can use to help is to keep a list of structures, where each structure contains the conversation ID, and all call parameters. This allows your program to keep all of the relevant information in one data structure.

Initialize_For_Incoming (CMINIC)

As you'll remember, starting up the client side of a program takes at least two calls. A conversation ID is obtained using an Initialize_Conversation() call, and a session is obtained with an Allocate() call. In between these two calls, conversation characteristics can be changed. One of these characteristics is called *return_control,* and it determines whether or not the Allocate() blocks, waiting for a session if one is not available.

A similar relationship can be used on the server side. A conversation ID can be obtained using the Initialize_For_Incoming() call. A second call, Accept_Incoming(), is used to know when an Attach has arrived. In between these two calls, conversation characteristics can be changed. One of these characteristics is called *processing_mode,* and it determines whether or not the Accept_Incoming() blocks, waiting for an Attach if one is not available.

Initialize_For_Incoming() is completely analogous to Initialize_Conversation() on the client side. It gives you a valid conversation ID and sets the default conversation characteristics. If you want your Accept call to be nonblocking, your program needs to use Initialize_For_Incoming() in combination with Set_Processing_Mode() and Accept_Incoming().

Here's the function prototype for the Initialize_For_Incoming() call:

```
CM_ENTRY                          /* Initialize_For_Incoming  */
cminic(unsigned char CM_PTR,      /* O: conversation_ID       */
       CM_RETURN_CODE CM_PTR);    /* O: return_code           */
```

The Initialize_For_Incoming() call can be used by your program so it can initialize values for various conversation characteristics before the conversation is actually accepted with an Accept_Incoming() call. Your program passes a pointer to an 8-byte field, and CPI-C returns a new conversation ID into that field. The return code is almost always CM_OK, unless CPI-C is all out of conversation IDs or unless CPI-C isn't loaded or available.

Accept_Incoming (CMACCI)

Use the Accept_Incoming() call to accept an incoming conversation that has previously been initialized with the Initialize_For_Incoming() call and to complete the initialization of the conversation characteristics. The combination of Initialize_For_Incoming() and Accept_Incoming() calls, without any intervening calls, is equivalent to calling just Accept_Conversation().

Before issuing the Accept_Incoming() call, a program has the option of issuing the Set_Processing_Mode() call to specify whether the Accept_Incoming() call, and subsequent calls, are to be processed in a blocking or nonblocking mode.

You'll find the nonblocking Accept_Incoming() call useful for creating server programs that handle multiple clients. The server program can always have an outstanding Accept and still process current conversations with its own outstanding send and receive operations.

Here's the function prototype for the Accept_Incoming() call:

```
CM_ENTRY                              /* Accept_Incoming        */
cmacci(unsigned char CM_PTR,          /* I: conversation_ID     */
       CM_RETURN_CODE CM_PTR);        /* O: return_code         */
```

You'll see the Initialize_For_Incoming() and Accept_Incoming() calls together in pairs. Although you can issue most of the Set calls between them, the one that's most interesting is Set_Processing_Mode() since it affects the operation of Accept_Incoming().

The program's current context is set to the newly created context when an Accept_Conversation() or Accept_Incoming() call completes with a return code of CM_OK. However, if Accept_Incoming() is issued with processing_ mode set to CM_NON_BLOCKING and returns with a CM_OPERATION_ INCOMPLETE return code, the program's current context is not changed. A new context is not created until the Accept_Incoming() call operation subsequently completes successfully as a result of the Wait_for_Conversation() call. The program can then use the Extract_Conversation_Context() call to determine the context assigned to the conversation. Because Wait_for_Conversation() does not cause a change of context, your program is responsible for issuing the appropriate node services call to establish the correct current context.

WINDOWS CPI-C EXTENSIONS FOR NONBLOCKING

In 1993, a team of vendors created the Windows CPI-C (WinCPIC) specification. The WinCPIC spec builds upon CPI-C 1.2, adding six additional calls to handle start-up and takedown, as well as nonblocking operations, in the Windows environment. These calls apply only when the local program is a Windows program; their use is invisible to the partner program. In order to use any of these six calls, your local CPI-C platform must support the WinCPIC 1.0 specification.

This section describes the six calls added by WinCPIC. These calls were designed for all WinCPIC implementations and versions of the Microsoft Windows graphical environment starting from Microsoft Windows version 3.x. They provide for Windows CPI-C platforms and applications in 16- and 32-bit operating environments.

Windows CPI-C allows multithreaded Windows-based processes. A process contains one or more threads of execution. All references to threads in this document refer to actual threads in multithreaded Windows environments. In environments that aren't multithreaded, such as the 16-bit Windows version 3.x graphical environment, "thread" is synonymous with "process." These six extensions for the Windows environment were added to the WinCPIC spec for, in Microsoft's words, "maximum Microsoft Windows programming compatibility and optimum application performance."

WinCPICStartup()

This call allows a Windows program to specify the version of Windows CPI-C it requires, and to retrieve details of the underlying Windows CPI-C platform it is using. This function *must* be called by a program before issuing any further WinCPIC calls, to register itself with the WinCPIC platform it is using. You'll probably want to place it at the top of your WinMain loop, or in your initialization code.

Here's the function prototype for the WinCPICStartup() call:

```
int
WinCPICStartup(WORD wVersionRequired,
               LPWCPICDATA lpwCPICData)
```

In order to support future Windows CPI-C platforms and programs that may have functional differences from WinCPIC version 1.0, a negotiation takes place in WinCPICStartup(). A program passes to WinCPICStartup() the WinCPIC version of which it can take advantage. If this version is numerically lower than the lowest version supported by the WinCPIC DLL, the DLL cannot support the program and the program's WinCPICStartup() call fails. Otherwise, the call succeeds and returns the highest version of WinCPIC supported by the DLL.

On the other hand, if this version is lower than the lowest version supported by the program, the program either fails its initialization or attempts to find another WinCPIC DLL on the system. This negotiation allows both a Windows CPI-C DLL and a program making WinCPIC calls to support a range of Windows CPI-C versions. A program can successfully use a DLL if there is any overlap in the versions. Table 26.1 gives examples of how WinCPICStartup() works in conjunction with different program and DLL versions.

TABLE 26.1   Example of Negotiation Between a Program and the WinCPIC DLL

WinCPIC calls used	DLL versions	To WinCPICStartup()	From WinCPICStartup()	Result
1.0	1.0	1.0	1.0	use 1.0
1.0 2.0	1.0	2.0	1.0	use 1.0
1.0	1.0 2.0	1.0	2.0	use 1.0
1.0	2.0 3.0	1.0	WCPICINVALID	fail
2.0 3.0	1.0	3.0	1.0	app fails
1.0 2.0 3.0	1.0 2.0 3.0	3.0	3.0	use 3.0

Details of the actual Windows CPI-C platform are described in the WHLL-DATA structure defined as follows:

```
typdef struct tagWCPICDATA {
    WORD wVersion;
    char szDescription[WCPICDESCRIPTION_LEN+1];
} WCPICDATA, * PWCPICDATA, FAR * LPWCPICDATA;

#define WCPICDESCRIPTION_LEN    127
```

The 2-byte wVersion parameter specifies the version of WinCPIC support required. The high-order byte specifies the minor version (revision) number; the low-order byte specifies the major version number.

The return value indicates whether the program has registered successfully and whether the WinCPIC platform can support the specified version number. It is zero if it has registered successfully and the specified version can be supported; otherwise it is one of the following return codes:

WCPICINVALID (0xF001).   The WinCPIC version specified by the local program is not supported by this DLL.

WCPICSYSNOTREADY (0xF003).   Indicates that the underlying network subsystem is not ready for network communication.

WCPICVERNOTSUPPORTED (0xF004). The version of WinCPIC support requested is not provided by this particular WinCPIC platform.

Each WinCPIC program must make a WinCPICStartup() call before issuing any other Windows CPI-C calls.

WinCPICCleanup()

The companion call to WinCPICStartup() is WinCPICCleanup(). After making its last WinCPIC call, a Windows program should call the WinCPICCleanup() routine. This call is used by a program to deregister itself from a WinCPIC platform. You'll probably want to put this call at the bottom of your WinMain loop, or in the cleanup code you call from your error-handling procedures.

Here's the function prototype for the WinCPICCleanup() call:

```
BOOL
WinCPICCleanup(void);
```

The return value indicates whether the program could deregister itself. It is nonzero if the program was successfully deregistered; otherwise it is zero.

Use the WinCPICCleanup() call to indicate deregistration of a Windows CPI-C program from a WinCPIC platform. This call can be used, for example, to free up resources allocated to the specific program.

WinCPICSetBlockingHook()

This call installs a new function which a WinCPIC platform should use to implement blocking CPI-C function calls.

This mechanism is provided to allow a Windows 3.x program to make blocking calls without blocking the rest of the system. Under Windows NT, by default a call that blocks suspends the calling program's thread, but not the entire system. Therefore, if a single-threaded program is targeted at both Windows 3.x and Windows NT and relies on this functionality, it should register a blocking hook even if the default hook would suffice.

Here's the function prototype for the WinCPICSetBlockingHook() call:

```
FARPROC
WinCPICSetBlockingHook(FARPROC lpBlockFunc)
```

A WinCPIC platform has a default mechanism by which blocking CPI-C calls are implemented. This call gives a program the ability to execute its own function at blocking time in place of the default function.

The lpBlockFunc parameter is the procedure instance address of the blocking function to be installed. The default blocking function is equivalent to the following:

```
BOOL DefaultBlockingHook(void) {
    MSG msg;

    /* get the next message, if any */
    if (PeekMessage(&msg, 0, 0, PM_NOREMOVE)) {
        if (msg.message == WM_QUIT) {
            /* let the application process WM_QUIT */
            return FALSE;
        }
        PeekMessage(&msg, 0, 0, PM_REMOVE);
        TranslateMessage(&msg);
        DispatchMessage(&msg);
    }

    /* TRUE if no WM_QUIT received */
    return TRUE;
}
```

The WinCPICSetBlockingHook() call allows programs to implement more complex message processing—for example, those employing the MDI (Multiple Document Interface) model.

A blocking function must return FALSE if it receives a WM_QUIT message, so WinCPIC can return control to the program to process the message and terminate gracefully. Otherwise, the function should return TRUE.

The return value of the WinCPICSetBlockingHook() call points to the procedure-instance of the previously installed blocking function. The program or library that calls WinCPICSetBlockingHook() should save this return value so that it can be restored if necessary. (If "nesting" is not important, the program may simply discard the value returned by WinCPICSetBlockingHook() and eventually use WinCPICUnhookBlockingHook() to restore the default mechanism.)

This function must be implemented on a per-thread basis. It thus provides for a particular thread to replace the blocking mechanism without affecting other threads.

WinCPICUnhookBlockingHook()

This call removes any previous blocking hook that has been installed and reinstalls the default blocking mechanism.

Here's the function prototype for the WinCPICUnhookBlockingHook() call:

```
BOOL
WinCPICUnhookBlockingHook(void)
```

The return value from this call is nonzero if the default blocking mechanism is successfully reinstalled; otherwise it is zero.

WinCPICIsBlocking()

This call allows a task to determine if it is executing while waiting for a previous blocking call to complete. This doesn't infer any information about a particular conversation, but is only intended to provide help to a program written to use the CM_BLOCKING characteristic of Set_Processing_Mode(). WinCPICIsBlocking() serves the same purpose as InSendMessage in the Windows API. Programs targeted at Windows 3.x that support multiple conversations must specify CM_NON_BLOCKING in Set_Processing_Mode() call so they can support multiple outstanding operations simultaneously. Programs are still limited to one outstanding operation per conversation in all environments.

Here's the function prototype for the WinCPICIsBlocking() call:

```
BOOL
WinCPICIsBlocking(void)
```

The return value from this call is nonzero if there is an outstanding blocking call awaiting completion; otherwise it is zero.

Although a call issued on a blocking function appears to a program as though it blocks, the WinCPIC DLL has to relinquish the processor to allow other programs to run. This means that it is possible for the program that issued the blocking call to be re-entered, depending on the message(s) it receives. In this instance, the WinCPICIsBlocking() call can be used to determine whether the program task currently has been re-entered while waiting for an outstanding blocking call to complete. Note that WinCPIC prohibits more than one outstanding blocking call per thread.

Specify_Windows_Handle (XCHWND)

This call sets the Windows handle to which a message is sent on completion of a CPI-C call in nonblocking mode. A program can set the processing mode by calling Set_Processing_Mode(). If the Windows handle is set to NULL or this call is never issued, then the program must call Wait_For_Conversation() to be notified when the outstanding operation completes.

Here's the function prototype for the Specify_Windows_Handle() call:

```
CM_ENTRY                           /* Specify_Windows_Handle   */
xchwnd(HWND,                       /* I: Windows handle        */
       CM_RETURN_CODE CM_PTR);     /* O: return_code           */
```

The input parameter, hwndNotify, specifies the Windows handle to be notified when the outstanding operation completes.

When an asynchronous operation is complete, the program's window hwnd-Notify receives the message returned by RegisterWindowMessage with "WinAsyncCPI-C" as the input string. The wParam value contains the conversation_return_code from the CPI-C call which is completing. Its value depends on which operation was originally issued. The lParam argument contains a CM_PTR to the conversation_ID specified in the original CPI-C call.

There may be a change to the conversation state. Whether or not there is a state change depends on the original CPI-C call which has now completed and its returned parameters.

Designing Servers with CPI-C

Every application we've shown so far in this book is a client/server application. The client program issues the Allocate() call and the server program issues the Accept_Conversation() or Accept_Incoming() call. In this chapter, we explain how to design servers which handle multiple clients when their resources are constrained.

The issue of resource constraints is what makes the information in this chapter important. When the number of clients is small and the transaction rate low, it is acceptable to dedicate a server program instance to each client. As the number of clients increases, platforms quickly run out of resources to support this operating model.

In this chapter, we show you how to improve your servers and work within resource constraints via two techniques: using short conversations and accepting multiple conversations. Short conversations allow your servers to interleave client requests and free up resources when not in use. Accepting multiple conversations allow your programs to handle new work from clients without incurring the overhead of program start-up.

CPI-C has been a great way to create portable client programs for years. However, before CPI-C 1.2, it was weak in the area of creating powerful server programs that handle many clients. The original specification and implementations of CPI-C only allowed a program to accept a single conversation. Creating servers to handle a large number of clients was difficult. Minimizing the operating system resources used by such servers was, thus, very difficult.

CPI-C 1.2 provides several new features which make things easier. These features make it possible to write efficient and portable servers which handle a large number of client requesters. The key feature making this possible is the ability to accept more than one conversation in a single server program.

In addition, we show you platform-specific ways to accept more than one conversation that you can use before CPI-C 1.2 is available on your platform.

USING SHORT CONVERSATIONS

Short conversations offer your server programs the ability to support more clients and increase server throughput.

For our purposes, we'll define a long conversation as one that is maintained even when no work is being done. Although a long conversation results in some amount of idle time, the start-up cost of initializing the conversation is performed only once.

An application using short conversations deallocates the conversation during idle times. This frees up the network and server resources for other clients or applications to use. The disadvantage of short conversations is the overhead of starting a conversation every time the client needs work from the server.

Advantages for server processing

On the server side, there are compelling reasons for us to use short conversations in our application design. Short conversations allow us to:

Support more clients.   Each server computer has a finite number of processes or threads that can be dedicated to serving clients. By using short conversations, we can "time share" our available tasks to the clients. If all available tasks are busy, the next client waits for a task to become available. But, since we're using short conversations, the wait is almost always short.

Increase server throughput.   To obtain the highest server throughput, we always want our server to have some work to perform. In fact, we would like a variety of tasks for our server to perform, to take advantage of the server platform's power (for example, disk I/O that can run in parallel with a calculation task).

By using short conversations, we reduce the amount of idle time in each of our server tasks. We increase our chances of having useful work to perform because we don't have to dedicate a task to waiting on an inactive client.

Reduce the number of server platform sessions.   Short conversations help in two ways:

- When many applications run between the client and server platforms, they can reuse sessions. Since each conversation is active for only a short period of time, your application can use the session while another application isn't using it. More applications can be run over fewer sessions.
- Sessions can actually be brought down when they haven't been used for a period of time. This is done by configuring your connection as a *limited resource.*

Provide recovery in case of connection failure. Short conversations result in less data that must be recovered in the event of a conversation failure. In addition, the code to restart a conversation is already written as part of your short conversation design, so your recovery logic is very similar to your mainline logic. This results in a more robust application.

Breaking up long conversations

When you first sit down to think about how your application will work, you will likely envision it as a long conversation. Upon further consideration, you may decide that you need the advantages that using short conversations will give you. So, how do you move from a long conversation model to a short conversation model?

The first step is to identify situations when the conversation is inactive. In most cases, you'll look for instances when the client is waiting for something to happen or to complete before issuing another request. Examples of things to look for are

- Waiting for user input
- Extensive processing of previously received data

You'll get the most advantage from short conversations if you can eliminate as much idle time as possible.

When breaking up long conversations, you should also determine the smallest transaction unit that can exist on its own in a single conversation. This transaction unit may span more than one request/reply, especially if the requests are related.

While breaking up long conversations, be sure that the conversation start-up cost does not become a significant portion of the total conversation time. If you make the conversations too short, the clients could spend most of their time starting conversations instead of getting work done.

To help illustrate how conversations can be broken up, let's look at an example file transfer program. This application sends a set of files from the client to the server. This application could be designed in a number of ways:

Long conversations. All files are sent on the same conversation.

1. The client connects to the server.
2. The client sends each file in succession.
3. The client requests confirmation of all files that were sent.
4. The conversation is deallocated.

The server program is tied up during the entire file transfer and cannot handle another client. If user input is required between files, there will be excessive idle time on the conversation.

One problem inherent in this design is how errors are handled. If only one of the files sent cannot be written to disk, the server cannot interrupt the client without stopping all files already in transit. The two choices for handling errors are:

- The server uses Send_Error() whenever the error occurs. The client has to resend files that were already in transit.
- The server has to receive the file that cannot be processed and discard the data. Network bandwidth is wasted if the file is large.

Short conversations.   Each file is sent on a separate conversation.

1. The client connects to the server.
2. The client sends a file.
3. The client requests confirmation that the file was stored successfully.
4. The conversation is deallocated.
5. The client goes through steps 1–4 for each file.

Shorter conversations.   Each data record of each file is sent on a separate conversation.

1. The client connects to the server.
2. The client sends a file data record.
3. The client requests confirmation.
4. The conversation is deallocated.
5. The client goes through steps 1–4 for each data record in the file.
6. The client repeats the process for each file.

Since we're not sending very much data on each conversation and confirming after each send, the conversation overhead is likely not worth the cost.

Excessively short conversations.   Each file byte is sent on a separate conversation.

1. The client connects to the server.
2. The client sends a 1-byte file data record.
3. The client requests confirmation.
4. The conversation is deallocated.
5. The client goes through steps 1–4 for each byte in the file.
6. The client repeats the process for each file.

The number of conversations started is equal to the number of bytes in all of the files combined. *Note:* This is definitely not the way you should design your applications.

Correlating short conversations

As we move to short conversations, we also need to be concerned with correlating transactions across the different conversations. For example, in the "shorter conversations" file transfer example, the server would have to know what to do with each data record when it arrives; for example, store it in the file to which the record belongs.

If you do need to correlate your short conversations you can either

- *Use an existing data item as a correlator.* In many instances, the resource that the server interacts with already has an identifier that could be used as a correlator. For example, a file server could use an operating system file handle as its correlator.
- *Develop a correlator for yourself.* If there is no acceptable existing data item to use, you may have to invent your own correlator. If you need to invent your own correlator, consider using a combination of the client's LU name (from the Extract_Partner_LU_Name() call) and a unique integer ID generated by the server program.

One way to avoid correlating short conversations is to design a stateless server. In a stateless server, each client request includes all of the information necessary to complete processing. Although this may result in more data in each request, the request can be handled independently of any other requests, past or future. In addition, the server is freed from having to maintain state information on each client. Thus, increasing the number of clients does not increase the server program's memory requirements.

Dealing with conversation start-up overhead

As we move toward using short conversations in our servers, we are also starting conversations more and more often. Thus, conversation start-up overhead becomes a more significant part of our performance concerns.

As we've already discussed in Chap. 23, the most troublesome part of conversation start-up is loading the server program. Now that we're looking for optimal performance and using short conversations, we absolutely cannot afford to start a copy of our server program for each conversation.*

As you may remember from "Estimating Conversation Start-up Overhead" in Chap. 23, starting the server program is usually the biggest part of conversation start-up overhead. To avoid program start-up costs, we would like to design our server program to accept multiple conversations without exiting. We discuss multiple accepts in the next sections.

---

* An exception is CICS, which is optimized to make program load blindingly fast.

SERVERS BEFORE CPI-C 1.2

Before talking about designing servers with CPI-C 1.2, let's start with how servers have been designed with CPI-C in the past.

The biggest problem designing servers with CPI-C before 1.2 was that there was no support for multiple Accept_Conversation() calls within a single program instance. That is, if a program issued the Accept_Conversation() call more than once, it would receive a return code of CM_PROGRAM_STATE_CHECK. As a result, every time a client connected to a server, it would talk to a new instance of the server program; a new process, task, or job would have to be started. The overhead of starting a new program instance for each conversation made using short conversations unfeasible.

To avoid the server program start-up costs, many client/server designs leaned toward using long conversations. In order to support many simultaneous clients, we had to resort to multiple server program instances running at the same time. Since we were using long conversations, it was difficult to support large numbers of clients, as our servers were limited in the number of tasks that the server could use. Overall, our servers used up much more resource than we would have liked.

USING ACCEPT MULTIPLE WITHOUT CPI-C 1.2

If you are writing programs for platforms that don't yet support the calls in CPI-C 1.2, there is still hope! On many platforms, you can use product-specific extensions or platform-specific calls to perform the multiple accepts. Here's a quick overview of what is available on selected platforms:

OS/2 Communications Manager/2 1.0 and 1.1.   CM/2 supports multiple accept. Simply reissue the Accept_Conversation() call, as in CPI-C 1.2.

Each Accept_Conversation() call in CM/2 creates a new TP instance identifier. In order to manage these TP instances, CM/2 also provides a number of extension calls:

- Start_TP (XCSTP)

- Extract_TP_ID (XCETI)

- Initialize_Conv_For_TP (XCINCT)

- End_TP (XCENDT)

The size of the CPI-C TP_ID parameter on each of these calls is 12 bytes.

Each Accept_Conversation() call creates a new CPI-C TP_ID. If your program loops on Accept_Conversation() without issuing End_TP(), eventually your program or the platform will run out of memory. Thus, on OS/2, your program should issue Accept_Conversation(), then Extract_TP_ID(). After the conversation is deallocated, your program should clean up the TP_ID using the End_TP() call.

Networking Services/DOS version 1.0.   The DOS environment does not provide a way for NS/DOS to detect when one program ends and another begins.

NS/DOS is in fact not able to restrict your programs to a single Accept_Conversation(). So your programs can simply issue multiple Accept_Conversation() calls.

APPC/VM. Applications that identify themselves as resource managers can accept multiple conversations. The application must use CPI-C extension calls to make use of this capability. In addition to multiple accept, your program uses a form of nonblocking facility to wait for one of a number of events to occur.

The applicable extension calls on APPC/VM are:

- Identify_Resource_Manager (XCIDRM)

- Wait_on_Event (XCWOE)

- Terminate_Resource_Manager (XCTRRM)

APPC/MVS. APPC/MVS allows you to use the same conversation ID on CPI-C and MVS product-specific API calls. Although you cannot issue multiple Accept_Conversation() calls, you can issue multiple ATBGETC calls instead. After accepting the conversation with ATBGETC, you can continue processing the conversation with portable CPI-C calls.

AIX SNA Server/6000. There is no mechanism for accepting multiple conversations from a CPI-C program.

OS/400. In OS/400, your program can accept multiple conversations if it is a prestart job.

When your application program is started, it should do as much initialization work as possible. When the program issues Accept_Conversation(), the call will wait for an incoming conversation to arrive.

After the conversation is over, the program can issue another Accept_Conversation() call. Your program cannot accept a new conversation while there is an existing active conversation.

Two OS/400 commands relevant to configuring and administering prestart jobs are

- Add Prestart Job Entry (ADDPJE)

- Start Prestart Jobs (STRPJ)

USING ACCEPT MULTIPLE IN CPI-C 1.2

Starting with CPI-C 1.2, your programs now have the ability to accept multiple conversations within a single program. Your programs can now handle multiple conversations or multiple clients without the overhead of program start-up for each conversation.

Accepting multiple conversations in CPI-C 1.2 is easy; just issue another Accept_Conversation() call. The easiest way to convert your programs to accept multiple conversations is to add a loop around your main processing:

```
-->
| Accept_Conversation
| process data
| Deallocate
loop
```

Your program should exit whenever an Accept_Conversation() call fails. An Accept_Conversation() failure usually indicates one of the following:

- *The program is running on an old CPI-C platform.* Since this platform doesn't support accept multiple, your program will never be able to accept a new conversation.

- *The TP definition for the server program isn't set up correctly to accept multiple conversations.* For example, on the OS/2 Communications Manager, a TP definition can specify that it is nonqueued. Nonqueued means that the attach manager should start a new instance of the program running for each incoming Attach. See "When Connecting an Attach to an Existing Application" in Chap. 23 for more information.

- *No incoming conversation arrived within a time-out period.* There wasn't an incoming Attach in a specified time period. Rather than tying up resources longer than necessary, you should end your program and free up those resources. Let the attach manager start a new server program when necessary. The time-out period is usually a configuration option.

In each of these cases, you don't have to worry about how new conversations will be serviced, since the attach manager will start new server programs as necessary.

To illustrate how to code your programs to accept multiple conversations, we've adapted the HELLO5D server program. Here's the source code:

```
/*------------------------------------------------------------
 *   CPI-C example program, displaying received records
 *   server side (file SERVER1D.C)
 *------------------------------------------------------------*/
#include <cpic.h>            /* conversation API library   */
#include <stdio.h>           /* file I/O                   */
#include <stdlib.h>          /* standard library           */
#include <string.h>          /* strings and memory         */

#define RECEIVE_SIZE (10)    /* receive 10 bytes at a time */

static void
process_incoming_data(
    unsigned char *  conversation_ID);

int main(void)
{
```

```
            unsigned char conversation_ID[CM_CID_SIZE];
            CM_RETURN_CODE cpic_return_code;

            setbuf(stdout, NULL);          /* assure unbuffered output    */

            do {

                cmaccp(                     /* Accept_Conversation         */
                    conversation_ID,        /* returned conversation ID    */
                    &cpic_return_code);     /* return code from this call  */

                if (cpic_return_code == CM_OK) {
                    printf("Accepted a conversation...\n");

                    process_incoming_data(
                        conversation_ID);
                }
                else {

                    fprintf(
                        stderr,
                        "Return code %lu on CMACCP.\n",
                        cpic_return_code);
                }

            } while (cpic_return_code == CM_OK);

            (void)getchar();                /* pause for a keystroke       */
            return(EXIT_SUCCESS);
        }

        static void
        process_incoming_data(
            unsigned char *  conversation_ID)
        {
            unsigned char data_buffer[RECEIVE_SIZE];
            CM_INT32 requested_length = (CM_INT32)sizeof(data_buffer);
            CM_INT32 received_length;
            CM_DATA_RECEIVED_TYPE data_received;
            CM_REQUEST_TO_SEND_RECEIVED rts_received;
            CM_STATUS_RECEIVED status_received;
            unsigned done = 0;
            CM_RETURN_CODE cpic_return_code;

            while (done == 0) {
                cmrcv(                      /* Receive                     */
                    conversation_ID,        /* conversation ID             */
                    data_buffer,            /* where to put received data  */
                    &requested_length,      /* maximum length to receive   */
                    &data_received,         /* returned data_received      */
```

```
                  &received_length,   /* length of received data    */
                  &status_received,   /* returned status_received   */
                  &rts_received,      /* ignore this parameter      */
                  &cpic_return_code); /* return code from this call */

        /*   replace the following block with the good algorithm
         *   that's shown in the program sketch in the text.
         */

        if ((cpic_return_code == CM_OK) ||
            (cpic_return_code == CM_DEALLOCATED_NORMAL)) {

            /* write the received string to stdout */
            (void)fwrite((void *)data_buffer, (size_t)1,
                        (size_t)received_length, stdout);
            if (data_received == CM_COMPLETE_DATA_RECEIVED) {
                /* write a newline character */
                (void)fputc((int)'\n', stdout);
            }
        }
        if (cpic_return_code != CM_OK) {
            done = 1;    /* CM_DEALLOCATED_NORMAL or unexpected */
        }
    }
}
```

We've modified the main loop to process the incoming data in a separate procedure. This just makes it easier to see how the accept conversation processing works. Another by-product of processing the data in a separate procedure is that it will be easier for us to convert this program to use multiple threads.

The only thing controlling how long the program stays active is the return code from the Accept_Conversation() call. As long as the return code is CM_OK, the program continues to accept conversations.

Specify_Local_TP_Name (CMSLTP)

The Specify_Local_TP_Name() call allows your server program to indicate that it wants to accept conversations for a certain TP name. This is useful in two cases.

The first case is when your server program is handling many different kinds of transactions, and each transaction type uses a different TP name. You may be trying to integrate many different existing servers into a single entity because they share code or need to share information. By using the Specify_Local_TP_Name() call, your program can accept conversations for multiple TP names.

The second case is when your server program is not started by the attach manager, but is started by the operator or automatically at platform start-up. Since the attach manager doesn't know your program's name, CPI-C can't process your program's Accept_Conversation() call. By using Specify_Local_TP_Name(), you can tell CPI-C and the attach manager the TP name your program is using.

Here's the function prototype for the Specify_Local_TP_Name() call:

```
CM_ENTRY                                /* Specify_Local_TP_Name      */
cmsltp(unsigned char CM_PTR,            /* I: TP_name                 */
       CM_INT32 CM_PTR,                 /* I: TP_name_length max 64 */
       CM_RETURN_CODE CM_PTR);          /* O: return_code             */
```

Release_Local_TP_Name (CMRLTP)

The Release_Local_TP_Name() call undoes the work done by the Specify_Local_TP_Name() call. Use this call when your program no longer wishes to process incoming conversations for a specific TP name.

Here's the function prototype for the Release_Local_TP_Name() call:

```
CM_ENTRY                                /* Release_Local_TP_Name      */
cmrltp(unsigned char CM_PTR,            /* I: TP_name                 */
       CM_INT32 CM_PTR,                 /* I: TP_name_length max 64 */
       CM_RETURN_CODE CM_PTR);          /* O: return_code             */
```

USING ACCEPT MULTIPLE WITH MULTIPLE THREADS

Although not specifically a CPI-C function, you can use multiple threads within your server to handle multiple conversations simultaneously. Using multiple threads allows your server to handle multiple clients without the overhead of multiple processes. More clients are serviced with fewer server resources.

There are many different ways you can use multiple threads in your server programs. We will concentrate on two of the most common approaches and examine how they affect your server behavior.

- *A main thread accepts conversations, then starts worker threads to process each conversation.* This allows your server to process all the client conversations that arrive, up to the system thread limit. This technique is useful if the number of conversations is not expected to grow beyond the thread limit. If your program does reach the thread limit, it is difficult to determine when threads are free to accept new conversations again.

- *A set of N threads is started. Each accepts and processes conversations in a loop.* This allows your program to explicitly specify how many threads and, thus, how much resource it will use up. The actual number of threads may be tuned to provide the best server throughput without overloading or thrashing the server platform.

Here is an example of the HELLO5D server program adapted to accept many conversations and start a thread to process each:

```
/*-------------------------------------------------------------
 *  CPI-C example program, displaying received records
 *  server side (file SERVER2D.C)
 *-------------------------------------------------------------*/
#include <cpic.h>                 /* conversation API library  */
#include <stdio.h>                /* file I/O                  */
#include <stdlib.h>               /* standard library          */
#include <string.h>              /* strings and memory        */

#include <process.h>

#define RECEIVE_SIZE (10)         /* receive 10 bytes at a time */

static void
process_incoming_data(
    void * void_conversation_ID);

int main(void)
{
    unsigned char *  conversation_ID;
    CM_RETURN_CODE   cpic_return_code;
    int              thread_id;

    setbuf(stdout, NULL);          /* assure unbuffered output    */

    do {
        conversation_ID = malloc(CM_CID_SIZE);

        if (conversation_ID != NULL) {
            cmaccp(                       /* Accept_Conversation */
                conversation_ID,     /* returned conv ID    */
                &cpic_return_code);

            if (cpic_return_code == CM_OK) {
                printf("Accepted a conversation...\n");

                thread_id = _beginthread(
                                process_incoming_data,
                                NULL, /* have C allocate the  */
                                      /* stack for the thread */
                                8192, /* specify stack size */
                                (void*)conversation_ID);

                if (thread_id == -1) {
                    perror("Error creating thread.");
                }
            }
            else {
                fprintf(
                    stderr,
                    "Return code %lu on CMACCP.\n",
                    cpic_return_code);
```

```
                }

            }
            else {
                printf("Error getting memory!\n");
                cpic_return_code = -1;

            }


        } while (cpic_return_code == CM_OK);

        (void)getchar();              /* pause for a keystroke        */
        return(EXIT_SUCCESS);
}

static void
process_incoming_data(
        void * void_conversation_ID)
{
        unsigned char data_buffer[RECEIVE_SIZE];
        CM_INT32 requested_length = (CM_INT32)sizeof(data_buffer);
        CM_INT32 received_length;
        CM_DATA_RECEIVED_TYPE data_received;
        CM_REQUEST_TO_SEND_RECEIVED rts_received;
        CM_STATUS_RECEIVED status_received;
        unsigned done = 0;
        CM_RETURN_CODE cpic_return_code;

        unsigned char *  conversation_ID =
            (unsigned char *) void_conversation_ID;

        while (done == 0) {
            cmrcv(                    /* Receive                      */
                conversation_ID,      /* conversation ID              */
                data_buffer,          /* where to put received data   */
                &requested_length,    /* maximum length to receive    */
                &data_received,       /* returned data_received       */
                &received_length,     /* length of received data      */
                &status_received,     /* returned status_received     */
                &rts_received,        /* ignore this parameter        */
                &cpic_return_code); /* return code from this call   */

            /*   replace the following block with the good algorithm
             *   that's shown in the program sketch in the text.
             */

            if ((cpic_return_code == CM_OK) ||
                (cpic_return_code == CM_DEALLOCATED_NORMAL)) {

                /* write the received string to stdout */
                (void)fwrite((void *)data_buffer, (size_t)1,
```

```
                                (size_t)received_length, stdout);
            if (data_received == CM_COMPLETE_DATA_RECEIVED) {
                /* write a newline character */
                (void)fputc((int)'\n', stdout);
            }
        }
        else {
            printf("unexpected error %lu\n", cpic_return_code);
        }

        if (cpic_return_code != CM_OK) {
            done = 1;    /* CM_DEALLOCATED_NORMAL or unexpected */
        }
    }
    free(conversation_ID);
}
```

USING CPI-C 1.2 NONBLOCKING AND ACCEPT MULTIPLE

Last, you can choose to write your server using CPI-C 1.2 nonblocking features as well as accept multiple.

Advantages of using nonblocking are

- The number of client conversations is limited by the number of sessions, rather than the number of threads or processes.

- Nonblocking frees your program from operating system dependencies, and is portable.

Disadvantages of using nonblocking are

- *Extra overhead for nonblocking processing.*   Although the overhead will be less than if you tried to implement nonblocking using threads, a nonblocking call is more expensive than a normal procedure call.

- *Your program must supply and maintain parameters for each nonblocking call it issues.*   CPI-C keeps the addresses of your parameters until the nonblocking call completes. If your program issues four nonblocking Receive() calls, you must have four sets of Receive() parameters, including four Receive() buffers. If you are using nonblocking calls, we recommend you use C structures to keep the sets of parameters together as one unit.

- *Your program must maintain complete state information for each conversation.*   When the nonblocking call completes, you are only told the conversation ID and the return code. It is up to your program to remember what CPI-C call actually completed and what call should be issued on that conversation next.

For information on how to use the nonblocking feature and calls, see Chap. 26.

Appendixes

CPI-C Return Codes, A Practical Guide

Every CPI-C call has a return code as its last parameter. The return code reports back from CPI-C on what happened on a call. Return codes don't just report success or failure; sometimes they report the arrival of a message from the partner, such as when the partner has issued a Send_Error() call.

The following is a description for each CPI-C return code. The return codes are listed in numerical order, since many CPI-C programs and utilities display or log the return code number and not its accompanying name.

After all the descriptions is a table that lets you map in the other direction; it lists the CPI-C return code names in alphabetical order, followed by their numerical value in decimal (and hexadecimal). Whenever you display a CPI-C return code or write it to a file, always use the decimal value. The days of making users deal with hex values should be gone by now!

CPI-C RETURN CODES (0 TO 99)

The following return codes apply to all programs that issue CPI-C calls.

0 CM_OK

A CPI-C call completed successfully.

Explanation. CPI-C executed the function that was requested.

Programmer action. This is usually an "expected" return code. No action is required. This return code should be handled as part of the mainline program logic for programs that issue CPI-C calls.

Operator action. None.

1 CM_ALLOCATE_FAILURE_NO_RETRY

A session cannot be obtained for a conversation, and human intervention will be needed to correct the problem.

Explanation. The local program issued an Allocate() call (CMALLC), but there was difficulty in activating a link or a session.

CPI-C replies with this return code when it has determined that it is impossible to allocate a session without some human intervention. For example, the local communications software can tell when there is no adapter in the local computer, making a conversation impossible.

If there is any hope that a conversation might be established, CPI-C responds with the CM_ALLOCATE_FAILURE_RETRY return code. For example, CPI-C cannot look in the remote computer and see if there is a communications adapter there or see if it is even powered on. CPI-C retains some hope that a conversation might still be established by simply retrying the Allocate() call.

When you get this return code in a production environment, the problem is frequently a transient link failure—which is recoverable. Retrying the Allocate will generally be successful. Contrast this with a test environment, where the conversation is being established for the first time. In a test environment, either return code is likely, and there is probably a setup problem with the network hardware or software.

The implication of this return code is that something is wrong at the local computer, but this is not necessarily always true. (Experience suggests that for any of these problems, it is likely both computers are set up wrong, as is the connection between them!)

This conversation with the partner is over.

Likely causes. There are thousands of reasons for this return code. The local computer is unable to set up the session it needs with the remote computer. Here are some likely causes:

- The partner LU name is not really in the network or cannot be reached.

- The partner LU name might be incorrect or the target computer is not active or is not reachable. Partner LU names are configured as part of the CPI-C side information, or set with a call to a Set_Partner_LU_Name().

- The mode name requested for this session is not configured or spelled correctly at the partner.

- There is no route through the network that satisfies the requirements of the mode name. For example, there isn't a secure route that meets the requirements associated with #INTERSC.

Programmer action. There are thousands of reasons for this return code. A specific reason for the failure can be found in the *SNA sense data* associated with this return code. To diagnose the problem, your program must provide this SNA sense data to its user, or indicate a way it can be obtained. You should consider directing your users to find sense data values in traces and error logs.

The local program should not try to allocate a session again until the condition is corrected.

The conversation is now in **Reset** state; the *conversation_ID* that was supplied in this CPI-C call is no longer valid.

Operator action. Examine any platform-related message logs and error logs at both locations to find more information about this problem. Look for equipment failures or setup problems related to the network components and the computers using them. Fix the problem, as indicated by any SNA sense data associated with this call. You may need to run the applications again with SNA tracing activated to get the sense data.

After correcting the problem, try running the pair of programs again, if appropriate.

2 CM_ALLOCATE_FAILURE_RETRY

A session cannot be obtained for a conversation; the problem may be temporary, but human intervention will probably be needed to correct the problem.

Explanation. The local program issued an Allocate() call (CMALLC), but the underlying network software was unable to obtain or activate a session.

CPI-C replies with this return code when it has determined that it cannot allocate a session for a conversation. If the Allocate() request is tried again at a later time, the session might be able to be obtained, without human intervention. For example, CPI-C cannot look in the remote computer and see if there is a matching communications adapter there. CPI-C retains some hope that a conversation might still be established by simply retrying the Allocate() call.

Although this return code has the word "RETRY" in it, the allocation request might never succeed, especially if the partner is never activated or has been configured wrong.

This conversation with the partner is over.

Likely causes. There are thousands of reasons for this return code. The local computer is unable to set up the session it needs with the remote computer. Here are some likely causes:

- The remote computer is not powered on or has no communications adapter.
- The underlying CPI-C or APPC software on the remote computer is stopped, has not been started or is not yet fully active, or is abended.
- The DLC at the remote computer is not configured correctly.
- One computer, using a dependent LU 6.2, is attempting to communicate with an independent LU 6.2.

Programmer action. There are thousands of reasons for this return code. A specific reason for the failure can be found in the *SNA sense data* associated with this return code. To diagnose the problem, your program must provide this SNA sense data to its user, or indicate a way it can be obtained.

The local program should try again (at least once) to allocate a session for a conversation. There are some conditions that cause a failure the first time and succeed every time after that. To avoid congesting the network with attempted allocation requests, the local program should pause or wait for a keystroke before repeatedly retrying the allocation, and limit the number of retries. The implication of this return code is that something is wrong at the partner location or with the connection between the two computers, but this is not necessarily always true.

The conversation is now in **Reset** state; the *conversation_ID* that was supplied in this CPI-C call is no longer valid.

Operator action.   Examine any platform-related message logs and error logs at both locations to find more information about this problem. Look for equipment failures or setup problems related to the network components and the computers using them. Fix the problem, as indicated by any SNA sense data associated with this call. You may need to run the applications again with SNA tracing activated to get the sense data.

After correcting the problem, try running the pair of programs again, if appropriate.

3 CM_CONVERSATION_TYPE_MISMATCH

The conversation type of the local program is not expected or supported by the partner.

Explanation.   The partner computer rejected the incoming Attach because it or the partner program does not support the specified conversation type. The local program set the *conversation_type* to CM_MAPPED_CONVERSATION or CM_BASIC_CONVERSATION, and the partner configuration does not support that type of conversation.

This conversation with the partner is over. This return code will recur until either the local program or the partner configuration is changed. CPI-C reports this return code on a conversation call issued after an Allocate() call.

(An Attach is the internal message that is created when an Allocate() call is successful. It contains the TP name to be sent to the partner, as well as the conversation type and sync level. It also contains any conversation security information.)

You may see this return code associated with SNA sense data 10086034.

Likely causes.   This is probably a configuration problem at the partner or a mismatched pair of programs. The TP definition at the partner must match the conversation type used by the local program.

Programmer action.   Decide what the correct conversation type should be (basic or mapped). Change the local program so it uses the correct conversation type.

The conversation is now in **Reset** state; the *conversation_ID* that was supplied in this CPI-C call is no longer valid.

Operator action. Change the TP definition at the partner to reflect the conversation type required by the local program. To allow any conversation type at the partner, configure the conversation type in the TP definition to allow "Either." The install and setup procedures for your application should not allow this return code to occur in a production environment.

5 CM_PIP_NOT_SPECIFIED_CORRECTLY

The partner expected PIP data, which cannot be sent using CPI-C.

Explanation. The partner computer rejected the incoming Attach because the partner is defined to expect one or more program initialization parameter (PIP) variables. No PIP data was sent, because it cannot be sent using CPI-C. This return code is returned only when the partner program is using a native APPC (LU 6.2) application programming interface and is not using CPI-C.

This conversation with the partner is over. This return code will recur until either the local program or the partner configuration is changed. CPI-C reports this return code on a conversation call issued after an Allocate() call.

(An Attach is the internal message that is created when an Allocate() call is successful. It contains the TP name to be sent to the partner, as well as the conversation type and sync level. It also contains any PIP data or conversation security information.)

You may see this return code associated with SNA sense data 10086032.

Likely causes. This is a configuration problem at the partner. The TP definition at the partner cannot require incoming PIP data for this conversation.

Programmer action. PIP data is an obsolete APPC concept, not supported by CPI-C. The partner program needs to be modified to receive initialization parameters as part of its initial data exchange with its partners.

The conversation is now in **Reset** state; the *conversation_ID* that was supplied in this CPI-C call is no longer valid.

Operator action. Change the partner's TP definition so that it does not expect PIP data.

6 CM_SECURITY_NOT_VALID

The conversation security fields sent by the local program are invalid for the partner.

Explanation. The partner computer rejected the user ID or password received on an incoming Attach.

This conversation with the partner is over. This return code will recur until either the values supplied by the local program or the partner configuration is changed. CPI-C reports this return code on a conversation call issued after an Allocate() call.

(An Attach is the internal message that is created when an Allocate() call is successful. It contains the TP name to be sent to the partner, as well as the conversation type and sync level. It also contains any conversation security information.)

You may see this return code associated with SNA sense data 080F6051.

Likely causes. This is probably a configuration problem at the partner or an incorrect user ID and password supplied to the local program. The cause differs depending upon the local *conversation_security_type* of the conversation that failed. There are three values for *conversation_security_type:*

- CM_SECURITY_NONE—the partner's TP definition has been configured to expect conversation security on the incoming Attach, but none was supplied by the local program.

- CM_SECURITY_SAME—this could be an access control problem. For example, the user ID is valid, but the local user does not have the authority to run the partner program.

  If using OS/2 Communications Manager, a likely cause is the use of *Enhanced_Security_Same.* The LAN (locally logged-on) user ID and password were sent automatically for you. The partner was obligated to check these, and rejected the attempt. The local program should retry the allocation request with CM_SECURITY_NONE.

  Commonly available CPI-C applications like APING, ATELL, and AREXEC default to using *conversation_security_type*(CM_SECURITY_SAME). This return code indicates that the partner does not accept the user ID and password that was sent. You may be able to get the applications to run by starting the local program with *conversation_security_type*(CM_SECURITY_NONE), by using the "-n" command line flag.

  Another possibility occurs when the local program issues an Allocate() call with CM_SECURITY_SAME, but the local platform downgrades the security level to CM_SECURITY_NONE and sends that to the partner. If the partner's TP definition has been configured to require security, this return code results.

- CM_SECURITY_PROGRAM—the combination of user ID and password were not accepted by the partner. For example, the partner is using OS/2 Communications Manager and its TP definition specifies conversation_security(YES). The partner's APPC attach manager searched its list of valid user IDs and passwords, but did not find the received combination.

User IDs and passwords are both case-sensitive. Ensure that the values sent by the local program match those expected by the partner's security configuration.

Programmer action. The Allocate() call made by the local program is using the wrong user_ID or password parameter, or the partner's configuration of allowed user IDs and passwords needs to be changed. In the local program, look at the values specified in the CPI-C Set_Conversation_Security_Type(),

Set_Conversation_Security_User_ID(), and Set_Conversation_Security_Password() calls. Verify that they specify user_ID and password values acceptable to the partner.

The conversation is now in **Reset** state; the *conversation_ID* that was supplied in this CPI-C call is no longer valid.

Operator action. If the problem is with the partner configuration, ensure that the user ID and password combination sent by the local program has been correctly defined there. User IDs and passwords are case-sensitive. Be sure that the combination of uppercase and lowercase letters configured at the partner matches those specified by the local program.

Assure that if these are required (see the partner's TP definition), they will be accepted by the partner LU (see the partner's definition of its partner LU).

7 CM_SYNC_LVL_NOT_SUPPORTED_LU

The partner's CPI-C platform does not support the sync_level used by the local program.

Explanation. The local computer rejected the Allocate() call (CMALLC) because the local program specified a *sync_level* of CM_SYNC_POINT, which the partner does not support. This return code is returned only for conversations with *sync_level* set to CM_SYNC_POINT (or set to CM_CONFIRM, if activating a session with IMS using its LU 6.1 adapter).

This conversation with the partner is over. This return code will recur until either the local program or the partner configuration is changed. CPI-C reports this return code on an Allocate() call.

Likely causes. The partner, as it is currently installed, does not support Resource Recovery (sync point) operations. The local program, which specifies sync point operation, may be incompatible with the current system software.

Programmer action. Since sync point is not available at the partner, consider designing your program logic to do the checkpointing it needs without using the CPI Resource Recovery (CPI-RR) functions.

The conversation is now in **Reset** state; the *conversation_ID* that was supplied in this CPI-C call is no longer valid.

Operator action. Upgrade the partner's system software, if possible, to a version that supports sync point operations.

8 CM_SYNC_LVL_NOT_SUPPORTED_PGM

The sync level of the local program is not expected by the partner.

Explanation. The partner computer rejected the incoming Attach because the local program specified a synchronization level (with the *sync_level* parameter) that the partner program does not support.

This conversation with the partner is over. This return code will recur until either the local program or the partner configuration is changed. CPI-C reports this return code on a conversation call issued after an Allocate() call.

(An Attach is the internal message that is created when an Allocate() call is successful. It contains the TP name to be sent to the partner, as well as the conversation type and sync level. It also contains any conversation security information.)

You may see this return code associated with SNA sense data 10086041.

Likely causes. This is probably a configuration problem at the partner or a mismatched pair of programs. For example, the local transaction program issued an Allocate() call with *sync_level* set to CM_CONFIRM, but at the partner computer, the TP definition was configured as sync_level(NONE).

Programmer action. Decide what the correct *sync_level* should be for the conversation. Change the local program, if necessary, so it uses the correct *sync_level*. The partner's TP definition should match the *sync_level* chosen by the local program.

The conversation is now in **Reset** state; the *conversation_ID* that was supplied in this CPI-C call is no longer valid.

Operator action. Change the TP definition at the partner to reflect the sync_level required by the local program.

9 CM_TPN_NOT_RECOGNIZED

The partner computer does not recognize the *TP_name* sent by the local program.

Explanation. The partner computer rejected the incoming Attach because the local program specified a *TP_name* that the partner LU does not recognize.

This return code can also indicate that the partner LU recognized the *TP_name,* but could not start the program for some reason. This can be caused by authorization problems. Some APPC products (like VM/ESA) check that three things match up: LU name, mode name, and TP name. These platforms check the incoming user_ID and password of each defined TP, and reject the incoming Attach with this return code if the Attach is not authorized to start a corresponding program on the partner computer.

This conversation with the partner is over. This return code will recur until either the local program or the partner configuration is changed. CPI-C reports this return code on a conversation call issued after an Allocate() call.

(An Attach is the internal message that is created when an Allocate() call is successful. It contains the TP name to be sent to the partner, as well as the conversation type and sync level. It also contains any conversation security information.)

You may see this return code associated with SNA sense data 10086021.

Likely causes. This is probably a configuration problem at the partner or an incorrect *TP_name* supplied to the local program. The *TP_name* parameter in the partner's TP definition is one of the APPC configuration fields that is case-sensitive. Be sure that the combination of uppercase and lowercase letters matches those specified in the program.

For example:

- Examine the TP definition at the partner. Its TP definition may have the *TP_name* spelled wrong or be using the wrong combination of uppercase and lowercase characters. The *TP_name* configured at the partner must exactly match the *TP_name* used by the local program. (The *TP_name* sent by the local program may be set up in the local side information file.)

- If the partner is using OS/2 Communications Manager, there may be no TP definition that corresponds to the incoming Attach. The attach manager on the partner computer will still attempt to start the program, using the parameters on the DEFINE_DEFAULTS statement (if present). Assure that the correct directory_for_inbound_attaches is specified, along with the correct default_tp_operation and default_tp_program_type.

- If the partner is using the VM operating system, this return code will be received if the remote VM AVS is not authorized via the "*IDENT" control statements in VM to send information to the TP Program. This return code is saying that there is no way to get to the TP Program on VM from OS/2.

- If the partner is using the VM operating system, this return code is returned if an attempt was made to run the partner program in a user's virtual machine (using a nondedicated private gateway), and the user ID and password were not specified correctly. User ID and password are case-sensitive fields; be sure they are specified in uppercase if that is what the partner expects.

Programmer action. The *TP_name* sent to the partner is either a field configured in the local CPI-C side information, or a parameter on a Set_TP_Name() call issued by the local program.

- Ask the program user if the correct *symbolic_destination_name* was supplied, if the *TP_name* was configured as part of the local CPI-C side information.

- Ensure that your program constructs the *TP_name* and *TP_name_length* parameter correctly, if it issues a Set_TP_Name() call. The characters in the *TP_name* are case-sensitive.

Check the designated partner LU and mode names, as well, if required by the partner.

The conversation is now in **Reset** state; the *conversation_ID* that was supplied in this CPI-C call is no longer valid.

Operator action. At the partner, check the list of TP names to be recognized. Ensure that they match the values supplied for the *TP_name* values on the Allocate() call in the local computer.

If this checks out (that is, you find the TP correctly defined at the partner), make sure that partner TP is correctly authorized for the user_ID and password sent on the Attach.

10 CM_TP_NOT_AVAILABLE_NO_RETRY

The partner cannot start the program that corresponds to the *TP_name* that was sent.

Explanation. The partner computer rejected the incoming Attach because it could not start the program that corresponds to the *TP_name* it received. Without correcting the partner's configuration or operating environment, retrying the Allocate() call will not succeed.

This conversation with the partner is over. CPI-C reports this return code on a conversation call issued after an Allocate() call.

(An Attach is the internal message that is created when an Allocate() call is successful. It contains the TP name to be sent to the partner, as well as the conversation type and sync level. It also contains any conversation security information.)

You may see this return code associated with SNA sense data 084C0000.

Likely causes. This is probably a configuration problem at the partner. There is a valid TP definition at the partner for the *TP_name* that was sent, but the executable program named in that TP definition could not be started. For example:

- The intended executable program does not exist at the partner location.

- The executable program exists at the partner, but not in the drive, path, or directory specified in the partner's TP definition.

- The executable program exists at the partner, but its name is spelled wrong in the partner's TP definition.

- The operating system, CPI-C, or APPC software at the partner has exhausted its available resources (such as memory, processes, queues, or threads). The partner is unable to start the program that corresponds with the incoming *TP_name*.

- If the partner is using OS/2 Communications Manager, the APPC attach manager at the partner location may have failed to start the program due to an OS/2 error on its internal DosExecPgm() or DosStartSession() function call. Any of the nonzero OS/2 return codes from these function calls may be causing this situation. For example, the partner location is using OS/2 Communications Manager and its TP definition indicates this program is to be attach-manager-started. If there is insufficient memory for the attach manager to start the program, the incoming Attach will be rejected with this return code. This could similarly occur if the partner's operating system finds that it has consumed all of its processes or screen groups.

Programmer action.   None. Until the partner configuration or operating environment is corrected, it is unlikely that this conversation can be completed.

The conversation is now in **Reset** state; the *conversation_ID* that was supplied in this CPI-C call is no longer valid.

Operator action.   Ensure that the intended program has been defined correctly at the partner (via the TP definition), and that it has been compiled and linked correctly for its operating system. If the partner is logging its attach manager errors, look at its error log for more information.

11 CM_TP_NOT_AVAILABLE_RETRY

The partner cannot now start the program that corresponds to the *TP_name* that was sent.

Explanation.   The partner computer rejected the incoming Attach because it could not start the program that corresponds to the *TP_name* it received. Because of timing conditions, retrying the conversation may succeed in causing the partner program to be started.

This conversation with the partner is over. CPI-C reports this return code on a conversation call issued after an Allocate() call.

(An Attach is the internal message that is created when an Allocate() call is successful. It contains the TP name to be sent to the partner, as well as the conversation type and sync level. It also contains any conversation security information.)

You may see this return code associated with SNA sense data 084B6031.

Likely causes.   This is probably a problem with the operating environment or configuration at the partner. There is a valid TP definition at the partner for the *TP_name* that was sent, but the executable program named in that TP definition could not be started. For example:

- The APPC attach manager associated with the partner LU is stopped. In OS/2 Communications Manager, this can be caused by a missing START_ ATTACH_MANAGER statement in the Communications Manager (.NDF) node definitions file.

- The incoming_allocate_timeout defined in the TP definition at the partner LU is 0 or is too short. This only applies if the partner TP is configured as Queued.

- The incoming_allocate_queue_depth configured in the TP definition at the partner LU is too small. This only applies if the partner TP is configured as Queued.

- At the partner, the incoming Attach was queued, waiting to be processed. The intended program was remotely started, but ended before it could process the queued incoming Attach. For example, it had not yet issued an Accept_Conversation() call (CMACCP).

Programmer action. Retry the Attach by reissuing the Initialize_Conversation() call (CMINIT) and Allocate() call (CMALLC). However, to avoid congesting the network with attempted allocation requests, the local program should pause or wait for a keystroke before retrying the conversation.

Check the Accept_Conversation() calls (CMACCP) made by the partner program. It may be failing to make these calls correctly.

The conversation is now in **Reset** state; the *conversation_ID* that was supplied in this CPI-C call is no longer valid.

Operator action. Start the APPC attach manager, increase the incoming_allocate_timeout, increase the incoming_allocate_queue_depth in the configuration at the partner, if appropriate.

17 CM_DEALLOCATED_ABEND

The partner has abruptly ended the conversation.

Explanation. This return code is returned under one of the following conditions:

- The partner program issued a Deallocate() call (CMDEAL) with *deallocate_type* set to CM_DEALLOCATE_ABEND, or the partner has done so because of a remote program abnormal-ending condition. If the conversation at the partner program was in **Receive** state when the call was issued, information sent by the local program and not yet received by the partner program is purged.

- The partner program terminated normally but did not deallocate the session before terminating. The CPI-C or APPC software used by the partner deallocated the conversation on behalf of the partner program.

This conversation with the partner is over. This return code is reported to the local program on a call the program issues for a conversation in **Send** or **Receive** state.

You may see this return code associated with SNA sense data 08640000.

Likely causes. The partner program encountered a condition that caused it to terminate unexpectedly, or it was stopped unexpectedly by a user. For example:

- The partner program was running on OS/2. A user terminated the partner program using Ctrl+Break or Ctrl+C, or any of the menu options for ending programs. OS/2's ExitList processing causes the Deallocate() call to be issued as part of cleaning up the process.

- The partner program was processing an error, and encountered another error. Rather than loop in its error-handling code, the partner program issued a Deallocate() call with *deallocate_type* set to CM_DEALLOCATE_ABEND.

Programmer action. None.

The conversation is now in **Reset** state; the *conversation_ID* that was supplied in this CPI-C call is no longer valid.

Operator action.   Correct the problem encountered by the partner program.

18 CM_DEALLOCATED_NORMAL

The partner program has ended the conversation.

Explanation.   The partner program issued a Deallocate() call (CMDEAL) with *deallocate_type* set to CM_DEALLOCATE_SYNC_LEVEL or CM_DEALLOCATE_FLUSH. If *deallocate_type* is CM_DEALLOCATE_SYNC_LEVEL, the *sync_level* is CM_NONE.

This conversation with the partner is over. This return code is reported to the local program on a call the program issues for a conversation in **Receive** state.

Likely causes.   This return code generally indicates the successful completion of a conversation.

Programmer action.   None.

If your program sees this return code on a Receive() call (CMRCV), it should examine the value of the *data_received* parameter. Although the conversation is over, data that the partner sent, but which was not yet received, may have been returned on the Receive() call.

The conversation is now in **Reset** state; the *conversation_ID* that was supplied in this CPI-C call is no longer valid.

Operator action.   None.

19 CM_PARAMETER_ERROR

The local program tried to allocate a session, using invalid parameter names.

Explanation.   The local program issued an Allocate() call (CMALLC) that references a parameter containing an invalid conversation characteristic. The source of the argument can be outside the scope of the local program, such as a field in the CPI-C side information that is referenced by the Initialize_Conversation() call.

The state of the conversation remains unchanged.

Note: Contrast this return code with the CM_PROGRAM_PARAMETER_CHECK return code, which indicates a syntax error in a parameter.

Likely causes.   This return code indicates a parameter value that is not valid on the local platform (for example, it has not been configured), or your program doesn't have the correct permission level to use that specific parameter value. This is usually a problem with the partner_LU_name, mode_name, or TP_name being used. It means that one or more fields in the local CPI-C side information are wrong, or a CPI-C Set call—issued after the Initialize_Conversation(), but before the Allocate() call—contained an invalid name. For example:

- The local program specified an all-blank symbolic destination name on its Initialize_Conversation() call, but the program failed to issue Set calls for the partner LU name, mode name, and TP name.

- The partner_LU_name, mode_name, or TP_name contain one or more characters that are not valid for these names on the local computer. For example, a tilde (~) is not a valid character in these names.

- The local program attempted to use one of APPC's special modes, CPSVCMG, CPSVRMGR, or SNASVCMG, which are not for use by application programs.

- The local program is using OS/2 Communications Manager. If you specified a partner_LU_name without a period, in the side information or on a Set_Partner_LU_Name() call, the Communications Manager interprets that name as a *partner_LU_alias*. If that *partner_LU_alias* is not configured on the local computer at the time of the Allocate() call, this return code results.

Programmer action.   If the local program is using CPI-C side information via a symbolic destination name, consider overriding the partner LU name or mode name values. If the partner LU name or mode name was set using the Set_Partner_LU_Name() or Set_Mode_Name() calls, consider requesting different names from the user.

You may want to consider checking the validity of the characters passed to CPI-C in the Set_Partner_LU_Name(), Set_Mode_Name(), and Set_TP_Name() calls, since CPI-C does no validity checking of these calls.

Receiving the return code does not invalidate the conversation ID. If you can set different names, given input from a user, you can retry the Allocate() call without issuing Initialize_Conversation() again.

Operator action.   Ensure that the partner LU name, mode name, and other conversation characteristics in the local CPI-C side information are set up properly, and correspond to the local APPC configuration.

20 CM_PRODUCT_SPECIFIC_ERROR

The local program made a CPI-C call that failed because of a platform-related condition.

Explanation.   An operational problem has been detected which relates to the CPI-C product that the local program is using. A description of the error has been written to the local CPI-C product's system error log. See the product documentation for an indication of conditions and state changes caused by this return code.

The state of the conversation remains unchanged.

Likely causes.   This return code generally indicates a problem with the underlying CPI-C software and the environment in which it is running, not the local program. For example:

- The underlying CPI-C or APPC software is stopped, has not been started or is not yet fully active, or is abended.

- CPI-C is unable to allocate needed memory for its internal control blocks. For example, no more conversation IDs are available.

- If the return code is from a call to Accept_Conversation() (CMACCP), it is likely that the program was started locally (for example, from the command line), but the program should have been started by the attach manager because of an incoming Attach.

- There is a CPI-C implementation bug.

Here are some other platform-specific examples of this return code.

On the OS/2 Communications Manager: If the local platform is OS/2 Communications Manager, the local TP may have been deactivated using Subsystem Management.

If the local platform is OS/2 Communications Manager, the APPCTPN environment variable was not set before calling Accept_Conversation().

On CICS/ESA: If the local platform is CICS/ESA, this return code results in one of the following informational error messages:

DFHCP0742	The session is not available for CPI-C, as it is already in use by another process.
DFHCP0743	CPI-C can not be used, as the transaction was initiated by ATI.
DFHCP0750	An unrecognized profile name was supplied in the partner resource *sym_dest_name*.

On MVS/ESA: If the local platform is MVS/ESA, the system writes a symptom record to SYS1.LOGREC to identify the error.

On VM/ESA: If the local platform is VM/ESA, the system writes a symptom record to CPICOMM LOGDATA to identify the error.

However, depending on the platform, there are some types of problems that are caused by an *application program*. For example:

- There is a multitasking interference problem. One way this can occur is for a multithreaded program to issue more than one CPI-C call for a given conversation at the same time.

Programmer action.   This return code generally indicates a problem that the local program cannot recover from without intervention. Since the state of the conversation generally is not changed by this call, the local program should issue a Deallocate() call (with *deallocate_type* set to CM_DEALLOCATE_ABEND, if possible) to end the conversation.

Operator action.   First, make sure the local CPI-C software is active. If the CPI-C software was active when this return code occurred, check the local

CPI-C product's system error log (and related message logs) for additional details about this problem.

CPI-C may be making calls to underlying APPC software. The details of these calls, including their control blocks and internal return codes, provide lots of diagnostic information. If possible, get a trace of these internal calls to see the return codes returned by APPC.

21 CM_PROGRAM_ERROR_NO_TRUNC

The partner program issued a Send_Error() call while it was in **Send** state.

Explanation. The partner program issued a Send_Error() call (CMSERR). The partner conversation was in **Send** state; the Send_Error() that it issued did not truncate a logical record. (No truncation occurs when a program issues a Send_Error() call before sending any logical records or after sending a complete logical record.) The local conversation is now in **Receive** state.

You may see this return code associated with SNA sense data 08890000.

Likely causes. The partner program issued a Send_Error() call. The partner program encountered a problem while it had the permission to send. This could be a problem with the data it was sending or building, or this could be a problem discovered by the partner program's logic.

Programmer action. The local program should issue a Receive() call to receive a logical record containing a description of the error from its partner. (This presumes that the partner program follows the recommended practice of sending a description of the error it has just encountered after issuing a Send_Error() call.)

The partner program may have been designed to call Send_Error() when it finds a bug in its own logic. Examine carefully why the partner issued Send_Error().

Operator action. The partner program generally issues a Send_Error() call when it has a problem with its logic or the data it is handling. It may be necessary to check the validity of the data being processed by the partner.

22 CM_PROGRAM_ERROR_PURGING

The partner program issued a Send_Error() call while the partner was in **Receive** or **Confirm** state.

Explanation. One of the following occurred:

- The partner program issued a Send_Error() call (CMSERR) while it was in **Receive** or **Confirm** state. The call may have caused information enroute to the partner program to be purged (discarded), but not necessarily.

    Purging occurs when the partner program issues a Send_Error() call for a conversation in **Receive** state before receiving all the information being sent by the local program. No purging occurs when the partner program issues a Send_Error() call for a conversation in **Receive** state if the partner program has already received all the information sent by the local program. Also, no purging occurs when the partner program issues Send_Error() for a conversation in **Confirm** state.

When information is purged, the purging can occur at the local system, the partner system, or both.

▪ The partner program issued a Send_Error() call. The conversation for the partner program was in **Send-Pending** state. No purging of data has occurred. This return code indicates that the partner program had the *error_direction* conversation characteristic set to CM_RECEIVE_ERROR when the Send_Error() call was made.

This return code is normally reported to the local program on a call the program issues after sending some information to the partner program. However, the return code can be reported on a call the program issues before sending any information, depending on the call and when it is issued. The local conversation is now in **Receive** state.

You may see this return code associated with SNA sense data 08890000.

Likely causes. The partner program issued a Send_Error() call. The partner program encountered a problem while the local program had the permission to send. This could be a problem with the data the partner was receiving or parsing, or this could be a problem discovered by the partner program's logic.

This can also indicate a "race" condition, where both programs issued a Send_Error() call at the same time. The local program lost the race.

Programmer action. The local program should issue a Receive() call, to receive a logical record containing a description of the error from its partner. (This presumes that the partner program follows the recommended practice of sending a description of the error it has just encountered after issuing a Send_Error() call.)

The partner program may have been designed to call Send_Error() when it finds a bug in its own logic. Examine carefully why the partner issued Send_Error().

Operator action. The partner program generally issues a Send_Error() call when it has a problem with its logic or the data it is handling. It may be necessary to check the validity of the data being processed by the partner.

23 CM_PROGRAM_ERROR_TRUNC

The partner program issued a Send_Error() call for a basic conversation, truncating a logical record it was sending.

Explanation. The partner program issued a Send_Error() call (CMSERR) while in **Send** state, and the Send_Error() truncated a logical record. Truncation occurs when a program begins sending a logical record and then issues a Send_Error() call before sending the complete logical record.

CPI-C reports this return code to the local program on a Receive() call (CMRCV), after receiving the initial portion of the truncated logical record. The local conversation remains in **Receive** state.

This return code is returned for basic conversations only.

You may see this return code associated with SNA sense data 08890001.

Likely causes. The partner program issued a Send_Error() call. The partner program was in the middle of sending a logical record, and it encountered a problem. This could be a problem with the data or a problem discovered by the partner program's logic.

Programmer action. The local program should issue a Receive() call to receive a logical record containing a description of the error from its partner. (This presumes that the partner program follows the recommended practice of sending a description of the error it has just encountered after issuing a Send_Error() call.)

The partner program may have been designed to call Send_Error() when it finds a bug in its own logic. Examine carefully why the partner issued Send_Error().

Operator action. The partner program generally issues a Send_Error() call when it has a problem with its logic or the data it is handling. It may be necessary to check the validity of the data being processed by the partner.

24 CM PROGRAM_PARAMETER_CHECK

The local program called CPI-C with an invalid parameter.

Explanation. The local program issued a CPI-C call with an error in one or more parameters. ("Parameters" include not only the parameters described as part of the call syntax, but also the CPI-C conversation characteristics associated with the *conversation_ID*.)

If the return code is from a call to Initialize_Conversation() (CMINIT), it is likely that the symbolic destination name supplied by the user was spelled wrong, or the name has not been configured in the local CPI-C side information.

The source of the error is considered to be under the control of the local program. This return code may be caused by the failure of the program to pass a valid parameter address. The program should not examine any other returned variables associated with the call.

The state of the conversation remains unchanged.

Likely causes. This can be caused by any incorrect parameter. All parameters passed to CPI-C must be valid pointers to variable fields of the proper length. Other examples of parameter errors are:

■ The symbolic destination name supplied on the Initialize_Conversation() call was not found in the local CPI-C side information.

Either the supplied symbolic destination name was spelled wrong (or the wrong mix of upper- and lowercase letters was used), or the supplied symbolic destination name has not been set up in the local CPI-C side information.

- The *conversation_ID* is invalid. This can easily occur if a program issues any CPI-C call after a conversation is over, using the old *conversation ID*.

- The length of a buffer to be sent or received is too large.

- A length field is too large or is out of range.

- An enumerated value is out of range.

- The requested *sync_level* is not supported by the local machine.

Programmer action. If your program gets its symbolic destination name from a user or an input file, it is likely that this return code is because of an error related to that name. Assure the proper combination of upper- and lowercase letters, numbers, and symbols (many platforms allow only uppercase letters and numbers). Also, have the user check to see that the symbolic destination name they provided is actually configured on the local computer in the CPI-C side information.

For any call other than Initialize_Conversation(), this return code indicates a bug or logic defect in the local program. Design your program so that users only see this return code when there is a bug to be reported and fixed. For example, do validity and range checking on length values before making CPI-C calls to diagnose potential problems,

Find the CPI-C call that failed, and carefully check the syntax of each parameter that is being supplied. Ensure that all parameters are valid pointers to valid fields, and that each of these fields has the proper size and value.

Operator action. Check that the symbolic destination name that was used is configured in the local CPI-C side information. Also, ensure that the symbolic destination supplied to the local program was spelled correctly, and used the correct combination of upper- and lowercase letters and numbers.

Otherwise, report this as a bug to the supplier of the program.

25 CM_PROGRAM_STATE_CHECK

The local program called CPI-C with the wrong call at this time.

Explanation. This return code is returned under one of the following conditions:

- The local program issued a CPI-C call in a conversation state that was not valid for that call.

- The local program issued a Wait_For_Conversation() call, and there were no outstanding operations for any conversations known to the local program.

- For a conversation with *sync_level* set to CM_SYNC_POINT, the conversation's context is in the *Backout-Required* condition. The call issued is not allowed for this conversation while its context is in this condition.

The state of the conversation remains unchanged.

Likely causes. For production-level (debugged) programs, this is usually caused when the wrong two programs are talking to one another. At the initiating side, this may be caused because the wrong symbolic destination name is specified by the initiating program. Similarly, the partner LU name or the TP name may be wrong. At the target side, TP definition may specify the wrong program to be started.

If your program has issued the Wait_For_Conversation() call, this return code should be handled as part of the mainline program logic. There were no conversations with outstanding calls on which to wait for completion.

Otherwise, this return code indicates a bug or logic defect in the local program. This generally occurs when CPI-C calls are issued in the wrong order, or when interactions with the partner program have been overlooked. For example:

- The Set_Mode_Name() call is only valid in **Initialize** state, that is, after issuing Initialize_Conversation() but before issuing Allocate(). If it is issued after Allocate() or Accept_Conversation(), CPI-C returns this return code.

- After receiving a return code that indicates the partner program has issued a Send_Error() call (for example, CM_PROGRAM_ERROR_NO_TRUNC or CM_PROGRAM_ERROR_PURGING), the local program is in **Receive** state. It can only issue CPI-C calls that are valid in **Receive** state.

On the OS/2 Communications Manager. This return code is also returned on an Accept_Conversation() call for the following reasons:

- The operator or program set a TP name in the APPCTPN environment variable that was incorrect; that is, it did not match the TP name on the incoming Attach.

- An operator-started program issued an Accept_Conversation() call, but the call expired before the incoming Attach arrived. The duration that a call waits for an incoming Attach is configured on the TP definition, using the *receive_allocate_timeout* field.

Programmer action. This is readily caused when the user of the initiating program specifies a valid, but wrong, symbolic destination name, which caused this program to be erroneously started. Convey the probable program mismatch to the program's user, and end the program using a Deallocate() call with *deallocate_type* set to CM_DEALLOCATE_ABEND.

If your program sees this on a Wait_For_Conversation() call, it should handle it as an expected return code. It means that there were no outstanding operations on any conversation. This can easily occur when all the conversations are using blocking mode, that is, their *processing_mode* conversation characteristic is set to the default value of CM_BLOCKING.

Otherwise, users of your program should never see this return code; to users, this return code indicates a bug. The program should report to its user that a bug has been encountered, and log the bug. The program should not examine any other returned variables associated with the call.

The conversation ID for this conversation is still valid. The local program can find the current state of the conversation by issuing the CPI-C Extract_Conversation_State() call. Refer to a CPI-C reference manual for a list of calls that are allowed in each conversation state.

Operator action. Ensure that the TP definition at the target computer specifies the correct program to be started for the arriving TP name. Also, ensure that the program on the initiating side has obtained the correct symbolic destination name, and that the side information for that entry is correct.

Otherwise, report this as a bug to the supplier of the local program.

26 CM_RESOURCE_FAILURE_NO_RETRY

The active conversation has been unexpectedly ended, and starting it again probably will fail.

Explanation. A permanent failure prematurely ended the conversation. The condition is not temporary; operator intervention is required to correct the problem.

This conversation with the partner is over. This return code can be reported to the local program on a call it issues for a conversation in any state other than **Reset** or **Initialize.**

Likely causes. The session or link used to get to the partner has been broken, or the partner program was abruptly stopped. For example:

- The local and partner LUs have been disconnected from each other. The link or session has been abruptly terminated.

- The partner program was deactivated while it was running. For example, if the partner is using OS/2 Communications Manager, this can be done using Communications Manager Subsystem Management.

- The partner computer may have violated internal SNA protocols.

Programmer action. Without human intervention, the conversation probably cannot be successfully restarted.

The conversation is now in **Reset** state; the *conversation_ID* that was supplied in this CPI-C call is no longer valid.

Operator action. Examine any platform-related message logs and error logs at both locations to find more information about this problem. Look for equipment failures or setup problems related to the network components and the computers using them. Fix the problem, as indicated by any SNA sense data associated with this call. You may need to run the applications again with SNA tracing activated to get the sense data.

After correcting the problem, try running the pair of programs again, if appropriate.

27 CM_RESOURCE_FAILURE_RETRY

The active conversation has been unexpectedly ended, and starting it again may be successful.

Explanation. A temporary failure prematurely ended the conversation.
This conversation with the partner is over. This return code can be reported to the local program on a call it issues for a conversation in any state other than **Reset** or **Initialize.**

Likely causes. Some aspect of the partner computer, needed for CPI-C communication, has been deactivated. Here are some examples of how this return code is caused.

- The partner computer was powered off or rebooted during the conversation.
- The partner computer stopped or unloaded its APPC software during the conversation.
- The partner computer deactivated its data link control (DLC) during the conversation.
- The local or partner LU deactivated the session in the middle of a conversation. In OS/2, for example, this can be done using Communications Manager Subsystem Management or issuing the CNOS verb.
- The local LU was notified of a session outage occurring in the network.

Programmer action. The local program should attempt to allocate a session again. It is possible for some permanent failures to be initially reported as temporary, but the allocation of subsequent conversations would also fail.
The conversation is now in **Reset** state; the *conversation_ID* that was supplied in this CPI-C call is no longer valid.

Operator action. Examine any platform-related message logs and error logs at both locations to find more information about this problem. Look for equipment failures or setup problems related to the network components and the computers using them. Fix the problem, as indicated by any SNA sense data associated with this call. You may need to run the applications again with SNA tracing activated to get the sense data.
After correcting the problem, try running the pair of programs again, if appropriate.

28 CM_UNSUCCESSFUL

The local program made a CPI-C call that could not complete its requested function.

Explanation. There are two CPI-C calls that can fail to complete their desired function when they are issued, but may succeed if issued later. For these two calls, this return code should be handled as part of the mainline program logic.

The state of the conversation remains unchanged.

Likely causes. This return code has different meanings, depending on whether the CPI-C call that was issued was Allocate() or Receive().

■ For an Allocate() call (CMALLC) with return_control(CM_IMMEDIATE), CPI-C could not obtain a contention-winner session to the partner computer, using the requested mode name.

■ For a Receive() call (CMRCV) with *receive_type* set to CM_RECEIVE_ IMMEDIATE, there is no data to receive, and the status_received value hasn't changed since the last Receive().

Programmer action. The requested call was unable to complete the function that was requested, but no explicit action is required. Retry the call as appropriate. If you are issuing these calls in a programmed loop, consider pausing slightly within the loop, to avoid hard CPU usage (thus allowing other programs a chance to run).

Operator action. If this return code is returned on an Allocate() call, it may indicate that there are a large number of simultaneous sessions between this computer and its partner using the same mode. These sessions might be spread among many programs that are running at the same time. Consider changing the mode definition on both computers for the mode name in question, so it has more contention-winner sessions available concurrently.

30 CM_DEALLOCATED_ABEND_SVC

The partner program was abnormally terminated, or it ended the conversation abnormally by issuing a Deallocate() call.

Explanation. This return code is returned under one of the following conditions:

■ The partner program, using a native APPC (LU 6.2) application programming interface and not using CPI-C, issued a DEALLOCATE verb specifying a TYPE parameter of ABEND_SVC. If the conversation for the partner program was in **Receive** state when the verb was issued, information sent by the local program and not yet received by the partner program is purged.

■ The partner program either terminated abnormally or terminated normally but did not deallocate the conversation before terminating. The CPI-C or APPC software used by the partner deallocated the conversation on behalf of the partner program.

This return code is returned for basic conversations only.

This conversation with the partner is over. This return code is reported to the local program on a call the program issues for a conversation in **Send** or **Receive** state.

You may see this return code associated with SNA sense data 08640000.

Likely causes. Here are some examples of how this return code is caused.

- If the partner program is running on OS/2, this return code is seen locally if the partner program ended unexpectedly because of a protection fault.

- If the partner program is running on the AS/400, this return code reports the absence of a valid routing entry in a subsystem. If no specific subsystem device or remote location name has been entered, check to see if the subsystem QCMN is active. If QCMN is active, be sure the routing entry for APPC programs (PGMEVOKE) is present in the subsystem. If a subsystem other than QCMN is being used and a specific communications entry or remote location name entry is being used, be sure a routing entry with PGMEVOKE is specified in the same subsystem. In both cases, the fix is to add a routing entry in a subsystem.

Programmer action.   None.

The conversation is now in **Reset** state; the *conversation_ID* that was supplied in this CPI-C call is no longer valid.

Operator action.   None.

31 CM_DEALLOCATED_ABEND_TIMER

The partner program ended the conversation abnormally by issuing a Deallocate() call.

Explanation.   The remote APPC transaction program issued a DEALLOCATE verb specifying a TYPE parameter of ABEND_TIMER. If the local conversation was in **Receive** state when the verb was issued, information sent by the local program and not yet received by the remote program is purged.

This return code is returned for basic conversations only. In addition, it is returned only when the remote transaction program is using a native APPC (LU 6.2) application programming interface and is not using CPI-C.

This conversation with the partner is over. This return code is reported to the local program on a call the program issues for a conversation in **Send** or **Receive** state.

Likely causes.   The partner program encountered a condition that caused it to choose to terminate abnormally.

Programmer action.   None.

The conversation is now in **Reset** state; the *conversation_ID* that was supplied in this CPI-C call is no longer valid.

Operator action.   None.

32 CM_SVC_ERROR_NO_TRUNC

The partner program issued a Send_Error() call while it was in **Send** state.

Explanation.   The partner program issued a Send_Error() call with a TYPE parameter of SVC. The partner conversation was in **Send** state; the

Send_Error() that it issued did not truncate a logical record. (No truncation occurs when a program issues a Send_Error() call before sending any logical records or after sending a complete logical record.) The local conversation is now in **Receive** state.

This return code is returned for basic conversations only. In addition, it is returned only when the remote transaction program is using a native APPC (LU 6.2) application programming interface and is not using CPI-C.

You may see this return code associated with SNA sense data 08890100.

Likely causes. The partner program encountered a problem while it had the permission to send. This could be a problem with the data it was sending or building, or this could be a problem discovered by the partner program's logic.

Programmer action. The local program should issue a Receive() call to receive a logical record containing a description of the error from its partner. (This presumes that the partner program follows the recommended practice of sending a description of the error it has just encountered after issuing a Send_Error() call.)

The partner program may have been designed to call Send_Error() when it finds a bug in its own logic. Examine carefully why the partner issued Send_Error().

Operator action. The partner program generally issues a Send_Error() call when it has a problem with its logic or the data it is handling. It may be necessary to check the validity of the data being processed by the partner.

33 CM_SVC_ERROR_PURGING

The partner program issued a Send_Error() call while it was in **Receive** or **Confirm** state.

Explanation. One of the following occurred:

- The partner program issued a Send_Error() call with a TYPE parameter of SVC. The conversation for the partner program was in **Receive** or **Confirm** state. The call may have caused information enroute to the partner program to be purged (discarded), but not necessarily.

    Purging occurs when the partner program issues a Send_Error() call for a conversation in **Receive** state before receiving all the information being sent by the local program. No purging occurs when the partner program issues a Send_Error() call for a conversation in **Receive** state if the partner program has already received all the information sent by the local program. Also, no purging occurs when the partner program issues Send_Error() for a conversation in **Confirm** state.

    When information is purged, the purging can occur at the local system, the partner system, or both.

- The partner program issued a Send_Error() call with a TYPE parameter of SVC. The conversation for the partner program was in **Send-Pending** state.

No purging of data has occurred. This return code indicates that the partner program had an *error_direction* characteristic set to CM_RECEIVE_ERROR when the Send_Error() call was made.

This return code is normally reported to the local program on a call the program issues after sending some information to the partner program. However, the return code can be reported on a call the program issues before sending any information, depending on the call and when it is issued. The local conversation is now in **Receive** state.

This return code is returned for basic conversations only. In addition, it is returned only when the remote transaction program is using a native APPC (LU 6.2) application programming interface and is not using CPI-C.

You may see this return code associated with SNA sense data 08890100.

Likely causes. The partner program encountered a problem while the local program had the permission to send. This could be a problem with the data it was receiving or parsing, or this could be a problem discovered by the partner program's logic.

Programmer action. The local program should issue a Receive() call to receive a logical record containing a description of the error from its partner. (This presumes that the partner program follows the recommended practice of sending a description of the error it has just encountered after issuing a Send_Error() call.)

The partner program may have been designed to call Send_Error() when it finds a bug in its own logic. Examine carefully why the partner issued Send_Error().

Operator action. The partner program generally issues a Send_Error() call when it has a problem with its logic or the data it is handling. It may be necessary to check the validity of the data being processed by the partner.

34 CM_SVC_ERROR_TRUNC

The partner program issued a Send_Error() call for a basic conversation, truncating a logical record it was sending.

Explanation. The partner program issued a Send_Error() call with a TYPE parameter of SVC. The conversation for the partner program was in **Send** state. The Send_Error() truncated a logical record. Truncation occurs when a program begins sending a logical record and then issues a Send_Error() call before sending the complete logical record.

CPI-C reports this return code to the local program on a Receive() call, after receiving the initial portion of the truncated logical record. The local conversation remains in **Receive** state.

This return code is returned for basic conversations only. In addition, it is returned only when the remote transaction program is using a native APPC (LU 6.2) application programming interface and is not using CPI-C.

You may see this return code associated with SNA sense data 08890100.

Likely causes. The partner program was in the middle of sending a local record, and it encountered a problem. This could be a problem with the data or a problem discovered by the partner program's logic.

Programmer action. The local program should issue a Receive() call to receive a logical record containing a description of the error from its partner. (This presumes that the partner program follows the recommended practice of sending a description of the error it has just encountered after issuing a Send_Error() call.)

The partner program may have been designed to call Send_Error() when it finds a bug in its own logic. Examine carefully why the partner issued Send_Error().

Operator action. The partner program generally issues a Send_Error() call when it has a problem with its logic or the data it is handling. It may be necessary to check the validity of the data being processed by the partner.

35 CM_OPERATION_INCOMPLETE

The local program issued a CPI-C call that has not yet completed.

Explanation. A nonblocking operation has been started on the conversation but is not complete. This return code is returned when *processing_mode* is set to CM_NON_BLOCKING for the conversation and the call is suspended waiting for incoming data, buffers, or other resources. A program must use the Wait_For_Conversation() call to wait for the operation to complete and to retrieve the return code for the completed operation.

The state of the conversation remains unchanged.

Likely causes. This is an "expected" return code. If your program is using nonblocking processing mode, this return code may be returned on any CPI-C call. Your program requested that CPI-C return immediately on each call, even if they have not completed. This is the return code your program sees is the call has not completed. For example:

- Your program issued a Receive() call with the *receive_type* set to CM_RECEIVE_AND_WAIT, and there is nothing yet to receive.

- Your program issued a Send_Data() call and the internal buffers are full and have not yet been sent.

Programmer action. This return code should be handled as part of the main-line program logic for programs that issue nonblocking calls. The local program was presumably designed to use nonblocking processing mode so that it could do other work rather than waiting on the completion of CPI-C calls. Your program should do whatever work it has available to do, then come back to this conversation and issue a Wait_For_Conversation() call.

Operator action.   None.

36 CM_SYSTEM_EVENT

A platform-specific event has canceled a Wait_For_Conversation() call issued by the local program.

Explanation.   A CPI-C Wait_For_Conversation() call was being executed by the local program when an event (such as a signal) occurred. This event was handled by the local program. Wait_For_Conversation() returns this return code to allow the program to reissue the Wait_For_Conversation() call or to perform other processing. It is the responsibility of the event-handling portion of the local program to capture sufficient information for the program to decide how to proceed when it sees this return code.
The state of the conversation remains unchanged.

Likely causes.   The local platform or product has determined that there is an event that your local program should handle. For example, keyboard input must be captured before continuing with a CPI-C Receive() call.

Programmer action.   Handle the interrupt raised by the local platform (in a product-specific manner), then issue a Wait_For_Conversation() call again.

Operator action.   All system-related events that cause this return code should be handled by the local program. When the local program cannot handle or repair an event-related condition, operator intervention may be required.

37 CM_OPERATION_NOT_ACCEPTED

The local program made a CPI-C call while a previously issued CPI-C call had not yet completed.

Explanation.   A previous CPI-C call on this conversation is incomplete. This return code is returned when there is an outstanding operation on the conversation, as indicated by the CM_OPERATION_INCOMPLETE return code to a previous call. On an operating system that supports multiple program threads, when one thread has started an operation that has not completed, this return code may be returned on a call made by another thread on the same conversation.
The state of the conversation remains unchanged.

Likely causes.   The local program issued a CPI-C call when another had not yet completed. This is a bug in the design or coding of the local program.

Programmer action. This return code indicates a bug or logic defect in the local program. Users of your program should not see this return code; to users, this return code signals a bug to be reported and fixed.

Operator action. Report this as a bug to the supplier of the local program.

CPI-RR RETURN CODES (100 AND HIGHER)

The following return codes apply only to CPI-C programs that use CPI Resource Recovery (CPI-RR) calls.

For programs using conversations with *sync_level* set to CM_SYNC_POINT, all return codes indicating that backout processing is required have numeric values equal to or greater than CM_TAKE_BACKOUT. This allows you to test for a range of return code values to determine if backout processing is required. An example is:

```
return_code>=CM_TAKE_BACKOUT
```

100 CM_TAKE_BACKOUT

A Backout() request has been made; the local program needs to handle it.

Explanation. The remote program, the local system, or the remote system issued a CPI-RR Backout() call, and the local application must issue a Backout() call to restore all protected resources for a context to their status as of the last synchronization point. The conversation's context is in the *Backout-Required* condition upon receipt of this return code. Once the local program issues a Backout() call, the conversation is placed in the state it was in at the time of the last sync point operation.

This return code is returned only for conversations with *sync_level* set to CM_SYNC_POINT.

Likely causes. The partner program issued a Backout() call.

Programmer action. Your program should return to the point where it last synchronized with its partners. The conversation state is now what it was then. To handle what has occurred since that time, all intervening logic and code must be executed again.

Operator action. None.

130 CM_DEALLOCATED_ABEND_BO

The partner has abruptly ended the conversation.

Explanation. The remote program issued a Deallocate() call (CMDEAL) with *deallocate_type* set to CM_DEALLOCATE_ABEND, or the remote system has done so because of a remote program abnormal-ending condition. If the conversation for the remote program was in **Receive** state when the call was issued, information sent by the local program and not yet received by the remote program is purged.

This conversation with the partner is over.

This return code is returned only for conversations with *sync_level* set to CM_SYNC_POINT.

Likely causes. The partner program encountered a condition that caused it to terminate unexpectedly, or it was stopped unexpectedly by a user. For example:

- The partner program was processing an error, and encountered another error. Rather than loop in its error-handling code, the partner program issued a Deallocate() call with *deallocate_type* set to CM_DEALLOCATE_ABEND.

Programmer action. The local conversation's context is in the *Backout-Required* condition and the program must issue a CPI-RR Backout() call to restore all of the context's protected resources to their status as of the last synchronization point.

The conversation is now in **Reset** state; the *conversation_ID* that was supplied in this CPI-C call is no longer valid.

Operator action. Correct the problem encountered by the partner program.

131 CM_DEALLOCATED_ABEND_SVC_BO

The partner program was abnormally terminated, or it ended the conversation abnormally by issuing a Deallocate() call.

Explanation. This return code is returned under one of the following conditions:

- The partner program, using a native APPC (LU 6.2) application programming interface and not using CPI-C, issued a DEALLOCATE verb specifying a TYPE parameter of ABEND_SVC. If the conversation for the partner program was in **Receive** state when the verb was issued, information sent by the local program and not yet received by the partner program is purged.

- The partner program either terminated abnormally or terminated normally but did not deallocate the conversation before terminating. The CPI-C or APPC software used by the partner deallocated the conversation on behalf of the partner program.

This return code is returned for basic conversations only. In addition, it is returned only for conversations with *sync_level* set to CM_SYNC_POINT.

This conversation with the partner is over. This return code is reported to the local program on a call the program issues for a conversation in **Send** or **Receive** state.

You may see this return code associated with SNA sense data 08640000.

Likely causes. Here are some examples of how this return code is caused.

■ This return code is seen locally if the partner program ended unexpectedly because of a protection fault or other operating system exception.

■ If the partner program is running on the AS/400, this return code reports the absence of a valid routing entry in a subsystem. If no specific subsystem device or remote location name has been entered, check to see if the subsystem QCMN is active. If QCMN is active, be sure the routing entry for APPC programs (PGMEVOKE) is present in the subsystem. If a subsystem other than QCMN is being used and a specific communications entry or remote location name entry is being used, be sure a routing entry with PGMEVOKE is specified in the same subsystem. In both cases, the fix is to add a routing entry in a subsystem.

Programmer action. The local conversation's context is in the *Backout-Required* condition and the program must issue a CPI-RR Backout() call to restore all of the context's protected resources to their status as of the last synchronization point.

The conversation is now in **Reset** state; the *conversation_ID* that was supplied in this CPI-C call is no longer valid.

Operator action. None.

132 CM_DEALLOCATED_ABEND_TIMER_BO

The partner program ended the conversation abnormally by issuing a Deallocate() call.

Explanation. The remote APPC (LU 6.2) transaction program issued a DEALLOCATE verb specifying a TYPE parameter of ABEND_TIMER. If the conversation for the remote program was in **Receive** state when the verb was issued, information sent by the local program and not yet received by the remote program is purged. This return code is reported to the local program on a call the program issues for a conversation in **Send** or **Receive** state.

This conversation with the partner is over.

This return code is returned for basic conversations only. In addition, it is returned only for conversations with *sync_level* set to CM_SYNC_POINT, and only when the remote transaction program is using a native APPC (LU 6.2) application programming interface and is not using CPI-C.

Likely causes. The partner program encountered a condition that caused it to choose to terminate abnormally.

Programmer action. The local conversation's context is in the *Backout-Required* condition and the program must issue a CPI-RR Backout() call to restore all of the context's protected resources to their status as of the last synchronization point.

The conversation is now in **Reset** state; the *conversation_ID* that was supplied in this CPI-C call is no longer valid.

Operator action. None.

133 CM_RESOURCE_FAIL_NO_RETRY_BO

The active conversation has been unexpectedly ended, and starting it again probably will fail.

Explanation. A failure occurred that caused the conversation to be prematurely terminated. For example, the session being used for the conversation was deactivated because of a session protocol error, or the conversation was deallocated because of a protocol error between the mapped conversation components of the systems. The condition is not temporary, and the program should not retry the transaction until the condition is corrected. This return code can be reported to the local program on a call it issues for a conversation in any state other than **Reset** or **Initialize.**

This conversation with the partner is over.

This return code is returned only for conversations with *sync_level* set to CM_SYNC_POINT.

Likely causes. The session or link used to get to the partner has been broken, or the partner program was abruptly stopped. For example:

- The local and partner LUs have been disconnected from each other. The link or session has been abruptly terminated.

- The partner program was deactivated while it was running.

- The partner computer may have violated internal SNA protocols.

Programmer action. The local conversation's context is in the *Backout-Required* condition and the program must issue a CPI-RR Backout() call to restore all of the context's protected resources to their status as of the last synchronization point.

The conversation is now in **Reset** state; the *conversation_ID* that was supplied in this CPI-C call is no longer valid.

Operator action. Examine any platform-related message logs and error logs at both locations to find more information about this problem. Look for equipment failures or setup problems related to the network components and the computers using them. Fix the problem, as indicated by any SNA sense data associated with this call. You may need to run the applications again with SNA tracing activated to get the sense data.

After correcting the problem, try running the pair of programs again, if appropriate.

134 CM_RESOURCE_FAILURE_RETRY_BO

The active conversation has been unexpectedly ended, and starting it again may be successful.

Explanation. A failure occurred that caused the conversation to be prematurely terminated. For example, the session being used for the conversation was deactivated because of a session outage such as a line failure, a modem failure, or a cryptography failure. The condition may be temporary, and the program can retry the transaction. This return code can be reported to the local program on a call it issues for a conversation in any state other than **Reset** or **Initialize.**

This conversation with the partner is over.

This return code is returned only for conversations with *sync_level* set to CM_SYNC_POINT.

Likely causes. Some aspect of the partner computer, needed for CPI-C communication, has been deactivated. Here are some examples of how this return code is caused.

- The partner computer was powered off or rebooted during the conversation.

- The partner computer stopped or unloaded its APPC software during the conversation.

- The partner computer deactivated its data link control (DLC) during the conversation.

- The local or partner LU deactivated the session in the middle of a conversation.

- The local LU was notified of a session outage occurring in the network.

Programmer action. The local program should attempt to allocate a session again. It is possible for some permanent failures to be initially reported as temporary, but the allocation of subsequent conversations would also fail.

The local conversation's context is in the *Backout-Required* condition and the program must issue a CPI-RR Backout() call to restore all of the context's protected resources to their status as of the last synchronization point.

The conversation is now in **Reset** state; the *conversation_ID* that was supplied in this CPI-C call is no longer valid.

Operator action. Examine any platform-related message logs and error logs at both locations to find more information about this problem. Look for equipment failures or setup problems related to the network components and the computers using them. Fix the problem, as indicated by any SNA sense data associated with this call. You may need to run the applications again with SNA tracing activated to get the sense data.

After correcting the problem, try running the pair of programs again, if appropriate.

135 CM_DEALLOCATED_NORMAL_BO

The local program issued a Send_Error() call, but the conversation with the partner had already been deallocated.

Explanation. When a Send_Error() call (CMSERR) is issued in **Receive** state, incoming information is purged by the system. This purged information may include a notification of Deallocate-Abend from the remote program or system. When such a notification is purged, CPI-C returns CM_DEALLO-CATED_NORMAL_BO instead of one of the following return codes:

- CM_DEALLOCATED_ABEND_BO
- CM_DEALLOCATED_ABEND_SVC_BO
- CM_DEALLOCATED_ABEND_TIMER_BO

This conversation with the partner is over.

This return code is returned only for conversations with *sync_level* set to CM_SYNC_POINT.

Likely causes. The partner program deallocated the conversation unexpectedly.

Programmer action. The local conversation's context is in the *Backout-Required* condition and the program must issue a CPI-RR Backout() call to restore all of the context's protected resources to their status as of the last synchronization point.

The conversation is now in **Reset** state; the *conversation_ID* that was supplied in this CPI-C call is no longer valid.

Operator action. None.

NAMES TO NUMBERS, IN ALPHABETICAL ORDER

Sometimes you have a return code's number; other times you have its name. The previous descriptions were listed in numerical order; the following list is in alphabetical order, so you can map from a return code's name to its numerical value.

```
CM_ALLOCATE_FAILURE_NO_RETRY         1   (X'01')
CM_ALLOCATE_FAILURE_RETRY            2   (X'02')
CM_CONVERSATION_TYPE_MISMATCH        3   (X'03')
CM_DEALLOCATED_ABEND                17   (X'11')
CM_DEALLOCATED_ABEND_BO            130   (X'82')
CM_DEALLOCATED_ABEND_SVC            30   (X'1E')
CM_DEALLOCATED_ABEND_SVC_BO        131   (X'83')
CM_DEALLOCATED_ABEND_TIMER          31   (X'1F')
CM_DEALLOCATED_ABEND_TIMER_BO      132   (X'84')
CM_DEALLOCATED_NORMAL               18   (X'12')
CM_DEALLOCATED_NORMAL_BO           135   (X'87')
CM_OK                                0   (X'00')
CM_OPERATION_INCOMPLETE             35   (X'23')
CM_OPERATION_NOT_ACCEPTED           37   (X'25')
CM_PARAMETER_ERROR                  19   (X'13')
CM_PIP_NOT_SPECIFIED_CORRECTLY       5   (X'05')
CM_PRODUCT_SPECIFIC_ERROR           20   (X'14')
CM_PROGRAM_ERROR_NO_TRUNC           21   (X'15')
CM_PROGRAM_ERROR_PURGING            22   (X'16')
CM_PROGRAM_ERROR_TRUNC              23   (X'17')
CM_PROGRAM_PARAMETER_CHECK          24   (X'18')
CM_PROGRAM_STATE_CHECK              25   (X'19')
CM_RESOURCE_FAILURE_NO_RETRY        26   (X'1A')
CM_RESOURCE_FAILURE_RETRY           27   (X'1B')
CM_RESOURCE_FAILURE_RETRY_BO       134   (X'86')
CM_RESOURCE_FAIL_NO_RETRY_BO       133   (X'85')
CM_SECURITY_NOT_VALID                6   (X'06')
CM_SVC_ERROR_NO_TRUNC               32   (X'20')
CM_SVC_ERROR_PURGING                33   (X'21')
CM_SVC_ERROR_TRUNC                  34   (X'22')
CM_SYNC_LVL_NOT_SUPPORTED_LU         7   (X'07')
CM_SYNC_LVL_NOT_SUPPORTED_PGM        8   (X'08')
CM_SYSTEM_EVENT                     36   (X'24')
CM_TAKE_BACKOUT                    100   (X'64')
CM_TPN_NOT_RECOGNIZED                9   (X'09')
CM_TP_NOT_AVAILABLE_NO_RETRY        10   (X'0A')
CM_TP_NOT_AVAILABLE_RETRY           11   (X'0B')
CM_UNSUCCESSFUL                     28   (X'1C')
```

Definitions for Five Predefined Modes

If the five modes aren't already defined on your system, the following table shows what the mode definitions should contain.

Mode name	Class-of-service name	Maximum RU size	Receive pacing window	Maximum negotiable session limit	Mode session limit	Minimum negotiable conwinners source
#INTER	#INTER	default RU size	7	8	8	4
#INTERSC	#INTERSC	default RU size	7	8	8	4
#BATCH	#BATCH	default RU size	3	8	8	4
#BATCHSC	#BATCHSC	default RU size	3	8	8	4
"all blanks"	#CONNECT	default RU size	2	8	8	4

The value "default RU size" means that the maximum RU size will be set dynamically to the largest value that can be transmitted on the link without segmentation.

CPI-C Header File <cpic.h>

```
/*
 * NOTE:
 * Before you use this file, you must set a supported operating
 * system constant.  Search on SYSTEM to find the list of
 * supported constants and how to set the appropriate one.
 */


/*
 *
 * This file is organized as follows:
 *   - product specific preprocessor directives that must be
 *     before all other declarations
 *   - Base CPI-C constants and type definitions
 *   - Base CPI-C function prototypes
 *   - Product specific constants and type definitions (enclosed
 *     in #if/#endif)
 *   - Product specific function prototypes (enclosed in
 *     #if/#endif)
 */

#ifndef _cpic_h
#define _cpic_h

/*
 * The macro SYSTEM should be changed in the following #define
```

```
* to an appropriate value for your platform.
* The following values are handled by this file:
*    CM_AIX
*    CM_DOS
*    CM_MVS
*    CM_OS2
*    CM_OS400
*    CM_VM
*
* This is necessary for the proper setting of
* CM_ENTRY and CM_PTR below.
*/


#if ! (defined(CM_AIX) || defined(CM_DOS) || defined(CM_MVS) || \
       defined(CM_OS2) || defined(CM_OS400) || defined(CM_VM)  \
       )
/*
 * Define the system ONLY if no system has been defined by the
 * program.  This avoids duplicate macro definition warnings and
 * allows this include file to be moved to other platforms more
 * easily.
 *
 * If you choose to move this include file to another platform,
 * we recommend that you define the CM_ constant for that
 * platform externally on the compiler command line.
 *
 * When this file is shipped with a platform product, the
 * following line should be changed to match the platform CM_
 * constant.  For example, if this file were shipping on MVS/ESA,
 * the following line would be changed to "#define CM_MVS"
 */

#define SYSTEM

#endif


/*
 * CPI-Communications Enumerated Constants
 */

/*
 * CM_INT32 should be a 32-bit, signed integer.  The following
 * #define is system dependent and may need to be changed on
 * systems where signed long int does not define a 32-bit, signed
 * integer.
 */

#define CM_INT32 signed long int
```

```
#if   defined( CM_OS2 )

#   if __IBMC__ >= 100

   /* C Set/2 or C Set++                              */
   /* To test for C Set++ only, use                   */
   /*      (__IBMC__ >= 200 || __IBMCPP__ >= 200)  */
#     define CM_ENTRY extern void _Far16 _Pascal
#     define CM_PTR * _Seg16
#     define STRUCT16 _Packed struct
#     pragma seg16(SIDE_INFO)

/*
 * NOTE: packing will be reset to default at the end of this file
 */
#pragma pack(1)

#   elif __BORLANDC__

   /* Borland C++ for OS/2 */
#     define CM_ENTRY extern void __far16 __pascal
#     define CM_PTR __far16 *
#     define STRUCT16 struct

#   elif (_MSC_VER >= 600) || __IBMC__

   /* Microsoft C 6.0 or IBM C/2 */
#     define CM_ENTRY extern void pascal far _loadds
#     define CM_PTR far *
#     define STRUCT16 struct

#   else

   /* Something else      */
   /* Use the defaults... */
#     define CM_ENTRY extern void
#     define CM_PTR *
#     define STRUCT16 struct

#   endif

#elif defined( CM_DOS)

/* Microsoft C 6.0 and IBM C/2 */
#     define CM_ENTRY extern void pascal far _loadds
#     define CM_PTR far *

#elif defined( CM_MVS ) || defined( CM_OS400 ) || \
      defined( CM_VM ) || defined(CM_AIX)
```

```
#       define CM_ENTRY extern void
#       define CM_PTR *


#else

/*
 * If we have gotten this far, a supported system constant has
 * not been defined.  We will produce a syntax error on the next
 * line that should help the user identify the problem.
 *
 * To correct this problem, a system constant should be defined
 * either above in this file, or externally with a compiler
 * option.
 */
INTENTIONAL_SYNTAX_ERROR define_a_system_in_cpic_h();

#endif


#if defined(CM_OS400) || defined(CM_MVS)
#define cmacci CMACCI
#define cmaccp CMACCP
#define cmallc CMALLC
#define cmcanc CMCANC
#define cmcfm  CMCFM
#define cmcfmd CMCFMD
#define cmcnvi CMCNVI
#define cmcnvo CMCNVO
#define cmdeal CMDEAL
#define cmecs  CMECS
#define cmect  CMECT
#define cmectx CMECTX
#define cmembs CMEMBS
#define cmemn  CMEMN
#define cmepln CMEPLN
#define cmesl  CMESL
#define cmesui CMESUI
#define cmetpn CMETPN
#define cmflus CMFLUS
#define cminic CMINIC
#define cminit CMINIT
#define cmptr  CMPTR
#define cmrcv  CMRCV
#define cmrltp CMRLTP
#define cmrts  CMRTS
#define cmscsp CMSCSP
#define cmscst CMSCST
#define cmscsu CMSCSU
```

```
#define cmsct  CMSCT
#define cmsdt  CMSDT
#define cmsed  CMSED
#define cmsend CMSEND
#define cmserr CMSERR
#define cmsf   CMSF
#define cmsld  CMSLD
#define cmsltp CMSLTP
#define cmsmn  CMSMN
#define cmspln CMSPLN
#define cmspm  CMSPM
#define cmsptr CMSPTR
#define cmsrc  CMSRC
#define cmsrt  CMSRT
#define cmssl  CMSSL
#define cmsst  CMSST
#define cmstpn CMSTPN
#define cmtrts CMTRTS
#define cmwait CMWAIT
#endif


/*
 *  - Base CPI-C constants and type definitions
 */

/* conversation ID */
typedef unsigned char CONVERSATION_ID [8];
typedef unsigned char CONTEXT_ID [32];
typedef unsigned char SECURITY_PASSWORD [10];
typedef unsigned char SECURITY_USER_ID [10];

typedef CM_INT32 CM_CONVERSATION_RETURN_CODE;    /* X/Open only */
typedef CM_INT32 CM_CONVERSATION_SECURITY_TYPE;
typedef CM_INT32 CM_CONVERSATION_STATE;
typedef CM_INT32 CM_CONVERSATION_TYPE;
typedef CM_INT32 CM_DATA_RECEIVED_TYPE;
typedef CM_INT32 CM_DEALLOCATE_TYPE;
typedef CM_INT32 CM_ERROR_DIRECTION;
typedef CM_INT32 CM_FILL;
typedef CM_INT32 CM_PREPARE_TO_RECEIVE_TYPE;
typedef CM_INT32 CM_PROCESSING_MODE;
typedef CM_INT32 CM_RECEIVE_TYPE;
typedef CM_INT32 CM_REQUEST_TO_SEND_RECEIVED;
typedef CM_INT32 CM_RETURN_CODE;
typedef CM_INT32 CM_RETURN_CONTROL;
typedef CM_INT32 CM_SEND_TYPE;
typedef CM_INT32 CM_STATUS_RECEIVED;
typedef CM_INT32 CM_SYNC_LEVEL;
```

```
/* X/Open typedefs for compatibilty  */
typedef CM_INT32 CONVERSATION_STATE;
typedef CM_INT32 CONVERSATION_TYPE;
typedef CM_INT32 CONVERSATION_SECURITY_TYPE;
typedef CM_INT32 DATA_RECEIVED_TYPE;
typedef CM_INT32 DEALLOCATE_TYPE;
typedef CM_INT32 ERROR_DIRECTION;
typedef CM_INT32 FILL;
typedef CM_INT32 PREPARE_TO_RECEIVE_TYPE;
typedef CM_INT32 RECEIVE_TYPE;
typedef CM_INT32 REQUEST_TO_SEND_RECEIVED;
typedef CM_INT32 CM_RETCODE;
typedef CM_INT32 RETURN_CONTROL;
typedef CM_INT32 SEND_TYPE;
typedef CM_INT32 STATUS_RECEIVED;
typedef CM_INT32 SYNC_LEVEL;
typedef CM_INT32 PROCESSING_MODE;


/*
 * Enumerated data types (enum) have not been used for the
 * constant values because the default type for an enum
 * is 'int'.  This causes type conflicts on compilers where
 * int is not the same size as CM_INT32.
 */

/*  conversation_state values  */

#define CM_INITIALIZE_STATE             (CM_CONVERSATION_STATE) 2
#define CM_SEND_STATE                   (CM_CONVERSATION_STATE) 3
#define CM_RECEIVE_STATE                (CM_CONVERSATION_STATE) 4
#define CM_SEND_PENDING_STATE           (CM_CONVERSATION_STATE) 5
#define CM_CONFIRM_STATE                (CM_CONVERSATION_STATE) 6
#define CM_CONFIRM_SEND_STATE           (CM_CONVERSATION_STATE) 7
#define CM_CONFIRM_DEALLOCATE_STATE     (CM_CONVERSATION_STATE) 8
#define CM_DEFER_RECEIVE_STATE          (CM_CONVERSATION_STATE) 9
#define CM_DEFER_DEALLOCATE_STATE       (CM_CONVERSATION_STATE) 10
#define CM_SYNC_POINT_STATE             (CM_CONVERSATION_STATE) 11
#define CM_SYNC_POINT_SEND_STATE        (CM_CONVERSATION_STATE) 12
#define CM_SYNC_POINT_DEALLOCATE_STATE (CM_CONVERSATION_STATE) 13
#define CM_INITIALIZE_INCOMING_STATE    (CM_CONVERSATION_STATE) 14


/*  conversation_type values  */

#define CM_BASIC_CONVERSATION           (CM_CONVERSATION_TYPE) 0
#define CM_MAPPED_CONVERSATION          (CM_CONVERSATION_TYPE) 1


/*  data_received values  */
```

```
#define CM_NO_DATA_RECEIVED              (CM_DATA_RECEIVED_TYPE) 0
#define CM_DATA_RECEIVED                 (CM_DATA_RECEIVED_TYPE) 1
#define CM_COMPLETE_DATA_RECEIVED        (CM_DATA_RECEIVED_TYPE) 2
#define CM_INCOMPLETE_DATA_RECEIVED      (CM_DATA_RECEIVED_TYPE) 3


/*  deallocate_type values  */

#define CM_DEALLOCATE_SYNC_LEVEL         (CM_DEALLOCATE_TYPE) 0
#define CM_DEALLOCATE_FLUSH              (CM_DEALLOCATE_TYPE) 1
#define CM_DEALLOCATE_CONFIRM            (CM_DEALLOCATE_TYPE) 2
#define CM_DEALLOCATE_ABEND              (CM_DEALLOCATE_TYPE) 3


/*  error_direction values  */

#define CM_RECEIVE_ERROR                 (CM_ERROR_DIRECTION) 0
#define CM_SEND_ERROR                    (CM_ERROR_DIRECTION) 1


/*  fill values  */

#define CM_FILL_LL                       (CM_FILL) 0
#define CM_FILL_BUFFER                   (CM_FILL) 1


/*  prepare_to_receive_type values  */

#define CM_PREP_TO_RECEIVE_SYNC_LEVEL  \
                                  (CM_PREPARE_TO_RECEIVE_TYPE) 0
#define CM_PREP_TO_RECEIVE_FLUSH       \
                                  (CM_PREPARE_TO_RECEIVE_TYPE) 1
#define CM_PREP_TO_RECEIVE_CONFIRM     \
                                  (CM_PREPARE_TO_RECEIVE_TYPE) 2


/*  processing_mode values  */

#define CM_BLOCKING                      (CM_PROCESSING_MODE) 0
#define CM_NON_BLOCKING                  (CM_PROCESSING_MODE) 1


/*  receive_type values  */

#define CM_RECEIVE_AND_WAIT              (CM_RECEIVE_TYPE) 0
#define CM_RECEIVE_IMMEDIATE             (CM_RECEIVE_TYPE) 1


/*  request_to_send_received values  */
```

```
#define CM_REQ_TO_SEND_NOT_RECEIVED     \
                            (CM_REQUEST_TO_SEND_RECEIVED) 0
#define CM_REQ_TO_SEND_RECEIVED         \
                            (CM_REQUEST_TO_SEND_RECEIVED) 1


/*  return_code values  */

#define CM_OK                           (CM_RETURN_CODE) 0
#define CM_ALLOCATE_FAILURE_NO_RETRY    (CM_RETURN_CODE) 1
#define CM_ALLOCATE_FAILURE_RETRY       (CM_RETURN_CODE) 2
#define CM_CONVERSATION_TYPE_MISMATCH   (CM_RETURN_CODE) 3
#define CM_PIP_NOT_SPECIFIED_CORRECTLY  (CM_RETURN_CODE) 5
#define CM_SECURITY_NOT_VALID           (CM_RETURN_CODE) 6
#define CM_SYNC_LVL_NOT_SUPPORTED_LU    (CM_RETURN_CODE) 7
#define CM_SYNC_LVL_NOT_SUPPORTED_PGM   (CM_RETURN_CODE) 8
#define CM_TPN_NOT_RECOGNIZED           (CM_RETURN_CODE) 9
#define CM_TP_NOT_AVAILABLE_NO_RETRY    (CM_RETURN_CODE) 10
#define CM_TP_NOT_AVAILABLE_RETRY       (CM_RETURN_CODE) 11
#define CM_DEALLOCATED_ABEND            (CM_RETURN_CODE) 17
#define CM_DEALLOCATED_NORMAL           (CM_RETURN_CODE) 18
#define CM_PARAMETER_ERROR              (CM_RETURN_CODE) 19
#define CM_PRODUCT_SPECIFIC_ERROR       (CM_RETURN_CODE) 20
#define CM_PROGRAM_ERROR_NO_TRUNC       (CM_RETURN_CODE) 21
#define CM_PROGRAM_ERROR_PURGING        (CM_RETURN_CODE) 22
#define CM_PROGRAM_ERROR_TRUNC          (CM_RETURN_CODE) 23
#define CM_PROGRAM_PARAMETER_CHECK      (CM_RETURN_CODE) 24
#define CM_PROGRAM_STATE_CHECK          (CM_RETURN_CODE) 25
#define CM_RESOURCE_FAILURE_NO_RETRY    (CM_RETURN_CODE) 26
#define CM_RESOURCE_FAILURE_RETRY       (CM_RETURN_CODE) 27
#define CM_UNSUCCESSFUL                 (CM_RETURN_CODE) 28
#define CM_DEALLOCATED_ABEND_SVC        (CM_RETURN_CODE) 30
#define CM_DEALLOCATED_ABEND_TIMER      (CM_RETURN_CODE) 31
#define CM_SVC_ERROR_NO_TRUNC           (CM_RETURN_CODE) 32
#define CM_SVC_ERROR_PURGING            (CM_RETURN_CODE) 33
#define CM_SVC_ERROR_TRUNC              (CM_RETURN_CODE) 34
#define CM_OPERATION_INCOMPLETE         (CM_RETURN_CODE) 35
#define CM_SYSTEM_EVENT                 (CM_RETURN_CODE) 36
#define CM_OPERATION_NOT_ACCEPTED       (CM_RETURN_CODE) 37
#define CM_TAKE_BACKOUT                 (CM_RETURN_CODE) 100
#define CM_DEALLOCATED_ABEND_BO         (CM_RETURN_CODE) 130
#define CM_DEALLOCATED_ABEND_SVC_BO     (CM_RETURN_CODE) 131
#define CM_DEALLOCATED_ABEND_TIMER_BO   (CM_RETURN_CODE) 132
#define CM_RESOURCE_FAIL_NO_RETRY_BO    (CM_RETURN_CODE) 133
#define CM_RESOURCE_FAILURE_RETRY_BO    (CM_RETURN_CODE) 134
#define CM_DEALLOCATED_NORMAL_BO        (CM_RETURN_CODE) 135


/*  return_control values  */
```

```
#define CM_WHEN_SESSION_ALLOCATED        (CM_RETURN_CONTROL) 0
#define CM_IMMEDIATE                     (CM_RETURN_CONTROL) 1


/*  send_type values   */

#define CM_BUFFER_DATA                   (CM_SEND_TYPE) 0
#define CM_SEND_AND_FLUSH                (CM_SEND_TYPE) 1
#define CM_SEND_AND_CONFIRM              (CM_SEND_TYPE) 2
#define CM_SEND_AND_PREP_TO_RECEIVE      (CM_SEND_TYPE) 3
#define CM_SEND_AND_DEALLOCATE           (CM_SEND_TYPE) 4


/*  status_received values  */

#define CM_NO_STATUS_RECEIVED            (CM_STATUS_RECEIVED) 0
#define CM_SEND_RECEIVED                 (CM_STATUS_RECEIVED) 1
#define CM_CONFIRM_RECEIVED              (CM_STATUS_RECEIVED) 2
#define CM_CONFIRM_SEND_RECEIVED         (CM_STATUS_RECEIVED) 3
#define CM_CONFIRM_DEALLOC_RECEIVED      (CM_STATUS_RECEIVED) 4
#define CM_TAKE_COMMIT                   (CM_STATUS_RECEIVED) 5
#define CM_TAKE_COMMIT_SEND              (CM_STATUS_RECEIVED) 6
#define CM_TAKE_COMMIT_DEALLOCATE        (CM_STATUS_RECEIVED) 7


/* sync_level values   */

#define CM_NONE                          (CM_SYNC_LEVEL) 0
#define CM_CONFIRM                       (CM_SYNC_LEVEL) 1
#define CM_SYNC_POINT                    (CM_SYNC_LEVEL) 2

/* conversation_security_type values */

#define CM_SECURITY_NONE        (CM_CONVERSATION_SECURITY_TYPE) 0
#define CM_SECURITY_SAME        (CM_CONVERSATION_SECURITY_TYPE) 1
#define CM_SECURITY_PROGRAM     (CM_CONVERSATION_SECURITY_TYPE) 2

/* maximum sizes of strings and buffers */

#define CM_CID_SIZE    (8)        /* conversation ID          */
#define CM_CTX_SIZE    (32)       /* context ID               */
#define CM_LD_SIZE     (512)      /* log data                 */
#define CM_MN_SIZE     (8)        /* mode name                */
#define CM_PLN_SIZE    (17)       /* partner LU name          */
#define CM_PW_SIZE     (10)       /* password                 */
#define CM_SDN_SIZE    (8)        /* symbolic destination name */
#define CM_TPN_SIZE    (64)       /* TP name                  */
#define CM_UID_SIZE    (10)       /* userid ID                */
```

```
/*
 *  - Base CPI-C function prototypes
 */

#ifdef __cplusplus
extern "C" {
#endif /* __cplusplus */

CM_ENTRY                                /* Accept_Incoming            */
cmacci(unsigned char CM_PTR,             /* conversation_ID           */
       CM_RETURN_CODE CM_PTR);           /* return_code               */
CM_ENTRY                                /* Accept_Conversation        */
cmaccp(unsigned char CM_PTR,             /* conversation_ID           */
       CM_RETURN_CODE CM_PTR);           /* return_code               */
CM_ENTRY                                /* Allocate                   */
cmallc(unsigned char CM_PTR,             /* conversation_ID           */
       CM_RETURN_CODE CM_PTR);           /* return_code               */
CM_ENTRY                                /* Cancel Conversation        */
cmcanc(unsigned char CM_PTR,             /* conversation_ID           */
       CM_RETURN_CODE CM_PTR);           /* return_code               */
CM_ENTRY                                /* Confirm                    */
cmcfm (unsigned char CM_PTR,             /* conversation_ID           */
       CM_REQUEST_TO_SEND_RECEIVED CM_PTR, /* RTS_received            */
       CM_RETURN_CODE CM_PTR);           /* return_code               */
CM_ENTRY                                /* Confirmed                  */
cmcfmd(unsigned char CM_PTR,             /* conversation_ID           */
       CM_RETURN_CODE CM_PTR);           /* return_code               */
CM_ENTRY                                /* Convert_Incoming           */
cmcnvi(unsigned char CM_PTR,             /* buffer                    */
       CM_INT32 CM_PTR,                  /* buffer length             */
       CM_RETURN_CODE CM_PTR);           /* return_code               */
CM_ENTRY                                /* Convert_Outgoing           */
cmcnvo(unsigned char CM_PTR,             /* buffer                    */
       CM_INT32 CM_PTR,                  /* buffer length             */
       CM_RETURN_CODE CM_PTR);           /* return_code               */
CM_ENTRY                                /* Deallocate                 */
cmdeal(unsigned char CM_PTR,             /* conversation_ID           */
       CM_RETURN_CODE CM_PTR);           /* return_code               */
CM_ENTRY                                /* Extract_Conversation_State */
cmecs (unsigned char CM_PTR,             /* conversation_ID           */
       CM_CONVERSATION_STATE CM_PTR,/* conversation_state             */
       CM_RETURN_CODE CM_PTR);           /* return_code               */
CM_ENTRY                                /* Extract_Conversation_Type  */
cmect (unsigned char CM_PTR,             /* conversation_ID           */
       CM_CONVERSATION_TYPE CM_PTR, /* conversation_type              */
       CM_RETURN_CODE CM_PTR);           /* return_code               */
CM_ENTRY                                /* Extract_Conversation_Context*/
cmectx(unsigned char CM_PTR,             /* conversation_ID           */
       unsigned char CM_PTR,             /* context_ID                */
       CM_INT32 CM_PTR,                  /* context_ID_length         */
```

```
                  CM_RETURN_CODE CM_PTR);      /* return_code              */
CM_ENTRY                                /* Extract_Maximum_Buffer_Size */
cmembs(CM_INT32 CM_PTR,                      /* maximum_buffer_size      */
       CM_RETURN_CODE CM_PTR);               /* return_code              */
CM_ENTRY                                /* Extract_Mode_Name            */
cmemn (unsigned char CM_PTR,                 /* conversation_ID          */
       unsigned char CM_PTR,                 /* mode_name                */
       CM_INT32 CM_PTR,                      /* mode_name_length         */
       CM_RETURN_CODE CM_PTR);               /* return_code              */
CM_ENTRY                                /* Extract_Partner_LU_Name      */
cmepln(unsigned char CM_PTR,                 /* conversation_ID          */
       unsigned char CM_PTR,                 /* partner_LU_name          */
       CM_INT32 CM_PTR,                      /* partner_LU_name_length   */
       CM_RETURN_CODE CM_PTR);               /* return_code              */
CM_ENTRY                                /* Extract_Sync_Level           */
cmesl (unsigned char CM_PTR,                 /* conversation_ID          */
       CM_SYNC_LEVEL CM_PTR,                 /* sync_level               */
       CM_RETURN_CODE CM_PTR);               /* return_code              */
CM_ENTRY                                /* Extract_Security_User_ID     */
cmesui(unsigned char CM_PTR,                 /* conversation_ID          */
       unsigned char CM_PTR,                 /* user_ID                  */
       CM_INT32 CM_PTR,                      /* user_ID_length           */
       CM_RETURN_CODE CM_PTR);               /* return_code              */
CM_ENTRY                                /* Extract_TP_Name              */
cmetpn(unsigned char CM_PTR,                 /* conversation_ID          */
       unsigned char CM_PTR,                 /* TP_name                  */
       CM_INT32 CM_PTR,                      /* TP_name_length           */
       CM_RETURN_CODE CM_PTR);               /* return_code              */
CM_ENTRY                                /* Flush                        */
cmflus(unsigned char CM_PTR,                 /* conversation_ID          */
       CM_RETURN_CODE CM_PTR);               /* return_code              */
CM_ENTRY                                /* Initialize_For_Incoming      */
cminic(unsigned char CM_PTR,                 /* conversation_ID          */
       CM_RETURN_CODE CM_PTR);               /* return_code              */
CM_ENTRY                                /* Initialize_Conversation      */
cminit(unsigned char CM_PTR,                 /* conversation_ID          */
       unsigned char CM_PTR,                 /* sym_dest_name            */
       CM_RETURN_CODE CM_PTR);               /* return_code              */
CM_ENTRY                                /* Prepare_To_Receive           */
cmptr (unsigned char CM_PTR,                 /* conversation_ID          */
       CM_RETURN_CODE CM_PTR);               /* return_code              */
CM_ENTRY                                /* Receive                      */
cmrcv (unsigned char CM_PTR,                 /* conversation_ID          */
       unsigned char CM_PTR,                 /* buffer                   */
       CM_INT32 CM_PTR,                      /* requested_length         */
       CM_DATA_RECEIVED_TYPE CM_PTR,         /* data_received            */
       CM_INT32 CM_PTR,                      /* received_length          */
       CM_STATUS_RECEIVED CM_PTR,            /* status_received          */
       CM_REQUEST_TO_SEND_RECEIVED CM_PTR,   /* RTS_received             */
       CM_RETURN_CODE CM_PTR);               /* return_code              */
```

```
         CM_ENTRY                                /* Release_Local_TP_Name     */
         cmrltp(unsigned char CM_PTR,            /* TP_name                   */
                CM_INT32 CM_PTR,                 /* TP_name_length            */
                CM_RETURN_CODE CM_PTR);          /* return_code               */
         CM_ENTRY                                /* Request_To_Send           */
         cmrts (unsigned char CM_PTR,            /* conversation_ID           */
                CM_RETURN_CODE CM_PTR);          /* return_code               */
         CM_ENTRY                        /* Set_Conversation_Security_Password */
         cmscsp(unsigned char  CM_PTR,           /* conversation_ID           */
                unsigned char  CM_PTR,           /* password                  */
                CM_INT32 CM_PTR,                 /* password_length           */
                CM_RETURN_CODE CM_PTR);          /* return_code               */
         CM_ENTRY                          /* Set_Conversation_Security_Type   */
         cmscst(unsigned char  CM_PTR,           /* conversation_ID           */
                CM_CONVERSATION_TYPE CM_PTR,     /* conv_security_type        */
                CM_RETURN_CODE CM_PTR);          /* return_code               */
         CM_ENTRY                          /* Set_Conversation_Security_User_ID */
         cmscsu(unsigned char  CM_PTR,           /* conversation_ID           */
                unsigned char  CM_PTR,           /* user_ID                   */
                CM_INT32 CM_PTR,                 /* user_ID_length            */
                CM_RETURN_CODE CM_PTR);          /* return_code               */
         CM_ENTRY                                /* Set_Conversation_Type     */
         cmsct (unsigned char CM_PTR,            /* conversation_ID           */
                CM_CONVERSATION_TYPE CM_PTR,     /* conversation_type         */
                CM_RETURN_CODE CM_PTR);          /* return_code               */
         CM_ENTRY                                /* Set_Deallocate_Type       */
         cmsdt (unsigned char CM_PTR,            /* conversation_ID           */
                CM_DEALLOCATE_TYPE CM_PTR,       /* deallocate_type           */
                CM_RETURN_CODE CM_PTR);          /* return_code               */
         CM_ENTRY                                /* Set_Error_Direction       */
         cmsed (unsigned char CM_PTR,            /* conversation_ID           */
                CM_ERROR_DIRECTION CM_PTR,       /* error_direction           */
                CM_RETURN_CODE CM_PTR);          /* return_code               */
         CM_ENTRY                                /* Send_Data                 */
         cmsend(unsigned char CM_PTR,            /* conversation_ID           */
                unsigned char CM_PTR,            /* buffer                    */
                CM_INT32 CM_PTR,                 /* send_length               */
                CM_REQUEST_TO_SEND_RECEIVED CM_PTR, /* RTS_received           */
                CM_RETURN_CODE CM_PTR);          /* return_code               */
         CM_ENTRY                                /* Send_Error                */
         cmserr(unsigned char CM_PTR,            /* conversation_ID           */
                CM_REQUEST_TO_SEND_RECEIVED CM_PTR, /* RTS_received           */
                CM_RETURN_CODE CM_PTR);          /* return_code               */
         CM_ENTRY                                /* Set_Fill                  */
         cmsf  (unsigned char CM_PTR,            /* conversation_ID           */
                CM_FILL CM_PTR,                  /* fill                      */
                CM_RETURN_CODE CM_PTR);          /* return_code               */
         CM_ENTRY                                /* Set_Log_Data              */
         cmsld (unsigned char CM_PTR,            /* conversation_ID           */
                unsigned char CM_PTR,            /* log_data,                 */
```

```
              CM_INT32 CM_PTR,              /* log_data_length,        */
              CM_RETURN_CODE CM_PTR);       /* return_code             */
CM_ENTRY                                /* Specify_Local_TP_Name       */
cmsltp(unsigned char CM_PTR,              /* TP_name                   */
              CM_INT32 CM_PTR,              /* TP_name_length          */
              CM_RETURN_CODE CM_PTR);       /* return_code             */
CM_ENTRY                                /* Set_Mode_Name               */
cmsmn (unsigned char CM_PTR,              /* conversation_ID           */
              unsigned char CM_PTR,         /* mode_name               */
              CM_INT32 CM_PTR,              /* mode_name_length        */
              CM_RETURN_CODE CM_PTR);       /* return_code             */
CM_ENTRY                                /* Set_Partner_LU_Name         */
cmspln(unsigned char CM_PTR,              /* conversation_ID           */
              unsigned char CM_PTR,         /* partner_LU_name         */
              CM_INT32 CM_PTR,              /* partner_LU_name_length  */
              CM_RETURN_CODE CM_PTR);       /* return_code             */
CM_ENTRY                                /* Set_Processing_Mode         */
cmspm (unsigned char CM_PTR,              /* conversation_ID           */
       CM_PROCESSING_MODE CM_PTR,         /* processing_mode           */
       CM_RETURN_CODE CM_PTR);            /* return_code               */
CM_ENTRY                                /* Set_Prepare_To_Receive      */
cmsptr(unsigned char CM_PTR,              /* conversation_ID           */
       CM_PREPARE_TO_RECEIVE_TYPE CM_PTR, /* prep_to_rcv_type          */
       CM_RETURN_CODE CM_PTR);            /* return_code               */
CM_ENTRY                                /* Set_Return_Control          */
cmsrc (unsigned char CM_PTR,              /* conversation_ID           */
       CM_RETURN_CONTROL CM_PTR,          /* return_control            */
       CM_RETURN_CODE CM_PTR);            /* return_code               */
CM_ENTRY                                /* Set_Receive_Type            */
cmsrt (unsigned char CM_PTR,              /* conversation_ID           */
       CM_RECEIVE_TYPE CM_PTR,            /* receive_type              */
       CM_RETURN_CODE CM_PTR);            /* return_code               */
CM_ENTRY                                /* Set_Sync_Level              */
cmssl (unsigned char CM_PTR,              /* conversation_ID           */
       CM_SYNC_LEVEL CM_PTR,              /* sync_level                */
       CM_RETURN_CODE CM_PTR);            /* return_code               */
CM_ENTRY                                /* Set_Send_Type               */
cmsst (unsigned char CM_PTR,              /* conversation_ID           */
       CM_SEND_TYPE CM_PTR,               /* send_type                 */
       CM_RETURN_CODE CM_PTR);            /* return_code               */
CM_ENTRY                                /* Set_TP_Name                 */
cmstpn(unsigned char CM_PTR,              /* conversation_ID           */
              unsigned char CM_PTR,         /* TP_name                 */
              CM_INT32 CM_PTR,              /* TP_name_length          */
              CM_RETURN_CODE CM_PTR);       /* return_code             */
CM_ENTRY                              /* Test_Request_To_Send_Received */
cmtrts(unsigned char CM_PTR,              /* conversation_ID           */
       CM_REQUEST_TO_SEND_RECEIVED CM_PTR, /* RTS_received             */
       CM_RETURN_CODE CM_PTR);            /* return_code               */
CM_ENTRY                                /* Wait_For_Conversation       */
```

```
        cmwait(unsigned char CM_PTR,          /* conversation_ID          */
                CM_RETURN_CODE CM_PTR,        /* conversation_ret_code    */
                CM_RETURN_CODE CM_PTR);       /* return_code              */


        #ifdef __cplusplus
        }
        #endif /* __cplusplus */

        /*
         *  - Product specific constants and type definitions
         */

        /*
         *     #pragma linkage directives
         *
         * Note: For OS/400, routine names must be all uppercase.
         */
        #if defined(CM_VM)
        #      pragma linkage (cmacci, OS)
        #      pragma linkage (cmaccp, OS)
        #      pragma linkage (cmallc, OS)
        #      pragma linkage (cmcanc, OS)
        #      pragma linkage (cmcfm,  OS)
        #      pragma linkage (cmcfmd, OS)
        #      pragma linkage (cmcnvi, OS)
        #      pragma linkage (cmcnvo, OS)
        #      pragma linkage (cmdeal, OS)
        #      pragma linkage (cmecs,  OS)
        #      pragma linkage (cmect,  OS)
        #      pragma linkage (cmectx, OS)
        #      pragma linkage (cmembs, OS)
        #      pragma linkage (cmemn,  OS)
        #      pragma linkage (cmepln, OS)
        #      pragma linkage (cmesl,  OS)
        #      pragma linkage (cmesui, OS)
        #      pragma linkage (cmetpn, OS)
        #      pragma linkage (cmflus, OS)
        #      pragma linkage (cminic, OS)
        #      pragma linkage (cminit, OS)
        #      pragma linkage (cmptr,  OS)
        #      pragma linkage (cmrcv,  OS)
        #      pragma linkage (cmrltp, OS)
        #      pragma linkage (cmrts,  OS)
        #      pragma linkage (cmscsp, OS)
        #      pragma linkage (cmscst, OS)
        #      pragma linkage (cmscsu, OS)
        #      pragma linkage (cmsct,  OS)
        #      pragma linkage (cmsdt,  OS)
        #      pragma linkage (cmsed,  OS)
```

```
#      pragma linkage (cmsend, OS)
#      pragma linkage (cmserr, OS)
#      pragma linkage (cmsf,   OS)
#      pragma linkage (cmsld,  OS)
#      pragma linkage (cmsltp, OS)
#      pragma linkage (cmsmn,  OS)
#      pragma linkage (cmspln, OS)
#      pragma linkage (cmspm , OS)
#      pragma linkage (cmsptr, OS)
#      pragma linkage (cmsrc,  OS)
#      pragma linkage (cmsrt,  OS)
#      pragma linkage (cmssl,  OS)
#      pragma linkage (cmsst,  OS)
#      pragma linkage (cmstpn, OS)
#      pragma linkage (cmtrts, OS)
#      pragma linkage (cmwait, OS)
#endif

#if defined(CM_OS400) || defined(CM_MVS)
#      pragma linkage (CMACCI, OS)
#      pragma linkage (CMACCP, OS)
#      pragma linkage (CMALLC, OS)
#      pragma linkage (CMCANC, OS)
#      pragma linkage (CMCFM,  OS)
#      pragma linkage (CMCFMD, OS)
#      pragma linkage (CMCNVI, OS)
#      pragma linkage (CMCNVO, OS)
#      pragma linkage (CMDEAL, OS)
#      pragma linkage (CMECS,  OS)
#      pragma linkage (CMECT,  OS)
#      pragma linkage (CMECTX, OS)
#      pragma linkage (CMEMBS, OS)
#      pragma linkage (CMEMN,  OS)
#      pragma linkage (CMEPLN, OS)
#      pragma linkage (CMESL,  OS)
#      pragma linkage (CMESUI, OS)
#      pragma linkage (CMETPN, OS)
#      pragma linkage (CMFLUS, OS)
#      pragma linkage (CMINIC, OS)
#      pragma linkage (CMINIT, OS)
#      pragma linkage (CMPTR,  OS)
#      pragma linkage (CMRCV,  OS)
#      pragma linkage (CMRLTP, OS)
#      pragma linkage (CMRTS,  OS)
#      pragma linkage (CMSCSP, OS)
#      pragma linkage (CMSCST, OS)
#      pragma linkage (CMSCSU, OS)
#      pragma linkage (CMSCT,  OS)
#      pragma linkage (CMSDT,  OS)
#      pragma linkage (CMSED,  OS)
```

```
#      pragma linkage (CMSEND, OS)
#      pragma linkage (CMSERR, OS)
#      pragma linkage (CMSF,   OS)
#      pragma linkage (CMSLD,  OS)
#      pragma linkage (CMSLTP, OS)
#      pragma linkage (CMSMN,  OS)
#      pragma linkage (CMSPLN, OS)
#      pragma linkage (CMSPM , OS)
#      pragma linkage (CMSPTR, OS)
#      pragma linkage (CMSRC,  OS)
#      pragma linkage (CMSRT,  OS)
#      pragma linkage (CMSSL,  OS)
#      pragma linkage (CMSST,  OS)
#      pragma linkage (CMSTPN, OS)
#      pragma linkage (CMTRTS, OS)
#      pragma linkage (CMWAIT, OS)
#endif



#if defined(CM_OS2) || defined(CM_DOS) || defined(CM_AIX)

/*
 * Conversation security extensions
 */

typedef CM_INT32 XC_CONVERSATION_SECURITY_TYPE;

/* conversation_security_type values */

#define XC_SECURITY_NONE        (XC_CONVERSATION_SECURITY_TYPE) 0
#define XC_SECURITY_SAME        (XC_CONVERSATION_SECURITY_TYPE) 1
#define XC_SECURITY_PROGRAM     (XC_CONVERSATION_SECURITY_TYPE) 2

#ifdef __cplusplus
extern "C" {
#endif /* __cplusplus */

#if !defined(CM_DOS) /* extract calls are not supported in DOS */



CM_ENTRY                  /* Extract_Conversation_Security_Type */
xcecst(unsigned char  CM_PTR,      /* conversation_ID           */
       CM_INT32 CM_PTR,            /* conv_security_type        */
       CM_RETURN_CODE CM_PTR);     /* return_code               */



CM_ENTRY              /* Extract_Conversation_Security_User_ID */
xcecsu(unsigned char  CM_PTR,      /* conversation_ID           */
```

```
           unsigned char  CM_PTR,        /* user_ID             */
           CM_INT32 CM_PTR,               /* user_ID_length      */
           CM_RETURN_CODE CM_PTR);        /* return_code         */
#endif


CM_ENTRY                       /* Set_Conversation_Security_Password */
xcscsp(unsigned char  CM_PTR,        /* conversation_ID     */
       unsigned char  CM_PTR,        /* password            */
       CM_INT32 CM_PTR,              /* password_length     */
       CM_RETURN_CODE CM_PTR);       /* return_code         */


CM_ENTRY                       /* Set_Conversation_Security_Type */
xcscst(unsigned char  CM_PTR,        /* conversation_ID     */
       CM_INT32 CM_PTR,              /* conv_security_type  */
       CM_RETURN_CODE CM_PTR);       /* return_code         */


CM_ENTRY                       /* Set_Conversation_Security_User_ID */
xcscsu(unsigned char  CM_PTR,        /* conversation_ID     */
       unsigned char  CM_PTR,        /* user_ID             */
       CM_INT32 CM_PTR,              /* user_ID_length      */
       CM_RETURN_CODE CM_PTR);       /* return_code         */

   /*
    * Since these platforms do not yet support the security calls
    * with their CPI-C 1.2 names, we'll map to them here.
    */
#undef  cmscsp
#undef  cmscst
#undef  cmscsu
#define cmscsp xcscsp
#define cmscst xcscst
#define cmscsu xcscsu

#ifdef __cplusplus
}
#endif /* __cplusplus */

#endif


#if defined(CM_OS2)
/*
 * Constants and prototypes for OS/2 side information calls
 */

typedef CM_INT32 XC_TP_NAME_TYPE;
/* TP_name_type values */
```

```
#define XC_APPLICATION_TP           (XC_TP_NAME_TYPE) 0
#define XC_SNA_SERVICE_TP           (XC_TP_NAME_TYPE) 1

/* End_TP type values  */

#define XC_SOFT                          (CM_INT32) 0
#define XC_HARD                          (CM_INT32) 1

/* side info structure used by xcmssi to define side info */
typedef struct side_info_entry {
    unsigned char    sym_dest_name[8];  /* sym dest name      */
    unsigned char    partner_LU_name[17];
    unsigned char    reserved[3];   /* currently not used    */
    XC_TP_NAME_TYPE  TP_name_type;  /* set to                */
                                    /* XC_APPLICATION_TP      */
                                    /* or XC_SNA_SERVICE_TP   */
    unsigned char    TP_name[64];
    unsigned char    mode_name[8];
    XC_CONVERSATION_SECURITY_TYPE
                     conversation_security_type;
                                      /* set to              */
                                      /*   XC_SECURITY_NONE   */
                                      /*   XC_SECURITY_SAME   */
                                      /*   XC_SECURITY_PROGRAM */
    unsigned char    security_user_ID[8];
    unsigned char    security_password[8];
} SIDE_INFO;

#ifdef __cplusplus
extern "C" {
#endif /* __cplusplus */


CM_ENTRY                             /* End_TP                */
xcendt(unsigned char CM_PTR,            /* cpic_tp_id          */
       CM_INT32 CM_PTR,                 /* type-XC_SOFT or XC_HARD */
       CM_INT32 CM_PTR);                /* return_code         */


CM_ENTRY                             /* Extract_TP_ID         */
xceti(unsigned char CM_PTR,             /* conversation_id     */
      unsigned char CM_PTR,             /* cpic_tp_id          */
      CM_INT32 CM_PTR);                 /* return_code         */


CM_ENTRY                             /* Initialize_Conv_For_TP */
xcinct(unsigned char CM_PTR,            /* conversation_ID     */
       unsigned char CM_PTR,            /* sym_dest_name       */
       unsigned char CM_PTR,            /* cpic_tp_id          */
       CM_INT32 CM_PTR);                /* return_code         */
```

```
CM_ENTRY                                /* Start_TP                    */
xcstp(unsigned char CM_PTR,              /* local_lu_alias             */
      CM_INT32 CM_PTR,                   /* local_lu_alias_length      */
      unsigned char CM_PTR,              /* tp_name                    */
      CM_INT32 CM_PTR,                   /* tp_name_length             */
      unsigned char CM_PTR,              /* cpic_tp_id                 */
      CM_INT32 CM_PTR);                  /* return_code                */


CM_ENTRY                                /* Set_CPIC_Side_Information    */
xcmssi(unsigned char CM_PTR,             /* key lock                   */
       SIDE_INFO CM_PTR,                 /* side info_entry            */
       CM_INT32 CM_PTR,                  /* side_info length           */
       CM_RETURN_CODE CM_PTR);           /* return_code                */


CM_ENTRY                                /*Extract_CPIC_Side_Information*/
xcmesi(CM_INT32 CM_PTR,                  /* entry_number               */
       unsigned char CM_PTR,             /* symbolic dest name         */
       SIDE_INFO CM_PTR,                 /* side_info_entry            */
       CM_INT32 CM_PTR,                  /* side_info_length           */
       CM_RETURN_CODE CM_PTR);           /* return_code                */


CM_ENTRY                                /* Delete_CPIC_Side_Information*/
xcmdsi(unsigned char CM_PTR,             /* key_lock                   */
       unsigned char CM_PTR,             /* symbolic dest name         */
       CM_RETURN_CODE CM_PTR);           /* return_code                */

#ifdef __cplusplus
}
#endif /* __cplusplus */
#endif

#ifdef CM_VM

/*
 * XC_INT32 should be a 32-bit, signed integer.  The following
 * #define is system dependent and may need to be changed on
 * systems where signed long int does not define a 32-bit, signed
 * integer.
 */

#define XC_INT32 signed long int
#define XC_ENTRY extern void
#define XC_PTR *


typedef XC_INT32 CMINT;
typedef CMINT *PCMINT;
```

```
typedef unsigned char CMCHAR;
typedef CMCHAR *PCMCHAR;


typedef XC_INT32 XC_RESOURCE_MANAGER_TYPE;
/*  resource_manager_type values  */
#define XC_PRIVATE              (XC_RESOURCE_MANAGER_TYPE) 0
#define XC_LOCAL                (XC_RESOURCE_MANAGER_TYPE) 1
#define XC_GLOBAL               (XC_RESOURCE_MANAGER_TYPE) 2
#define XC_SYSTEM               (XC_RESOURCE_MANAGER_TYPE) 3

typedef XC_INT32 XC_SERVICE_MODE;
/*  service_mode values  */
#define XC_SINGLE               (XC_SERVICE_MODE) 0
#define XC_SEQUENTIAL           (XC_SERVICE_MODE) 1
#define XC_MULTIPLE             (XC_SERVICE_MODE) 2

typedef XC_INT32 XC_SECURITY_LEVEL_FLAG;
/*  security_level_flag values  */
#define XC_REJECT_SECURITY_NONE     (XC_SECURITY_LEVEL_FLAG) 0
#define XC_ACCEPT_SECURITY_NONE     (XC_SECURITY_LEVEL_FLAG) 1

typedef XC_INT32 XC_CONVERSATION_SECURITY_TYPE;
/*  conversation_security_type values  */
#define XC_SECURITY_NONE    (XC_CONVERSATION_SECURITY_TYPE) 0
#define XC_SECURITY_SAME    (XC_CONVERSATION_SECURITY_TYPE) 1
#define XC_SECURITY_PROGRAM (XC_CONVERSATION_SECURITY_TYPE) 2

typedef XC_INT32 XC_EVENT_TYPE;
/*  event_type values  */
#define XC_ALLOCATION_REQUEST       (XC_EVENT_TYPE) 1
#define XC_INFORMATION_INPUT        (XC_EVENT_TYPE) 2
#define XC_RESOURCE_REVOKED         (XC_EVENT_TYPE) 3
#define XC_CONSOLE_INPUT            (XC_EVENT_TYPE) 4
#define XC_REQUEST_ID               (XC_EVENT_TYPE) 5
#define XC_USER_EVENT               (XC_EVENT_TYPE) 6

CM_ENTRY                          /* Extract_Conversation_LUWID  */
xcecl( unsigned char CM_PTR,        /* conversation_ID           */
       unsigned char CM_PTR,        /* luwid                     */
       CM_INT32 CM_PTR,             /* luwid_length              */
       CM_RETURN_CODE CM_PTR);      /* return_code               */
CM_ENTRY              /* Extract_Conversation_Security_User_ID */
xcecsu(unsigned char CM_PTR,        /* conversation_ID           */
       unsigned char CM_PTR,        /* security_user_ID          */
       CM_INT32 CM_PTR,             /* security_user_ID_length */
       CM_RETURN_CODE CM_PTR);      /* return_code               */
CM_ENTRY                    /* Extract_Conversation_Workunitid */
xcecwu(unsigned char CM_PTR,        /* conversation_ID           */
       CM_INT32 CM_PTR,             /* workunitid                */
```

```
                   CM_RETURN_CODE CM_PTR);        /* return_code            */
CM_ENTRY                      /* Extract_Local_Fully_Qualified_LU_Name */
xcelfq(unsigned char CM_PTR,         /* conversation_ID        */
       unsigned char CM_PTR,         /* local_fq_LU_name       */
       CM_INT32 CM_PTR,              /* local_fq_LU_name_length */
       CM_RETURN_CODE CM_PTR);       /* return_code            */
CM_ENTRY                      /* Extract_Remote_Fully_Qualified_LU_Name */
xcerfq(unsigned char CM_PTR,         /* conversation_ID        */
       unsigned char CM_PTR,         /* remote_fq_LU_name      */
       CM_INT32 CM_PTR,              /* remote_fq_LU_name_length*/
       CM_RETURN_CODE CM_PTR);       /* return_code            */
CM_ENTRY                             /* Extract_TP_Name        */
xcetpn(unsigned char CM_PTR,         /* conversation_ID        */
       unsigned char CM_PTR,         /* TP_name                */
       CM_INT32 CM_PTR,              /* TP_name_length         */
       CM_RETURN_CODE CM_PTR);       /* return_code            */
CM_ENTRY                             /* Identify_Resource_Manager */
xcidrm(unsigned char CM_PTR,         /* resource_ID            */
       CM_INT32 CM_PTR,              /* resource_manager_type  */
       CM_INT32 CM_PTR,              /* service_mode           */
       CM_INT32 CM_PTR,              /* security_level_flag    */
       CM_RETURN_CODE CM_PTR);       /* return_code            */
CM_ENTRY                 /* Set_Conversation_Security_Password */
xcscsp(unsigned char CM_PTR,         /* conversation_ID        */
       unsigned char CM_PTR,         /* security_password      */
       CM_INT32 CM_PTR,              /* security_password_length*/
       CM_RETURN_CODE CM_PTR);       /* return_code            */
CM_ENTRY                     /* Set_Conversation_Security_Type */
xcscst(unsigned char CM_PTR,         /* conversation_ID        */
       CM_INT32 CM_PTR,              /* conv_security_type     */
       CM_RETURN_CODE CM_PTR);       /* return_code            */
CM_ENTRY                  /* Set_Conversation_Security_User_ID */
xcscsu(unsigned char CM_PTR,         /* conversation_ID        */
       unsigned char CM_PTR,         /* security_user_ID       */
       CM_INT32 CM_PTR,              /* security_user_ID_length */
       CM_RETURN_CODE CM_PTR);       /* return_code            */
CM_ENTRY                             /* Set_Client_User_ID     */
xcscui(unsigned char CM_PTR,         /* conversation_ID        */
       unsigned char CM_PTR,         /* client_user_ID         */
       CM_RETURN_CODE CM_PTR);       /* return_code            */
CM_ENTRY                             /* Signal_User_Event      */
xcsue( unsigned char CM_PTR,         /* event_ID               */
       unsigned char CM_PTR,         /* user_data              */
       CM_INT32 CM_PTR,              /* user_data_length       */
       CM_RETURN_CODE CM_PTR);       /* return_code            */
CM_ENTRY                             /* Terminate_Resource_Manager */
xctrrm(unsigned char CM_PTR,         /* resource_ID            */
       CM_RETURN_CODE CM_PTR);       /* return_code            */
CM_ENTRY                             /* Wait_On_Event          */
xcwoe( unsigned char CM_PTR,         /* resource_ID            */
```

```
              unsigned char CM_PTR,        /* conversation_ID       */
              CM_INT32 CM_PTR,             /* event_type            */
              CM_INT32 CM_PTR,             /* info_input_length     */
              unsigned char CM_PTR,        /* console_input_buffer  */
              CM_RETURN_CODE CM_PTR);      /* return_code           */

#     pragma linkage (xcecl,  OS)
#     pragma linkage (xcecsu, OS)
#     pragma linkage (xcecwu, OS)
#     pragma linkage (xcelfq, OS)
#     pragma linkage (xcerfq, OS)
#     pragma linkage (xcetpn, OS)
#     pragma linkage (xcidrm, OS)
#     pragma linkage (xcscsp, OS)
#     pragma linkage (xcscst, OS)
#     pragma linkage (xcscsu, OS)
#     pragma linkage (xcscui, OS)
#     pragma linkage (xcsue,  OS)
#     pragma linkage (xctrrm, OS)
#     pragma linkage (xcwoe,  OS)

#endif


/*
 * These macros allow you to write programs that are easier to
 * read, since you can use the full name of the CPI-C call rather
 * than its 6 character entry point.
 *
 * When porting code that uses these macros, you will have to
 * ensure that the macros are defined on the target platform.
 */

#ifdef READABLE_MACROS
#define Accept_Conversation(v1,v2)              \
          cmaccp(v1,v2)
#define Accept_Incoming(v1, v2)                 \
          cmacci(v1,v2)
#define Allocate(v1,v2)                         \
          cmallc(v1,v2)
#define Cancel_Conversation(v1,v2)              \
          cmcanc(v1,v2)
#define Confirm(v1,v2,v3)                       \
          cmcfm(v1,v2,v3)
#define Confirmed(v1,v2)                        \
          cmcfmd(v1,v2)
#define Convert_Incoming(v1,v2,v3)              \
          cmcnvi(v1,v2,v3)
#define Convert_Outgoing(v1,v2,v3)              \
          cmcnvo(v1,v2,v3)
```

```
#define Deallocate(v1,v2)                              \
          cmdeal(v1,v2)
#define Extract_Conversation_Context(v1,v2,v3,v4) \
          cmectx(v1,v2,v3,v4)
#define Extract_Conversation_State(v1,v2,v3)   \
          cmecs(v1,v2,v3)
#define Extract_Conversation_Type(v1,v2,v3)    \
          cmect(v1,v2,v3)
#define Extract_Maximum_Buffer_Size(v1,v2)     \
          cmembs(v1,v2)
#define Extract_Mode_Name(v1,v2,v3,v4)         \
          cmemn(v1,v2,v3,v4)
#define Extract_Partner_LU_Name(v1,v2,v3,v4)   \
          cmepln(v1,v2,v3,v4)
#define Extract_Security_User_ID(v1,v2,v3,v4)  \
          cmesui(v1,v2,v3,v4)
#define Extract_Sync_Level(v1,v2,v3)           \
          cmesl(v1,v2,v3)
#define Extract_TP_Name(v1,v2,v3,v4)           \
          cmetpn(v1,v2,v3,v4)
#define Flush(v1,v2)                           \
          cmflus(v1,v2)
#define Initialize_Conversation(v1,v2,v3)      \
          cminit(v1,v2,v3)
#define Initialize_For_Incoming(v1,v2)         \
          cminic(v1,v2)
#define Prepare_To_Receive(v1,v2)              \
          cmptr(v1,v2)
#define Receive(v1,v2,v3,v4,v5,v6,v7,v8)       \
          cmrcv(v1,v2,v3,v4,v5,v6,v7,v8)
#define Release_Local_TP_Name(v1,v2,v3)        \
          cmrltp(v1,v2,v3)
#define Request_To_Send(v1,v2)                 \
          cmrts(v1,v2)
#define Send_Data(v1,v2,v3,v4,v5)              \
          cmsend(v1,v2,v3,v4,v5)
#define Send_Error(v1,v2,v3)                   \
          cmserr(v1,v2,v3)
#define Set_Conversation_Security_Password(v1,v2,v3,v4) \
          cmscsp(v1,v2,v3,v4)
#define Set_Conversation_Security_Type(v1,v2,v3) \
          cmscst(v1,v2,v3)
#define Set_Conversation_Security_User_ID(v1,v2,v3,v4) \
          cmscsu(v1,v2,v3,v4)
#define Set_Conversation_Type(v1,v2,v3)        \
          cmsct(v1,v2,v3)
#define Set_Deallocate_Type(v1,v2,v3)          \
          cmsdt(v1,v2,v3)
#define Set_Error_Direction(v1,v2,v3)          \
          cmsed(v1,v2,v3)
```

```
#define Set_Fill(v1,v2,v3)                          \
            cmsf(v1,v2,v3)
#define Set_Log_Data(v1,v2,v3,v4)                   \
            cmsld(v1,v2,v3,v4)
#define Set_Mode_Name(v1,v2,v3,v4)                  \
            cmsmn(v1,v2,v3,v4)
#define Set_Partner_LU_Name(v1,v2,v3,v4)            \
            cmspln(v1,v2,v3,v4)
#define Set_Prepare_To_Receive_Type(v1,v2,v3)       \
            cmsptr(v1,v2,v3)
#define Set_Processing_Mode(v1,v2,v3)               \
            cmspm(v1,v2,v3)
#define Set_Receive_Type(v1,v2,v3)                  \
            cmsrt(v1,v2,v3)
#define Set_Return_Control(v1,v2,v3)                \
            cmsrc(v1,v2,v3)
#define Set_Send_Type(v1,v2,v3)                     \
            cmsst(v1,v2,v3)
#define Set_Sync_Level(v1,v2,v3)                    \
            cmssl(v1,v2,v3)
#define Set_TP_Name(v1,v2,v3,v4)                    \
            cmstpn(v1,v2,v3,v4)
#define Specify_Local_TP_Name(v1,v2,v3)             \
            cmsltp(v1,v2,v3)
#define Test_Request_To_Send_Received(v1,v2,v3)     \
            cmtrts(v1,v2,v3)
#define Wait_For_Conversation(v1,v2,v3)             \
            cmwait(v1,v2,v3)

#endif

#if   defined( CM_OS2 )

#   if __IBMC__ >= 100

/* reset default packing */
#   pragma pack()

#   endif

#endif

#endif
```

A Guide to Helpful Information

This is where you might find a traditional bibliography. We thought we'd offer you the best we know in related books, on-line forums, classes, conferences, and other information.

SPECS, BOOKS, AND MANUALS

We've split this section into the CPI-C specs, other related CPI-C programming books, books on APPC and APPN, our favorite books on C programming, and some books on data conversion. CPI-C was a creation of IBM, and many of the best CPI-C and APPC books are IBM books. We include details at the end of this section on how to get IBM books easily over the phone or by fax.

CPI-C specifications

From the list of CPI-C specifications, pick the one that's appropriate for the platforms you're coding to.

- *IBM SAA CPI Communications Reference,* IBM document number SC26-4399-06, March 1993. This is the current **CPI-C 1.1** spec, with the detailed product information for the following IBM platforms: CICS/ESA, IMS/ESA, MVS/ESA, OS/2 Communications Manager, OS/400, VM/ESA CMS, Networking Services/DOS, and AIX SNA Services/6000.

- *Common Programming Interface Communications Specification,* IBM document number SC31-6180-00, March 1993. This is the **CPI-C 1.2** spec. It contains no product information.

- *Microsoft Windows CPI-C Specification, version 1.0.* This is the **WinCPIC** spec, available for downloading from CompuServe. The ZIPped, softcopy file is in Microsoft *Word for Windows* format. You can download the WinCPIC spec by itself, or the entire WinSNA spec, which includes WinCPIC along with 4 other APIs.

"GO APPC" to reach the APPC Forum.

Download file "WINCPI.ZIP" from the Technical Papers library. This is the WinCPIC specification only.

"GO WINSDK" to reach the Microsoft Windows SDK Forum.

Download file "WINSNA.ZIP" from the COMM API/Networking library. This is the entire specification for all five parts of the Windows SNA definition.

- *X/Open CAE Specification, CPI-C,* Document Number C210, February 1992, ISBN 1-872630-35-9. This is the X/Open XPG4 CPI-C standard for Mainframe Internetworking. To obtain a copy, contact:

X/Open Company Ltd.
1010 El Camino, Suite 380
Menlo Park, California 94025 U.S.A.
telephone: 415-323-7992

- *IBM SAA CPI Resource Recovery Reference,* IBM document number SC31-6821-01. This is the **CPI-RR** spec, discussing the two calls involved with syncpoint operation. CPI-RR support is a separate programming interface; support for it is not required to fully support CPI-C 1.1 or later.

No matter what spec you get, be sure to get a current copy of *The Best of APPC, APPN, and CPI-C* CD-ROM from IBM, IBM order number SK2T-2013-02. This contains a collection of up-to-date product and architecture documents, sample source code, running programs, all back copies of *The APPC Connection* newsletter, and so on. It is available for a nominal charge (around U.S. $20), and is updated several times a year with the latest technical information. On our diskette, we've listed the table of contents for the current version; you'll see it's quite a deal.

CPI-C books

- *APPC and CPI-C Product Implementations,* IBM redbook number GG24-3520-01.

- *Introduction to CPI-C Programming in an AIX SNA Environment,* IBM document number GG22-9510-00.

- *AS/400 CPI Communications Selected Topics,* IBM redbook number GG24-3722-00. Contains source code for several example CPI-C applications, all written in the language RPG/400.

- *Application Development: Writing Servers for APPC/MVS,* IBM document number GC28-1070. Explains how CPI-C can handle multiple incoming Accepts, using the server facility in MVS/ESA 4.3.

- *VM/ESA CPI Communications User's Guide,* IBM document number SC24-5595.

- *Encina PPC Support to CPI-C and CPI-RR,* IBM document number SC23-2463-00.

- *Client/Server Programming with OS/2 2.1—Third Edition,* Robert Orfali and Dan Harkey, 1993, New York, N.Y.: Van Nostrand Reinhold, ISBN 0-442-01833-9.

APPC and APPN books

- *APPC: Introduction to LU 6.2,* Alex Berson, 1990, New York, N.Y.: McGraw-Hill, ISBN 0-07-005075-9.

- *Client/Server Architecture,* Alex Berson, 1992, New York, N.Y.: McGraw-Hill, ISBN 0-07-005076-7.

- *APPN Architecture and Product Implementations,* IBM document number GG24-3669.

- *APPN Networks,* Jesper Nilausen, Chichester, 1994: John Wiley & Sons, ISBN 0-471-94447-5.

- *SAA: IBM's Systems Applications Architecture,* Stephen J. Randesi and Donald H. Czubek, 1991, New York, N.Y.: Van Nostrand Reinhold, ISBM 0-44200-468-0.

- *SAA/LU 6.2 Distributed Networks and Applications,* John J. Edmunds,1991, New York, N.Y.: McGraw-Hill, ISBN 0-07019-022-4.

- *SNA Architecture, Protocols, and Implementation,* Atul Kapoor, 1991, New York, N.Y.: McGraw-Hill, ISBN 0-07033-727-6.

- *The APPC Resource Book,* IBM document number G325-0055. If you're doing anything related to APPC, APPN, CPI-C, or LU 6.2, be sure to get this book. It contains extensive information on education, manuals, applications, development tools, and platforms. The latest softcopy can be downloaded from the APPC Forum on CompuServe.

- *SNA Formats,* IBM document number GA27-3136-13. This book is usually only used by those who implement APPC platforms. It also contains a description of the log_data format and descriptions for all architected sense data.

- Watch for the upcoming book on APPN from McGraw-Hill by Steve Joyce and Tim Huntley.

C programming books

These three books should be part of every C programmer's library:

- *The C Programming Language, Second Edition,* Brian W. Kernighan and Dennis M. Ritchie, 1988, Englewood Cliffs, N.J.: Prentice-Hall, ISBN 0-13-110370-9.

- *The Elements of C Programming Style,* Jay Ranade and Alan Nash, 1993, New York, N.Y.: McGraw-Hill, ISBN 0-07-051278-7.
- *Writing Solid Code,* Steve Maguire, 1993, Redmond, Washington: Microsoft Press, ISBN 1-55615-551-4. An excellent book! A "must-read" book for every C programmer. We can't recommend it strongly enough.

Data conversion books

- *DBCS Design Guide and Information for OS/2 Programming,* IBM document number GA18-7284.
- *DBCS Design Guide—System/370 Software,* IBM document number GG18-9095.
- *System/370—DBCS Application Primer,* IBM document number GG18-9059.
- *National Language Information and Design Guide,* volumes 1 and 2, IBM document numbers SE09-8001 and SE09-8002.

Ordering IBM publications

You can now order IBM documents, CD-ROMs, redbooks, brochures, and other publications by fax or over the telephone. You can use a VISA, Master Card, or Diners Club credit card for your order, or you can use your IBM customer number.

- By fax, call 800-284-4721, toll free in the U.S.A. You can get the form you need from your IBM branch office, or you can make up your own form. Be sure to include the following information:

  Publication numbers of what you're ordering

  Credit card type, number, and expiration date—or your IBM customer number (if you have one)

  Name, phone number, and fax number of the person placing the order

  "Ship to" address, including the name of person to receive the order

- By telephone, call 800-879-2755, toll-free in the U.S.A. You will reach "IBM Software Manufacturing and Delivery." Despite the odd name, you're in the right place. Select option 1, and follow the directions.

For many of the IBM books we've listed in the previous sections, we've added the last two digits of the book number. These indicate the most current release of the book that we know about. For example, the last two digits of the *SNA Formats* book is now *-13*. These versions are the ones we're working from; if you're not at least up to these versions, we recommend them to you.

ON-LINE INFORMATION

The places where you can find on-line information and support for CPI-C continues to grow. Here are some of the best sources we know of.

The APPC Forum on CompuServe

The APPC Info Exchange Forum on CompuServe provides you with the latest information and help on APPC, 24 hours a day. This forum gives you direct access to APPC experts from both IBM and other companies. You can also use this forum to access sample programs and tools, get recent technical papers on APPC application design, and read catalogs on APPC education and products. Most of the resources listed in this section are available in this forum.

You can try CompuServe and the APPC Info Exchange Forum with no risk or obligation. To get a free introductory membership:

- In the United States and Canada, phone 800-848-8199.
- In the United Kingdom, phone 0800-289-378.
- In Germany, phone 0130-37-32.
- In the rest of Europe, phone 44-272-255-111.
- Elsewhere, phone 614-457-0802 in the U.S.A.

To access the APPC Forum, type "GO APPC" (or "GO APPN") at the ! prompt.

When you get to the APPC forum, be sure to search the libraries with the keyword "CPI-C." You'll find dozens and dozens of sample programs and documents to download. CPI-C programs in many different languages, like REXX, COBOL, and SmallTalk, are to be found there.

We'll also keep the latest version of the diskette that accompanies this book in the APPC Forum. Go to the Sample Programs [5] library, and download the CPICC1.ZIP file. As you find bugs or have code suggestions, check first to be sure that you have the latest version of the diskette.

APPC newsgroup on the Internet: APPC-L

To subscribe, send mail to listserv@auvm.bitnet, with the following line as the first line of the note:

```
SUBSCRIBE APPC-L your_name
```

To post a message to the forum, send mail to:

```
appc-l@auvm.bitnet
```

The IBM Communications Manager BBS

This bulletin board service is for customers of IBM's OS/2 Communications Manager. This is a good place to report on bugs, and to download bug fixes for the OS/2 Communications Manager.

BBS number: 919-543-8200

IBMLINK CFORUMs

The OS/2 BBS is implemented on the IBM Information Network (IIN) and the IBMLink facility. Any customer can acquire and register for this service.

IBMLINK number: 800-547-1283.

The CPI-C Implementers' Workshop

The CPI-C Implementers' Workshop (CIW) is a forum of architects, implementers, and users of CPI-C. Its purpose is to define enhancements to CPI-C, to promote the implementation and use of CPI-C, and to move CPI-C toward consideration for standardization. Participation in the CIW is open to any person with an interest in CPI-C as an implementer or user. For additional information about the CIW, send an Internet note to ciw-chair@ibmstandards. cary.ibm.com.

The CIW conducts much of its business between meetings via Internet e-mail lists. The same system also serves as a repository for the CIW document library files and for other files related to the CIW. These files include copies of presentations, architecture proposals, and other documentation. The files are available to anyone with Internet access via anonymous ftp.

The following instructions on using ftp assume direct connection to the Internet. If you access the Internet via a gateway or firewall system, the instructions will probably require modification.

1. ftp to the ibmstandards.cary.ibm.com system:

   ```
   ftp ibmstandards.cary.ibm.com
   ```

2. When prompted for userid, enter:

   ```
   anonymous
   ```

3. When prompted for password, enter your e-mail address.

4. Enter the following ftp commands, substituting the appropriate string for <desired-directory> and <file-name>.

   ```
   cd <desired-directory>
   mode i              /* mode i sets mode to image, which is
                          required for binary files such as
                          postscript. This step is not required
                          if the file is plain ascii. */
   get <file-name>
   .
   . <other ftp commands>
   .
   quit                /* end ftp session */
   ```

The technical work items, schedules for their completion, and publication plan of the CIW are described in the CIW Technical Plan, available in the CIW document library as /ciw/general/ciwtech.ps.

A list with descriptions of the documents currently in the CIW document library is available in the CIW document library as /ciw/general/doclist.txt.

IBM'S APPC MARKET ENABLEMENT TEAM

IBM's APPC Market Enablement team provides a variety of education and information on APPC, APPN, and CPI-C.

Conferences

One of the best sources for education are the annual APPC Application Developers Conferences sponsored by the APPC Market Enablement team. The tutorials conducted at these conferences give you the in-depth knowledge you need to write applications using CPI-C and APPC. Conference sessions include case studies from customer and consultants who have designed and developed APPC applications in many different settings. For more information on these conferences, phone APPC Market Enablement at 919-254-4957. For information on registering for these conferences, phone Technology Transfer Institute at 310-394-8305.

Classes

Two IBM classes address the development of CPI-C applications.

- Course G3792, "Designing Client/Server Applications Using APPC," is designed for application programmers who need practical skills in developing, coding, and testing CPI-C applications.

- Course G3860, "Distributing CICS 3270 Applications with APPC," is designed to help 3270 application programmers make the transition to CPI-C programming.

For more information or to register for these classes, phone Skill Dynamics at 800-IBM-TEACh (426-8322) or 703-412-2354.

Newsletter

The APPC Connection newsletter is designed to answer your questions and give you the latest news on APPC, APPN, and CPI-C. This free, bimonthly newsletter includes feature articles on industry news and trends, tips and techniques for programmers, case studies of businesses that are using APPC and APPN, and other helpful information.

Softcopies of *The APPC Connection* are also available for download in the News/Announcements library of the APPC Forum on CompuServe, and on the *Best of . . .* CD-ROM.

To subscribe to this free newsletter or for any assistance from the APPC Market Enablement team, send your name and mailing address to:

IBM APPC Market Enablement
Department E42
P.O. Box 12195
Research Triangle Park, North Carolina 27709-2195 U.S.A.
telephone: 919-254-4957
fax: 919-254-6050

Internet: appcmrkt@vnet.ibm.com

IBM VNET: APPCMRKT at RALVM6

CompuServe: "GO APPC" or "GO APPN" at any ! prompt

Index

#BATCH mode, 65, 140, 232, 441
#BATCHSC mode, 65, 140, 358, 441
#INTER mode, 57, 65, 139, 441
#INTERSC mode, 65, 139, 358, 441

A2E.C, 342
A2EMACRO.H, 345
A2ETABLE.C, 343
Accept multiple, 394–402
Accept_Conversation (cmaccp), 145
Accept_Incoming (cmacci), 378, 381
Advanced Peer-to-Peer Networking (APPN),
    11, 291
Advanced Program-to-Program Communica-
    tion (APPC), 10
AIX SNA Server/6000, 53, 395
Alert, 278
All-blank mode name, 65, 140, 441
All-blank symbolic destination name, 125,
    305, 308
Allocate (cmallc), 128, 330, 378, 406,
    407
alloc_cpic_buffer(), 263
Already verified, 361, 362, 365
Anonymous, 375
APING, 49, 65, 263, 295, 364
APPC, 10
APPC Connection, 473
APPC Market Enablement, 473–474
Application, definition of, 24
APPN, 11, 291
ASCII, 42, 339, 340
ascii_to_ebcdic_table[], 343
assert(), 45, 118
ATBCMC, 50
ATBGETC, 395
Attach, 60, 106, 128, 144, 151, 323
Attach contents, 144
Attach manager, 143, 144, 149, 323–333
Authentication, 360
Authorization, 360

Backout(), 134
Basic conversation, 132–133, 149, 205
Batch send, 232
Begging, 201
_beginthread(), 400
Best of APPC, APPN, and CPI-C CD-ROM, 5,
    7, 468
Big endian, 206, 348
Bind, 60
BIND program, 54
Blocking calls, 270
Borland C compiler, 6, 7
Buffer size, 150, 156, 265
Buffering, 101–113
Buffering guidelines, 102, 158
Building blocks, 117
Byte order, 338, 347

Call overhead, 266, 330
Call speed, 269
Cancel_Conversation (cmcanc), 380
Carriage-return character, /r, 238, 340
CD-ROM, 5, 7, 468
CDROM.TXT, 5, 7, 468
Characteristics, 130, 147, 315
Checkpoint, 279
CICS/ESA, 53, 393
Classic transactions, 211–253
Client, 24, 121, 305
CM, 42
cmacci() (Accept_Incoming), 378, 381
cmaccp() (Accept_Conversation), 145
cmallc() (Allocate), 128, 330, 378, 406, 407
cmcanc() (Cancel_Conversation), 380
cmcfm() (Confirm), 102, 162, 186, 260, 378
cmcfmd() (Confirmed), 187, 378
cmcnvi() (Convert_Incoming), 341
cmcnvo() (Convert_Outgoing), 341
CMCOBOL, 50
CMD.EXE, 332
cmdeal() (Deallocate), 102, 194, 378

cmecs() (Extract_Conversation_State), 76, 148

cmect() (Extract_Conversation_Type), 149

cmectx() (Extract_Conversation_Context), 148

cmembs() (Extract_Maximum_Buffer_Size), 150, 265

cmemn() (Extract_Mode_Name), 150

cmepln() (Extract_Partner_LU_Name), 41, 151, 393

cmesl() (Extract_Sync_Level), 152

cmesui() (Extract_Security_User_ID), 152, 365

cmetpn() (Extract_TP_Name), 153

cmflus() (Flush), 102, 158, 257, 261, 378

cminic() (Initialize_For_Incoming), 381

cminit() (Initialize_Conversation), 122, 330

CMPASCAL, 50

cmptr() (Prepare_To_Receive), 161, 259, 378

cmrcv() (Receive), 102, 166, 265, 378

CMREXX, 50

cmrltp() (Release_Local_TP_Name), 399

cmrts() (Request_To_Send), 202, 204, 378

cmscsp() (Set_Conversation_Security_Password), 367

cmscst() (Set_Conversation_Security_Type), 360, 366

cmscsu() (Set_Conversation_Security_User_ID), 366

cmsct() (Set_Conversation_Type), 132

cmsdt() (Set_Deallocate_Type), 194, 267

cmsed() (Set_Error_Direction), 190

cmsend() (Send_Data), 156, 191, 265, 266, 070

cmserr() (Send_Error), 102, 188, 191, 261, 283, 286, 378

cmsf() (Set_Fill), 207, 267

cmsld() (Set_Log_Data), 208

cmsltp() (Specify_Local_TP_Name), 398

cmsmn() (Set_Mode_Name), 139

cmspln() (Set_Partner_LU_Name), 41, 137

cmspm() (Set_Processing_Mode), 379, 382

cmsptr() (Set_Prepare_To_Receive_Type), 162, 267

cmsrc() (Set_Return_Control), 133

cmsrt() (Set_Receive_Type), 169, 267

cmssl() (Set_Sync_Level), 134

cmsst() (Set_Send_Type), 159, 267

cmstpn() (Set_TP_Name), 141

cmtrts() (Test_Request_To_Send_Received), 204

cmwait() (Wait_For_Conversation), 380

CM_ALLOCATE_FAILURE_NO_RETRY, 130, 275, 280, 406

CM_ALLOCATE_FAILURE_RETRY, 130, 276, 280

CM_BASIC_CONVERSATION, 150

CM_BLOCKING, 378, 379

CM_BUFFER_DATA, 159

CM_CID_SIZE, 40

CM_COMPLETE_DATA_RECEIVED, 97, 167

CM_CONFIRM, 134, 153

CM_CONFIRM_DEALLOCATE_STATE, 149

CM_CONFIRM_DEALLOC_RECEIVED, 168, 187

CM_CONFIRM_RECEIVED, 168, 187

CM_CONFIRM_SEND_RECEIVED, 168, 187

CM_CONFIRM_SEND_STATE, 149

CM_CONFIRM_STATE, 149

CM_CONVERSATION_TYPE_MISMATCH, 107, 275, 327, 332, 408

CM_CTX_SIZE, 40

CM_DATA_RECEIVED, 97, 167

CM_DEALLOCATED_ABEND, 198, 277, 416

CM_DEALLOCATED_ABEND_BO, 198, 277, 433

CM_DEALLOCATED_ABEND_SVC, 198, 277, 427

CM_DEALLOCATED_ABEND_SVC_BO, 198, 277, 434

CM_DEALLOCATED_ABEND_TIMER, 198, 277, 428

CM_DEALLOCATED_ABEND_TIMER_BO, 198, 277, 435

CM_DEALLOCATED_NORMAL, 198, 275, 417

CM_DEALLOCATED_NORMAL_BO, 198, 275, 437

CM_DEALLOCATE_ABEND, 195

CM_DEALLOCATE_CONFIRM, 195

CM_DEALLOCATE_FLUSH, 195

CM_DEALLOCATE_SYNC_LEVEL, 195

CM_DEFER_DEALLOCATE_STATE, 149

CM_DEFER_RECEIVE_STATE, 149

CM_ENTRY, 52

CM_FILL_BUFFER, 207

CM_FILL_LL, 207

CM_IMMEDIATE, 134

CM_INCOMPLETE_DATA_RECEIVED, 97, 167, 178, 278

CM_INITIALIZE_INCOMING_STATE, 149

CM_INITIALIZE_STATE, 149

CM_INT32, 38

CM_LD_SIZE, 40

CM_MAPPED_CONVERSATION, 150

CM_MN_SIZE, 40

CM_NONE, 134, 153

CM_NON_BLOCKING, 378, 379, 382

CM_NO_DATA_RECEIVED, 97, 167

CM_NO_STATUS_RECEIVED, 168

CM_OK, 275, 405

CM_OPERATION_INCOMPLETE, 378, 382, 431

CM_OPERATION_NOT_ACCEPTED, 432

CM_PARAMETER_ERROR, 125, 137, 275, 417

CM_PIP_NOT_SPECIFIED_CORRECTLY, 107, 275, 332, 409

CM_PLN_SIZE, 40
CM_PREP_TO_RECEIVE_CONFIRM, 162
CM_PREP_TO_RECEIVE_FLUSH, 162
CM_PREP_TO_RECEIVE_SYNC_LEVEL, 162
CM_PRODUCT_SPECIFIC_ERROR, 276, 418
CM_PROGRAM_ERROR_NO_TRUNC, 190,
    275, 420
CM_PROGRAM_ERROR_PURGING, 190,
    275, 286, 420
CM_PROGRAM_ERROR_TRUNC, 190, 275,
    421
CM_PROGRAM_PARAMETER_CHECK, 148,
    276, 422
CM_PROGRAM_STATE_CHECK, 146, 148,
    161, 276, 394, 423
CM_PTR, 51
CM_PW_SIZE, 40
CM_RECEIVE_AND_WAIT, 170
CM_RECEIVE_ERROR, 191
CM_RECEIVE_IMMEDIATE, 170
CM_RECEIVE_STATE, 149
CM_REQ_TO_SEND_NOT_RECEIVED, 205
CM_REQ_TO_SEND_RECEIVED, 205
CM_RESOURCE_FAILURE_NO_RETRY, 276,
    282, 425
CM_RESOURCE_FAILURE_RETRY, 276,
    282, 426
CM_RESOURCE_FAILURE_RETRY_BO, 276,
    436
CM_RESOURCE_FAIL_NO_RETRY_BO, 276,
    436
CM_SDN_SIZE, 40, 123
CM_SECURITY_NONE, 360, 363, 366, 368
CM_SECURITY_NOT_VALID, 107, 275, 328,
    332, 363, 375, 409
CM_SECURITY_PROGRAM, 361, 366, 368
CM_SECURITY_SAME, 361, 366, 367
CM_SEND_AND_CONFIRM, 159
CM_SEND_AND_DEALLOCATE, 159
CM_SEND_AND_FLUSH, 159
CM_SEND_AND_PREP_TO_RECEIVE, 159
CM_SEND_ERROR, 191
CM_SEND_PENDING_STATE, 149
CM_SEND_RECEIVED, 168
CM_SEND_STATE, 149
CM_SVC_ERROR_NO_TRUNC, 190, 275, 429
CM_SVC_ERROR_PURGING, 190, 275, 429
CM_SVC_ERROR_TRUNC, 190, 275, 430
CM_SYNC_LVL_NOT_SUPPORTED_LU, 275,
    411
CM_SYNC_LVL_NOT_SUPPORTED_PGM,
    107, 275, 332, 411
CM_SYNC_POINT, 134, 153, 169, 195
CM_SYNC_POINT_DEALLOCATE_STATE,
    149

CM_SYNC_POINT_SEND_STATE, 149
CM_SYNC_POINT_STATE, 149
CM_SYSTEM_EVENT, 432
CM_TAKE_BACKOUT, 275, 433
CM_TAKE_COMMIT, 168
CM_TAKE_COMMIT_DEALLOCATE, 168
CM_TAKE_COMMIT_SEND, 168
CM_TPN_NOT_RECOGNIZED, 107, 275, 332,
    412
CM_TPN_SIZE, 40
CM_TP_NOT_AVAILABLE_NO_RETRY, 107,
    275, 281, 329, 332, 414
CM_TP_NOT_AVAILABLE_RETRY, 107, 276,
    281, 329, 332, 415
CM_UID_SIZE, 40
CM_UNSUCCESSFUL, 134, 169, 275, 426
CM_WHEN_SESSION_ALLOCATED, 134
Code page, 339, 346, 470
Coding style, 54
Combined functions, 266
Commit(), 134
Communications Manager, OS/2, 53, 137, 277,
    291, 309, 394, 471
Compiler optimization, 45
Compiler warning levels, 44
Compiling, 44
Compression, 359
CompuServe, 8, 468, 471
Configuration, 55–68, 256, 294, 363
Confirm (cmcfm), 102, 162, 186, 260, 378
Confirmed (cmcfmd), 187, 378
Confirmed delivery, 218
Connection-oriented, 127
Constants, 38, 51
context_ID, 148, 382
Control point (CP), 66
Conversation, 25, 58
Conversation characteristics, 130, 147, 315
Conversation security, 327, 360
Conversation start-up overhead, 329–331
Conversation state, 70, 76, 148
Conversation state table, 70, 75
Conversational reply, 243
conversation_ID, 28, 42, 122, 123, 306–309
conversation_return_code, 379, 380
conversation_security_type, 360, 367
conversation_type, 132, 149, 327
convert_ascii_to_ebcdic_field(), 342
convert_ebcdic_to_ascii_field(), 343
convert_from_ascii(), 345
convert_get_int16_from_buffer(), 350
convert_get_int32_from_buffer(), 351
Convert_Incoming (cmcnvi), 341
Convert_Outgoing (cmcnvo), 341
convert_store_int16_in_buffer(), 349

convert_store_int32_in_buffer(), 350
convert_to_ascii(), 345
copy_sym_dest_name(), 314
Correlator, 393
CPI-C Implementers Workshop, 17, 472
CPI-C include file (cpic.h), 44, 50, 443–466
CPI-C library, 46, 53
CPI-C side information, 56, 57, 136
CPI-C version 1.0, 17, 147
CPI-C version 1.1, 5, 18, 147, 467
CPI-C version 1.2, 5, 18, 147, 340, 467
CPI-C version 2.0, 19
CPI-RR, 14, 169, 433–438, 468
CPIC.H, 44, 50, 443–466
CPIC.LIB, 53, 54
CPICC1.ZIP, 8, 471
CPICCC environment variable, 47
CPICLIB environment variable, 47
CPICLINK environment variable, 47
CPICNSDR.LIB, 54
CPICPLAT.TXT, 7
CPICRC.INF, 7
Credit-check transaction, 218
CREDIT.C, 220
CREDITD.C, 223

Daemon, 27
Data buffering, 101–113
Data conversion, 337–356
Data encoding, 356
Data structure, 355
Database-update transaction, 243
Datagram, 212
data_buffer, 99, 262
data_received, 92, 96, 98, 167, 278
DBCS (double-byte character set), 339, 346, 470
Deallocate (cmdeal), 102, 194, 378
Deallocate-Abend, 196, 261, 380
deallocate_type, 193
Debug version, 45, 158
Debugging, 331, 332
Default LU, 66
DEFINETP.NDF, 7
DEFINETP.NSD, 7
DEFINE_TP verb, 326, 332
DISPLAY verb, 291
DISPLAY_APPN verb, 291
DLC layer, 61, 291
DLC window, 256
DLL, 383
DOCPIC.C, 118
DOCPIC.H, 118
Dollar sign, 346
Double-byte character set (DBCS), 339, 346, 470
do_accept_conversation(), 146

do_allocate(), 128
do_blank_sym_dest_name(), 126
do_build_an_ll(), 206
do_error_cleanup(), 87, 199
do_initialize_conversation(), 123
do_receive_credit(), 180
do_receive_generic(), 173
do_receive_inquiry(), 182
do_receive_pipe(), 178
do_send_data(), 157
do_set_mode_name(), 140
do_set_partner_lu_name(), 137
do_set_tp_name(), 142
do_sync_level_confirm(), 135

E-mail program, 218
EBCDIC, 42, 339, 340
EBCDIC_HOST, 345
ebcdic_to_ascii_table[], 344
Encryption, 359
End_TP (xcendt), 394
Enhanced security same, 362, 363
Entry point, 52
Environment variable, 47
Error description, 189
Error log, 278
Error reply, 189
Error-handling, 84, 271–287
exit(), 194, 199
Extension calls, 43
Extract_Conversation_Context (cmectx), 148
Extract_Conversation_State (cmecs), 76, 148
Extract_Conversation_Type (cmect), 149
Extract_Maximum_Buffer_Size (cmembs), 150, 265
Extract_Mode_Name (cmemn), 150
Extract_Partner_LU_Name (cmepln), 41, 151, 393
Extract_Security_User_ID (cmesui), 152, 365
Extract_Sync_Level (cmesl), 152
Extract_TP_ID (xceti), 394
Extract_TP_Name (cmetpn), 153

Family API, 53
File transfer transaction, 232
FILEX.C, 234
FILEXD.C, 238
Finite state machine, 70
First-failure data capture, 291
Floating point, 353
Flow control, 103
FLTSAMP.C, 353
Flush (cmflus), 102, 158, 257, 261, 378
FLUSH.C, 107
FLUSHD.C, 110

Footprint, 290
force_connection(), 373
Frame, 61, 256
free(), 155, 166
Function prototypes, 51

GDS variable, 208
General-purpose receive, 170, 177
get_conversation_ID(), 312

handle_cpic_rc(), 85
handle_error(), 84
handle_receive_error(), 86
Handling errors, 84, 271–287
HELLO1.C, 28
HELLO1D.C, 29
HELLO1S symbolic destination name, 28, 83
HELLO2.C, 33
HELLO2D.C, 34
HELLO2S symbolic destination name, 33, 83
HELLO3.C, 72
HELLO3D.C, 73
HELLO3S symbolic destination name, 72, 83
HELLO3T.C, 300
HELLO4D.C, 81
HELLO5.C, 94
HELLO5D.C, 95

I: (input parameter), 28
IBM C compiler, 6, 7
Identify_Resource_Manager (xcidrm), 395
IEEE floating point, 353
Implicit confirmation, 261
Implicit target, 49
Improving performance, 255–270
Initialize_Conversation (cminit), 122, 330
Initialize_Conv_For_TP (xcinct), 394
Initialize_For_Incoming (cminic), 381
init_with_security(), 370
Inquiry transaction, 226
INQUIRY.C, 227
INQUIRYD.C, 229
INTCONV.C, 349
Integers, 38, 347
Internet, 8, 471
INTSAMP.C, 351
IPMD (debugger), 333
is_partner_lu_name_valid(), 315

Language independence, 3
Lengths, 39
Library, 46, 53
Limited resource, 390
Line flows, 269
Link, 59, 67

Linking, 46
Little endian, 348
LL field, 205–207
Local LU, 309
Logical length (LL), 205–207
Logical record, 61, 91
Logical unit (LU) name, 66
log_data, 208
Long conversation, 268, 390, 391
Long name, 27, 42, 53, 131, 147
LOOP, 287
LPINIDEA.C, 196
LPINIT.C, 126
LU name, 66
LU-LU password, 359
LU-LU security, 359

MAKE, 49
Makefile, 7, 46
malloc(), 155, 166
Mapped conversation, 132–133, 149, 205
Maximum size, 40
mblen(), 347
mbstowcs(), 347
mbtowc(), 347
Message queuing, 16
Microsoft C compiler, 6, 7, 47, 353
Mode definition, 441
mode_name, 57, 64, 66, 139, 150
MSC6.CMD, 47
Multibyte character, 347
Multiple accept, 394–402
MVS include file (ATBCMC), 50
MVS/ESA, 50, 52, 53, 395, 468

National language, 339, 346, 470
NetBIOS, 14
Network name, 62
Network name registry, 62
Networking Services/DOS, 53, 394
Newline character, /n, 156, 238, 340
NMAKE, 49
Nonblocking, 377–387, 402
Nonblocking calls, 378
NS/DOS (Networking Services/DOS), 53, 394
Null character, \0, 24, 40, 123, 148, 156, 340

O: (output parameter), 28
One-way bracket, 213
Optimization, 45
OS/2 Communications Manager, 53, 137, 277, 291, 309, 394, 471
OS/2 shared data buffer, 262, 265
OS/400, 52, 278, 395
Outstanding operation, 378

Pacing window, 103, 256
Packets, 101
partner_LU_name, 57, 61, 137, 151
Password, 367, 374, 375
pause_before_retrying(), 173
Performance, 255–270
Permission-to-send, 75, 161
Persistent verification, 361, 362, 364
Physical security, 365
PIPE.C, 214
PIPED.C, 216
Pipeline transaction, 212
Pointers, 38, 51
Pound sign, 346
Prepare_To_Receive (cmptr), 161, 259, 378
Processing overlap, 257
processing_mode, 378, 381
process_data(), 173
process_incoming_data(), 397, 401
Production version, 45, 158
Program, definition of, 23
prompt_for_security_info(), 373

rand(), 226
Rarely-used techniques, 201–208
READABLE_MACROS, 53
README.TXT, 7, 43
Receive (cmrcv), 102, 166, 265, 378
Receive processing, 99
Receive wrappers, 170, 177
Receive-Immediate, 169, 202
received_length, 99
receive_double(), 354
receive_int32(), 352
Record, 61, 91
Release number, 296
Release_Local_TP_Name (cmrltp), 399
Remote procedure call, 16, 226
Reporting failures, 289–301
Request unit (RU), 61, 256
request-and-reply, 226
request-to-send, 202
Request_To_Send (cmrts), 202, 204, 378
request_to_send_received, 99
Resource Recovery (CPI-RR), 14, 169, 433–438,
    468
Retry guidelines, 279, 282
return_code, 28, 30, 87, 98, 167, 273, 292, 331
return_code categories, 274
return_control, 133
Route security, 358
RPC (remote procedure call), 16, 226
RU (request unit), 61, 256

Security, 357–375
SECURITY.TXT, 7, 362

Send_Data (cmsend), 156, 191, 265, 266, 378
send_double(), 353
Send_Error (cmserr), 102, 188, 191, 261, 283,
    286, 378
send_error_loop(), 284
send_int32(), 351
SENSDATA.INF, 7
Sense data, 7, 277, 406, 407
SERRLOOP.C, 284
SERRLOOP.H, 284
SERROR.C, 283
SERRORD.C, 285
Server, 24, 143, 389–402
SERVER1D.C, 396
SERVER2D.C, 400
Service TP name, 309
Session, 60, 127, 268
Session security, 359
Setup, 55–68, 256, 294, 363
Set_Conversation_Security_Password (cmscsp),
    367
Set_Conversation_Security_Type (cmscst), 360,
    366
Set_Conversation_Security_User_ID (cmscsu),
    366
Set_Conversation_Type (cmsct), 132
Set_Deallocate_Type (cmsdt), 194, 267
Set_Error_Direction (cmsed), 190
Set_Fill (cmsf), 207, 267
Set_Log_Data (cmsld), 208
Set_Mode_Name (cmsmn), 139
Set_Partner_LU_Name (cmspln), 41, 137
Set_Prepare_To_Receive_Type (cmsptr), 162, 267
Set_Processing_Mode (cmspm), 379, 382
Set_Receive_Type (cmsrt), 169, 267
Set_Return_Control (cmsrc), 133
set_security_program(), 369
Set_Send_Type (cmsst), 159, 267
Set_Sync_Level (cmssl), 134
Set_TP_Name (cmstpn), 141
SET_UP_CONV structure, 310
set_up_conversation(), 309
set_up_mode_name(), 316
set_up_partner_lu_name(), 316
set_up_tp_name(), 318
Shared data buffer, 262, 265
Short conversation, 268, 390, 392
Short name, 27, 42, 53, 131, 147
show_conversation_state(), 76
show_cpic_return_code(), 88
show_data_received(), 98
show_status_received(), 89
Side information, 56, 57, 136
SIDEINFO.NDF, 7
SIDEINFO.NSD, 7
Signaling, 201

SIZE constants, 40
SNA Formats, 278, 469
SNA sense data, 277, 406, 407
Source debugger, 332
Specify_Local_TP_Name (cmsltp), 398
Specify_Windows_Handle (xchwnd), 386
Square brackets, 339
Stack size, 46
Start_TP (xcstp), 394
State table, 70, 75
status_received, 89, 99, 168, 279
Strings, 39
string_reverse(), 74
strlen(), 40, 347
symbolic_destination_name, 28, 56, 67, 123, 306
Sync point, 14, 169
Synchronization, 186
sync_level, 32, 134, 152, 195, 326

Terminate_Resource_Manager (xctrrm), 395
Testing, 283
Test_Request_To_Send_Received (cmtrts), 204
Thread, 399
Time-out, 396
TP definition, 63, 67, 83, 325, 396
TP_ID, 394
TP_name, 57, 63, 67, 141, 153, 324, 399
TRACE.C, 297
TRACE.H, 299
trace_close(), 299
trace_init(), 298
trace_log(), 299
trace_set_filename(), 298
trace_set_level(), 298
Tracing, 296–301
Transactions, 211

Trust, 361, 362, 365
TSTSETUP.C, 320
Typedefs, 51

Unicode, 339
UPDATE.C, 244
UPDATED.C, 249
Upward compatibility, 296
user_ID ,152, 374, 375

Version number, 296
VM/ESA, 53, 137, 279, 395, 469

Wait_For_Conversation (cmwait), 380
Wait_On_Event (xcwoe), 395
Warning levels, 44
wchar_t, 347
wcstombs(), 347
wctomb(), 347
WinCPIC, 5, 18, 53, 377, 382, 468
WINCPIC.DEF, 7
WINCPIC.H, 7, 382
WinCPICCleanup(), 384
WinCPICIsBlocking(), 386
WinCPICSetBlockingHook(), 384
WinCPICStartup(), 383
WinCPICUnhookBlockingHook(), 386
Writing Solid Code, 118, 470

X/Open CPI-C, 5, 18, 468
XC (extension call), 43
xchwnd() (Specify_Windows_Handle), 386
xcscsp(), 367
xcscsu(), 367
XID (exchange identifier), 60

Zero-length record, 157

Table 1   CPI-C Calls and Conversation Characteristics

Short name	Long name	CPI-C version	Page
CMACCP	Accept_Conversation	1.0	145
CMACCI	Accept_Incoming	1.2	381
CMALLC	Allocate	1.0	128
CMCANC	Cancel_Conversation	1.2	380
CMCFM	Confirm	1.0	186
CMCFMD	Confirmed	1.0	187
CMCNVI	Convert_Incoming	1.2	341
CMCNVO	Convert_Outgoing	1.2	341
CMDEAL	Deallocate	1.0	194
CMECS	Extract_Conversation_State	1.1	148
CMECT	Extract_Conversation_Type	1.0	149
CMECTX	Extract_Conversation_Context	1.2	148
CMEMBS	Extract_Maximum_Buffer_Size	1.2	150
CMEMN	Extract_Mode_Name	1.0	150
CMEPLN	Extract_Partner_LU_Name	1.0	151
CMESUI	Extract_Security_User_ID	1.2	152
CMESL	Extract_Sync_Level	1.0	152
CMETPN	Extract_TP_Name	1.2	153
CMFLUS	Flush	1.0	158
CMINIT	Initialize_Conversation	1.0	122
CMINIC	Initialize_For_Incoming	1.2	381
CMPTR	Prepare_To_Receive	1.0	161
CMRCV	Receive	1.0	166
CMRLTP	Release_Local_TP_Name	1.2	399
CMRTS	Request_To_Send	1.0	204
CMSEND	Send_Data	1.0	156
CMSERR	Send_Error	1.0	188
CMSCSP	Set_Conversation_Security_Password	1.2	367
CMSCST	Set_Conversation_Security_Type	1.2	366
CMSCSU	Set_Conversation_Security_User_ID	1.2	366
CMSCT	Set_Conversation_Type	1.0	132
CMSDT	Set_Deallocate_Type	1.0	194
CMSED	Set_Error_Direction	1.0	190
CMSF	Set_Fill	1.0	207
CMSLD	Set_Log_Data	1.0	208
CMSMN	Set_Mode_Name	1.0	139
CMSPLN	Set_Partner_LU_Name	1.0	137
CMSPM	Set_Processing_Mode	1.2	379
CMSPTR	Set_Prepare_To_Receive_Type	1.0	162
CMSRT	Set_Receive_Type	1.0	169
CMSRC	Set_Return_Control	1.0	133
CMSST	Set_Send_Type	1.0	159
CMSSL	Set_Sync_Level	1.0	134
CMSTPN	Set_TP_Name	1.0	141
CMSLTP	Specify_Local_TP_Name	1.2	398
CMTRTS	Test_Request_To_Send_Received	1.0	204
CMWAIT	Wait_For_Conversation	1.2	380

Table 2   CPI-C Conversation Characteristics

This table shows all of the CPI-C conversation characteristics, their default values, and the page number where their Set and Extract calls are discussed.

Characteristic	Default value on the client side	Default value on the server side	Set call	Extract call
Conversation security type	CM_SECURITY_SAME (or from side info)	Inherited from client	366	N/A
Conversation state	CM_SEND_STATE, after Allocate() call	CM_RECEIVE_STATE, after Accept_Conversation() or Accept_Incoming() call	N/A	148
Conversation type	CM_MAPPED_CONVERSATION	Inherited from client	132	149
Deallocate type	CM_DEALLOCATE_SYNC_LEVEL	CM_DEALLOCATE_SYNC_LEVEL	194	N/A
Error direction	CM_RECEIVE_ERROR	CM_RECEIVE_ERROR	190	N/A
Fill	CM_FILL_LL	CM_FILL_LL	207	N/A
Log data	0 length buffer	0 length buffer	208	N/A
Mode name	0 length string, or value from side information	Inherited from client	139	150
Partner LU name	1 blank character, or value from side information	Inherited from client	137	151
Prepare to receive type	CM_PREP_TO_RECEIVE_SYNC_LEVEL	CM_PREP_TO_RECEIVE_SYNC_LEVEL	162	N/A
Processing mode	CM_BLOCKING	CM_BLOCKING	379	N/A
Receive type	CM_RECEIVE_AND_WAIT	CM_RECEIVE_AND_WAIT	169	N/A
Return control	CM_WHEN_SESSION_ALLOCATED	Not applicable	133	N/A
Security password	0 length string, or value from side information	Not applicable	367	N/A
Security user ID	0 length string, or value from side information	Inherited from client	366	152
Send type	CM_BUFFER_DATA	CM_BUFFER_DATA	159	N/A
Sync level	CM_NONE	Inherited from client	134	152
TP name	1 blank character, or value from side information	Inherited from client	141	153

ABOUT THE AUTHORS

JOHN Q. WALKER II manages architecture, development, and marketing departments responsible for APPC, CPI-C, and APPN at IBM in Research Triangle Park, North Carolina. He recently managed one of the teams responsible for this software on OS/2. He lectures and teaches worldwide on programming and communications technology.

PETER J. SCHWALLER is currently a member of IBM's APPC market enablement group, responsible for making APPC, CPI-C, and APPN easier to use. In 1989, he joined IBM in Research Triangle Park, North Carolina, where he helped define the APPN architecture, and later moved to developing the first CPI-C and APPN product for OS/2.

ABOUT THE SERIES

The J. Ranade Workstation Series is McGraw-Hill's primary vehicle for providing workstation professionals with timely concepts, solutions, and applications. Jay Ranade is also Series Editor in Chief of more than 100 books in the J. Ranade IBM and DEC Series and Series Advisor to the McGraw-Hill Series on Computer Communications.

Jay Ranade, Series Editor in Chief and best-selling computer author, is a Senior Systems Architect and Assistant V. P. at Merrill Lynch.